# Lincoln

## AND THE
## AMERICAN MANIFESTO

*Let us re-adopt the Declaration of Independence, and with it, the practices, and policy, which harmonize with it. Let north and south—let all Americans—let all lovers of liberty everywhere—join in the great and good work. If we do this, we shall not only have saved the Union, but we shall have so saved it, as to make, and to keep it, forever worthy of the saving.*
—Abraham Lincoln, 16 October 1854

*I have often inquired of myself, what great principle or idea it was that kept this Confederacy [nation] so long together. It was . . . something in that Declaration giving liberty, not alone to the people of this country, but hope to the world for all future time . . . that all should have an equal chance. This is the sentiment embodied in that Declaration of Independence. . . . I would rather be assassinated on this spot than to surrender it.*
—Abraham Lincoln, 22 February 1861

# Lincoln

## AND THE
## AMERICAN MANIFESTO

### ALLEN JAYNE

**Prometheus Books**

59 John Glenn Drive
Amherst, New York 14228-2197

Published 2007 by Prometheus Books

Inquiries should be addressed to
Prometheus Books
59 John Glenn Drive
Amherst, New York 14228–2197
VOICE: 716–691–0133, ext. 207
FAX: 716–564–2711
WWW.PROMETHEUSBOOKS.COM

11  10  09  08  07     5  4  3  2  1

Library of Congress Cataloging-in-Publication Data

Jayne, Allen.
    Lincoln and the American manifesto / Allen Jayne.
        p.  cm.
    Includes bibliographical references and index.
    ISBN 978–1–59102–502–3 (alk. paper)
    1. Lincoln, Abraham, 1809–1865—Political and social views. 2. Lincoln, Abraham, 1809–1865—Religion. 3. Lincoln, Abraham, 1809–1865—Oratory. 4. United States. Declaration of Independence. 5. Jefferson, Thomas, 1743–1826—Political and social views. 6. Jefferson, Thomas, 1743–1826—Religion. 7. Deism—United States—History. 8. Religion and politics—United States—History. 9. United States—Politics and government—1775–1783. 10. United States—Politics and government—1783–1865. I. Title.

E457.2.H39 2007
973.7—dc22

                                                                    2006102523

Printed in the United States on acid-free paper

*To Linda*

# Contents

# Preface

*O*ne of the two principal subjects of this work is the Declaration of Independence and how Thomas Jefferson made the egalitarian ecumenical God of deism, who gives "rights" to "all men" regardless of color or religious belief, the foundational truth of the Declaration. Jefferson took this step because he was acutely aware—as were many in the Age of Enlightenment of which he was part—that the God of mainstream Judeo-Christian theology is partial to those of certain religious views and oppressive to others. Therefore, the Judeo-Christian God is not the source of the Declaration's political theory based on "rights" that God gives equally to each individual regardless of religious belief or disbelief, as many claim, but is opposed to that theory. Abraham Lincoln, who, like Jefferson, was imbued with deism, was very much aware of and in accord with this deistic aspect of the Declaration. It is among the reasons he used the universal, all are included, moral idealism of the Declaration of Independence as his main moral weapon in the struggle against slavery, which is the second principal subject of this work.

Although the ideas contained in this work are historical, they are relevant today. They explain how the deistic idealism of the Declaration of Independence, when implemented by the Constitution and Bill of Rights of the United States, put religion under man-made law and thereby tamed the despotism and violent excesses of religion that had plagued the West for over one thousand years. This extraordinary achievement within the United States—which is largely ignored, taken for granted, and sometimes maligned today—was the contribution of the Founding Fathers of American civilization, especially Thomas Jefferson and James Madison. Its contribution to religious peace is especially significant at this time since it is being attacked from within, as well as from outside the United States, by those who fervently believe in the medieval notion that government and law are and should be of God and by God via scripture or church

11

or clergy, which is theocracy, rather than of the people and by the people, which is democracy. If they succeed in their efforts to have God-centered rather than human-centered government, conflicts within and between civilizations—that history demonstrates have resulted from such government—could once again emerge. Only this time, with the aid of modern weaponry, they could well disrupt or destroy civilized life on the planet in an unprecedented way.

I am indebted to Bhek Pati Sinha, a world court jurist, philosopher, and professor of American government, for reading and commenting on this work. Any errors it contains, however, are mine. I am also indebted to the UCLA Library where much of the research on this work was done. Special thanks go to Jane Ehrenhart at the new Abraham Lincoln Library in Springfield, Illinois, for making available portions of the library that were closed. I owe similar gratitude to Peter Fox and the University Library at Cambridge University, where I received a PhD in intellectual history, for waiving normal admission procedures during a quick trip to England thereby allowing me maximum use of limited time.

# Introduction

The Declaration of Independence, the charter of the American Revolution, was the idealistic "lode-star of Lincoln's life," according to legal scholar Charles Black.[1] Lincoln himself described the Declaration as "my ancient faith" and "our ancient faith" as well as "the father of all moral principal in" Americans, which provides three reasons why he regarded the Declaration not only as his but the nation's "lodestar."[2] One purpose of this book is to explain why Lincoln described the Declaration in this way and, thereby, why he exalted the moral idealism of the Declaration along with Thomas Jefferson, its principal author. If Lincoln were alive today, however, his exaltation of the Declaration and Jefferson would place him at odds with a trend among scholars, who, for several decades, have engaged in an ascending order of criticism of the American Revolution and what it "intended and accomplished"—criticism that even extends to the Declaration of Independence itself.[3] A principal criticism is that despite the Declaration's "all men are created equal" idealism of Equality in the sense that each human being has the God-given "unalienable rights" of "Life, Liberty and the Pursuit of Happiness" and "that to secure these Rights, Governments are instituted among Men," this idealism did not extend to "all Men" during and after the Revolutionary War. Blacks, most of whom were slaves, did not enjoy the right of "Liberty" the Revolutionaries fought to obtain for themselves. This and the fact that prominent Revolutionaries, including George Washington, Thomas Jefferson, and James Madison, all former presidents, were slave owners and continued to be slave owners after the Revolution is something critics are quick to point out.[4] Harry Jaffa, however, is critical of many critics, especially those who condemn the Founders' prudential compromise with slavery at the nation's beginning as the "portrayal of a 'racist' American Founding" and "a necessary preamble to the disavowal of any authority to the principles of the Revolution . . . enshrined in the

Declaration of Independence." He calls such critics "later-day abolitionist historians."[5] Yet Jefferson would not have been surprised at
criticism of the Revolution, the Declaration, or himself. The nation
he helped found is based on the Age of Enlightenment value of
critical scrutiny,[6] and the right to make public criticism is protected
by the Bill of Rights that Jefferson, while serving as Minister Plenipotentiary in France, insisted his friend James Madison add to the
Constitution.[7]

Even though criticism is appropriate and indeed encouraged in
the American system, especially in the academic community whose
function is to criticize, it has, in the last several decades, often led to
a distorted view of the American Revolution and its heroes as a
result of emphasizing their shortcomings and largely ignoring their
extraordinary achievements. Seldom, for example, have critics explained that the values of Liberty and Equality of the Declaration
and Revolution, although borrowed by America from the European
Age of Enlightenment, were not actualized in Europe to any great
extent in the eighteenth century—even among white males—as they
were in America. This lack of explanation has caused many Americans to have little or no understanding of the positive impact the
Age of Enlightenment had on the American Revolution, the Declaration of Independence, and indeed America itself. Nor has it been
fully explained that the God of the Declaration, as Jefferson wrote
that document, granted the right of "Liberty" to "all Men" equally
regardless of religion, gender, or race. Indeed the God of the Declaration, in Jefferson's version before editing by the Continental Congress, specifically granted that right of "Liberty" to blacks, as we shall
see. And, since the Declaration states that the purpose of government is to secure the rights that the Declaration's God granted to "all
Men" including blacks, the Declaration is antislavery, as Jefferson
wrote it. Therefore, the problem in 1776 America, and even now to
a lesser extent, was not with its all-inclusive idealistic theory contained in the Declaration, but rather putting that theory into practice. Despite this problem, however, the Declaration was and continues to be an extraordinary document, because no other civilization began with such all-inclusive idealism. Significantly, Abraham
Lincoln was aware of the all-inclusiveness of the Declaration and

emphasized it again and again in his speeches in his struggle against slavery. To put it another way, Lincoln put the Enlightenment ideas and ideals of the Declaration of Independence—which he called the "enlightened beliefs" of the Founders—to work in his efforts to alter the mind-set of Americans on slavery, as we shall see.[8]

At the time of the bicentennial celebration of the Declaration of Independence, in 1976, Henry Steele Commager did his best to increase the people's understanding of the positive impact the Age of Enlightenment had on the American Revolution and America in 1776. He emphasized that principles and values originating in the European Enlightenment, but not practiced there to any great extent, were made America's foundational truths in the Declaration of Independence.[9] Commager also pointed out that the Revolution's achievements are often judged by what is commonplace in today's. America rather than 1776 America. In addition, he pointed out that this practice of presentism is commonplace among today's critical scholars even though many condemn it and maintain that judgment of the past should be based on the standards and circumstances of the period judged. Jefferson scholar Peter Onuf, however, justifies presentism as well as passionate "forays into Jefferson's private life" on the grounds that "historians want to make sense of Jefferson" and "grasp exactly what it was that the Revolutionary founders intended and accomplished." Even though Onuf acknowledges that this presentism and passion approach "sometimes strains the scholarly standards of dispassion and disinterest," he stopped short of concluding that judging by eighteenth-century standards and a dispassionate disposition would better enable scholars "to make sense of Jefferson" as well as what the "founders intended and accomplished."[10] Commager, in contrast to Onuf, pointed out that if the American Revolution is judged by what was practiced in eighteenth-century Europe, its accomplishments are extraordinary. As he put it in his *Empire of Reason: How Europe Imagined and America Realized the Enlightenment*:

> We tend increasingly to interpret the American Revolution and Enlightenment not in eighteenth- but in twentieth-century terms, to see it not against the background of eighteenth-century Europe

but against the foreground of our own time, and to be more conscious of its limitations than of its spectacular achievements. We take for granted what neither Americans nor Europeans took for granted in the eighteenth century; not only have we lost that sense of astonishment and exultation that animated Jefferson's generation, we have almost lost our ability to understand it. It is not perhaps surprising that we should be skeptical of a society that preached liberty and practiced slavery, but it is surprising that we should be equally skeptical of a society that achieved a larger degree of political and social democracy, constitutional order, effective limits on the pretensions of government, freedom of religion, freedom of the press, civil liberties, popular education, and material well being than any other on the globe.[11]

An effect of being "more conscious" of the Revolution's "limitations" than "its spectacular achievements" as a result of contemporary criticism is the diminished status of Revolutionary heroes and even the Declaration itself. Simultaneously, this criticism has caused Lincoln's status to rise in comparison. Lincoln would be pleased with his increase in stature, since being remembered favorably was important to him.[12] He would, however, be displeased with the diminished stature of the Revolution and its heroes, and especially the Declaration of Independence, the charter of the Revolution, since no one ever paid higher tribute to the Revolution, its participants, and its Enlightenment values stated in the Declaration than he did. This is seen in his address to the Young Men's Lyceum of Springfield in January of 1838, where he stated in a way that parallels the aforementioned comment of Commager:

We find ourselves under the government of a system of political institutions, conducing more essentially to the ends of civil and religious liberty, than any of which the history of former times tells us. . . . We toiled not in the acquirement or establishment of them—they are a legacy bequeathed us, by a *once* hardy, brave, and patriotic, but *now* lamented and departed race of ancestors. Theirs was the task (and nobly they performed it) to possess themselves, and through themselves, us, of this goodly land; and to uprear upon its hills and its valleys, a political edifice of *liberty and equal rights*. [My italics][13]

In the same address, which Dwight Anderson tells us was heavily influenced by Mason Locke Weems's *The Life of Washington* that Lincoln read as a young man,[14] Lincoln referred to the Revolutionary generation as "pillars of the temple of liberty" who needed to be replaced "with other pillars, hewn from the solid quarry of sober reason." "Cold calculating, unimpassioned reason," elaborated Lincoln, "*must* furnish *all the materials* for our future support and defense," and "sound morality" was one of those materials (my italics). It was, however, reason and reason-based morality that was emphasized here, not the morality of religion, church, or scripture, and Lincoln's stress on reason conformed to the principal thrust of the Age of Enlightenment.[15]

The Lyceum address also stated that "establishing and maintaining civil and religious liberty" was the purpose, indeed the cause of the Revolution, which Lincoln described as "the noblest of cause."[16] Significantly, he maintained that this cause was still being fought for in the Civil War in January 1863 when he wrote of "imploring the gracious favor of the God of Nations upon the struggles our people are making for the preservation of their precious birthright of *civil and religious liberty* [my italics]."[17] Lincoln's great lament in his Lyceum address, however, was his own prediction that the accomplishments and idealism of the Revolution and its heroes would "fade upon the memory of the world, and grow more and more dim by the lapse of time" while he simultaneously hoped they "will be read of, and recounted, so long as the bible shall be read."[18] These comments, made to his nineteenth-century Bible-loving audience, tell us the great importance Lincoln attached to the Revolution and its idealistic Enlightenment values stated in the Declaration. They state in effect that the Declaration's ideals and moral values are as important as those in the Bible. Indeed, Lincoln's extensive use of the Declaration's moral idealism of God-given equal rights in his struggle against slavery rather than the Judeo-Christian morality of the Ten Commandments and Sermon on the Mount indicates he believed that the Declaration's morality was in some respects superior to that of the Bible, which in fact he did, as we shall see.

Consistent with Lincoln's praise of the accomplishments of the

American Revolution and his high esteem for reason and the moral values of "liberty and equal rights" of the Enlightenment found in the Declaration of Independence, *a principal purpose of this book is to demonstrate the profound influence the Age of Enlightenment had on Lincoln and how his understanding of that movement was similar to Thomas Jefferson's, since there are different and conflicting views of the Enlightenment.* More specifically, a purpose of this work is to demonstrate that Lincoln had a concept of God, human reality, and the Declaration of Independence and its significance similar to Jefferson's Enlightenment views that emphasized individual reason—not faith or non-reason-based belief—as each individual's principal guide and authority in life and religion, and that Lincoln cultivated these views as a young man and continued to hold them his entire life. Another purpose is to explain Lincoln's reasons for maintaining that the Declaration's moral idealism of equal rights extends to blacks, whites, persons of all religious persuasions, and both sexes, and that he got those reasons from reading Jefferson. Finally, in a very broad sense, a purpose of this work is to point out that Lincoln realized, as did Jefferson, that the Declaration of Independence made hypocrites of anyone who subscribed to the Declaration's universal, none-are-excluded equal rights idealism—which most Americans did—if they did not respect and uphold the equal rights of others. To put it another way, Lincoln saw that the Declaration made hypocrites of virtually all Americans, because virtually all of them either owned slaves, favored slavery, or condoned its practice even if they were opposed to it, while simultaneously subscribing to the principles of the Declaration. Knowing this and knowing that virtually all humans do not want to be hypocrites, Lincoln put these facts to work by repeatedly referring to the Declaration's moral idealism of equal rights in his speeches in his struggle against slavery. This was his way of constantly reminding Americans that they were hypocrites and would continue to be hypocrites until either slavery or the Declaration of Independence was abolished.

By arguing, as I do in this work, that Lincoln, as well as Jefferson, subscribed to the Age of Enlightenment idea that human reason is the most important guide to humans in all matters, I differ from

Garry Wills, who argues that while Jefferson was a man of the Enlightenment, Lincoln "was a man of his own age; but his age was the romantic era."[19] Richard Tarnas tells us, Romantics "valued man . . . for his imaginative and spiritual aspirations, his emotional depths, his artistic creativity and powers of individual self expression"—all manifest in the poet.[20] And Lincoln wrote poetry—not very good poetry—in the 1840s, as Wills points out. Yet Lincoln's poetic expression was relatively minor and short-lived. Therefore, his efforts to write poetry and poetry's influence on him, in my view, should not be overemphasized. Moreover, Lincoln's interests in poetry could well have been the result of reading Benjamin Franklin's *Autobiography*,[21] which stated that writing poetry developed the capacity to express oneself well.[22] Since Lincoln did aspire to express himself well,[23] he probably wrote poetry as a means to accomplish this end and not because of an extraordinary love of poetry, as is evidenced by his short-lived poetry-writing efforts.

I also differ from Stewart Winger, who maintains that the influence of the Romantic poets, which Lincoln read, plus the influence of Romantic culture in America during the decades prior to the Civil War, caused Lincoln to come back to the faith of his parents and grandparents that he had practiced as a boy and abandoned as a young man. That ancestral faith emphasized predestination and Providence. To Winger, this Romantic influence resulted in Lincoln's "creedal definition of American nationality that was evident in *all* [my italics] his nationalistic utterances," especially his Second Inaugural Address, in which he reflected "on a predetermined providential world."[24] While I reject the views of Wills and Winger, I do not deny that Lincoln had a Romantic personality facet and could express his thoughts in ways that appealed to Romantics, for Lincoln mastered the art of Romantic appeal. Yet I do maintain, and will explain why I do so, that the Romantic facet in Lincoln's personality was subordinate to his rational Enlightenment facet that dominated his life.

As Tarnas explained, the Enlightenment's measure of man "rested on his unequaled rational intellect and its power to comprehend the laws of nature." This is why those whose perceptions of truth and actions were founded on reason—that is, on rational calculations based on sensory perceived facts—were highly esteemed by the Enlightenment.[25] This is manifest in the Enlightenment's exaltation of men like Bacon, Newton, Locke, and Franklin. Romantics, on the other hand, exalted poets or men like Blake, Wordsworth, Coleridge, Shelley, Keats, Byron, Emerson, Thoreau, and Whitman.[26] I maintain that Lincoln fell squarely in the Enlightenment category since he, like the men of the Enlightenment, was governed by the limits of fact-based reason whereas Romantics revolted against these limits "established by Locke" and sought to extend them with imagination, emotion, and even will. Indeed, Romantics maintained that humans can, to a great extent, will their lives to be the way they want them to be and, therefore, did not have to live and act within limits established by the factual circumstances of their lives. To Enlightenment figures, this willful romantic approach would lead one away from truth, which, in order to be truth, had to be consistent with and verified by facts.[27] Moreover, many in the Enlightenment maintained that willful romantic action not based on truth supported by fact would have destructive rather than constructive consequences, which would eventually lead to disaster. It should be emphasized, however, that many rational human beings, which Lincoln was, have a Romantic personality facet. As Tarnas stated of the Romantic and Enlightenment dispositions, these "two sensibilities"—imagination, emotion, and will on one hand, and sense perceptions and reason on the other—"were present in varying proportion in every reflective individual of the modern West."[28] As has been stated, in Lincoln's case his Enlightenment disposition or facet dominated his actions, not his Romantic facet. Indeed, Walt Whitman, a Romantic poet and transcendentalist who knew Lincoln, said as much by stating that Lincoln led "a life often" dominated "by temporary but most urgent materialistic reasons" or facts.[29] Lincoln, therefore, had his feet firmly on the ground of Enlightenment values and did not allow Romantic willful imagination and fancy to run his life.

## THE AMERICAN MANIFESTO

An underlying theme of this work is that both Jefferson and Lincoln regarded the Declaration of Independence as the American Manifesto or public statement of the American worldview, motives, and intentions. Few Americans, however, think of the Declaration of Independence as a manifesto, even though many are aware that major political movements have manifestos. For example, the well-known *Communist Manifesto*, written in 1848 by Karl Marx and Friedrich Engels, specifies a Communist blueprint for the world.[30] It states that Communism is the only political truth and ultimately everyone must and will conform to Communism. Nazism, too, had its manifesto, which is found in Adolf Hitler's well-known *Mein Kampf*, published in 1925, which outlined the Nazi plan for world order.[31] Like Communism, Nazism claims that it is the only political truth and ultimately everyone must conform to Nazism. Not so well known is the Fascist Manifesto written in 1915 by Benito Mussolini, if indeed Mussolini or Italian Fascism under him ever had a meaningful manifesto, because his ideas constantly changed and contradicted each other.[32] What finally emerged under Mussolini as Fascism, however, was a totalitarian state with Mussolini wielding all the power. The creed of that state, which Giovanni Gentile helped to formulate, was: nothing outside of the state's or Mussolini's power, nothing against it, and everything for it; in other words, the complete subordination of individual Italians to the state's or Mussolini's power.[33] This is in effect saying that Fascism is the only and absolute political power, and whatever that power says is true must be true.

With claims that they alone have political truth as their basis, each of these three political systems—Communism, Nazism, and Fascism—manifested itself in a single party with the head of that party having absolute, arbitrary political power. With that power, dissenting views on political truth were ruthlessly suppressed by these three political systems because they were considered untruth. Germany, Italy, Russia, and China all suffered from this affliction on a massive scale in the twentieth century.

Manifestos, however, are not confined to political systems. Religions have them too. You find them in Judaism, Christianity, and Islam. The Jewish Manifesto is found in the Torah or Old Testament. There, the God of the Jews gave the worldview, motive, and intentions of Judaism, which claims to be the only religious truth as revealed by God to Moses, the greatest of all past or future prophets. As Moses Maimonides, the Jewish philosopher of the twelfth century, put it: "Remember that ours is the only true and authentic Divine religion, revealed to us through Moses, the master of the former as well as the later prophets."[34] The Christian Manifesto is also contained in the Old Testament, at least partly, but mostly in the New Testament, where Jesus Christ—God incarnate in human form—and Paul—his apostle—gave the Christian worldview, motive, and intention based on the idea that Christianity is the only religious truth. As Jesus said in John 14:6, "I am the way, the truth, and the life: no man cometh unto the Father, but by me." Finally, the Islamic Manifesto is contained in the Qur'an, which states the worldview, motive, and intention of Islam as revealed by Allah, the God of Islam, to Mohammed, His principal prophet. Islam claims that Mohammed's revelations are the latest, the greatest, and supercede all others. It also claims that those revelations are final and conclusive. Islam, therefore, in a manner similar to Judaism and Christianity, also claims to have the only religious truth. As a result of their claims, both Christianity and Islam, unlike Judaism, have the concept of triumphalism or the view that their religion will ultimately be the faith of the entire world. All three religions, however, have subjected or still subject their followers, and many nonfollowers as well, to religious authority in the form of scripture, temple, church, mosque, and clergy. Such authorities have frequently been backed by the coercive power of the state. To put it another way, as Communism, Nazism, and Fascism do not allow dissent on political truth, Judaism, Christianity, and Islam do not allow dissent on religious truth and God if you are a follower of these religions and frequently even if you are a nonfollower. And, as Nazism, Communism, and Fascism have ruthlessly repressed political dissent, the three religions that originated in the Middle East have often ruthlessly repressed religious dissent, which they call heresy. Accounts of such repression are found in the Old Testament (Joshua 8:28) and the history of Christianity and Islam.[35]

An underlying theme of this book is that the Declaration of Independence, or American Manifesto, is against all manifestos of systems claiming to have the only truth and authority over individual human beings, including systems and individuals that claim the superiority and authority of any race over any other race. It is the Declaration's idealism of the natural "unalienable rights" of "Life, Liberty and the Pursuit of Happiness" that the God of the Declaration gave equally to each individual, combined with its idea that governments are "instituted" to "secure" these rights, which opposes and indeed nullifies such truth and authority claims. In other words, each individual, with his or her right of "Liberty" secured by "government," can reject the truth and authority claims of any philosophy, political theory, religion, race, or other individual with impunity.

In the course of this book, I will demonstrate that Lincoln was indebted to several thinkers for his Enlightenment views and idealism but most of all to Jefferson, whose idealism in the Declaration of Independence was praised by Lincoln, despite the fact that William Herndon, Lincoln's law partner, once said, as Allen Guelzo pointed out: "Mr. Lincoln hated Thomas Jefferson as a man" as well "as a politician."[36] Herndon's statement is not to be relied on, however, at least about Lincoln's hating Jefferson "as a politician," since Lincoln himself praised Jefferson as "the most distinguished politician of our history" in a speech at Peoria, Illinois, in 1854.[37] Moreover, Leonard Swett, a friend and colleague of Lincoln in law, contradicted Herndon by stating that Lincoln was "a very poor hater"— a statement that Herndon himself put in his book *Herndon's Life of Lincoln*.[38] And, even if Lincoln did hate Jefferson as a personality, in praising the ideas and ideals Jefferson put in the Declaration of Independence, which he did again and again, as we shall see, he manifested the critical Enlightenment method of using reason to accept truth and reject untruth wherever he found it. This method ruled out fallacious ad hominem logic, which rejects ideas if their source is disliked or hated without examining the truth or merit of those ideas.

In order to show that Lincoln shared many of Thomas Jefferson's Enlightenment ideas and ideals, especially those of the Declaration of Independence, the first chapter reveals the source of Jefferson's critical, empirical, reason-based, deistic religion and his use of that religion, a product of Age of Enlightenment critical thought, as the foundation of the political theory of the Declaration of Independence. The second chapter presents the sources of Lincoln's deistic, critical, Enlightenment, reason-based religious ideas and demonstrates that he was very much aware of the deistic element of the Declaration and subscribed to its concept of a universal God who smiles on everyone regardless of their religious beliefs, even if those beliefs are agnostic or atheistic. To put it another way, the deistic God of Jefferson, Lincoln, and the Declaration of Independence does not condemn any human being to hell or bar them from heaven for not believing a certain way, as does Jehovah, Lord Jesus Christ, and Allah. The third chapter explores Jefferson's and Lincoln's rejection of original sin and how they both subscribed to a moral sense view of human nature that makes each individual a moral agent who can attain accurate moral knowledge and behave according to that knowledge independent of God, scripture, church, and clergy. It also considers the implications of this view, as well as the original sin view, in democratic or republican political theory and practice. The first three chapters taken together supply the background necessary to fully understand Lincoln's as well as Jefferson's indebtedness to the critical Enlightenment approach to theology and religion and the exposure of both men to similar unorthodox concepts of God and human reality that made an enormous impact not only on their religious but also on their political thought. In addition, these three chapters provide the basis for demonstrating that Lincoln never abandoned the basic unorthodox ideas on religion he was exposed to in his earlier years even though his use of the Bible and more orthodox Christian beliefs for political purposes in his speeches and letters often made him sound orthodox. The fourth chapter details Lincoln's defense of the ideology of the Declaration of Independence against revisionist interpretations that were used to justify slavery and his use of the Declaration as a moral weapon against that evil institution. Moreover, it explains his view that the Supreme Court of the United States has too much power and how he used Jefferson's similar ideas in arguments against the Court's proslavery Dred Scott decision. Finally, it explains Lincoln's method for overturning Supreme Court decisions that are unjust in any president's view provided his view is supported by the majority of the people and their representatives and senators in Congress. The fifth chapter presents Lincoln's Gettysburg Address, which was arguably his greatest defense of the ideology contained in the Declaration of Independence. It explores what he meant by Liberty and Equality as well as his exaltation of the democratic, homocentric, or human-centered "government of the people, by the people, for the people," which he used as an argument justifying the Civil War. It also explores his views on the nature and extent of American government as opposed to those of John C. Calhoun, whose ideas were the ideological basis of the Confederacy. The sixth chapter covers Lincoln's Second Inaugural Address. It explains his use of orthodox Christian theology there with its God-centered of-God-by-God-for-God ideas on the government of humans to justify the Civil War as well as an argument for the immediate and total abolition of slavery. It also explains how his use of this theology does not mean he abandoned the democratic, people-centered "government of the people, by the people, for the people" thrust of the Gettysburg Address in favor of theocratic government in the Second Inaugural. Moreover, it explains his justification for breaking or stretching the law in order to preserve the state or nation and that this reason-of-state method was advocated by Jefferson in his writings, which Lincoln read. Finally, it explains how Lincoln stated in the Second Inaugural itself his disbelief in the theology he used in that address.

A major element of this work has to do with Lincoln's religious views. The literature on this subject, however, is vast. Therefore, describing it adequately would be tedious to most.[39] Yet I wish to point out, as Stephen Oates did in *Abraham Lincoln,* that Josiah

Gilbert Holland's *The Life of Abraham Lincoln*, first published in 1866, portrayed Lincoln as a "true Christian," while William Herndon's *The Life of Lincoln*, first published in 1889, portrayed him as a religious skeptic. These two books started a "war" of conflicting interpretations of Lincoln's religious views that persists to this day.[40] However, far more authors have portrayed Lincoln as a mainstream or "true Christian" than as skeptical or heterodox in his views. This is because, as Merrill Peterson stated: "From the hour of his death Protestant ministers portrayed the Martyr President as an exemplary Christian."[41] In addition, Glen Thurow, in *Abraham Lincoln and the American Political Religion*, wrote: "A host of books were written in the late nineteenth and early twentieth centuries seeking to show that Lincoln was a conventional believer of one sort or another."[42] Since this work falls more in the Herndon than Holland camp, it will no doubt antagonize many who deem it important that Lincoln be considered a "true Christian" in an orthodox way. Yet in his own radically heterodox way, Lincoln believed he was a "true Christian," as we shall see.

# Chapter 1

# JEFFERSON, DEISM, AND THE DECLARATION OF INDEPENDENCE

By 1775, Thomas Jefferson had copied some ten thousand words on religious criticism and deism from Henry St. John, Lord Viscount Bolingbroke's *Philosophical Works* in his commonplace book. Gilbert Chinard maintains that these writings made a profound and lasting impression on Jefferson and that many of the "ideas" he "expressed in his correspondence with John Adams during the last twelve years of his life, could be illustrated with quotations taken from the abstracts of Bolingbroke in his commonplace book."[1] This is also true of correspondents other than Adams to whom Jefferson wrote on religion. Certainly Bolingbroke was the principal source of Jefferson's deism, which is the subject of this chapter that will explain why Jefferson made the deistic "Nature's God" the foundational truth of the Declaration of Independence.

Bolingbroke was an extraordinary figure of the English Enlightenment in the first half of the eighteenth century. He began a career in politics when he entered Parliament in 1700. After becoming one of Queen Anne's secretaries of state, he negotiated the Treaty of Utrecht in 1713 that established peace between England and Holland. As a Tory, his political future looked bright. Then in 1714, the Whigs took control of Parliament. Fearing violent Whig reprisals because he had opposed their rise to power, Bolingbroke fled to France. There he remained for ten years, at which time he cultivated the friendship of Voltaire and Montesquieu and became a bridge between the English and French Enlightenment. An extremely learned man, Bolingbroke studied classical, Renaissance humanist, and Enlightenment authors. Among those who influenced him were deists Lord Herbert of Cherbury, Anthony Collins, Benedict Spinoza, and John Toland. Among more secular writers, he was indebted to John Locke, Anthony Ashley Cooper (Earl of Shaftesbury), Pierre Bayle, Nicolas Malebranche, and Samuel Pufendorf.[2] Bolingbroke's own writings were published posthumously in 1754.[3] They created a huge uproar among people of faith because of their critical challenge of the truth of Christian doctrine and much of what is contained in the Old and New Testaments. After reading them, Dr. Samuel Johnson described Bolingbroke as "a scoundrel for charging a blunderbuss against religion and morality" and "a coward" because he had not done it while living.[4]

The first passage Jefferson copied—all Bolingbroke quotations in this text are from Jefferson's commonplace book—set the critical tone found in the remaining passages: "It is said that the sacred authors writ agreeably to all the vulgar notions of the ages and countries in which they lived, out of regard to their ignorance and to the gross conceptions of the people."[5] This was a sweeping challenge to the writings of the "sacred authors" of all "ages and countries." To Bolingbroke, they were not interested in truth. They merely accommodated what they wrote to the people's ignorance and superstition. This criticism hit particularly hard at Protestantism because it is based on scripture written by "sacred authors." Yet Bolingbroke also challenged the ability of tradition or verbal transmission of historical religious events to deliver the truth emphasized by Catholicism. To him, "the least reflection on human nature" demonstrates that it is not safe to rely on "memory alone," the basis of tradition, in passing "facts and circumstances" to future generations. This was because the "weakness of the human mind" will surely lead to inaccuracies, omissions, and distortions. Moreover, the "human heart," which gives rise to passions and interests, will suggest altering the facts to suit those passions and interests. In addition, "the authors of authentic history may be known; but those of tradition, whether authentic or inauthentic, are not known." This makes it impossible to check the credibility of the authors of tradition, and Bolingbroke maintained that what made history authentic were credible witnesses of good character.[6]

A major problem with tradition, which Bolingbroke also pointed out, was that if it was very old, its age alone made its truth content doubtful. As he put it, tradition "furnishes very precarious anecdotes" and because many were put in written form "at great distances of time," it made it "difficult, nay impossible, to ascertain the authority even of books that were written" based on tradition. Such books, he concluded, "may be neither received nor rejected on grounds absolutely sure."[7] This uncertainty caused the same tradition to be "rejected at one time [as untruth], and received at another [as truth]." He cited the "adventure of the apocalypse" as an example because the council of Laodicea left it "out of the canon in the year 860," while the "the council of Carthage put it into the canon in the year 397."[8] What especially bothered Bolingbroke about tradition was that even though its truth content was questionable or even contrary to factual evidence, if it was repeated again and again, it often became accepted as truth. He gave historical examples of this when he said: "The court of Rome has established many maxims and claims of right, by affirming them constantly and boldly against evident existent proofs of the contrary. The jewish and the christian church have proceeded by the same rule of policy."[9]

## LOCKEAN EPISTEMOLOGY

The religious claim that the Bible's divinely inspired or revealed words gave truth not only about God but also about science became increasingly doubtful in early modern times. As the sensory empiricism of Francis Bacon, which was elaborated on by John Locke, gained a greater foothold in Western civilization, it demonstrated that much of what the Bible said about science was false. Moreover, since Erasmus had found errors, omissions, and additions in the Vulgate or Catholic Bible compared to the original texts translated by Jerome in the fourth century, its content apart from science was suspect. For many deists, the solution to this problem was for religion to adopt the same theory of knowledge as science—which they did by using Locke's theory of knowledge, the basis of later deism.[10] In his *Essay concerning Human Understanding*, Locke denied the existence of René Descartes's God-given innate ideas and stated that the mind of every human was empty at birth. From that moment, however, ideas are placed in the mind by sense perceptions of objects in the world outside of one's self. These sensory-based ideas are the foundation of reason-based conclusions or knowledge, conclusions that must correspond to sensory-based ideas or facts. Therefore, if some fact does not correspond with a conclusion, that conclusion must be rejected and a new one formed which explains that fact along with others related to the conclusion. As Bolingbroke put it, "No hypothesis [or conclusion] ought to be maintained if a single phenomenon stands in direct opposition to it," a premise that he and other deists applied to the Bible when seeking knowledge of God as well as of science.[11]

When it came to science, Bolingbroke observed that, according to Genesis, God created the earth as the center of the universe and man as its most important creature. He was aware that this Ptolemaic idea was opposed to sensory-observed facts, which demonstrated conclusively that the earth was not the center of the universe. In fact, the earth was not even the center of its solar system—a position occupied by the sun. This caused Bolingbroke to label Genesis's account of creation "absurd" and to challenge the idea that Moses, who wrote it, was inspired by God. If Moses were so inspired, why would God inspire him with such absurd falsity, Bolingbroke argued? Was God merely accommodating His inspired revelations to the low level of understanding of the people as some rationalized the deficiencies of Genesis? Bolingbroke did not think so and countered this argument by asking: "Was it necessary to that purpose . . . that he [God] should, give them an absurd account, since he thought fit to give them one, of the creation of our physical, and may we say, of our moral system?"[12] This line of thought led to the conclusion that either Moses was not inspired by God but pretended he was, which made him a fraud, or if he was inspired, God gave him false information, which made God a deceiver. It was such thinking that caused deists to reject the Bible as the word of God and view it as a human document written by men who passed themselves off as "sacred authors" but merely catered to "all the vulgar notions of the ages and countries in which they lived, out of regard to their ignorance and to the gross conceptions of the people," as Bolingbroke stated.

Consistent with the deistic Lockean theory of knowledge, a major premise of deism is that if you want to know God, don't use scripture or tradition because they are full of imposture and untruth. More reliable knowledge is gained by examining God's works or creation with the senses from which the reality of God can then be deduced. To put it another way, true knowledge of God, like true knowledge of science, is discovered by using sensory-based perceptions of the world and reason-based conclusions born of contemplating on those perceptions. By observing such things as nature's intricate patterns and structures—like those in plants and animals— one can deduce that an intelligent God, called nature's God, was nature's creator. Moreover, Isaac Newton's discovery of the laws of gravity by using the scientific method gave support to the deistic idea that the laws of nature that govern the world and universe were placed there by an intelligent God at the time of creation. Indeed, to deists, discovery of scientific law, which was the same as God's law of nature, proved the existence of God.[13] Jefferson himself used this scientific deistic approach to proving the existence of God:

> I hold (without appeal to revelation) that when we take a view of the universe, in its parts, general or particular, it is impossible for the human mind not to perceive and feel a conviction of design, consummate skill, and indefinite power in every atom of its composition. The movements of the heavenly bodies, so exactly held in their course by the balance of centrifugal and centripetal forces; the structure of our earth itself, with its distribution of lands, waters,

and atmosphere; animal and vegetable bodies, examined in all their minutest particles; insects, mere atoms of life, yet as perfectly organized as man or mammoth; . . . it is impossible, I say, for the human mind not to believe, that there is in all this, design, cause and effect, up to an ultimate cause, a Fabricator of all things from matter and motion.[14]

Another premise of most deists is that once God put his laws of nature in the universe at creation, He left His creation alone and let His laws govern exclusively. Deists used the clock and clock-maker analogy to illustrate this point. Creation was the clock and God the clock maker. Scientific law or God's laws of nature were analogous to the springs and mechanism God put in His clock that enabled it to run itself. Because of this view, many deists argued that God does not intervene in His creation with miracles because they are against natural law or the laws of motion God put in His creation. A miracle, by definition, is a momentary suspension or defiance of natural law and for God to go against His laws this way was for God to go against Himself. Moreover, deists argued that God was perfect and, therefore, put perfect law in His creation capable of governing it at all times and under all circumstances. Therefore, if God ever found it necessary to intervene in His creation with miracles and thereby went against His laws, this was a de facto admission by God that His laws were inadequate, and that He, therefore, was not perfect. Bolingbroke expressed this deistic view when he wrote: "Nothing can be less reconcilable to the notion of an all-perfect being, than the imagination that he undoes by his power in particular cases [miracles] what his wisdom [law born of God's wisdom], to whom nothing is future, once thought sufficient to be established for all cases."[15]

Bolingbroke concluded that without laws governing creation, there would be chaos. To him, therefore, the real miracles were God's laws of nature established at the time of creation that maintain order in creation. Those laws never needed to be changed, suspended, or redirected with other miracles. On the other hand, Bolingbroke maintained that miracles described in biblical revelation, unverified by credible witnesses and repugnant to universal human experience, should not be accepted as true by blind, unexamined, or unquestioned faith. Rather they should be scrutinized critically with reason and denied as false if there is no evidence to support them from credible witnesses.[16] Moreover, once these miracles were denied, theology based on them should also be denied. On the other hand, the objectively verifiable laws of nature or scientifically discovered laws, which were true miracles according to Bolingbroke, proved the existence of God. As he put it:

> The missionary of supernatural religion [revelation] appeals to the testimony of men he never knew, and of whom the infidel he labors to convert never heard, for the truth of those extraordinary events [miracles] which prove the revelation he preaches: and it is said that this objection was made at first to Austin the monk by Ethereld the saxon king. But the missionary of natural religion can appeal at all times, and every where, to present and immediate evidence, to the testimony of sense intellect, for the truth of those miracles which he brings in proof: the constitution of the mundane system [laws of nature] being in a very proper sense an aggregate of miracles.[17]

In the light of Bolingbroke's comments, it becomes understandable why Jefferson deleted all miracles when he edited the four gospels later in life that became known as *The Jefferson Bible*.

## WHAT KIND OF GOD?

An Age of Enlightenment value, to which Bolingbroke and Jefferson both subscribed, was that an unexamined God was not worth believing in or worshiping. As a result of this value, both men critically examined the Gods of the Old and New Testaments and found them unworthy of either belief or worship. To put it another way, they found these biblical Gods bad Gods, while they found the deistic God of natural theology a good God who was, therefore, worthy of belief and worship. Both men thereby passed moral judgment on God, which was commonplace among those who subscribed to Enlightenment values. To people of faith, however, this was blasphemy because they maintained humans should never pass judgment on God.

The idea of humans judging God brings up a theological dilemma, which, as Mark Goldie pointed out, has its roots in classical thought. Socrates mentioned it when he asked Euthyphro: Is something "just" solely because God willed it, or did God will it because that something is just by its very nature? If justice is nothing more than the will of God expressed in His revealed commands or laws, it has no essential element. It is known by gaining knowledge of God's commands or laws. Voluntarism or nominalism is the name for this unthinking, uncritical approach to justice, which is found in the Bible where God told Abraham to kill his son Isaac. To Abraham, this act of killing was both just and moral simply because God commanded it, which made it a reflection of God's will. At risk in this theological approach, which leaves God's will supreme, is God's reasonableness. Is it reasonable and just, according to reason, for God to order Abraham to kill his own son? Many would say no. Therefore, although the will of God is supreme in His command that Abraham kill Isaac, that supremacy takes toll of God's reasonableness and justice too if justice has an essential nature that can be found with reason. As Goldie also pointed out, Thomas Hobbes secularized the voluntarist view by making justice and morality the will of the sovereign expressed in his proclaimed rules or laws.[18]

Enter the New Testament logos God in this theological dilemma. The logos God is found in the first verse of John: "In the beginning was the Word and the Word was with God, and the Word was God." This language identifies God with "Word" and the "Word" is revealed and set forth in scripture—a reflection of God's will. Voluntarism and nominalism is, therefore, upheld in this verse of John. Indeed, in the original Greek version of this verse, logos means "Word." Yet logos also means reason and if reason is substituted for "Word" in this verse, it becomes: "In the beginning was Reason and Reason was with God and Reason was God." Although this substitution equates God with reason, some Enlightenment figures, Jefferson included, said this makes more sense than to equate God with "Word" or will, as the New Testament translation does, since only a rational intelligent God could, "in the beginning," create the universe with all its intricacies and laws. Moreover, God as reason instead of word or will makes God conform to reason along with His justice and morality, since reason is His very being. And, if God conforms to reason, so does His will.[19] Clearly, Jefferson came down on the reason side of this dilemma because he insisted that God should and would conform to justice, which had an essential nature discoverable with reason combined with the moral sense, as we shall see in chapter 3. And, if human reason could discover justice, God and His justice could be judged by reason.

There is, however, still another problem in humans passing moral judgment on God. The effect of original sin renders them morally incompetent to do this. After Adam and Eve ate the forbidden fruit from the tree of knowledge in the Garden of Eden, they fell away from their original righteousness and became morally tainted. This made them incapable of accurately determining what is moral independent of God, His scripture, His church, and His clergy. All humans inherit this moral taint as a result of original sin as well as the guilt of Adam and Eve for their disobedience to God in the Garden of Eden, according to predominating versions of Christianity by principal Christian theologians both Catholic and Protestant.[20] Bolingbroke, however, denied original sin. He maintained it put God in a very unfavorable light. How could an all-good, all-powerful, all-knowing, or perfect God create a man and a woman who would disobey Him, thereby demonstrating that His creation was imperfect from the start? Moreover, how could God, if He were just, punish all successive generations of males with earning their bread by hard labor and all females with pain at childbirth as well as obedience to their husbands—the same punishments He imposed on Adam and Eve for committing the original sin?[21] These successive generations issuing from Adam and Eve did not disobey God. Yet He punished them as if they had. Moreover, how could He punish all humans after original sin with eternal damnation unless He sent His innocent son, Lord Jesus Christ— God incarnate in the form of the second person of the Trinity—to die on the cross to atone for the guilt each person inherited from Adam and Eve for original sin, as Christian theology of major denominations states? A just God would not have done any of these things, concluded Bolingbroke by stating that they were "absolutely irreconcilable to every idea we can frame of wisdom, justice, and goodness, to say nothing of the dignity of the supreme being."[22] Bolingbroke was especially critical of the Christian doctrine of atonement or satisfaction where the innocent Jesus became the sacrificial Lamb of God and suffered, as a substitute, the punishment guilty humans deserved in order to satisfy God's justice. As he put it:

> God sent his only begotten son, who had not offended him, to be sacrificed by men, who had offended him, that he might expiate their sins, and satisfy his own anger. Surely our ideas of moral attributes will lead us to think that god would have been satisfied, more agreeably to his mercy and goodness, without any expiation, upon the repentance of the offenders, and more agreeably to his justice with any other expiation rather than this.[23]

Bolingbroke then ridiculed the doctrine of atonement and satisfaction by describing how absurd an earthly king would look if he offered his own innocent son as a substitute to receive punishment deserved by his wicked and offensive people the way God the Father did with Jesus:

> Let us suppose a great prince governing a wicked and rebellious people. He had it in his power to punish, he thinks fit to pardon them. But he orders his only and beloved son to be put to death to expiate their sins, and to satisfy his royal vengeance.[24]

Jefferson also rejected and ridiculed original sin, especially the idea that it caused humans to be morally tainted. If God created humankind capable of original sin or in any way that would cause them to become morally tainted, then God must have been "a pitiful bungler," according to Jefferson.[25] Jefferson also rejected the doctrine of atonement and satisfaction with his denial of original sin, which is the basis of atonement and satisfaction. Without original sin there is no need for Jesus to atone for human guilt due to original sin. Moreover, like many deists, Jefferson rejected the divinity of Jesus along with his miraculous virgin birth and resurrection offered as proof of his divinity, because that divinity is linked to the doctrine of atonement and satisfaction which states that God sent Jesus, His only begotten son, to die on the cross to atone for the guilt each human inherits as a result of original sin.[26]

When judging the God of the Old Testament, Bolingbroke called attention to Deuteronomy 13:5, which states that any "prophet, or that dreamer of dreams," who speaks in a way that would "turn *you* away from the LORD your God" "shall be put to death." Verses 6 through 9 say the same punishment applies to anyone, including family and friends:

> 6 If thy brother, the son of thy mother, or thy son, or thy daughter, or the wife of thy bosom, or thy friend, which *is* as thine own soul, entice thee secretly, saying, Let us go and serve other gods, which thou hast not known, thou, nor thy fathers:
> 7 *Namely*, of the gods of the people which *are* round about you, nigh unto thee, or far off from thee, from the *one* end of the earth even unto the *other* end of the earth;
> 8 Thou shalt not consent unto him, nor hearken unto him; neither shall thine eye pity him, neither shalt thou spare, neither shalt thou conceal him:
> 9 But thou shalt surely kill him; thine hand shall be first upon him to put him to death, and afterwards the hand of all the people.

No tolerance, compassion, or mercy must be shown to those who influence individuals to worship other gods. Similar treatment is prescribed for cities that believe in and serve other gods where individuals live who are trying to influence Jews to do the same, as is stated in verses 15 and 16:

> 15 Thou shalt surely smite the inhabitants of that city with the edge of the sword, destroying it utterly, and all that *is* therein, and the cattle thereof, with the edge of the sword.
> 16 And thou shalt gather all the spoil of it into the midst of the

street thereof, and shalt burn with fire the city, and all the spoil
thereof every whit, for the LORD thy God: and it shall be all heap
for ever; it shall not be built again.

What the God of the Old Testament commands in Deuteronomy
13 is murder, assassination, and even the extermination of people
who try to influence His followers to turn away from Him or worship another god. Bolingbroke said such commands or laws were
against the moral laws of nature and the deistic God of natural theology who placed those natural laws in the world at the time of creation. Therefore, he condemned laws like those in Deuteronomy 13
along with the God who commanded them as "unjust"[27] while
simultaneously praising the deistic God of natural theology and His
moral law of nature:

> I say that the law of nature is the law of god. Of this I have the
> same demonstrative knowledge, that I have of the existence of god,
> the all-perfect being [of natural theology]. I say that the all-perfect
> being cannot contradict himself; that he would contradict himself
> if the laws contained in the thirteenth chapter of Deuteronomy, to
> mention no others here, were his laws, since they contradict those
> of nature; and therefore that they are not his laws. Of this I have as
> certain, as intuitive [knowledge], as I have that two and two are
> equal to four, or that the whole is bigger than a part.[28]

Bolingbroke's condemnation of the Gods of the Old and New
Testaments was also due to the doctrine of predestination, which
arose out of Paul's quote in Romans 9:11–13 (New Testament) of
God's statement in Malachi 1:2–3 (Old Testament) about Jacob and
Esau to their mother, Rebecca, while she carried these twins in her
womb: "Yet I loved Jacob, And I hated Esau." What Paul stressed
with this statement is that in the prebirth state, it was God's election
or grace that determined salvation, not works, because the unborn
Jacob and Esau had not yet performed any works. According to
Christian predestination, just as the Old Testament God loved Jacob
and hated Esau for no reason while they were in their mother's
womb, the New Testament God gave saving grace to some and with-

held it from others for no reason while in the womb. Those who were elected for salvation, however, still had the inclination to sin as a result of moral taint due to original sin. Yet according to the doctrine of predestination, predestinating grace gave them God's strength to restrain their sinful inclinations. The test of being an elect or predestined, therefore, was living a moral life free of sin.[29]

Although Catholicism did not officially subscribe to predestination, the doctrine was part of the North African Church in the third century, which expelled those unable to restrain their sinful inclinations because they were presumed to be nonelect and, therefore, hell-bound. At that time, Pope Callistus of the Roman Church, in contrast to the North African Church, decided to retain both the elect and the nonelect as members of the Church, indicating that he believed in predestination. He is said to have quoted Jesus' words "Let the tares grow along with the wheat" to support this position.[30] In addition, predestination was believed by many of the Catholic Church's most prominent theologians. Augustine, who lived in the fourth and fifth centuries, subscribed to predestination and fully explained it, as did Thomas Aquinas. So did the Counter-Reformation leader Ignatius Loyola, who argued that predestination should not be talked about because it encouraged immorality in humans. Loyola maintained that there was no motive to be good if you felt you were an elect or refrain from evil if you were a nonelect: your actions would have no impact on your salvation since the issue was already decided by God's having granted or withheld grace while you were in your mother's womb. The principal Reformation theologians—Martin Luther, John Calvin, and Huldreich Zwingli—also subscribed to predestination. Moreover, they emphasized it. Luther even quoted Jesus in John 13:18 and 6:44 to support predestination: "I speak not to you all: I know whom I have chosen" and "No man can come to me, except the Father which hath sent me draw him."[31]

Bolingbroke was appalled by the doctrine of predestination because of the partiality and injustice of the New Testament God arbitrarily granting grace to some while withholding it from others before they were born. Moreover, he railed against the viciousness of the Old Testament God, which was manifest in His commands in

Deuteronomy 13. He also railed against the Old Testament God's partiality, which was manifest in His granting grace exclusively to the seed of Abraham, Isaac, and Jacob, thereby making them His chosen people while simultaneously rejecting Jacob's twin brother, Esau, and his seed. Bolingbroke compared the partiality of the gods of both Christianity and Judaism with the impartiality of the deistic God of natural theology, who loved and treated all humans equally regardless of their beliefs or nonbeliefs. The deistic nature's God thereby acted in accord with the justice of His moral law of nature rather than the vicious biblical laws born of the biblical God's willful commands. To Bolingbroke, therefore, it was the natural religion God of deism that was worthy of belief and worship, not the Gods of either the Old or New Testament. As he put it:

> Natural religion represents an all perfect being to our adoration and to our love; and the precept "thou shalt love the lord thy god with all thy heart["]; will be effectual in this system. Can any man now presume to say that the god of Moses, or the god of Paul, is this amiable being? The god of the first is partial, unjust, and cruel; delights in blood, commends assassinations, massacres and even exterminations of people. The god of the second elects some of his creatures to salvation, and predestines others to damnation, even in the womb of their mothers.[32]

Following Bolingbroke's lead, Jefferson judged and condemned the partial Gods of the Old and New Testaments with similar language. He called the God of the Jews the "family God of Abraham, of Isaac, and of Jacob, and the local God of Israel."[33] He was also aware of Deuteronomy, which he referred to during a law case in 1771.[34] That awareness gave him knowledge of the Old Testament God's cruel and bloody commands in chapter 13. As a result, he stated that the Jewish religion "had presented for the object of their worship, a Being of terrific character, cruel, vindictive, capricious and unjust."[35] The God of the New Testament was similar, according to Jefferson. He knew that predestination extended beyond Calvinism, which emphasized this doctrine, since Anglicanism, the faith in which he was raised, included predestination in its Thirty-nine Articles.[36] Yet he singled out Calvin when he criticized predestination by stating that Calvin was

> an atheist, which I can never be; or rather his religion was one of daemonism. If ever man worshipped a false god, he did. The Being described in his 5 points [which included predestination], is not the god whom you and I acknowledge and adore, the Creator and benevolent Governor of the world; but a daemon of malignant spirit. It would be more pardonable to believe in no God at all, than to blaspheme Him by the atrocious attributes of Calvin.[37]

Like Bolingbroke, who praised the "all perfect being" or deistic God of "natural religion" as worthy "of our adoration" but condemned the "unjust and cruel" God of the Old Testament and the predestinator God of the New Testament, Jefferson did the same. He called the God of the Jews "cruel" and "unjust"[38] and the God of Predestination "a daemon of malignant spirit." As he wrote to John Adams, neither of these gods was the God "whom you and I acknowledge and adore," thereby reiterating the Enlightenment value of examining God before you believe in or worship Him to see if he is worthy of either. Yet even though Jefferson rejected the Gods of the Old and New Testaments, he did "acknowledge and adore" the deistic God of natural theology, "the Creator and benevolent Governor of the world," as he stated to Adams.[39]

## THE GOD OF JUSTICE, REASON, FREEDOM, AND TOLERANCE

A prerequisite of justice is impartiality symbolized by the blindfold worn by the goddess of justice who was derived from the classical Greek and Roman goddesses Themis and Justitia. She holds scales in one hand and a sword in the other with which she meticulously weighs the actions of humans without seeing who they are and then metes out the exact punishment due. Everyone is thereby judged by the same standard, with no one receiving partial, biased, or preferential treatment. The blindfold thereby depicts that partiality is incom-

patible with justice. Consistent with this concept of justice, both Bolingbroke and Jefferson maintained that if God was partial to some, He
was also unjust as well as parochial, narrow-minded, and bigoted.
Therefore, both men rejected any sectarian God that favored some religion, church, or temple and saved only persons who believed in its
doctrines, participated in its worship, and partook of its sacraments,
because this was a manifestation of partiality and therefore injustice
on the part of God. Diametrically opposed to a partial, sectarian God
was the deistic God of natural theology. He was an impartial universal
God who treated all peoples and persons the same no matter what
they believed or disbelieved and was, thereby, just. In addition, individual humans created by the deistic God were not morally tainted by
original sin and, therefore, were incapable of attaining salvation
without God's divine intervention or grace. Indeed, Jefferson's deistic
"Nature's" God endowed each person with a moral sense, which made
them independent morally competent agents who could earn salvation by good works, which will be discussed in chapter 3. Therefore,
the God of Deism and natural theology did not require that humans
believe in a certain set of doctrines, worship at a certain church or
temple, receive grace, or participate in certain sacraments as prerequi-
sites to salvation. The deistic God did not care if you were a Catholic,
a Protestant, a Jew, a Muslim, an agnostic, or even an atheist. The fact
that you did not believe in Him, or could not make up your mind
whether or not to believe in Him, or believed in another God, did not
concern Him. He was not a jealous God. He was the antithesis of
narrow-mindedness and jealousy. He was the universal God of reason,
freedom, and tolerance. As such, He respected the reason and freedom
of each person to make up their own minds what to believe or disbelieve about God and religion. Instead of stating, as the Judeo-Christian God did in the Ten Commandments: "Thou shalt have no other
gods before me. . . . For I the LORD thy God *am* a jealous God"
(Exodus 20:3–5) and later on in Exodus: "Thou shalt worship no
other god: for the LORD, whose name *is* Jealous, *is* a jealous God"
(Exodus 34:14), the deistic God in effect states: "You choose with your
own reason what God to believe or not to believe in, and I will not
favor you or punish you no matter what you choose, for I the Lord thy

God am not a jealous God." Jefferson described this disposition of the deistic God when he wrote his nephew Peter Carr:

> Question with boldness even the existence of a God; because, if there be one, he must more approve of the homage of reason, than that of blindfolded fear. . . . Your own reason is the only oracle given you by heaven, and you are answerable, not for the rightness, but the uprightness of the decision. . . . Read all the histories of Christ, as well as those whom the council of ecclesiastics have decided for us, to be Pseudo-evangelists, as those they named Evangelists. Because these Pseudo-evangelists pretended to inspiration, as much as the others, and you are to judge their pretensions by your own reason, and not by the reason of those ecclesiastics.[40]

In his later years, Jefferson edited the four gospels in order to bring Jesus and Christianity in accord with deism, "liberty, science, and the freest expansion of the human mind," as well as religious pluralism and peace that results from allowing freedom in religion. What remained, after his editing, were Jesus' moral teachings without any doctrine.[41] Among Jesus' statements Jefferson deleted were those he deemed "rags" or imposture that were posited on Jesus' moral teachings by the early followers of Jesus or priests of the church, which made Jesus and Christianity authoritarian, doctrinaire, creedal, and violent. Since humans fought and killed each other over doctrine and creed, such statements, as Jefferson put it, "made of Christendom a slaughter-house" and "Aceldama" or field of blood.[42] Jesus' authoritarian comment "I am the way, the truth, and the life: no man cometh unto the Father, but by me" (John 14:6), which in effect states that individuals must follow Jesus and Christian doctrine in order to reach God and heaven, was one of Jesus' statements that Jefferson deleted. So was "Think not that I am come to send peace on earth: I came not to send peace, but a sword" (Matthew 10:34). Another was where Jesus gave "the keys of the kingdom of heaven" (Matthew 16:18–19) to Peter and his successors as heads or popes of the Church, which made it necessary to be part of the Church and receive its sacraments in order to gain entrance to heaven. Jefferson also deleted all miracles contradicting the laws of nature that govern the material world, including virgin birth and resurrection, as well as Jesus' anti-Semitic authoritarian statements in John 8:42–47, where Jesus accused Jews, and in effect all who did not accept his teachings, of being children of the devil:

> 42 If God were your father, ye would love me: for I proceeded forth and came from God; neither came I of myself, but he sent me.
>
> 43 Why do ye not understand my speech? *even* because ye cannot hear my word.
>
> 44 Ye are of *your* father the devil, and the lusts of your father ye will do. He was a murderer from the beginning, and abode not in the truth, because there is no truth in him. When he speaketh a lie, he speaketh of his own: for he is a liar, and the father of it.
>
> 45 And because I tell *you* the truth, ye believe me not.
>
> 46 Which of you convinceth me of sin? And if I say the truth, why do ye not believe me?
>
> 47 He that is of God heareth God's words: ye therefore hear *them* not, because ye are not of God.[43]

Deist George Washington,[44] Lincoln's hero, captured the essence of the deistic God's disposition with a statement that is antithetical to Jesus' authoritarian comments and exactly antithetical to Jesus' statements in John 8:42-47:

> Shall I . . . set up my judgment as the standard of perfection? . . . Shall I arrogantly pronounce that whoever differs from me, must discern the subject through a distorting medium, or be influenced by some nefarious design? The mind is so formed in different persons as to contemplate the same object in different points of view. Hence originates the difference in questions of the greatest import, both human and divine.[45]

Washington maintained men were bound to think differently because: "Men's minds are as variant as their faces, and where the motives of their actions are pure, the operation of former is no more to be imputed to them as a crime than the appearance of the latter; for both, being the work of nature, are equally unavoidable."[46]

Jefferson, too, had the idea that differences in human minds were the "work of nature" and made differences of opinion "unavoidable," as Washington stated, but added that they were "the work of our Creator." As he put it: "The varieties in the structure and action of the human mind as in those of the body, are the work of our Creator, against which it cannot be a religious duty to erect the standard of uniformity."[47]

Both Washington and Jefferson manifested deistic tolerance to those of all religious as well as nonreligious beliefs. This can be seen in letters they wrote to Jews who were often discriminated against by law in America prior to the Revolution. As Washington stated in 1790 to one of the first American Jewish congregations in Newport, Rhode Island, emphasizing that government would enforce deistic tolerance by protecting the rights, including the religious freedom rights, of all citizens:

> The citizens of the United States of America have a right to applaud themselves for having given to mankind examples of an enlarged and liberal policy—a policy worthy of imitation. All possess alike liberty of conscience and immunities of citizenship.
>
> It is now no more that toleration is spoken of as if it were the indulgence of one class of people that another enjoyed the exercise of their inherent natural rights, for, happily, the government of the United States, which gives to bigotry no sanction, to persecution no assistance, requires only that they who live under its protection should demean themselves as good citizens in giving it on all occasions their effectual support. . . .
>
> May the children of the stock of Abraham who dwell in this land continue to merit and enjoy the good will of the other inhabitants; while every one shall sit in safety under his own vine and fig tree and there shall be none to make him afraid.[48]

Jefferson's comments to Mordecai M. Noah, a prominent American Jew, were similar. Yet he believed governmental or legal enforcement of tolerance was not enough. Tolerance should be ingrained in the mind-set of the people:

Your sect [Jews] by its sufferings has furnished a remarkable proof of the universal spirit of religious intolerance inherent in every sect, disclaimed by all while feeble and practiced by all while in power. Our laws have applied the only antidote to this vice, protecting our religions, as they do our civil rights by putting all on equal footing. But more remains to be done. For altho' we are free by the law, we are not so in practice. Public opinion erects itself into an inquisition, and exercises its office with as much fanaticism as fans the flames of an *Auto da fe*. The prejudice still scowling on your section of our religion, altho' the elder one, cannot be unfelt by yourselves. It is hoped that individual dispositions will at length, mould themselves to the model of the law, and consider the moral basis on which all our religions rest, as the rallying point which unites them in a common interest; while the peculiar dogmas branching from it are the exclusive concern of the respective sects embracing them, and no rightful subject of notice to any other.[49]

Although the deistic God was not concerned with what you believed or disbelieved, simultaneously, since He created humans as free moral agents, He required moral behavior on their part in order to attain salvation, which had to be earned through good works. This made the deistic God just, not partial, whimsical, and capricious when it came to salvation. In a statement reflecting these ideas, Jefferson said: "Were I to be founder of a new sect, I would call them Apiarians, and after the example of the bee, advise them to extract the honey of every sect. My fundamental principle would be the reverse of Calvin's, that we are to be saved by our good works which are within our power, not by our faith [determined by grace in Calvinism] which is not within our power."[50]

Jefferson made similar comments, which reflect his rejection of sectarian dogmatic religion. When paraphrasing the views of a Quaker, he said, "that in heaven, God knew no [creedal or doctrinal] distinctions, but considered all good men as his children, and as brethren of the same family." Then, continuing his paraphrase, he stated: "I believe, with the Quaker preacher, that he who steadily observes those moral precepts in which all religions concur, will never be questioned at the gates of heaven, as to the dogmas in which they all differ."[51] One year later, still paraphrasing the Quaker preacher, Jefferson wrote:

> That, on entering that [heaven's] gate, we leave those badges of schism [religious affiliation] behind, and find ourselves united in those [moral] principles only in which God has united us all. Let us not be uneasy then about the different roads we may pursue, as believing them the shortest, to that our last abode; but, following the guidance of a good conscience, let us be happy in the hope that by these different paths we shall all meet in the end.[52]

Bolingbroke's impartial, all-inclusive, universal deistic God of reason, freedom, tolerance, and justice was the basis of his own "belief in some sort of a universal religion" not limited to one religious point of view, as Gilbert Chinard pointed out.[53] "Theism" was the term Bolingbroke used for this natural theology, deistic approach to religion. And, while he criticized the "partiality" of the Gods of Old and New Testament theology, which he called "artificial theology," because they were not born of observing nature, he emphasized that "partiality" was something "which theism will never impute to the supreme being."[54]

## DEISM AND THE DECLARATION OF INDEPENDENCE

Jefferson placed the natural theology impartial, none-are-excluded, universal, all-inclusive God of deism in the Declaration of Independence as the foundation of the egalitarian republican political theory of that document as is seen in the first sentence:

> When in the Course of human events, it becomes necessary for one People to dissolve the Political Bands which have connected them with another, and to assume among the Powers of the Earth, the separate and equal Station to which the *Laws of Nature and of Nature's God* [my italics] entitle them, a decent Respect to the Opinions of Mankind requires that they should declare the causes which impel them to the Separation.[55]

This sentence is taken from the first official printed copy of the Declaration approved by the Continental Congress in 1776. In quotations of the Declaration contained in this work, this text is used. And, in order to demonstrate that the ideas of each quote are Jefferson's and not Congress's or the other four members of the Declaration's drafting committee of five appointed by the Congress, each quote is referenced to show that its language was unaltered from Jefferson's rough draft that the drafting committee designated him to write or that alterations were his, or, if not his, did not change the meaning of his language.

The partiality of the Old Testament God, who chose the Jewish people and nation above all others, is repudiated in the first sentence of the Declaration. As Jefferson put it, the "Nature's God" of deism and His "Laws of Nature" entitle every "People" to a "separate and *equal* [my italics] Station" or nation "among the Powers of the Earth." This God-given equality among all peoples and nations was an argument against any claims of imperialism, colonialism, or dominion by any people or nation—aimed at the English people and nation—over other peoples, territories, or nations. Indeed, the deistic "Nature's God" content of Jefferson's language even applied to religious imperialism or the claim of any religion that a certain city or place is the spiritual center of the world from which all religious truth emanates, thereby giving that city or place spiritual authority over the world. As the impartial "Nature's God" would not choose any people, nation, individual, or doctrinal belief system as special, privileged, or sacred, neither would He choose a particular place in this way. Bolingbroke expressed this by pointing out conflicting claims as to who were good Christians coming from various geographical locations and even from the same location at different times. Obviously, all these claims could not be true, and since none could be proved to the satisfaction of all the others, all of them were highly questionable. Moreover, if each one was considered in the context of all others, it gave the impression of being self-servingly sectarian and subjective. Implicitly echoing Locke's view that there was no authority on earth that could determine orthodoxy or what was correct in religion, Bolingbroke said:

Who are to be reputed good Christians? Go to Rome, they are papists. Go to Geneva, they are Calvinists. Go to the north of Germany, they are Lutherans. Come to London, they are none of these. Orthodoxy is a mode. It is one thing at one time and in one place. It is something else at another time, and in another place, or even in the same place: for in this religious country of ours, without seeking proofs in any other, men have been burned under one reign, for the very same doctrines they were obliged to profess in another.[56]

To the deistic God, Rome or Geneva, Jerusalem or Mecca, Boston or Salt Lake City are not chosen, designated, or blessed by God with religious authority any more than any other place. Thus the deistic theology of the Declaration of Independence is against any form of religious, as well as political, imperialism or dominion.

In the second paragraph of the Declaration, Jefferson took the partial-to-none, none-are-privileged-or-excluded egalitarianism of "Nature's God" that applied to each and every "People" and nation in the first paragraph and applied it to each and every individual. In a succinct expression of the political theory of the Declaration of Independence, he wrote:

We hold these Truths to be self-evident, that all Men are created equal, that they are endowed by their Creator with certain unalienable Rights, that among these are Life, Liberty, and the Pursuit of Happiness. That to secure these Rights, Governments are instituted among Men, deriving their just powers from the Consent of the Governed, that whenever any Form of Government becomes destructive to these Ends, it is the Right of the People to alter or to abolish it, and to institute new Government, laying its Foundation on such Principles and organizing its Powers in such Form, as to Them shall seem most likely to effect their Safety and Happiness.[57]

Compare this egalitarian "All Men are created equal" theology with Calvin's statement, "For all are not created in equal condition; rather, eternal life is foreordained for some, eternal damnation for others."[58] Yet even in the medieval period, long before the Reformation and Calvin, as D. E. Luscombe and G. R. Evans point out, humans were considered unequal because of the inequality of God's grace and angelic protection.[59] In marked contrast, Jefferson's "Nature's God" of the Declaration made His egalitarianism manifest by endowing each person at the time of creation with the equal "unalienable Rights" of "Life, Liberty and the Pursuit of Happiness" and by giving each the moral capacity—discussed in chapter 3—to earn salvation without grace. Indeed the impartial, egalitarian, deistic God was antigrace, since grace is a partial or special favor granted by God to some but not to others for no reason.

Apart from Jefferson's two deistic references to God—"Nature's God" in the first paragraph and "all Men are created equal" by the "Creator" in the second paragraph—there are two other references to God in the Declaration. Both are in the last paragraph and both have orthodox Judeo-Christian implications. They are: "appealing to the Supreme Judge of the World for the Rectitude of our Intentions" and "with a firm reliance on the Protection of divine Providence." However, Jefferson did not make these last paragraph references. They were made and inserted by the Continental Congress in which the vast majority of delegates were not deists.[60] The question then arises: Why did the Congress approve the deism Jefferson placed in the succinctly stated political theory of the first two paragraphs? In answering this question, it should be kept in mind that the Colonies and England were already at war in July of 1776 and had been since the skirmishes at Lexington and Concord in 1775. And, because the colonies were opposing the superior military might of the British, the key to a successful revolution was military alliance with a foreign power. Without a formal Declaration of Independence, however, other nations would not accept an ambassador to negotiate an alliance.[61] Indeed, without a Declaration of Independence, there was no American national entity with which a foreign nation could make an alliance. The Second Continental Congress that finally made the Declaration dealt with this political problem with delegates who were, for the most part, practical-minded political men, not theologians. As such, many delegates, perhaps most, were unaware of the deistic thrust of the Declaration's first two paragraphs. And if they were aware of the Declaration's deism, being practical-minded they did not object to the deistic "Nature's God" because it served the purpose of declaring an independent nation or, as Jefferson put it, "the separate and equal Station to which the Laws of Nature and of Nature's God entitle" a "People." As to why the committee of five, appointed by Congress to draft the Declaration that in turn appointed Jefferson its draftsman, approved the deism Jefferson placed in the Declaration before it submitted its draft to Congress for final approval, Benjamin Franklin was a deist and John Adams was a religious liberal. Neither, therefore, was offended by the Declaration's deism. As for Roger Sherman and Robert Livingston, the other two members of the drafting committee besides Jefferson, whatever their views were on the Declaration's deism, if they had any, they approved Jefferson's draft without suggesting any changes, according to Jefferson's account.[62]

## THE DECLARATION'S ALL-INCLUSIVE DEFINITION OF HUMANITY

Consistent with the Declaration's impartial, egalitarian, universal, all-inclusive deistic theology that Jefferson placed there, the language of the second paragraph contains the Declaration's most extraordinary feature—an all-inclusive universal definition of common humanity extending to all races, both sexes, and people of all theistic, atheistic, or agnostic persuasions. The phrase "All Men are created equal" and endowed with the right of "Liberty" provides that definition. Deists would have recognized this element of the Declaration because of the impartial, all-inclusive, none-are-excluded theological aspect of the deistic "Nature's God."

Apart from this deistic, all-inclusive theological element of the Declaration, Jefferson's rough draft contained a provision deleted by the Continental Congress that makes it clear he specifically included blacks and women in the "All Men" language of that document. It states that King George III

> has waged cruel war against human nature itself, violating it's most
> sacred rights of life & liberty in the persons of a distant people who

never offended him, captivating & carrying them into slavery in another hemisphere, or to incur miserable death in their transportation thither. This piratical warfare, the opprobrium of *infidel* powers, is the warfare of the *CHRISTIAN* king of Great Britain. Determined to keep open a market where MEN should be bought & sold. He has prostituted his negative for suppressing every legislative attempt to prohibit or restrain this execrable commerce: and that this assemblage of horrors might want no fact of distinguished die, he is now exciting those very people to rise in arms among us, and to purchase that liberty of which *he* has deprived them, by murdering the people upon whom *he* also obtruded them: thus paying off former crimes committed against the *liberties* of one people, with crimes which he urges them to commit against the *lives* of another.[63]

Scholars have seen this provision differently. Herbert Friedenwald says that it is "unquestionably one of the most forceful clauses that issued from Jefferson's pen."[64] Henry Steele Commager, on the other hand, described it as "bad history" and "rhetorical without being passionate."[65] Certainly to blame King George III for having "obtruded" slavery on the colonies was not in accordance with fact, because that evil institution was established in America before his reign. The same is true of blaming him for having "deprived" blacks of "liberty" in America, because obviously many colonists were slave owners before his coronation. Yet Commager also states that there is an element of truth in Jefferson's accusations against George III. In the decade prior to the Revolutionary War, some colonies did pass legislation "to prohibit and restrain" the slave trade, as Jefferson stated in his deleted provision. The British Board of Trade, however, repeatedly disallowed such legislation, and King George III had indeed "prostituted his negative" or veto power to override the Board's decisions, as Jefferson stated. In other words, he let the Board of Trade's veto of colonial anti–slave-trade legislation stand.[66]

An important feature of Jefferson's deleted provision, however, is that it is antislavery in addition to being anti–slave trade. In the second paragraph of the Declaration, Jefferson stated that the purpose of government is to secure individual rights "among" which are

"Life" and "Liberty." Then, in the deleted provision, he said blacks have the "sacred rights of life & liberty." Since the purpose of government, according to the Declaration, is to secure the rights of "Life" and "Liberty," and blacks have these rights, the Declaration, as Jefferson drafted it, is antislavery. Jefferson was certainly aware of this. He was highly intelligent, extremely well educated, and, as an experienced lawyer, meticulous in selecting language when writing anything. This was especially true of the Declaration, which can be seen in the many alterations he made in his rough draft. There were, however, several other intelligent well-educated men in the Continental Congress, many of whom were from the South. They would have immediately grasped the antislavery implications of Jefferson's provision because it was alien to their interest in slavery. As a Virginian who was keenly aware of the proslavery disposition of many of his fellow Virginians, Jefferson had to have known his antislavery provision would provoke them as well as others who profited from slavery. Yet he still put it in the Declaration. He thereby ran the risk of alienating some colonies and perhaps jeopardized the success of the Revolutionary War should any have withdrawn their support over his anti–slave trade, antislavery provision. Therefore, even though Commager *may* be right that the language of this provision is "rhetorical without being passionate," nonetheless it tells us Jefferson was antislavery when he wrote the Declaration and took risks to make the Declaration antislavery.

Jefferson's deleted provision also makes it clear that he meant species not gender when he wrote "All Men are created equal" and endowed with "Liberty." Therefore, women are included in the Declaration's all-inclusive definition of common humanity. To many in this era of gender-neutral pronouns inclusive of both men and women, "All Men" is objectionable, which of course was not the case in Jefferson's time. However, with one exception, the phrases that designate blacks in the deleted provision are gender neutral and include both sexes. "Human nature itself" is used instead of "All Men" when stating that blacks have the "most sacred rights of life & liberty," and "Persons of a distant people" is used to designate blacks whose "sacred rights" were violated. The only place Jefferson used

"MEN" in this provision is his reference to a "[slave] market" where blacks were "bought and sold." Obviously, "MEN" in this instance refers to species not gender since men, women, and children were "bought and sold" at slave markets. However, because Jefferson used "MEN" here to designate both men and women, it is clear he did the same with "Men" in the second paragraph's "All Men are created equal."[67] Therefore, "all Men" refers to species and includes women.

Even apart from the Declaration, Jefferson stated that women have equal rights with men. He did this in his only book, *Notes on the State of Virginia*, where he wrote: "It is civilization alone which replaces women in the enjoyment of their natural equality. That [civilization] first teaches us to subdue the selfish passions and to respect those rights in others, which we value in ourselves." Although *Notes* was written in 1781, the ideas expressed and materials presented there were held and gathered by Jefferson before the Declaration of Independence. Indeed, notes he made before the Declaration of Independence reflect this.[68]

Not only blacks and women were included in "All Men are created equal" and endowed with the right of "Liberty," but also those of any and all religious or theistic, irreligious or atheistic, and nonreligious or agnostic persuasions. The freedom to be a theist, an agnostic, or an atheist was granted by the deistic "Nature's God" of the Declaration without impacting salvation, which Jefferson in effect stated when he wrote his nephew Peter Carr: "Question with boldness even the existence of a God; because, if there be one, he must more approve of the homage of reason, than that of blindfolded fear," as has been mentioned. There is, however, no specific reference to religious liberty in the Declaration. Yet it *is* included in the right of "Liberty." This is made abundantly clear in Jefferson's research and notes on religion of 1776 and the Virginia Statute for Religious Freedom he drafted in 1777 based on that research and notes.[69] Moreover, Jefferson linked religious freedom to intellectual freedom, which is also included in the right of "Liberty." This is seen in his Virginia Statute for Religious Freedom, where he wrote "all men shall be Free to profess *and by argument maintain* [my italics], their opinions in matters of religion" as well as his research notes of 1776.[70]

Jefferson's inclusion of blacks, women, and those of all religious persuasions in "All Men are created equal" and endowed with the right of "Liberty" demonstrates that he meant this phrase to be a universal, all-inclusive definition of common humanity. This is a unique feature of the Declaration of Independence, the first American document, since no other nation or civilization began with all-inclusive universal idealism. All others began with the idea, explicitly or implicitly expressed, that those of a particular tribe, race, gender, religion, or belief system were favored.

## THE UTOPIAN DECLARATION

The universal all-inclusive idealism of the Declaration, was, of course, practiced nowhere in the world in 1776, including the United States. It was therefore utopian, or, as Theodore Parker and other Transcendentalists would later say, outside of or transcendental to history. Jefferson himself was aware of the nowhere or utopian aspect of the Declaration as can be seen in his statement: "Mine, after all, may be an Utopian dream; but. . . I have thought I might indulge in it till I go to the land of dreams, and sleep there with the dreamers of all past and future times."[71] Yet Jefferson did more than just dream his utopian dream. He sought to make it a reality. He made more than a dozen legislative attempts to get rid of slavery.[72] Most of them were in his state of Virginia, but at least one was on the national level. His efforts in this respect far exceeded those of George Washington and James Madison, who both owned slaves as he did. They also exceeded those of John Adams, who made little or no effort to eradicate slavery even though he owned no slaves and was against slavery. In addition, Jefferson initiated legislation in Virginia that abolished entails and primogeniture, which, as he stated, "laid the axe to the root of Pseudo-aristocracy" based on land ownership and was, therefore, progress toward a more egalitarian society.[73] He also drafted the Virginia Statute for Religious Freedom that provided religious liberty by separating church and state.[74] Moreover, he converted his friend James Madison into an

enthusiastic supporter of adding a bill of rights to the federal Constitution and insisted that such a bill include religious and intellectual freedom (freedom of the press), which of course it did when
finally adopted.[75] He thereby contributed to the First Amendment
freedoms even though he was absent from the Constitutional Con-
ventions overseen by Madison, the architect of the Constitution and
Bill of Rights. Among Jefferson's suggestions to Madison was that
the Bill of Rights include "restriction against monopolies," which
was not included.[76] Finally, Jefferson, along with his friend
Madison, was in the forefront of resistance to the notoriously repressive and unconstitutional Alien and Sedition Acts of 1798, signed
into law by President John Adams, that enabled the federal government to jail and expel aliens without due process as well as jail and
fine those who criticized the government or its officeholders.

Although law was the principal method used by Jefferson to
actualize and expand the Declaration's all-inclusive utopian idealism, he was aware of its limitations in a democratic republic where
it would ultimately reflect public opinion. If such opinion was unfavorable, progressive legislation seldom passed or, if by some
unusual circumstance it did pass, it did not survive in ensuing legislation. The only recourse when unfavorable public opinion blocked
progressive legislation was to change that opinion. As Jefferson
stated to Charles Clay in 1790, "You are too well informed a politician, too good a judge of men, not to know, that the ground of liberty is to be gained by inches, that we must be contented to secure
what we can get, from time to time, and eternally press forward for
what is yet to get. It takes time to persuade men to do even what is
for their own good."[77] In 1814 he said much the same thing to
Thomas Cooper: "To do our fellow men the most good in our
power, we must lead where we can, follow where we cannot, and
still go with them, watching always the favorable moment for
helping them to another step."[78] Both of these statements demonstrate that Jefferson was progress oriented. Certainly, his ideas on
public opinion applied to the antislavery legislation he sought on
both state and federal levels. Yet, even though these legislative efforts
failed because public opinion was against them, one he made in

1784 inspired the similar Northwest Ordinance passed in 1787 that outlawed slavery in one-half of the United States.

Public opinion was not only generally proslavery and against emancipation in Jefferson's time, it had not changed appreciably in Lincoln's time, even in New England, which prided itself on being more progressive and civilized than the rest of the nation. Theodore Parker, the Boston Unitarian-Transcendentalist preacher and contemporary of Lincoln, complained of this. In his biography on Parker, Henry Steele Commager described New England during this period:

> New England went for slavery . . . Massachusetts went for slavery, . . . Boston went for slavery, . . . The Press pled for slavery. . . . The Courier and the Advertiser [newspapers] urged the proscription of lawyers who dared to defend fugitive slaves. . . . Even the Church preached slavery, Brattle Street and Old South taking for their text the "Southside View," and Andover reconciling "Conscience and the Constitution." Slavery in the State House, slavery in the Court House, slavery on Beacon Hill, the city of Hancock and Adams faithless to her past. . . . When the Fugitive Slave Bill was passed, Boston greeted it with a salute of a hundred guns. . . . Charles Follen was dropped from Harvard College for his abolitionism, and when he died the Federal Street Church would not allow its own Doctor Channing to hold services for him. Richard Dana espoused abolition and lost his clients; Doctor Bowditch walked arm in arm with Frederick Douglass and lost his patients. . . . Well might James Freeman Clarke say, "When I came back to Boston, it was harder to speak of slavery than it had been in Kentucky." Well might Garrison write that here he had found "contempt more bitter, opposition more active, detraction more relentless, prejudice more stubborn, and apathy more frozen than among slave owners themselves."[79]

Commager's comment, "Even the Church pled slavery," was affirmed by abolitionist Stephen S. Foster's similar statement in his pamphlet *The Brotherhood of Thieves, or a True Picture of the American Churches and Clergy*, written in 1843:

*They have publicly defended the slave system as an innocent and Heaven-ordained institution, and have thrown the sacred sanctions of religion around it, by introducing it into the pulpit, and to the communion table!* At the South, nearly the entire body of the clergy publicly advocate the perpetuity of slavery, and denounce the abolitionists as fanatics, incendiaries, and cut-throats; and the churches and clergy of the North still fellowship them, and palm them off upon the world as the ministers of Christ. I know it will be said that there are exceptions to this charge; but if there be any, I have yet to learn of them. I know not of a single ecclesiastical body in the country which has excommunicated any of its members for the crime of slaveholding, since the commencement of the anti-slavery enterprise, though most of them have cast out the true and faithful abolitionists from their communion.[80]

Some churches, like Theodore Parker's, preached abolition. Yet the overall view of public opinion on slavery, even in the churches, was not a pretty picture! It calls attention to the stark reality that public opinion was a major problem that impeded the efforts of abolitionists like Parker, Foster, and Abraham Lincoln.

The fact that Jefferson was painfully aware of the massive contradiction between slavery, which was protected by law under the Constitution, and the deistic, utopian, all-inclusive idealism of the Revolution stated in the Declaration of Independence is reflected in his letter to Jean Nicholas Demeunier, written while Minister Plenipotentiary to France in 1786, where he made one of his few references to the vengeance of a just God—perhaps hyperbole considering that Jefferson was a deist and most deists did not believe that God intervened in the world. Demeunier had been critical of the Virginia legislature's failure to pass a law abolishing slavery. In response, Jefferson, after pointing out that a minority in the legislature who favored such law was overwhelmed by the majority who opposed it, stated:

What a stupendous, what an incomprehensible machine is man! Who can endure toil, famine, stripes, imprisonment or death itself in vindication of his own liberty, and the next moment be deaf to all those motives whose power supported him thro' his trial, and inflict on his fellow men a bondage, one hour of which is fraught with more misery than ages of that which he rose in rebellion to oppose. But we must await with patience the workings of an over-ruling providence, and hope that that is preparing the deliverance of these our suffering brethren. When the measure of their tears shall be full, when their groans shall have involved heaven itself in darkness, doubtless a god of justice will awaken to their distress, and by diffusing light and liberality among their oppressors, or at length by his exterminating thunder, manifest his attention to the things of this world, and that they are not left to the guidance of a blind fatality.[81]

Another of Jefferson's rare references to the vengeance of a just God—again over slavery—was made earlier in *Notes on the State of Virginia*, written in 1781 in response to the queries of another Frenchman, Francois Marbois:

And can the liberties of a nation be thought secure when we have removed their only firm basis, a conviction in the minds of the people that these liberties are of the gift of god? That they are not to be violated but with his wrath? Indeed *I tremble for my country when I reflect that God is just* [my italics]: that his justice cannot sleep for ever: that considering numbers, nature and natural means only, a revolution of the wheel of fortune, an exchange of situa-tion, is among possible events: that it may become probable by supernatural interference! The Almighty has no attribute which can take side with us in such a contest.—But it is impossible to be temperate and to pursue this subject through the various consider-ations of policy, of morals, of history natural and civil. We must be contented to hope they will force their way into every one's mind. I think a change already perceptible, since the origin of the present revolution. The spirit of the master is abating, that of the slave rising from the dust, his condition mollifying, the way I hope preparing, under the auspices of heaven, for a total emancipation, and that this is disposed, in the order of events, to be with the con-sent of the masters, rather than by their extirpation.[82]

What Jefferson stated in these passages from *Notes*, which Lincoln read, since he quoted, "I tremble for my country when I reflect that

God is just" in his 1859 speech at Columbus, Ohio, is that "total emancipation" was called for by the "liberties of a nation"—"liberties" that were specified in the God-given, equal, unalienable rights enumerated in the Declaration of Independence. Indeed, these passages from *Notes* stated that "total emancipation" would take place. Thus Jefferson held the idea of progressive actualization of the universal utopian idealism contained in the Declaration. More specifically, he maintained that idealism mandated the complete eradication of slavery.

## "ENLIGHTEN THE PEOPLE GENERALLY"

A peaceful or nonviolent method of eradicating slavery, according to Jefferson, was by increasing knowledge among the people, or, as he said to Demeunier, "by diffusing light and liberality among their [the slaves'] oppressors." Like others of the Enlightenment, Jefferson believed that certain ideas or the lack of certain ideas that men have in their minds determine their actions. If, therefore, people are ignorant and full of untruth and superstition, they will act against their own freedom as well as that of others. They will do things, or will follow others who will cause them to do things, that are destructive to freedom. That is why Jefferson maintained that education was the remedy for ignorant, partial, biased, and prejudiced public opinion that blocked liberalizing legislation designed to eradicate and prevent exploitation and oppression. A staunch supporter of the Age of Enlightenment value that knowledge leads to progress and liberation in all fields, especially in government and religion, he said:

> *Enlighten the people generally* [my italics], and the tyranny and oppressions of body and mind will vanish like evil spirits at the dawn of day. Although I do not, with some enthusiasts, believe that the human condition will ever advance to such a state of perfection as that there shall no longer be pain or vice in the world, yet I believe it susceptible of much improvement, and most of all, in matters of government and religion; and that the diffusion of

knowledge among the people is to be the instrument by which it is to be effected.[83]

Education would enable humans to think for themselves in religion as well as in politics, according to Jefferson. It would give them knowledge necessary to establish and maintain freedom. This is why he believed the key to progressive legislation and a truly republican government, as well as insurance that the people would maintain control of such government, was public secular education. He maintained that church-controlled education produced indoctrinated sheeplike followers who would obey their clergy in politics as well as in religion. Such people, who had received such education, would merely echo the political preferences of their clergy at the polls and thereby establish a de facto oligarchy of the clergy. This would in effect destroy a democratic republican form of government. Jefferson's views on the effect of public secular education designed to teach people to read and think for themselves is reflected in his letter to Thomas Seymour: "It would seem impossible that an intelligent people, with the faculty of reading and right thinking, should continue much longer to slumber under the pupilage of an interested aristocracy of priests and lawyers, persuading them to distrust themselves, and to let them think for them."[84] Equating lawyers with priests in this statement demonstrates that Jefferson was against anyone who had and used the capacity to persuade the "people" "to distrust themselves and, to let them think for them." And, in a letter to his friend and former law teacher, George Wythe, requesting support for his Virginia bill for public secular education, he stressed the importance of people who could think for themselves in republican government.

> Preach, my dear Sir, a crusade against ignorance; establish and improve the law for educating the common people. Let our countrymen know, . . . that the tax which will be paid for this purpose, is not more than the thousandth part of what will be paid to kings, priests and nobles, who will rise up among us if we leave the people in ignorance.[85]

Lincoln, like Jefferson, was imbued with the Enlightenment idea that knowledge through reading enables people to think for themselves and that this leads to freedom and progress. Indeed, both men experienced this impact of reading in their own lives, because both, despite the fact that Jefferson was formally educated and Lincoln was not, had cultivated the habit of reading to attain knowledge early in their lives.[86] Lincoln's views on the importance of reading leading to freedom of thought are seen in his comment on the impact of the printing press in his lecture on discoveries and inventions delivered on 11 February 1859—a comment full of Enlightenment values such as the "habit of freedom of thought" among individuals comprising the populace:

> I will venture to consider *it* [the printing press], the true termination of that period called "the dark ages." Discoveries, inventions, and improvements followed rapidly, and have been increasing their rapidity ever since. . . . It is very probable—almost certain— that the great mass of men, at that time, were utterly unconscious, that their *conditions*, or their *minds* were capable of improvement. They not only looked upon the educated few as superior beings; but they supposed themselves to be naturally incapable of rising to equality. To immancipate [*sic*] the mind from this false and under estimate of itself, is the great task which printing came into the world to perform. It is difficult for us, *now* and *here*, to conceive how strong this slavery of the mind was; and how long it did, of necessity, take, to break it's shackles, and to get a habit of *freedom of thought* [my italics] established.[87]

Lincoln's value of education through reading is also seen in his first campaign address made when he unsuccessfully ran for the state legislature in 1832. His rival for the affections of Ann Rutledge, John McNamar, helped him write that address. So did Mentor Graham, the schoolteacher who assisted him in his self-education through reading.[88] Echoing Jefferson's idea that cultivating the "faculty of reading" in people was essential to a republican form of government, he said:

> Upon the subject of education, not presuming to dictate any plan or system respecting it, I can only say that I view it as the most

important subject which we as a people can be engaged in. *That every man may receive at least, a moderate education, and thereby be enabled to read the histories of his own and other countries, by which he may duly appreciate the value of our free institutions, appears to be an object of vital importance* [my italics], even on this account alone, to say nothing of the advantages and satisfaction to be derived from all being able to read the scriptures and other works, both of a religious and moral nature, for themselves. For my part, I desire to see the time when education, and by its means, morality, sobriety, enterprise and industry, shall become much more general than at present, and should be gratified to have it in my power to contribute something to the advancement of any measure which might have a tendency to accelerate the happy period.[89]

Lincoln's mention of "all being able to read the scriptures and other works, both of a religious and moral nature, for themselves" implies that this would lead people to think and make conclusions about religious truth "for themselves," which is what happened in his case, as we shall see in the next chapter.

That the foundation of a republic is an educated people was as much a part of Lincoln's thinking as it was in Jefferson's is seen in William Herndon's letter to John C. Henderson of 4 April 1895. Herndon, echoing Jefferson's statements on education, wrote that Lincoln often stated in essence "that the very best, firmest, and most enduring basis of our republic was the education, the thorough and the universal education of the great American people; and that the intelligence of the mass of our people was the light and life of the republic."[90]

When it came to eradicating slavery, Lincoln had his own method of educating or diffusing "knowledge among the people," to use Jefferson's phrase. That method was his continuous teaching and preaching the idealism of the Declaration of Independence, which he believed included blacks, as we shall see. Moreover, Lincoln was aware of Jefferson's utopian idea of progressive actualization of the Declaration's idealism and that Jefferson maintained such actualization necessitated eradicating slavery, since these ideas were contained in passages from *Notes on the State of Virginia*, which Lincoln quoted in 1859 at Columbus, as has been mentioned. Yet Garry Wills argues that nineteenth-century Romantic Transcendentalist interpretations of the Declaration as a nonhistorical goal or idealism to be actualized in history as much as possible coming from Theodore Parker and George Bancroft was what influenced Lincoln's ideas on progressive actualization of the principles of the Declaration.[91] The Transcendentalist, outside of history, view of the Declaration, however, is essentially the same as Jefferson's utopian or "nowhere" in the world or history perspective. Transcendentalism, therefore, did not provide any revolutionary ideas in the way the Declaration was perceived by Lincoln and the way it should impact American civilization or slavery, as Wills claims. As a result, when Lincoln made the following statement in his 1857 speech on the proslavery Dred Scott decision of the Supreme Court, he merely restated Jefferson's views:

> I think the authors of that notable instrument [the Declaration] intended to include *all* men, but they did not intend to declare all men equal *in all respects*. They did not mean to say all were equal in color, size, intellect, moral developments, or social capacity. They defined with tolerable distinctness, in what respects they did consider all men created equal—equal in "certain inalienable rights, among which are life, liberty, and the pursuit of happiness." This they said, and this meant. They did not mean to assert the obvious untruth, that all were then actually enjoying that equality, nor yet, that they were about to confer it immediately upon them. In fact they had no power to confer such a boon. They meant simply to declare the *right*, so that the *enforcement* of it might follow as fast as circumstances should permit. They meant to set up a standard maxim for free society, which should be familiar to all, and revered by all; constantly looked to, constantly labored for, and even though never perfectly attained, constantly approximated, and thereby constantly spreading and deepening its influence, and augmenting the happiness and value of life to all people of all colors everywhere.[92]

The thrust of this statement—that the intent of the Declaration was to extend and actualize its values "to all people of all colors everywhere"—is similar to the thrust of Jefferson's statement made 24 June 1826, just ten days before his death:

> May it [the Declaration] be to the world, what I believe it will be, (to some parts sooner, to others later, but finally to all,) the signal of arousing men to burst the chains under which monkish igno-rance and superstition had persuaded them to bind themselves, and to assume the blessings and security of self-government. That form which we have substituted, restores the free right to the unbounded exercise of reason and freedom of opinion. All eyes are opened, or opening, to the rights of man. The general spread of the light of science has already laid open to every view the palpable truth, that the mass of mankind has not been born with saddles on their backs, nor a favored few booted and spurred, ready to ride them legitimately, by the grace of God. These are grounds of hope for others.[93]

The fact that Lincoln's interpretation of the Declaration followed Jefferson's universal, partial-to-none, all-are-included utopian ide-alism derived from the universal, partial-to-none, all-inclusive deistic "Nature's God" of the Declaration becomes more under-standable considering that Lincoln, like Jefferson, was imbued with deism—the subject of the next chapter.

# Chapter 2

# LINCOLN, DEISM, AND THE DECLARATION OF INDEPENDENCE

*I*t is well known that Abraham Lincoln had extensive knowledge of the Bible.[1] He constantly quoted or alluded to it in his speeches. To the predominantly Christian-oriented common people of nineteenth-century America, this had great appeal. Lincoln was keenly aware of this and used it to his advantage in politics by publicly projecting the image of a mainstream Christian. Yet privately he was a religious radical. This can even be seen in some of his biblical-oriented speeches that sound orthodox, at least on the surface, as we shall see in chapter 6. When read carefully, however, they reveal elements of skepticism or religious heterodoxy that he subscribed to from his early adulthood. What was that heterodoxy? To answer this question, we must look to the testimony of those who knew Lincoln well and the writings of those who influenced him most, like deist Thomas Paine and modified deist Theodore Parker, because, unlike Jefferson, who wrote a great deal on his own religious views, Lincoln did not. And, unlike Jefferson, whose religious writings survived, what little Lincoln wrote did not. In the early lives of Jefferson and Lincoln, however, the radical religious influence of deism ran a parallel course.

As a young man, Lincoln authored a book on his religious radicalism. Fortunately for his political career, because it would have offended his Christian constituency, that book was never published. One of his friends burned it. According to several who knew him well, in 1834 Lincoln wrote a pamphlet or small book in which he denied the miraculous immaculate conception of Jesus, the miraculous inspiration of biblical revelation, and much of its truth content as well. William Herndon, Lincoln's friend and former law partner, who gathered testimony about Lincoln after his assassination, heard that Samuel Hill, another of Lincoln's friends, had burned the book. Hill was convinced that if Lincoln's views on religion had been published, they would have destroyed his political future. Samuel Hill, however, was dead by the time Herndon heard of the incident, so he interviewed Hill's son John about it and memorialized the results in a letter:

> Lincoln, one day after the book was finished, read it to Mr. Hill— his good friend. Hill tried to persuade him not to make it public— not to publish it. Hill at that time saw in Mr. Lincoln a rising man, and wished him success. Lincoln refused to destroy it—said it should be published. Hill swore it should never see the light of day. He had an eye to Lincoln's popularity—his present and future success; and believing that, if the book were published, it would kill Lincoln forever, he snatched it from Lincoln's hand, when Lincoln was not expecting it, and ran it into an old-fashioned ten-plate stove, heated as hot as a furnace.[2]

Douglas Wilson, in *Honor's Voice*, stated the evidence that Lincoln wrote the book Samuel Hill wanted destroyed is "very strong" and quoted a letter from John Hill to Herndon of 29 May 1865 further describing his childhood and young adulthood memories of hearing of the book burning. That letter, Wilson argues, "is replete with indications" that the incident actually took place. Three of those indications were: Hill's "recollections" that "his father and others frequently" retold the incident; the impact on Hill of hearing "the words 'infidelity,' 'Paine,' and 'Voltaire'" over and over in the retelling described in the letter; and Hill's recollection that "his father seemed . . . uncharacteristically concerned about manifestations of irreligion" because his father entertained and discussed "heretical ideas."[3]

Herndon first heard of the book burning from Hardin Bale, who was among Lincoln's circle of friends when he lived in New Salem, Illinois, where the incident took place. As Bale described the incident: "About the year 1834 A Lincoln wrote a work on infidelity, denying the divinity of the Scriptures and was persuaded by his friends—particularly by Saml [Hill] to burn it which was done."[4] Another of Lincoln's friends who commented on the book was Isaac Cogdal, who stated, "I do know that Mr Lincoln did write a letter, pamphlet—book or what not on faith as I understand he held—denying special & miraculous Revelation—Inspiration and Conception."[5]

Herndon, Bale, and Cogdal, however, were not witnesses to the book or its burning. Nor did they state that Lincoln told them about it. Bale and Cogdal, however, were "part of the New Salem network for local news," so their testimony cannot be discounted.[6] Yet, James H. Matheny, another of Lincoln's friends, stated: "Mr. Lincoln did tell me *that he did write* a little Book on Infidelity." Lincoln, however, made Matheny promise he would never say anything about the book. At first, Matheny kept his promise. Then he made the mistake of telling Herndon that he knew something about Lincoln that he had promised not to tell. After that, Herndon relentlessly pressured Matheny to reveal his secret, which he finally did, much to his regret, since in so doing he broke his promise. As Herndon stated, "after strong & repeated solicitation from me," Matheny, "under protest told it to me—evidently hating to do it."[7] Matheny's testimony, however, as well as John Hill's, is based on statements they witnessed that came from individuals who saw Lincoln's book on infidelity—namely Lincoln himself and Hill's father, Samuel.

Apart from the book-burning incident, Matheny's testimony tells us much about Lincoln's religious views:

I knew Mr Lincoln as Early as 1834–37—Know he was an infidel—have heard Lincoln call Christ a bastard—He & Wm D. Herndon used to talk Infidelity in the Clerks office in this city about the years 1837–40. Lincoln attacked the Bible & new Testament on two grounds—1st From the inherent or apparent contradiction under its lids & 2nly From the grounds of Reason—sometimes he ridiculed the Bible & New Testament—sometimes seemed to Scoff it, though I shall not use that word in its full & literal sense. . . . Sometimes Lincoln bordered on absolute Atheism: he went too far that way & often shocked me. . . . Lincoln was Enthusiastic in his infidelity. As he grew older he grew more discrete—didn't talk much before strangers about his religion, but to friends—close bosom ones he was always open & avowed—fair & honest, but to strangers he held them off from Policy.[8]

Herndon said that Matheny "knew Lincoln as well as I did" and therefore valued his testimony.[9] Another of Lincoln's friends, John T. Stuart, who helped him get started in law and politics, echoed Matheny's comments by stating that Lincoln "was an avowed and open Infidel. . . . Lincoln went further against Christian beliefs—& doctrines & principles than any man I ever heard: he shocked me."[10]

Although Cogdal and Herndon claimed no firsthand knowledge of the book burning or that Lincoln told them of it, they did claim firsthand knowledge of Lincoln's heterodox religious views, which is seen in Herndon's account of his interview with Cogdal containing Herndon's parenthetical notes:

I have often talked to Mr Lincoln on the question of Religion in his own office & in your presence too (This is true). Mr Lincoln believed in God—and all the great substantial groundworks of Religion—Believed in the progress of man and of nations—He believed that nations—like individuals were punished for their Sins—there [sic] violations of fundamental rights—&c—

He did not believe in Hell—Eternal punishment as the christians say—his idea was punishment as Education. He was a Universalist tap root & all in faith and sentiment. I have talked this often and often with him Commencing as Early as 1834 and as late down as 1859—(This is correct). He did not believe in the orthodox Theologies of the day. . . . Lincoln thought that God predestined things—and governed the universe by Law—nothing going by accident. He could not believe [God] created a world and that the result of that would be Eternal damnation &c—His mind was full of terrible Enquiry—and was skeptical in a good sense—[11]

Although Cogdal states that "Lincoln thought that God predestined things," it is clear he was speaking of predetermination, not the Christian doctrine of predestination. According to predestination, as has been stated in the previous chapter, many are not given predestinating saving grace by God while in their mother's womb and therefore are condemned to "Eternal punishment" in "Hell." Yet, as Cogdal said, Lincoln "did not believe in Hell." Nor did he believe in eternal damnation or punishment since he was a "Universalist" who thought everyone would be saved. Cogdal also stated in effect that Lincoln did not believe a moral and just God would condemn humans to suffer eternal damnation, especially when in their mother's womb before they did anything. As he put it, Lincoln "could not believe [God] created the world and that the result of that would be Eternal damnation &c." It was God after all who created humans, and Lincoln did not believe God would create something and then condemn it even if that creation was immoral. And, if humans were immoral, then it was God's fault because He created them capable of immorality. Therefore, Lincoln held several views incompatible with predestination: his disbelief in hell, his belief in universal salvation, and his belief in a just, moral, and competent God.

## THOMAS PAINE'S CRITICISM OF THE OLD TESTAMENT

Matheny said that "Lincoln attacked the Bible & New Testament on two grounds": "contradiction" in the text and critical analysis "From the grounds of Reason." This is exactly what Thomas Paine did in his *Age of Reason*, published in 1794, a principal source of Lincoln's radical religious views. Paine's in-your-face revolutionary disposition is reflected in this deistic work filled with scathing criticism of Judaism and Christianity. Paine was therefore condemned by both Jews and Christians, as Voltaire was earlier in the eighteenth century and Spinoza was in the seventeenth century for their religious criticisms. Indeed, Paine acknowledged indebtedness to Spinoza for some of the ideas in the *Age of Reason*.[12] Among freethinking individuals like Lincoln in the nineteenth century, however, Paine's book was well received. As Herndon described the *Age of Reason's* influence on Lincoln:

> In 1834, while still living in New Salem and before he [Lincoln] became a lawyer, he was surrounded by a class of people exceedingly liberal in matters of religion. Volney's *Ruins* and Payne's [*sic*] *Age of Reason* passed from hand to hand, and furnish food for the evening's discussion in the tavern and village store. Lincoln read both of these books and thus assimilated them into his own being.[13]

Paine and other deists were of course part of the Age of Enlightenment, which maintained that any truth, including religious truth, should be able to withstand critical scrutiny with reason. Anything that failed this test should be rejected as untruth. Judaism, Christianity, and Islam were among the casualties of this approach because deists found traditional and scriptural foundations of these religions riddled with fabrications, inconsistencies, contradictions, and absurdities. Despite this, deists did not abandon religion and God altogether. They constructed a new God and religion based on the authority of individual human reason, not God's revelation to prophets or through an incarnation. As Paine summed up the impact of this approach on his own beliefs:

> I do not believe in the creed professed by the Jewish church, by the Roman church, by the Greek church, by the Turkish [Islamic] church, by the Protestant church, nor by any church that I know of. *My own mind is my own church* [my italics].
>
> All national institutions of churches, whether Jewish, Christian or Turkish [Moslem], appear to me no other than human inventions, set up to terrify and enslave mankind, and monopolize power and profit. . . . I shall, in the progress of this work [*Age of Reason*], declare . . . my reasons for not believing them.[14]

One of the reasons for Paine's disbelief was miracles. Jews and Christians maintained that the miracles described in the Old and New Testaments proved the truth of their religions. According to Paine, they were lies. He explained his rejection of miracles in general by stating:

> As we are to suppose a miracle to be something so entirely out of the course of what is called nature, that she must go out of that

course to accomplish it, and we see an account given of such miracle by the person who said he saw it, it raises a question in the mind very easily decided, which is, is it more probable that nature should go out of her course, or that a man should tell a lie? We have never seen, in our time, nature go out of her course; but we have good reason to believe that millions of lies have been told in the same time; it is, therefore, at least millions to one, that the reporter of a miracle tells a lie.[15]

Paine had more specific reasons for rejecting certain Old Testament miracles. For example, Joshua 10:14 says the sun and moon stood still in the valley of Ajalon on Joshua's command. Paine argued that if this had happened, it would have been reported "all over the world" because "One half [of the world] would have wondered why the sun did not rise, and the other why it did not set." Yet, as Paine stated, "there is not a nation in the world that knows anything about it [none have reported it]."[16]

The belief that Moses was miraculously inspired by God to write the first five books of the Bible or Pentateuch was also attacked by Paine. He maintained that those books contained so many contradictions that they could not have been written by the same author or inspired by the same God. In his analysis of Genesis, for example, he noticed that the book of Judges stated that the town called Laish in Moses' time was named Dan after the death of Joshua, Moses' successor as leader of the Jews. Yet, Genesis refers to Laish as Dan. How could that be if Moses authored Genesis before the name was changed, asked Paine? He concluded that Moses did not write Genesis. Someone wrote it after the death of Joshua, which ruled out Moses, whose death preceded Joshua's. Paine went on to demonstrate that the Pentateuch and the entire Old Testament was full of such inconsistencies and contradictions. After calling attention to several of them, he came to the conclusion that "every book in the Bible, from Genesis to Judges, is without authenticity."[17]

Paine not only claimed that the truth of the Old Testament was discredited by contradictions and false miracles but also that it was morally discredited by its numerous accounts of violence, criminality, and atrocities. He sarcastically stated that the book of Ruth was "one of the best books in the Bible," as he referred to the Old Testament, "for it is free from murder and rapine," despite being a "bungling story, foolishly told . . . about a strolling country girl creeping slyly into bed with her cousin Boaz."[18] What especially distressed Paine was the criminality of some of the Bible's central personalities, with Moses, whose "character . . . is the most horrid that can be imagined," being one of the worst offenders.[19] According to biblical accounts, stated Paine, "he [Moses] was the wretch that first began and carried on wars on the score and pretence of religion; and under that mask, or that infatuation, committed the most unexampled atrocities."[20] He pointed out that Moses commanded the "Jewish army" to commit barbarous acts after they "returned from one of their plundering and murdering excursions" by quoting "Numbers, chapt. xxxi., ver.13":

> Moses, and Eleazar the priest, and all the princes of the congregation, went forth to meet them [the returning Jewish army] without the camp; and Moses was wroth with the officers of the host, . . . which came from the battle; and Moses said unto them, *Have ye saved all the women alive?* behold, these caused the children of Israel, through the council of Balaam, to commit trespass against the Lord in the matter of Peor, and there was a plague among the congregation of the Lord. *Now, therefore, kill every male among the little ones, and kill every woman that hath known a man by lying with him; but all the women-children, that have not known a man by lying with him, keep alive for yourselves.*[21]

"Here was an order," said Paine, "to butcher the boys, to massacre the mothers, and debauch the daughters," which made Moses rank "among the detestable villains in any period of the world."[22]

Joshua, too, committed horrendous atrocities, according to Paine, who quoted Joshua 8:28, which says Joshua burned the city of Ai and "made it a heap forever" after he had first killed its inhabitants[23]—the exact punishment that God commanded for idolatrous cities in chapter 13 of Deuteronomy, quoted in the last chapter.

Apart from the crimes and atrocities of Moses and Joshua, Paine called attention to other grisly crimes described in the Old Testament, specifically those described in the tenth chapter of the second book of Kings:

> Two baskets full of children's heads, seventy in number, being exposed at the entrance of the city; they were the children of Ahab, and were murdered by the order of Jehu, whom Elisha, the pretended man of God, had anointed to be king over Israel, on purpose to commit this bloody deed, and assassinate his predecessor. And in the account of the reign of Menahem, one of the kings of Israel who had murdered Shallum, who had reigned but one month, it is said, II. Kings chap. xv., ver. 16, that Menahem smote the city of Tiphsah, because they opened not the city to him, *and all the women therein that were with child he ripped up.*[24]

Unproved miracles, inconsistencies, and incidents of brutality and barbarism in the Old Testament caused Paine to call it "a book of lies and contradictions, and a history of bad times and bad men."[25] Moreover, he maintained that reading it had an immoral influence because "it abounds with too many ill examples to be made a rule for moral life, and were a man to copy after the lives of some of its most celebrated characters, he would come to the gallows."[26]

## PAINE'S CRITICISM OF CHRISTIANITY

When it came to Christianity, Paine was critical of Christian doctrine. This was especially true of the Fall as well as atonement and satisfaction, according to which God incarnate in the form of Jesus Christ, the innocent son, who was begotten by God, came to earth to shed his blood on the cross to atone and give satisfaction to God for the guilt that each individual inherited from Adam and Eve because they ate the forbidden fruit from the tree of knowledge. Paine's criticism was in the form of ridicule and his perspective was cosmic:

> From whence, then, could arise the solitary and strange conceit [on the part of man] that the Almighty who had millions of worlds

equally dependent on his protection, should quit the care of all the
rest, and come to die in our world, because, they say, one man and
one woman had eaten an apple? And, on the other hand, are we to
suppose that every world in the boundless creation had an Eve, an
apple, a serpent, and a redeemer? In this case, the person who is
irreverently called the Son of God, and sometimes God himself,
would have nothing else to do than to travel from world to world,
in an endless succession of deaths, with scarcely a momentary
interval of life.[27]

James H. Matheny, as has been mentioned, said that Lincoln,
who loved humor, "ridiculed" and indulged in "scoff" when
expressing his "Infidelity" in "the years 1837–40." He also said that
"Lincoln was Enthusiastic in his Infidelity."[28] Paine's comments
show the same style and disposition in the *Age of Reason*, as the
aforementioned statements, full of ridicule, scoff, and enthusiasm
for infidelity, demonstrate.[29]

Paine's disbelief in the Fall, however, was based on more than
ridicule and scoff. When scrutinizing the New Testament, he noticed
that "Jesus never speaks of Adam himself, of the Garden of Eden,
nor what is called the fall of man."[30] Nor did he speak of the serpent,
or say that each person was morally tainted, or that they were as
guilty as Adam and Eve for eating the forbidden fruit from the tree
of knowledge. Paine thought this absence in Jesus' comments was
extraordinary. If indeed Jesus was God incarnate, the redeemer, who
came to earth to shed his blood on the cross to atone for Adam and
Eve's transgression and satisfy the anger of God the Father over
human guilt resulting from the Fall, he surely would have said so in
no uncertain terms, according to Paine. Moreover, Paine's examination and research led him to conclude that the story of the Fall originated from a Persian fable that had nothing to do with Moses or
Christianity—a fable later distorted by Judaism and Christianity.

During the Babylonian captivity, the Jews, according to Paine,
came in contact with the "cosmogony of the Persians, or at least of
getting some ideas how to fabricate one to put at the head of their
own history after their return from captivity." He also noticed that
other books of the Old Testament—those written before the cap-

tivity—did not mention the cosmogony of Genesis or even Adam.[31] Therefore, he concluded: Genesis had a Persian origin and was written "after the return of the Jews from the Babylonian captivity" and then added as an introduction to the books written previously. Moreover, although he noticed that Adam was mentioned in the book of Chronicles, written after the captivity, he pointed out that other books written during this period did not mention Adam or the unusual events of Genesis. Therefore, Paine concluded, those events did not happen. If they had, they would have been mentioned again and again in the later books and even in the ones Moses wrote earlier if he was the author of Genesis. As he put it:

> If the extraordinary things related in it [Genesis] such as the cre-
> ation of the world in six days, the tree of life, and of good and evil,
> the story of Eve and the talking serpent, the fall of man and his
> being turned out of paradise, were facts or even believed by the
> Jews to be facts, they would be referred to as fundamental matters,
> and that very frequently, in the books of the Bible [Old Testament]
> that were written by various authors afterwards [after the captivity];
> whereas there is not a book, chapter, or verse of the Bible, from the
> time Moses is said to have written the book of Genesis, to the book
> of Malachi, the last book in the Bible, including a space of more
> than a thousand years, in which there is any mention made of
> these things or any of them, nor are they so much as alluded to.[32]

Consistent with this, Paine dismissed the Fall as "no other than a fable borrowed from and constructed upon the religion of Zoroaster, or the Persians, of the annual progress of the sun through the twelve signs of the zodiac."[33] The Persian version, however, referred to the fall season—not the moral Fall of man. Paine stated that during the fall of the year, according to Zoroastrianism, the "*evil of winter*" is "announced by the ascension of the autumnal constellation of the *serpent* of the zodiac."[34] In addition, he pointed out that:

> Adam and Eve are names taken from the cosmogony of the Per-
> sians. Henry Lord, in his book, written from Surat . . . says, that in
> the Persian cosmogony, the name of the first man was *Adamoh*, and

of the first woman *Hevah*. From hence comes the Adam and Eve of the book of Genesis.[35]

Paine then argued that the serpent, Adam, Eve, and the fall season were all adapted to describe the moral fall of mankind by the Jewish author or authors of Genesis. Moreover, even the association of the apple, the fruit forbidden to Adam and Eve according to tradition, was in accord with the Persian fall season fable. As Paine explained, "The fall of the year is the season of gathering and eating the new apples of that year. The [Persian] allegory [of the fall season in Genesis], therefore, holds with respect to the fruit, which it would not have done had it been and early summer fruit."[36] Paine went on to state that the fall season fable

> holds also with respect to clothing, and temperature of the air. It is said in Genesis, chapt. iii., ver 21, "*Unto Adam and his wife did the Lord make coats of skins, and clothed them.*" But why are coats of skins mentioned? This cannot be understood as referring to any thing of the nature of *moral evil*. The solution of the allegory gives again the answer to this question, which is, that the *evil of winter*, which follows the *fall of the year*, fabulously called in Genesis the *fall of man*, makes warm clothing necessary.[37]

The entire biblical account of the Fall, therefore, was fiction, allegory, or fable, according to Paine. Augustine agreed with him, which Paine pointed out by stating, "Augustine . . . acknowledges, in his *City of God*, that the adventure of Eve and the serpent, and the account of Paradise, were generally considered fiction or allegory."[38]

Paine also considered it strange that God, according to the Fall, made knowledge a sin by forbidding men to eat from the tree of knowledge. Roman Emperor Julian, who Paine quoted, maintained Genesis garbled God's command: "If there ever had been, or could be, a Tree of knowledge," said Julian, "instead of God forbidding man to eat thereof, it would be that of which he would order him to eat the most."[39] Paine agreed. Why then did Genesis get it wrong by forbidding knowledge? Paine, like others of the Enlightenment, argued that the Jewish and Christian religions were easily proved false if examined in the light of knowledge. However, they also maintained that the clergy of these religions got their financial support from ignorant and unthinking people of faith. Therefore, it was in the clergy's interests to outlaw knowledge and the exercise of reason that provided it, because if the people became knowledgeable thinking people they would not support religious untruth that served the interests of the clergy. This caused the priestcraft or clergy, not God, to give the command in the name of God in Genesis not to eat from the tree of knowledge. It was their way of keeping the people in ignorance. Paine expressed this idea by stating: "As priestcraft was always the enemy of knowledge, because priestcraft supports itself by keeping people in delusion and ignorance." He added: "It was consistent with its [the priestcraft's] policy [of keeping the people in ignorance] to make the acquisition of knowledge a real sin."[40] With these arguments, Paine believed he had explained why the Persian fable of the fall season, distorted to mean moral fall, caused by eating the sinful forbidden fruit of knowledge, was placed in Genesis by the Jewish priestcraft and made the foundation of New Testament theology by the Christian priestcraft.

Denial of the Fall, however, went hand in hand with denial of the Christian doctrine of Redemption and Atonement that was based on the Fall. Paine's logic was simple. If the Fall was fiction, it was unnecessary for God to beget a son, Jesus Christ, God incarnate in human form, and that the son shed his blood on the cross in order to redeem mankind and atone for or satisfy God for human guilt resulting from the Fall. As Paine put it: "If what is called the fall of man in Genesis be fabulous or allegorical, that which is called redemption in the *New Testament* can not be fact."[41] To Paine, therefore, the doctrine of Redemption was fable just like the Fall. As he stated: "Redemption is the fable of priestcraft invented since the time the *New Testament* was compiled."[42]

## CHRISTIAN MIRACLES

According to Christian theologians, there were two miracles that proved that Jesus Christ was the Son of God or God incarnate in the form of the second person of the Trinity. The first was Jesus' immaculate conception and the second was his resurrection from the dead after his crucifixion. Paine attacked the veracity of both. The immaculate conception or virgin birth was prophesized in Isaiah 7:14 of the Old Testament: "Behold, a virgin shall conceive, and bear a son, and shall call his name Immanuel." This statement, as Paine stated, was made some seven hundred years before Jesus' time. Yet the book of Matthew of the New Testament (1:23) repeated it almost verbatim as prophecy of the birth of Jesus: "Behold, a virgin shall be with child, and shall bring forth a son, and they shall call his name Emmanuel, which, being interpreted, is, God with us."[43] As Paine pointed out, however, this prediction of birth, which originated in the Old Testament, was a sign given by the prophet Isaiah to King Ahaz of Judah and Jerusalem that he would win his war against the combined forces of Syria and Israel. In those days, signs from God of the success of some great endeavor about to begin were extremely important. Therefore, the prophet Isaiah stated to King Ahaz, "The Lord himself shall give you a sign," which was followed by verse 7:14: "Behold a virgin shall conceive, and bear a son, and shall call his name Immanuel." Significantly, however, this was followed by: "For before the child shall know to refuse the evil, and choose the good, the land that thou abhorest [lands ruled by the kings of Syria and Israel who Ahaz was fighting] shall be forsaken of both her kings." To Paine, this clearly prophesized Ahaz's impending war and victory. It had nothing to do with Jesus' birth and childhood seven hundred years later since the sign Ahaz was promised—in order to be meaningful—had to refer to a birth that would take place before Ahaz's war started.

Paine also said the word translated as "virgin" from the Hebrew language of the book of Isaiah is more accurately translated as "young woman." Therefore, the prophecy was that a "young woman," not necessarily a virgin, would bear a child. Paine then argued that the "young woman" referred to by Isaiah was the prophet's own wife or mistress. Verses 8:2–3 of Isaiah were evidence of this where Isaiah said: "And I took unto me faithful witnesses to record, Uriah the priest and Zechariah the son of Jebedhiah. And I went unto the prophetess; and she conceived and bare a son." Then in 8:18, Isaiah told of the birth referred to as Ahaz's sign: "Behold, I and the children whom the Lord hath given me for signs and for wonders in Israel."[44] Paine maintained that these verses demonstrated conclusively that the prophet Isaiah was not referring to the virgin birth of Jesus in 7:14.

Consistent with such analysis, Paine went on to examine various other prophecies concerning the birth of Jesus and to demonstrate that they were false or, at the very least, highly questionable.[45] Moreover, he observed that the only testimony of the virgin birth of Jesus in the New Testament came from Mary and Joseph who claimed they were informed of this miracle by angels. In Luke, Mary was told by her angel, who appeared when she was wide-awake, that she would "bring forth a son" called "Jesus." She responded by asking, "How shall this be, seeing I know not a man?" (1:34). The angel then said: "The Holy Ghost shall come upon thee, and the power of the Highest shall over shadow thee: therefore also that holy thing which shall be born of thee shall be called the son of God" (1:35). Paine saw similarities between this account and some in pagan literature where the gods fathered children—like "Jupiter and Leda" or "Jupiter and Europa" or in any of Jupiter's "amorous adventures."[46] He also maintained with ridicule and scoff that the New Testament account of the virgin birth was "blasphemously obscene," because it made Mary and Joseph, and especially God, parties to a libertine love triangle— something not allowed by Christian morality. As he put it:

> It gives an account of a young woman engaged to be married, and while under this engagement she is, to speak in plain language debauched by a ghost under the impious pretence (Luke, chap. i., ver. 35), that *"the Holy Ghost shall come upon thee, and the power of the Highest shall overshadow thee."* Notwithstanding which, Joseph afterward marries her, cohabits with her as his wife, and in turn rivals the ghost.[47]

Paine emphasized that only Mary and Joseph witnessed the angels who told of the miraculous conception. Since they were engaged at that time, Paine maintained their accounts of the angels reeked of self-serving denials of a premarital affair during which Mary became pregnant. To Paine, only third-party witnesses, other than Mary and Joseph, could give credible testimony of Mary's miraculous conception. Moreover, Joseph claimed he received his knowledge of the "immaculate conception" from an angel in a dream. Mary's angel, as has been stated, told her in waking state. All of this was too much for the skeptical Paine, who said:

> Either Joseph or Mary was the worst evidence that could have been thought of, for it was others that should have testified *for them* and not they for themselves [but there were no other witnesses]. Were any girl that is now with child to say, and even to swear it, that she was gotten with child by ghost, and that an angel told her so, would she be believed? Certainly she would not. Why, then, are we to believe the same thing of another girl, whom we never saw, told by nobody knows who, nor when, nor where?[48]

Considering these passages concerning Jesus' birth, Lincoln's contact with the *Age of Reason* makes it understandable, although not excusable, why he shocked and offended James H. Matheny by referring to Jesus as a "bastard," as has been mentioned—something even Paine did not do.

As the immaculate conception was not true, according to Paine, neither was the Resurrection because of the conflicting accounts given in the Gospels. Matthew states that the disciples went to Galilee to see the resurrected Jesus after Mary and Mary Magdalene were the first to see Him not far from His sepulcher where He told them He would be in Galilee—information they passed on to the disciples (Matthew 28:1–20). John, on the other hand, states the disciples never went to Galilee. They were hiding in fear, at which time Jesus appeared to them (John 20:1–31). Luke gives a third conflicting account by stating that "certain" persons saw the risen Jesus inside the sepulcher but that they did not recognize him until he had walked and eaten with them (Luke 24:22–31). Mark adds to the conflicting accounts by stating that after the risen Jesus first appeared to Mary Magdalene, he reappeared in another form to two unnamed persons who told the disciples that Jesus was alive. The disciples rejected this testimony after which the resurrected Jesus appeared to them (Mark 16:9–14). These conflicting Gospel testimonies caused Paine to argue, as a lawyer would, that they impeached each other. As he put it, "The evidence given in these books destroys each other."[49]

There was one point on which the authors of the four Gospels did agree, according to Paine. The resurrected Jesus revealed himself to very few people. This was strange, according to Paine. Why didn't Jesus manifest himself to as many people as possible, because part of his mission was to prove his divinity by his miraculous resurrection?[50] Paul's claim that the risen Jesus was seen by more than five hundred people at the same time made more sense from this perspective (1 Corinthians 15:6). However, it was only Paul who said this. There was no mention of it by any of the five hundred. Moreover, Paine ridiculed Paul's testimony by pointing out that Paul originally denied Christ and therefore his statements about the five hundred who saw the risen Jesus "is like that of a man who comes into a court of justice to swear that what he had sworn before is false."[51] Paine concluded that Jesus' resurrection was nothing more than a ghost story, which, typical of such stories, evolved into conflicting accounts:

> The story of Jesus Christ appearing after he was dead is the story of apparition, such as timid imaginations can always create in vision, and credulity believe. Stories of this kind had been told of the assassination of Julius Caesar, not many years before; and they generally have their origin in violent deaths, or in the execution of innocent persons. In cases of this kind, compassion lends its aid and benevolently stretches the story. It goes on a little and a little further till it becomes *a most certain truth*. Once start a ghost and credulity fills up the history of its life, and assigns the cause of its reappearance! One tells it one way, another another way, till there are as many stories about the ghost and about the proprietor of the ghost, as there are about Jesus Christ in these four books [the Gospels].[52]

Commenting on basic Christian doctrine—the Fall, the redemption of man by the crucifixion of God incarnate, and His resurrection—and the idea that belief in this doctrine was necessary for salvation, Paine again resorted to ridicule: "That man should redeem himself from the sin of eating an apple, by committing a murder on Jesus Christ, is the strangest system of religion ever set up."[53] In a more elaborate ridicule, he said much the same thing but added that Christian doctrine degrades God because it involves Him in a struggle with the devil, who "outwits" Him:

> The Christian religion is derogatory to the Creator in all its articles. It puts the Creator in an inferior point of view, and places the Christian Devil above him. It is he, according to the absurd story in Genesis, that outwits the Creator in the garden of Eden, and steals from him his favorite creature, man, and at last obliges him to beget a son, and put that son to death, to get man back again, and this the priests of the Christian religion call redemption.[54]

## PAINE'S NATURAL THEOLOGY AND DEISM

Paine concluded that those who regarded the Jewish and Christian religions as true were living in illusion because of the inconsistencies, fabrications, and absurdities found in the Old and New Testaments upon which these religions are based. This caused him to look for another scripture upon which to base religion, one that was true and also pure in the sense of not being fabricated, corrupted, or adulterated by humans, especially the priestcraft. He, like other deists, found one in "Creation" or the universe itself that he maintained was the real "word of God." This scripture of "Creation" or works of God, argued Paine, had the advantage of being presented in a universal language that everyone can read or observe compared to a written scripture in a particular language. Moreover, the scripture of "Creation" cannot be altered to suit human interests, like those of the priestcraft, or refused publication, as can scriptures based on written words. As he put it:

The Creation speaketh an universal language, independently of human speech or human language, multiplied and various as they may be. It is an ever existing original, which every man can read. It cannot be forged; it cannot be counterfeited; it cannot be lost; it cannot be altered; it cannot be suppressed. It does not depend on the will of man whether it shall be published or not; it publishes itself from one end of the earth to the other. It preaches to all nations and to all worlds; and this *word of God* reveals to man all that is necessary for man to know God.[55]

On how observance of "Creation" or God's works gives knowledge of God, Paine said:

Do we want to contemplate his [God's] power? We see it in the immensity of the Creation. Do we want to contemplate his wisdom? We see it in the unchangeable order by which the incomprehensible WHOLE is governed [natural law]. Do we want to contemplate his munificence? We see it in the abundance with which he fills the earth. Do we want to contemplate his mercy? We see it in his not withholding that abundance even from the unthankful.[56]

Paine went on to state, "In fine, do we want to know what God is? Search not the written or printed books," which any human hand might make, "but the scripture called the *Creation*."[57] With this line of thought, Paine makes any written scripture, or any organized religion such as Judaism, Christianity, or Islam based on written scripture, a highly questionable source of knowledge of God or religious truth, as did Bolingbroke.[58] It also explains Paine's famous comment previously mentioned, "My own mind is my own church," and, more important, it gives us a reason why Abraham Lincoln never joined a church.

Paine's deistic God, like Bolingbroke and Jefferson's, was a moral and just God. This caused him to criticize the God of the Old Testament for the immoral and unjust commands in Deuteronomy 13 to make "horrid butcheries of men, women, and children."[59] Bolingbroke and Jefferson made similar criticism, which was mentioned in the last chapter. To attribute such vicious commands to God was blasphemy, according to Paine, since they made God a murderer. This is why he said: "It was the duty incumbent on every true Deist, that he vindicate the moral justice of God against the calumnies of the Bible."[60] In other words, the biblical passages alien to God's justice and morality should be rejected as untrue. Paine was especially critical of the immorality and injustice of the Christian doctrine that God sent his innocent son Jesus Christ to shed his blood on the cross in order to wash away human guilt resulting from original sin or the Fall. Echoing Bolingbroke and Jefferson, he said:

> Moral justice cannot take the innocent for the guilty, even if the innocent would offer itself. To suppose justice to do this, is to destroy the principle of its existence, which is the thing itself; it is then no longer justice, it is indiscriminate revenge.[61]

A part of the deistic God's justice was His revelation of His truth in the form of His Creation, unmediated by any prophet, incarnation, scripture, or clergy. This gave everyone since the beginning of time direct access to the "scripture called the *Creation*," as Paine called it. It enabled everyone to gain knowledge of God by observing His works or nature. Therefore, the God of creation did not favor any people or nation with a particular revelation mediated by a particular prophet, incarnation, scripture, language, or clergy. This impartiality of God makes Him just because a vital element of justice is impartiality, as was mentioned in chapter 1. The deistic God also provided the bounty of His creation to all creatures, not just humans. This was another manifestation of His impartiality. Paine, sounding like Bolingbroke, made this impartiality of the deistic God explicit by stating: "The creation preaches a different doctrine to this [the partiality of God contained in biblical revelation]. We see there that the care and goodness of God [His bounty] is extended *impartially* [my italics] over all the creatures he has made."[62] Consistent with His impartiality, the deistic God gave access to the doors of heaven to all persons of any belief. As Paine stated, when denying the Catholic Church's claim that it alone had the keys to heaven and could refuse entrance to anyone by excommunication, "The key to heaven is not in the safekeeping of any sect, nor ought the road to [salvation] be obstructed by any."[63] Paine had the Universalist all-will-be-saved element, as did Lincoln, as has been stated, which Lincoln could well have acquired by reading the *Age of Reason*.

Paine maintained that all religions except deism were tinged with cultural bias and partiality. Simultaneously, he maintained that "Deism," born of the "scripture called the *Creation*," "is the only profession of religion that admits of worshipping and reverencing God in purity [unadulterated by imposture from partial, self-interested priestcraft], and the only one on which the thoughtful mind can repose with undisturbed tranquility." He added that in Christianity, with its emphasis on Jesus, "God is almost forgotten. . . . Every thing, even the creation, is ascribed to the son of Mary."[64]

Consistent with Paine's de-emphasis of Jesus, Lincoln "rarely mentioned the words Jesus Christ" at any time or on any occasion private or public, according to Wayne Temple.[65] William Herndon said he "never heard" Lincoln "use of the name of Jesus" except "to confute the idea that he was the Christ."[66] This applies to Lincoln's speeches, including his Farewell Address, delivered at Springfield in 1861; his Gettysburg Address, when he said "under God"; and even his sermonlike Second Inaugural, which will be discussed in chapter 6. Yet it can be argued that Lincoln refrained from using Jesus in his speeches because they were political. But this does not explain why he did not refer to Jesus in his private letters except "to confute the idea that he was the Christ," as Herndon stated.

Yet, in a general way, Lincoln did sound very Christian on many occasions. Indeed, he considered himself a good Christian even though he never joined a church, as Mary Todd Lincoln tells us, and even though he continued to be radical and heterodox in religion, as Matheny stated.[67] Paradoxical as this may seem, it is consistent with Herndon's statement that Lincoln "was a Theist, somewhat after the order of Theodore Parker" whose religious ideas were based on Enlightenment criticism, as were Paine's, and who, like Paine, influenced Lincoln.[68] Jesse W. Fell, a lawyer who had a long and close political as well as personal relationship with Lincoln, beginning in the mid-1830s, said Lincoln was highly influenced by Parker.

After stating that Lincoln told him "the writings of Theodore Parker" were "furnished him" by "Mr. Herndon," Fell said:

> No religious views with him Seemed to find any favor except of the practical & rationalistic order; & if from my recollections on this subject I were called upon to designate an author whose views most nearly represented Mr. Lincoln's, on this Subject, I would say that author was Theodore Parker.[69]

## THEODORE PARKER'S INFLUENCE

Theodore Parker, an extraordinary personality of nineteenth-century America, was born in 1810, a year after Lincoln, into a distinguished patriotic family. His grandfather was Captain John Parker, who commanded the militia that fought British troops in the first battles of the Revolutionary War at Lexington and Concord in 1775. Theodore Parker's calling, however, was not the military. He became a Unitarian minister after attending Harvard College and Harvard Divinity School. In addition to his ministry, or as part of it, he became an extremely learned and able scholar. He studied philosophical and theological works in the languages in which they were written. As Henry Steele Commager states, "No man in America was more learned, more widely read. He took pride in his reputation as a scholar, he was vain of the number of languages with which he was familiar."[70]

Parker's Christianity was uniquely radical. It had an element of cold, critical deism and the added dimension of transcendentalism with its reverence and mysticism.[71] Parker was by far the most intellectually profound among American Transcendentalists, far more than Ralph Waldo Emerson, Henry David Thoreau, and Walt Whitman. Although relatively unknown today, in Lincoln's time, he was very well known. Yet unlike Emerson, Parker did not leave the Unitarian Church when he began to have Transcendentalist inclinations. However, his religious views were so radical that they almost proved too much to take even for the liberal Unitarians, who were themselves regarded as radical by Catholic and predominating Protestant denominations because they had no doctrinal or creedal requirements and were committed to freedom of conscience. Despite their liberal views on doctrine, however, Unitarians seriously considered expelling Parker. In the end, they kept him and allowed him freedom of the pulpit that went hand in hand with freedom from doctrine and creed.

Parker rejected conventional Christian theology. He called it popular theology, which he maintained consisted of five false doctrines:

> [1] The false idea of God, as imperfect in power, wisdom, justice, benevolence, and holiness; [2] the false idea of man, as fallen, depraved, and by nature lost; [3] the false idea of the relation between God and man, a relation of perpetual antagonism, man naturally hating God, and God hating "fallen" and "depraved" man; [4] the false idea of inspiration, that it comes only by a miracle on God's part, not by normal action on man's [part]; [5] and the false idea of salvation, that it is from the "wrath of God" who is "a consuming fire," by the "atoning blood of Christ," that is by the death of Jesus of Nazareth, which appeased "the wrath of God" and on condition of belief in this popular theology, especially of the five false ideas.[72]

These five points succinctly express Parker's critical approach to Christian theology based on the Fall. The first implies the Enlightenment view that if the Fall is fact, it is God's fault because He created humans. They are His "failure" if the Fall is true or, as Parker stated: "All things which God made work well except human nature; and that worked so badly that it fell as soon as it was put together."[73] A competent, intelligent, just, and moral God would not have created humans who would fall or be capable of falling. Hence, in the second doctrine of popular theology, the Fall is labeled as false, which helped to eliminate the idea that God "is imperfect in power, wisdom, justice, benevolence, and holiness"—the first false doctrine—because he created imperfect humans. Moreover, without the Fall, there is no "perpetual antagonism" between God and the "fallen" and "depraved" man, as Parker stated in his third false doctrine of popular theology. Nor is there any need for salvation "by the blood of Christ" in order to appease God's anger and save mankind from the "wrath of God" over original sin mentioned in the fifth false doctrine.

While Paine emphasized how the Fall made Christian theology degrading to God, as has been stated, Parker emphasized how it was degrading to man.[74] And, in his fourth false doctrine of popular theology, he upgrades man by denying that inspiration "comes only by a miracle on God's part" and affirming that it can also arise from "normal action on man's [part]." This has vast implications regarding the origin of religion. If a man or woman can be the cause of their own inspiration by "normal action," he or she can develop their own religion arising from their own nature, since they don't need "a miracle on God's part" for religious inspiration. Nor do they need inspired prophets or incarnations through which God expresses religious truth. In short, they don't need extra human sources or intermediaries to know God's truth or religion. They have resources in their own nature to find it themselves. This is a major premise of Parker's radical or heterodox Christianity.

Parker spoke of the religious nature in humans and seldom referred to it without mentioning its three "spiritual Faculties" or components: the intellectual, the affectional, and the moral judgments of reason. He used the term "manliness" to describe the harmonious relationship between these three. He called religion arising from them "the four forms of piety" or devotion, which were: "[1] piety of the mind, the love of truth . . . ; [2] piety of conscience, the love of right . . . ; [3] love of men or piety of the heart"; and [4] piety of the soul which implies love of God.[75] To Parker, the source of religion was not "the traditional claims of miraculous revelation," according to which God worked through prophets or an incarnation; it was "the spiritual nature of man himself."[76]

While many deists emphasized sensory observation of God's works or creation and critical reason in the construction and analysis of religion and theology at the exclusion of intuition, Parker maintained that both reason and intuition were necessary to find religious and theological truth. Sensory observation and critical reason could determine that an intelligent being designed and created the universe. Critical reason could also be used to find and eliminate errors in religion and theology. Intuition, on the other hand, gave universals and general principles on God and religion that were perceived within one's own consciousness. Intuition, however, if not restrained by critical reason, could lead humans astray. It could cause Romantic feelings, dreams, and imaginings contrary to objectively verified reality to be regarded as truth. Therefore, Parker maintained that if what is intuited, or even what was revealed, was contrary to sensory observed facts and conclusions based on those facts, it should be rejected as untruth. Critical reason thereby performed a restraint or check on intuition. Parker thus synthesized deism or early Enlightenment critical empiricism in religion and theology emphasized in deism with later Enlightenment Romanticism that emphasized intuition in reaction to rigid empiricism. As he described the function of this synthesis in a theologian:

> He must direct his eye inward on what passes there, studying the stars of that inner firmament, as the astronomer reads the phenomena of the heavens. He must also look outward on the face of nature and of man, and thus read the primitive gospel God wrote on the heart of his child, and illustrated in the earth and the sky and the events of life. Thus from observations made in the external world, made also in the internal world, comprising both the reflective and the intuitive faculties of man, he is to frame the theory of God, of man, of the relation between God and man, and of the duties that grow out of this relation, for with these four questions we suppose theology is exclusively concerned. This is the philosophical method, and it is strictly legitimate.[77]

Parker, echoing Paine's "scripture called the *Creation*," summed up Paine's observation of this "scripture" method of finding God and religion and added the contribution of inner human nature when he said, "It is not the Bible, but the universe is the only scripture of God—material nature is its Old Testament, human nature the New, and in both fresh leaves get written over every day."[78] This synthesis of deism and mystical transcendentalism in religion and theology was the basis of Parker's own heterodox version of Christianity, which emphasized individual authority in religion, that he described as "Christianity as old as Creation" in a sermon title echoing almost verbatim the title of deist Matthew Tindal's eighteenth-century book *Christianity as Old as the Creation*.[79]

Parker could be scornfully deistic and Paine-like in his rejection of any religious belief or scripture not in accord with science. When commenting on the creationist theory of Genesis, for example, he said:

> Modern science has show[n] that the [biblical] theological astronomy, geology and geography are mixed with whims, which overlay their facts; that the theological history [of the Bible] is false in its chief particulars, relating to the origin and development of mankind; that its metaphysics are often absurd, its chief premises false; that the whole tree is of gradual growth; and still men have the hardihood to pretend it [biblical revelation] is all divine, all true, and that every truth in the science and morals of our times, nay, any piety and benevolence in human consciousness has come from the miraculous revelation, and this alone! Truly it is a teacher's duty to expose this claim, so groundless, so wicked, so absurd, and refer men to the perpetual revelation from God in the facts of this world of matter and of men.[80]

When commenting on why intelligent, enlightened, and knowledgeable persons could not believe the five false doctrines of popular theology, Parker said in a way consistent with Enlightenment critics of religion:

> How can you ask men of large reason, large conscience, large affections, large love for the good God, to believe any one of the numerous schemes of the Trinity, the miracles of the New or the Old Testament; to believe in the existence of a devil whom God has made, seeking to devour mankind? How can you ask such men to believe in the existence of an angry god, jealous, capricious, selfish, and revengeful, who has made an immeasurable hell under his feet wherein he designs to crowd down ninety-nine thousand nine hundred and ninety-nine out of every hundred thousand of

his children? Will you ask Humboldt, the greatest of living philosophers to believe that a wafer is "the body of God," as the Catholics say or M. [Auguste] Compte [Comte, the father of sociology] to believe that the Bible is "the word of God," as the Protestants say? Will you ask a man of great genius, of great culture, to lay his whole nature in the dust, and submit to some little man [clergyman], with no genius, who only reads to him a catechism which was dreamed by some celibate monks in the dark ages of human history? You cannot expect such men to assent to that: as well might you ask the whole solar system to revolve around the smallest satellite that belongs to the planet Saturn.[81]

To Parker, religion and theology had to be constantly revised in the light of current knowledge. If they were not, they lost all meaning and significance. They became dead relics of the past, which, according to Parker, "the art of the embalmer preserves in the church . . . to cumber the ground for centuries."[82]

Like Paine, whose "own mind" was his "own church," Parker stressed an individualistic rational approach to religious truth. He denounced any kind of sectarian authority that compelled conformity to any creed or set of doctrines in the name of Christianity or any religion: "Surely," he said, "no man, no sect, no book nor oracle is master to a single soul."[83] Moreover, he said that Christianity, that is, his version of Christianity,

allows perfect freedom. It does not demand all men to *think* alike, but to think uprightly, and get as near as possible at truth; not all men to *live* alike, but to live holy, and get as near as possible to a life perfectly divine. Christ set up no Pillars of Hercules, beyond which we must not sail the *sea* in quest of truth. He says, "I have many things to say unto you, but ye cannot bear them now. . . . Greater works than these ye shall do." Christianity lays no rude hand on the sacred peculiarity of the individual genius and character. But there is no Christian sect which does not fetter a man. It would make all men think alike, or smother their conviction in silence.[84]

There were, according to Parker, two kinds of Christianity, "the transient and the permanent." The permanent is eternal and unchanging while the transient is the constantly changing, finite, temporal representations of the eternal, which, being eternal, cannot be completely or even adequately represented in finite or temporal terms. The transient was the "Christianity of sects, of the pulpit, of society," which "is ephemeral—a transitory fly" because it is constantly changing.[85] "*Doctrines* and *forms*" comprise the transient and "since men will always differ" in "total growth in wisdom, virtue, and piety," the finite or temporal "form religion takes, the doctrines wherewith she is girded, can never be the same in any two centuries or two men."[86] Here, Parker embraced the perspective approach to religious truth or the idea that each person perceives religion and the infinite eternal reality of God differently because the limited temporal consciousness of each occupies a different point of growth from which their perception is made. As a result, when human conscience and consciousness develops and grows, the forms and doctrines of religion and finite temporal representations of God change as well in order to adapt to changing conscience and consciousness or become "suited to the aspect of the changing times."[87] Parker maintained, in contrast to the claim of each sect, that its forms and doctrines contain the whole of religious truth, that "each will represent something of truth, but no one the whole. It seems the whole race of man is needed to do justice to the whole of truth."[88] The idea expressed here that the cumulative total of all different views of Christianity "of the whole race of man" represents the truth of Christianity far more than any single view of any individual, sect, denomination, or church is extremely radical. Its effect is more than mere tolerance of different religious views. It results in appreciation of each because all are needed to have "the whole of truth." It explains Lincoln's respect and reverence for all forms of Christianity and indeed all different religions because Parker's principle of cumulative perceptions of Christianity comprise the whole can be applied to all religious views.

Parker's "permanent" or eternal, unchanging Christianity had an intuitive or mystical element, which he described as "attaining oneness with God." The "method" he prescribed to attain "oneness" was living "a good life of piety within, of purity without."[89] These internal and external disciplines constituted "the whole extent of Christianity" as respects what should be practiced. They were "so well summed up in the command" of Jesus quoted by Parker: "Thou shalt love the Lord thy God with all thy heart, and with all thy soul, and with all thy mind—thou shalt love thy neighbor as thyself."[90] Love of God, as Jesus mentions here, comes from within—from the "heart," "soul," and "mind." This is "piety within." "Purity without," on the other hand, involves one's relations with one's fellow human beings external to one's self. Such relations attain the "purity" Parker mentions only if one seeks nothing from them. As soon as some selfish advantage, pleasure, or gain is sought, the person from whom it is sought becomes an object to be manipulated for selfish reasons and "purity" in that relationship is lost. "Purity," therefore, can only come through love in the sense of identifying with another person or, as Jesus put it, "Thou shalt love your neighbor as yourself." Such identification will cause one to want what is good for that person more than any selfish advantage, pleasure, or gain that person can provide.

From a moral perspective, Parker's "purity without" necessitated treating others according to moral norms and, therefore, involved attaining moral perfection, which he believed humans could attain. In this he departed substantially from the moral taint concept of original sin in orthodox versions of Christianity discussed previously that maintained tainted human nature does not change and moral perfection is, therefore, impossible. The basis for Parker's belief in moral perfection is found in his statement that "the first book of the Old Testament tells man he is made in the image of God; the first of the New Testament gives us the motto, Be Perfect as your Father in heaven."[91] It was because God is perfect and man is made in His image that Jesus instructed men to live according to the perfect image in which they were made, according to Parker.

"Love thy neighbor as thyself," however, was too general, too vague, and too abstract to describe what was needed in order to manifest moral perfection. So was "Be Perfect as your Father in heaven." Therefore, Parker prescribed ten specific duties as the measure of moral perfection: "humility, reverence, sobriety, gentleness, charity, forgiveness, fortitude, resignation, faith, and active love,"[92] all of which were manifest in Lincoln's character.

Echoing the bad God–good God analysis of theology found in Bolingbroke and Jefferson—Paine had this element as well—Parker maintained that orthodox denominations of Christianity made "Christ the despot of the soul" by deifying him and imposing doctrines in his name when actually he was our "elder brother" or human and did not impose himself or his teachings on humankind.[93] Moreover, Parker denounced the jealous, partial elements of Judeo-Christian theology, which caused God to take vicious wrathful vengeance against those who did not worship Him or go along with His belief systems, as "that old barbaric theology which suited the rudeness of a savage age."[94] He also deplored the concept of hell and a God who created imperfect humans who could not behave and then condemned millions of them to this infernal region when he said, "What is the Russian's subjection to a Czar compared to a Christian's worship of a conception of God who creates millions of millions of men only for the pleasure of squelching them down in bottomless and eternal hell!"[95] Parker emphasized that "there is no 'wrath of God' [over original sin] to be saved from; no 'vicarious atonement' to be saved by."[96] Simultaneously, he described the impartial good God, desired by philosophers, philanthropists, and all humankind, who loves all humans equally regardless of their faith, race, or gender:

> The philosopher wants a theology as comprehensive as his science— a God with wisdom and with power immanent in all the universe, and yet transcending that. The philanthropist wants it not less, *a God who loves all men* [my italics]. Yea, men and women all throughout the land desire a theology like this, which shall legitimate the instinctive emotions of reverence, and love, and trust in God, that to their spirits, careful and troubled about many things, shall give the comfort and the hope and peace for which they sigh![97]

After stressing that Jesus was not God but "our brother" who "went before" us and thereby showed all mankind how to attain "oneness with God" by the example of his life, Parker stated:[98]

Jesus stood and looked up to God. There was nothing between him and the Father of all; no old world, be it of Moses or Esaias, of a living rabbi, or sanhedrin of rabbis; no sin or perverseness of the finite will. As a result of this virgin purity of soul and perfect obedience, the light of God shone down into the very depths of his soul, bringing all of the Godhead which the flesh can receive. He would have us do the same; worship with nothing between us and God; act, think, feel, live, in perfect obedience to him [God]; and we never are *Christians* as he was *Christ*, until we worship as Jesus did, with no mediator, with nothing between us and the Father of all.[99]

By making Jesus human instead of God, Parker downgraded Jesus and simultaneously emphasized God, which Thomas Paine also did, as has been mentioned. It is also clear that Paine's and Parker's stress on God rather than on Jesus impacted Lincoln, since Jesus was rarely mentioned by him in his speeches or correspondence, as has also been mentioned.

To Parker, real Christianity "makes us outgrow any form or any system of doctrines."[100] Indeed, his unmediated, direct-to-God interpretation of Christianity denies the authority of all intermediaries in religion such as prophets, incarnations, churches, traditions, scriptures, and clergymen that give rise to and require belief in doctrine. Simultaneously, his unmediated approach to Christianity asserts the authority and responsibility of the individual as to what to believe in religion, but only for one's self and no one else.

Both Paine's and Parker's influence can be seen in Lincoln's life. As a younger man, he made shocking, Paine-like criticisms of Christianity—which Parker had in his writings to a lesser extent—as we have seen. Yet, as he matured, Lincoln mellowed and began to manifest all four of Parker's pieties. He always loved the truth, the first of Parker's four pieties, and therefore did not abandon Paine-like criticism in religion that Parker emphasized as well, which helped attain truth in religion by eliminating error. In his later years, however, Lincoln confined his critical religious comments to his close friends, according to Matheny, as has been mentioned. Lincoln also manifested love of righteousness—the piety of conscience—as Parker called the second piety, which contributed to his ultimate insistence on the complete abolition of slavery. Lincoln's love of humanity, the third of Parker's pieties, which he called piety of the heart, is a well-known attribute of Lincoln. And finally, Lincoln loved God, as we shall see, which was Parker's fourth category of piety, the piety of the soul.

The fact that Lincoln shared both Parker's disdain for doctrine and his simultaneous value of love or piety is illustrated in Henry Deming's "Eulogy of Abraham Lincoln." Deming, a congressman, visited Lincoln about a year before his death. The two men began reciting biblical passages. Deming, impressed with Lincoln's knowledge of the Bible and his interest in religion, could not help but ask why he was not a member of any church. Lincoln explained that he could not go along with the "Confessions of Faith" or doctrine that were "long complicated statements" required by churches. He then said, "When any church will inscribe over its altar, as its sole qualification for membership . . . 'Thou shalt love the Lord thy God with all thy heart, and with all thy soul, and with all thy mind, and thy neighbor as thyself,' that church will I join with all my heart and all my soul."[101] Here Lincoln echoed Parker, who said that this great commandment of Jesus "so well summed up" "the whole extent of Christianity."[102]

Dr. William Jayne, a Springfield friend of Lincoln, who Lincoln made the governor of the Dakota Territory, also gave testimony of Lincoln's piety and rejection of creed:

> Lincoln was by nature a deeply religious man. But I have no evidence that he ever accepted the formulated creed of any sect or denomination. I know that all churches had his profound respect and support. . . . It is now beyond the realm of controversy that Lincoln loved, honored, and revered Almighty God.[103]

Lincoln's "profound respect and support" for all "churches" is consistent with Parker's idea that each sect or religion comprises a part of the whole truth of Christianity.

Leonard Swett, in a letter to Herndon, gives still another Parkeresque account of Lincoln's mature religious views in the carefully chosen words of a good lawyer that tell us Lincoln manifested

Parker's four pieties—love of truth, rightness, mankind, and God. Swett also refers to Lincoln's "natural religion" born of his own nature—the source of religion according to Parker:

> You ask me whether he [Lincoln] changed his religious opinions towards the close of his life. I think not. As he became involved in matters of the gravest importance, full of great responsibility and great doubt, a feeling of religious reverence, and belief in God—his justice and overruling power—increased upon him. He was full of *natural religion* [my italics]; he believed in God as much as the most approved Church member; Yet he judged of Providence by the same system of great generalization as of everything else. He had in my judgment very little faith in ceremonials and forms. Whether he went to Church once a month or once a year troubled him but very little. He failed to observe the Sabbath very scrupulously. I think he read "Petroleum V. Nasby" [the humorist] as much as he did the Bible. He would ridicule the Puritans, or swear in a moment of vexation; but yet his heart was full of *natural and culti-vated religion* [my italics]. He believed in the great laws of truth [love of truth], the rigid discharge of duty, his accountability to God, the ultimate triumph of right, and the overthrow of wrong [love of righteousness]. If his religion were to be judged by the line and rule of Church Creeds and unexceptionable language, he would fall far short of the standard; but if by the higher rule of purity of conduct, of honesty of motive, of unyielding fidelity to the right and acknowledging God as the Supreme Ruler, then he filled all the requirements of true devotion [love of God] and love of his neighbor as himself [love of mankind].[104]

It seems clear from the remarks of Deming, Jayne, and Swett that Lincoln did, as Parker stated a "real" Christian would, "outgrow any form or any system of doctrines we have devised, and approach still closer to the truth."[105] It seems equally clear that as Lincoln matured, piety or love had become more important to him than criticism in religion while simultaneously not abandoning criticism by going back to more conventional faith in the sense of blind, unques-tioned, or uncritical belief in doctrine. These aspects of Lincoln's religious disposition justify Herndon's comment that Lincoln "was a Theist, somewhat on the order of Theodore Parker," as well as Fell's that Theodore Parker's "views most nearly represented Mr. Lincoln's" on the subject of religion.[106]

## LINCOLN AND THE DECLARATION OF INDEPENDENCE

As Bolingbroke's deism influenced Jefferson, Paine's deism along with Parker's mystical transcendentalism grounded in rational deism influenced Lincoln. This resulted in Lincoln's belief in a universal, impartial, all-inclusive God who included all individuals, peoples, nations, races, religions, irreligions, and nonreligions in His love and benevolence. Being completely impartial, this universal God did not favor any person or group of persons. He treated them all equally. In this sense Lincoln's God was exactly like the deistic, impartial "Nature's God" Jefferson placed in the Declaration of Independence. Moreover, by reading Paine's deistic natural theology in the *Age of Reason*, Lincoln would have been familiar with the phrase "Nature's God" because Paine used these exact words to describe the deistic God as Jefferson had done in the Declaration of Independence. When comparing religions based on the revealed "Word of God" or scripture with deism based on observations of nature and rational conclusions drawn from those observations, Paine wrote in a way reminiscent of Bolingbroke and Jefferson by stating that you cannot trust "revealed religion" or scripture-based religion, you can only trust nature-based *"natural religion"*:

> Books, whether Bibles or Korans, carry no evidence of being the work of any other power than man. It is only that which man cannot do that carries the evidence of being the work of a superior power. Man could not invent and make a universe—he could not invent nature, for nature is of divine origin. It is laws by which the universe is governed. When, therefore, we look through nature up to *nature's God* [my italics], we are in the right road of happiness, but when we trust to books as the Word of God, and confide in them as revealed religion, we are afloat on the ocean of uncertainty, and shatter into contending factions. The term, therefore,

*natural religion,* explains itself to be *divine religion,* and the term *revealed religion* involves in it the suspicion of being *artificial.*[107]

Even Paine sounds a bit mystical and transcendental here with the phrase "look through nature up to nature's God" or the God that created nature. In addition, he succinctly mentions his awareness of how particular mediators between God and man, such as scriptures, churches, temples, mosques, or clergymen, accepted as central authorities in religion, made humans "shatter into contending factions" with each believing in different doctrine and each claiming that theirs alone was true and, therefore, that God favored them. Bolingbroke, Jefferson, and Parker, as well as Paine, were also aware of this. All four men saw how this doctrinal approach caused religions or sects to make God jealous, partial, narrow, and small-minded—indeed a bigot who favored their religion or sect and frowned on all others. As a result, all four rejected theology where God required belief in a particular set of doctrines as the only way to salvation. Lincoln also took this approach, as the aforementioned comments of Deming, Jayne, and Swett make abundantly clear.

As was stated in chapter 1, the disposition of the deistic God has egalitarian democratic political implications that were used by Jefferson in the Declaration of Independence. The universal, impartial, all-inclusive "Nature's God" of the first paragraph did not choose any people or nation over others as a result of His all-inclusiveness and impartiality. Indeed, according to Him, all peoples and nations are entitled to a "separate and equal Station among the powers of the earth." Then in the second paragraph, "Nature's God" treated all individuals equally and impartially by giving each person equal rights when they were created: "We hold these Truths to be self-evident, that All Men are created equal, that they are endowed by their Creator with certain unalienable Rights, among which are Life, Liberty, and the Pursuit of Happiness."

As we have seen, Jefferson included black men in the universalism and egalitarianism of the Declaration of Independence in two of its provisions. The first was his anti–slave trade, antislavery passage deleted by the Continental Congress that specifically stated blacks have the God-given rights of "life & liberty." Lincoln was aware of this passage because he read and quoted from Jefferson's *Autobiography*, which contains a copy of the Declaration as Jefferson drafted it prior any deletions, additions, or alterations made by the Congress or members of the drafting committee.[108] The second provision was of course where the all-inclusive, none-are-excluded, deistic "Nature's God" of the Declaration "created" "All Men" equal by endowing each individual with the "unalienable Rights" of "Life, Liberty, and the Pursuit of Happiness."

Considering Lincoln's knowledge of Jefferson's anti–slave trade and antislavery passage as well as the all-inclusive deistic theology succinctly stated in that document, it is understandable that again and again he publicly stated that blacks were included in the Declaration of Independence, which will be discussed in subsequent chapters. Moreover, when it came to politics, on 22 February 1861 in Philadelphia, he gave a speech in which he stated that all his political feelings and sentiments were derived from the Declaration of Independence and that its universal principles gave promise not only to American blacks, but also to "*all*" oppressed people everywhere:

> I have never had a feeling politically that did not spring from the sentiments embodied in the Declaration of Independence. . . . I have often inquired of myself, what great principle or idea it was that kept this Confederacy so long together. It was not the mere matter of the separation of the colonies from the mother land; but something in that Declaration giving liberty, not alone to the people of this country, but hope to the world for all future time. It was that which gave promise that in due time the weights should be lifted from the shoulders of *all* [my italics] men, and that *all* should have an equal chance. This is the sentiment embodied in that Declaration of Independence.[109]

Lincoln went further than this the day before when he addressed the New Jersey Senate. There he stated that the "Union," the "Constitution," and the "liberties of the people *shall* [my italics] be perpetuated in accordance with" the "original idea" contained in the Declaration of Independence as to why the Revolutionary War was fought.

Since he knew that blacks, indeed all people, were included in the "original idea" of the Declaration which stated that "All Men are created equal" in the sense that God gave every human being the right of "Liberty" and that "to secure" that right "governments are instituted among Men," Lincoln was in effect saying that it was his aim to abolish slavery, which was protected by constitutional law in the United States. He even said that it would please him—indeed, make him happy—if he could be God's and the people's "humble" instrument to accomplish this aim:

> I am exceedingly anxious that this Union, the Constitution, and the liberties of the people shall be perpetuated in accordance with the original idea [contained in the Declaration of Independence] for which that struggle [the Revolutionary War] was made, and I shall be most happy indeed if I shall be an humble instrument in the hands of the Almighty, and of this, *his almost chosen people* [my italics], for perpetuating the object of that great struggle.[110]

In his efforts to be "an humble instrument" "for perpetuating" the nation "in accordance with the original idea [of the Declaration]," which was "to secure" the rights of "all Men" with "governments" that were "instituted among Men" by "Men," Lincoln implied his concept of human nature that was alien to orthodox Christianity's original sin concept but in accord with Jefferson's heterodox view. This heterodox view of human nature is the subject of the next chapter.

# Chapter 3

# Moral-Sense Theory in Jefferson and Lincoln

Thomas Jefferson and Abraham Lincoln not only held the same concept of God—an impartial, egalitarian ecumenical God. They also held the same concept of human nature. Both rejected the morally tainted original sin concept subscribed to by orthodox Christianity. Yet unlike orthodoxy, both subscribed to the moral-sense view of human reality articulated by deistic Scottish Enlightenment thinkers, which is the cornerstone of the political theory Jefferson placed in the Declaration of Independence discussed in this chapter. Henry Home, Lord Kames was the principal Scottish influence on Jefferson whereas Thomas Brown provided similar influence on Lincoln, which will also be discussed in this chapter.

As we have seen, deism is based on natural law or laws that govern the motion of physical objects in the universe like planets and stars. There is, however, another type of natural law—the type that governs social relationships. Both types were God-given at the time of creation, according to deists. The first makes the universe self-governing. The second, according to some deists, makes human beings self-governing because each individual has a moral sense or conscience, which along with reason gives the capacity to easily detect the moral laws of nature independent of God, His church, His scripture, or His clergy, and, in addition, gives each individual the capacity to regulate their behavior according to those laws. Moreover, it is the ability to easily perceive the moral law of nature that enables the people to establish governments whose purpose is to help regulate human behavior in accordance with that law. Indeed, this ability is what enables the people to pass judgment on their government as to whether it fulfills its purpose and to terminate that government and form a new one if their judgment is adverse.

This human self-governing element of deism was a radical departure from Catholicism and predominating versions of Protestantism, which maintain that original sin caused Adam and Eve to fall from righteousness and become morally tainted. All humans somehow inherit this effect of the Fall, which renders them morally defective. Therefore, no one can attain trustworthy moral knowledge without God, His church, His scripture, or His clergy. In politics, however, morally defective humans pose a problem. How can you give them political authority and have a moral state? Medieval political thought and practice, dominated by Christianity, said you couldn't. People need God, mediated by His church or His scripture or His clergy or a Christian king, anointed or deputized by God via the church, to supply moral direction to the state. Hence the dominion of a Christian king or church or both king and church together, as the moral and political authority in medieval times.[1] Even the political thought of reformers Martin Luther and John Calvin was based on God-given authority over the people. Luther said the purpose of that authority was "to preserve peace, punish sin, and restrain the wicked" and Calvin said it "has been divinely ordained that we should be defended by the hand and protection of the magistrate against the outrages and injustices of the wicked, and so be able to live our lives in peace and safety."[2]

Some would argue that Protestantism and Calvinism initiated modern democracy. This may be true of radical Calvinist Protestants and Puritans such as John Locke. Yet mainstream Protestants and Calvinists believed in and followed the authority of scripture or God's word administered to by a church or a clergy, the custodians of scripture, who were, in many instances, as authoritarian as monarchs. It was scripture and its custodians, not the people, which were the supreme authority in Calvin's Bible commonwealth of Geneva and the Puritan governments of colonial New England.

John Locke departed from the original sin concept of human nature and the authoritarian political systems it entailed. In his *Second Treatise on Government*, where he gave ultimate political authority to the people over king, church, scripture, or clergyman, Locke maintained that individual humans could detect easily and independently the moral laws of nature with demonstrative reason based on sense perceptions. People were morally competent in this respect. Therefore, they could supply the moral direction of the state, which, as John Dunn points out, was the cornerstone of Locke's *Second Treatise* in which the people, not kings or church, had ultimate political authority.[3] However, Locke's demonstrative-reason method of gaining knowledge of the moral laws of nature involved a step-by-step process similar to that found in Euclidian Geometry in which simple "self-evident" things, acknowledged as truth immediately upon perception, like one plus two equals three, were used to prove something more complex and not immediately recognizable as truth, like the "Agreement or Disagreement in bigness, between the three Angles of a Triangle, and two right ones."[4] Although Locke's demonstrative-reason approach to moral knowledge sounded feasible, he soon found it was not. He was never able to determine the moral laws of nature using this method, as he claimed he could.[5] This failure left his political thought an abstraction because its foundational premise did not work. Jefferson was aware of Locke's failure but used Lockean political thought in the Declaration of Independence anyway because he maintained that he found another method whereby individuals could easily and independently find the moral laws of nature.[6]

## HENRY HOME, LORD KAMES

Enter Scottish jurist, deist, and moral-sense philosopher Henry Home, Lord Kames, who made a profound impression on Jefferson that lasted all his life.[7] A member of the Scottish Enlightenment, Kames explained how individuals could easily attain knowledge of the moral laws of nature. He argued that each person has a moral sense or conscience that perceives what is moral in a situation as soon as that situation is perceived. Moreover, he argued that this moral sense is a God-given faculty that enforces moral behavior. Kames thereby made humans morally competent in contrast to Catholic and Protestant orthodoxy that claimed all humans were morally defective or tainted. As Kames put it when describing the inner moral sense or conscience in his *Principles of Equity* that Jefferson read as a law student:

> By perception alone, without reasoning, we acquire the knowledge of right and wrong, of what we may do, of what we ought to do, and of what we ought to abstain from: and considering that we have thus a greater certainty of the moral laws than of any proposition discovered by reasoning, man may well be deemed the favorite of Heaven. . . . The moral sense or conscience may well be held the voice of God within us, constantly admonishing us of our duty; and requiring on our part no exercise of our faculties but attention merely. The celebrated Locke ventured what he thought a bold conjecture, that the moral duties may be capable of demonstration: how great his surprise to have been told, that they are capable of much higher evidence.[8]

In Kames's analysis of human nature in his *Essays on the Principles of Morality and Natural Religion*, which Jefferson read in his early adulthood along with Kames's *Elements of Criticism*, Kames synthesized the opposing views of Thomas Hobbes, who claimed humans were motivated by selfishness, and the Third Earl of Shaftesbury, who claimed humans were motivated by altruism.[9] He maintained that each person had five "principles of action" that supply the will or motivating force for human action. The first two, self-preservation and self-love, were selfish while the last three, fidelity, gratitude, and benevolence, were altruistic or involved obligations to others. Self-preservation, the first principle, according to Kames, is "the strongest of all instincts." The second, self-love, is "the desire of our own happiness and good" and "is a stronger principle than benevolence, or love bestowed on others; and is wisely ordered," according to Kames, "because every man has more power, knowledge, and opportunity to promote his own good, than that of others." Therefore, Kames concluded, "the good of individuals is principally trusted to their own care." Fidelity, the third principle, has to do with the "performance of promises . . . and in general the executing of trusts," like the "love of children, who by nature are entrusted to our care." "Friendship, which supposes a mutual [trust] engagement," also falls under fidelity. The fourth principle is gratitude, which is "universally acknowledged," according to Kames, and involves a duty to those to whom we are grateful. The fifth, benevolence, "exerts itself more vigorously, or more faintly in proportion to the distance of particular objects." To put it another way, we are more inclined to perform benevolent acts to those in close proximity than those far away. In addition, we are more apt to manifest benevolence "to those in distress" rather than "promote" the "positive good" of those not in distress.[10]

A major premise of Kames's moral thought is that the five principles of action are regulated by the moral sense or conscience itself that tells us "which of our principles of action we may indulge and which of them we must restrain."[11] Another major premise is that the moral sense is the instrument that enables individuals to easily find the moral laws of nature. Although Kames downgraded the role of reason in gaining knowledge of natural law compared to Locke's complicated deduction method, it did play a small part in acquiring such knowledge when used simultaneously with the moral sense. As Kames put it:

> In searching for these laws [of nature], it must be obvious that we may falsely indulge every principle of action, where the action is not disapproved of by the moral sense, and that we ought to perform every action which the moral sense informs us to be our duty. From this short proposition, may be readily *deduced* all the laws of nature which govern human actions [my italics].[12]

The fact that the laws of nature were "readily" or easily "deduced" after the moral sense approved or disapproved of an action is another way of saying the amount of reason involved was minimal. This made the moral law easily known to virtually every human being and gave a huge impetus to Lockean political thought where easy access to moral knowledge was essential. In democratic republics especially, Kames's ideas could be used as the basis of granting ultimate moral and political authority to the people because they made the people morally competent and thereby capable of supplying moral direction to the state. Although Christian precepts like "Thou shalt not kill," "Thou shalt not steal," and "Thou shalt not commit adultery" are easily determined with the moral sense and minimal reason in Kames's system, many deists clung to the idea that Christ's mission on earth was to specifically state the moral laws of nature that God prescribed at the time of creation.[13]

## JUSTICE AND BENEVOLENCE

One of the principal elements of Kamesean moral thought is the difference between justice and benevolence. The moral sense or conscience itself, Kames maintained, gives each person a sense of justice, which is an inner feeling that tells us not to harm others as well as what harms them. In addition, the moral sense makes justice or refraining from harmful acts a duty and enforces that duty.[14] Benevolence or doing something good to someone, on the other hand, is not a duty unless it will cure distress in others without harming one's self.[15] Therefore, benevolence is discretionary if it cannot be done without harming one's self.[16] Kames's logic in making justice a duty and benevolence to a great extent discretionary was that God made humans sociable, and although society can exist without benevolence, it cannot exist without justice because individuals would constantly inflict harm on each other, making social relations destructive to humankind.[17]

According to Kames, the enforcement of justice by the moral sense or conscience was the result of feelings of "remorse of conscience" in one's self when one harmed others. Kames maintained that this punishment had historically proven to be "the most severe of all tortures."[18] It gave the moral sense or conscience "the most complete character of a law" because punishment is essential to law. Kames also maintained that the moral sense or conscience rewards benevolent acts with feelings of "approbationary pleasure" that gives greater satisfaction than being just, which itself gives some pleasure.[19]

The duty of justice and limitations on the duty of benevolence in Kames put Jefferson, who sounded like Kames on this issue, in the Lockean liberal camp rather than in the communitarian camp. According to the liberal camp, individuals, for the most part, have no duties to the community or to the individuals of the community other than to respect each individual's rights. In contrast, communitarians, for the most part, say the community has duty claims on individuals that take precedence over individual rights. In his 1782 letter to James Monroe, Jefferson expressed his preference for liberalism over communitarianism by writing:

> If we are made in some degree for others, yet in a greater are we made for ourselves. It were contrary to feeling and indeed ridiculous to suppose a man had less right in himself than one of his neighbors or all of them put together. This would be slavery and not that liberty which the bill of rights has made inviolable and for the preservation of which our government has been changed.[20]

In mentioning "that liberty which the bill of rights has made inviolable and for the preservation of which our government has been changed," Jefferson reiterated the purpose of government stated in the Declaration of Independence where he wrote: "Governments are instituted among men" in order "to secure" the individual "Rights" of "Life, Liberty, and the Pursuit of Happiness." Using Kamesean logic, Jefferson's statement to Monroe says in effect that the purpose of government, according to the Declaration, would be defeated if benevolence were always a duty because it would give every distressed person or persons who needed help claims on others to come to their aid even to the detriment of those providing aid or at the expense of their rights. The result, as Jefferson concluded, "would be slavery," not "liberty."

In 1816, Jefferson was still emphasizing justice as a prerequisite to society, as Kames did, when he said it was linked to God's will, design, or final cause at the time of creation in a syllogistic argument: "Assuming the fact that the earth has been created in time, and consequently the dogma of final causes, we yield, of course, to this short syllogism. Man was created for social intercourse; but social intercourse cannot be maintained without a sense of justice; then man must have been created with a sense of justice."[21]

Another element of Kamesean thought is that the moral sense or conscience is strengthened by reading good literature and attending good plays because, as Kames maintained, the feelings in our mind or moral sense become emotionally attracted to moral characters and repelled by immoral characters. As a result, repeated exposure to good literary works and plays gradually intensifies these moral-sense feelings of attraction and repulsion. This is like strengthening a muscle through repeated exercise, according to Kames, who said:

> Nothing conduces so much to improve the mind [moral feelings], and confirm it in virtue, as being continually employed in surveying the actions of others, entering into the concerns of the virtuous, approving of their conduct, condemning vice, and showing an abhorrence at it; for the mind acquires strength by exercise, as well as the body.[22]

Jefferson expressed the same thought in his 1771 letter to Robert Skipwith, his nephew, in which he enclosed a list of books he recommended for purchase that included several literary works and plays as well as the writings of Kames:

> Every thing is useful which contributes to fix us in the principles and practice of virtue. When any signal act of charity or of gratitude, for instance, is presented either to our sight or imagination, we are deeply impressed with its beauty and feel a strong desire in ourselves of doing charitable and grateful acts also. On the contrary when we see or read of any atrocious deed, we are disgusted with its deformity and conceive an abhorrence of vice. Now every emotion of this kind is an exercise of our virtuous dispositions;

and dispositions of the mind, like limbs of the body, acquire strength by exercise. But exercise produces habit; and in the instance of which we speak, the exercise being of the moral feelings, produces a habit of thinking and acting virtuously. We never reflect whether the story we read be truth or fiction.[23]

## THE COMMON STANDARD OF MORALITY

There were, according to Kames, many different and conflicting views on what was moral throughout the world. Yet, simultaneously there was a uniform common standard of morality, as he explained in his *Essays on the Principles of Morality and Natural Religion* and *Elements of Criticism*, both of which Jefferson read when a student. That common standard originated in what Kames called the "common nature of man." Because of this common nature, humans could perceive the common moral standard notwithstanding cultural differences on what constituted morality.[24] Kames maintained that each individual of each species has an "internal" constitution that manifests itself in a certain uniformity of conduct peculiar to each species that was the basis of "the laws of our nature." Any act, in order to be "considered regular and good," had to be in accord with the internal "common nature of the species" that gave rise to the common standard. Any person who violated this standard was looked upon as a "monster," as if he had "two heads or four hands."[25] Late in his life, Jefferson made reference to this uniform common standard in Kames's *Essays* that he read some "fifty years" earlier: "A man owes no duty to which he is not urged by some impulsive feeling. This is correct, if referred to the *standard of general feeling* [my italics] in the given case, and not the feeling of an individual."[26] In other words, although individuals could find the moral laws of nature, they could not be subjective. Their findings had to conform to the common standard of morality based on similar findings by the vast majority of human beings.

According to Kames, old civilizations and cultures provided the most perfect examples of the uniform universal common standard of morality because of their subjection to moral-sense education and culture for longer periods of time than other civilizations and cultures. This is what refined the moral sense and morals of their people even though there were exceptions manifest in some individuals, which Kames referred to as "aberrations" that harkened back to ancient times when men were "originally savage and brutal." This general moral refinement of "men in their more perfect [or civilized] state" in old civilizations was reflected in the "rules of morality" of the common standard as well as in laws that were in accord with this standard. Moreover, only laws that were the "most universal and the most lasting" from old civilizations and cultures should be included in the common standard. Meaning, even old and largely moral nations or civilizations could have an immoral law or two on its books not found in other largely moral nations or civilizations. In addition, new laws could have been added, the morality of which had not yet stood the test of time. These old and new laws were excluded from the common standard since they were not among the "most universal and most lasting," according to Kames. "In this very manner," he said of this method of selecting moral norms and laws, "a standard for morals has been ascertained with a good deal of accuracy, and is daily apply'd by able judges with general satisfaction."[27] As individuals could not be subjective in what was moral in Kames's system, neither could nations and civilizations.

## LINCOLN'S MORAL-SENSE IDEAS

A source of Lincoln's moral-sense ideas came from reading Thomas Brown (1878–1920). Joshua Speed, one of Lincoln's few close friends, stated that Lincoln read "Brown's philosophy" or his *Lectures on the Philosophy of the Human Mind.*[28] Brown was a deist and a professor of moral philosophy at the University of Edinburgh in Scotland. He was a product of and sympathetic to the Age of Enlightenment with its ideas of progress. His *Lectures* consist of three volumes of critical analysis of the ideas of several thinkers of the seventeenth-

and eighteenth-century English, Scottish, and French Enlightenment mixed with some ideas of his own. Classical thinkers Cicero and Seneca are frequently quoted along with many poets, especially Alexander Pope, in order to support his arguments. As might be expected, because Brown was a professor of moral philosophy at a Scottish university, the moral philosophy of Scottish thinkers was emphasized. Francis Hutcheson, a moral-sense thinker, David Hume, Thomas Reid, and, of course, Adam Smith were among the Scottish philosophers Brown discussed. Even though Henry Home, Lord Kames was not mentioned, Brown sounded like Kames in many of his statements. This is seen in Brown's idea that the moral sense or conscience is what gives individuals moral direction by giving knowledge of right and wrong as well as rewards for righteous acts and punishment for those that are wrong:

> Nature has . . . made it delightful to man to be active; and, not content with making it delightful to him to be merely active,— since this propensity to action, which of itself might lead him sometimes to benefit others, might of itself also lead him to injure as well as to benefit,—she has, as we have seen, directed him *how* to act, by that voice of conscience which she has placed within his breast; and given still greater efficacy to that voice by the pain which she has attached to disobedience, and the pleasure that is felt in obeying it.[29]

Like Kames, Brown made a distinction between justice, or refraining from harming others, and benevolence, or doing what benefits others, which he referred to as negative and positive duties respectively.[30] Elaborating on how conscience gives pleasure when our actions are virtuous and pain when they are opposed to virtue, Brown, again sounding like Kames, who said "remorse of conscience" is one of "the most severe of all tortures," said:

> The power of conscience does, indeed, what consciousness [reason] does not. It truly doubles all our feelings, when they have been such as virtue inspired; . . . and it multiplies them in a much more fearful proportion, when they have been of an opposite kind—arresting, as it were every moment of guilt, which, of itself, would have passed

away, as fugitive as our other moments, and suspending them forever before our eyes, in fixed and terrifying reality.[31]

Four factors, plus the way he argued against slavery, make Lincoln's
ideas similar to those of Kames and Jefferson's use of Kames. First,
he made a comment exactly like one Kames made in his *Essays on the
Principles of Morality and Natural Religion*. Second, he loved Shakespearean plays that exercised conscience or the moral sense in the
manner described by Kames. Third, he spoke of the moral sense as
the measure of human or legislated law—a premise of Jefferson's
substitution of Kames's moral-sense method of finding the moral
law of nature that made Locke's political thought contained in the
Declaration of Independence effective. Locke maintained that legislated law had to be in accord with the moral laws of nature in order
to be binding and that the people themselves, since they had knowledge of the moral law of nature, were the ultimate judge as to
whether or not legislated law corresponded with natural law.[32]
Fourth, Lincoln believed in the doctrine of necessity and he
described it the same way Kames did.

Lincoln's Kamesean-like statement had to do with the idea that
actions born of self-love to further one's selfish interests are acceptable
to the moral sense as long as they are in accord with justice or do not
harm others—with self-preservation as the exception. As Kames put it:

> We meet with no obstruction from the moral sense when we prefer
> our own interest to that of others. The same will hold with regard
> to our particular appetites, passions and affections. But here comes
> a remarkable limitation, that we are not to indulge self-love at the
> expense of harming others, whether in their person, goods or rep-
> utation. The moral sense, in every case, *self-preservation excepted* [my
> italics], lays us under an absolute restraint with regards to these
> particulars. This restraint is felt as our indispensable duty and the
> transgression of this duty never fails to be attended with remorse,
> and a dread of merited punishment.[33]

Here Kames allows that self-preservation, "the strongest of all
instincts," is the exception to the moral-sense duty not to harm

others, meaning that one's self has precedence over others and we can inflict harm on them in order to preserve our own self or life. To put it another way, justice or the duty not to harm others can be suspended for self-preservation in many circumstances. To illustrate his point, Kames used the analogy of two shipwrecked men on a plank that could support only one, which justified either man pushing the other off in order to keep from drowning:

> With regard to our principles of action, self-preservation being the leading principle, it is hard to say that any means, strictly speaking, are unlawful, to attain that end. If two men in a ship-wreck get hold at the same instant of a plank, which is not bulky enough to support both, it is lawful for the one to thrust off the other, in order to save his own life. This action is not condemned by the moral sense: It is not attended with any feeling of wrong.[34]

Lincoln used the same analogy with the same meaning and implications. In his speech at New Haven, Connecticut, 6 March 1860, when arguing against some in the Democratic Party who maintained that there is a basic struggle going on between white and black men in which one must enslave the other, Lincoln said:

> There is no such struggle! It is merely an ingenious falsehood, to degrade and brutalize the negro. Let each let the other alone, and there is no struggle about it. If it was like *two wrecked seamen on a narrow plank, when each must push the other off or drown himself* [my italics] I would push the negro off or a white man either, but it is not; the plank is large enough for both. This good earth is plenty broad enough for white man and negro both, and there is no need of either pushing the other off.[35]

This statement leaves no doubt that Lincoln was aware of the difference and sometimes delicate balance existing between the motivating force or will in human nature arising from the moral sense of justice on the one hand and self-interest and self-preservation on the other. In fact, he made another more specific reference to this difference in his speech at Springfield, Illinois, in 1857: "Will springs from the two elements of moral sense and self interest." This comment is in accord with Kames, who maintained that will is born of the moral sense and also the principles of action, one of which is self-interest born of "self-love."[36]

The second of Lincoln's four similarities to Kamesean thought is the type of Shakespearean plays he preferred. These preferences correspond with Kames's idea that good plays and literature exercise and strengthen the moral sense or conscience. As a young man, Lincoln read Shakespeare, according to Dennis F. Hanks, James H. Matheny, Joshua F. Speed, and John Stuart.[37] When mature, he maintained his affection for Shakespeare, as a letter he wrote to Shakespearean actor James H. Hackett while president demonstrates:

> Some of Shakespeare's plays I have never read; while others I have gone over perhaps as frequently as any unprofessional reader. Among the latter are Lear, Richard Third, Henry Eighth, Hamlet and especially Macbeth. I think nothing equals Macbeth. It is wonderful. Unlike you gentlemen of the profession, I think the soliloquy in Hamlet commencing "O, my offense is rank" surpasses that commencing "To be, or not to be." But pardon this small attempt at criticism. I should like to hear you pronounce the opening speech of Richard the Third. Will you not soon visit Washington again?[38]

Lincoln always thought himself ugly. So did Donn Piatt, a soldier, journalist, and finally a judge, who said, "Mr. Lincoln was the homeliest man I ever saw."[39] This is no doubt why Lincoln wanted to hear the opening soliloquy of *Richard the Third* because Richard was ugly and in his first lines of the play manifested bitterness over that fact:

> Cheated of feature by dissembling nature,
> Deform'd, unfinish'd, sent before my time
> Into this breathing world, scarce half made up,
> And that so lamely and unfashionable
> That dogs bark at me as I halt by them.[40]

Angry at his appearance and those who found it revolting, Richard was "determined to prove a villain," an aspiration he abundantly fulfilled.[41] Lincoln, on the other hand, joked about his own ugliness, displaying what James McPherson described as "his endearing . . . self mocking sense of humor."[42] When speaking at an editor's banquet, Lincoln said that as a noneditor "he felt out of place."[43] He then compared this feeling to the time he met "a woman on horseback in the woods." "As I stopped to let her pass," he continued, "she also stopped and looking at me intently, said, 'I do believe your are the ugliest man I ever saw.'" Lincoln responded: "Madam, you are probably right but I could not help it," to which she replied, "No, you can't help it, but you might stay home."[44]

From a Kamesean perspective, *Richard the Third*, like most of Shakespeare's plays Lincoln mentioned in his letter to Hackett, gave an account of how guilt-ridden conscience tormented those who committed injustice by murdering or doing harm to others, thus instructing and thereby strengthening the conscience or moral sense of those attending or reading the play, as Kames said good plays would. Richard himself was an example. Haunted and unnerved toward the end of the play by a dream in which the ghosts of numerous people he murdered in his bloody rise to power cursed him, Richard lamented, "O coward conscience, how dost thou afflict me!" He then described his conscience-induced afflictions in more detail:

> My conscience hath a thousand several tongues!
> And every tongue brings in a several tale,
> And every tale condemns me for a villain.
> Perjury, perjury, in the high'st degree;
> Murder, stern murder, in the direst degree;
> All several sins, all used in each degree;
> Throng to the bar, crying all, "Guilty! Guilty![45]

*Henry the Eighth*, another of Lincoln's favorite plays mentioned in his letter to Hackett, provides another example of conscience instruction involving Cardinal Wolsey, a tragic figure in the play. Wolsey's ambition made him try to serve the king's interests as well as those of the Church, which finally resulted in his execution when the two interests conflicted and because of his conscience Wolsey went against Henry and took the side of the Church. Yet during the time between his falling out with Henry and his execution, Wolsey enjoyed what he described as "a still and quiet conscience" because he no longer had to offend it by serving the king's interests when they went against his conscience.[46] Here again, the importance of a remorseless or "quiet" conscience is emphasized and thereby exercised in this play, as Kames said it was in many plays.

Another Kamesean exercise of conscience is in *Macbeth*, Lincoln's favorite Shakespeare play according to his letter to Hackett, where Macbeth, along with his wife, murder Duncan, then king of Scotland, so that they could be king and queen. Lady Macbeth, so ruthless at the beginning of the play, is reduced to a madwoman at the end, given to rubbing her hands because she imagines Duncan's blood is on them, causing her to comment famously, "Out, damned spot! out, I say!" and "Here's the smell of the blood still. All the perfumes of Arabia will not sweeten this little hand."[47] In a sober reflective moment she stated her conscience tortured her to the extent that she would have been better off as the victim rather than the perpetrator of her crime: "Where our desire is got without content, 'Tis safer to be that which we destroy, Than by destruction dwell in doubtful joy."[48] Macbeth himself expresses the same thoughts after his tortured conscience afflicted him with bad dreams:

> In the affliction of these terrible dreams
> That shake us nightly. Better be with the dead
> Whom we, to gain our peace, have sent to peace,
> Than on the torture of the mind to lie:
> In restless ecstasy.[49]

Lincoln's favorite *Hamlet* soliloquy, mentioned in his letter to Hackett, is another lament from a villain whose conscience is tortured. Hamlet's uncle, who ascended the throne by murdering his brother who was then king as well as Hamlet's father, delivered it:

> O, my offence is rank, it smells to heaven;
> It had the primal eldest curse upon't,
> A brother's murder. Pray can I not,

Though inclination be sharp as will.
My stronger guilt defeats my strong intent;
And, like a man to double business bound,
I stand in pause where I shall first begin,
And both neglect. What if this cursed hand
Were thicker than itself with brother's blood,
Is there not rain enough in the sweet heavens
To wash it white as snow?[50]

Perceiving his victim's blood on his own hands, Hamlet's uncle, echoing Lady Macbeth's hand-wringing "Out damned spot," decries in these lines how he cannot turn to prayer for relief from his conscience because of his intense feeling of guilt. Elaborating on this state of mind, he said in Lincoln's favorite soliloquy:

But, O, What form of prayer
Can serve my turn? "Forgive me my foul murder"?
That cannot be; since I am still possess'd
Of those effects for which I did murder,
My crown, mine own ambition, and my queen.
May one be pardon'd and retain the offence?
In the corrupted currents of this world
Offence's gilded hand may shove by justice,
And oft 'tis seen the wicked prize itself
Buys out the law: but 'tis not so above;
There is no shuffling, there the action lies
In his true nature; and we ourselves compell'd,
Even to the teeth and forehead of our faults,
To give in evidence. What then? what rests?
Try what repentance can. What can it not?
Yet what can it when one can not repent?
O wretched state! O bosom black as death!
O limed soul, that, struggling to be free,
Art more engaged![51]

Here the murderer makes it clear that he has no place to hide from his conscience. It won't let him forget what he has done. And, as long as he has the ambition that caused his crime along with the fruits it brought him—the crown, the kingdom, even the queen of his murdered brother who he married shortly after his crime—how could he repent, how could he pray to a just God to forgive him? Indeed, the conscience inflicted miseries so graphically depicted in this soliloquy that Lincoln said surpassed Hamlet's "To be, or not to be" in his aforementioned letter to Hackett tells us how much it instructed or, as Kames would say, exercised Lincoln's own conscience.

The third similarity between Lincoln's and Kames's ideas has to do with the moral sense as the measure of legislated or human-made law, as Jefferson used Kames to support Lockean political thought. According to Kames, as has been stated, individuals of the populace can easily detect the moral laws of nature using the moral sense and minimal reason, which enabled them to judge whether legislated law was in accord with natural law. This judgment capacity was an essential element of Locke's *Second Treatise*, as has also been stated. That Lincoln had similar ideas is seen in his First Inaugural: "The moral sense of the people imperfectly supports the law itself." Lincoln used the word "imperfectly" to describe the impact of "the moral sense of the people" on the law because, as he explained, "One section of our country believes slavery is *right*, and ought to be extended, while the other believes it is *wrong*, and ought not to be extended." Then, in a way consistent with the Lockean view that ultimately people will revolt against government and law they judge immoral, Lincoln cited two mild examples of such revolt: the "fugitive slave" law and the "law for the suppression of the foreign slave trade." In the South, he stated that the foreign slave trade was "now imperfectly suppressed" despite law against it. This was because many Southern people thought slavery was morally right. On the other hand, in the North "fugitive" or runaway slaves were not always surrendered so they could be returned to their owners as the Fugitive Slave law required because many Northerners thought slavery was morally wrong. Lincoln pointed out that these mild revolutions against law judged morally wrong would be complete *"after the separation of the sections [North and South]"* at which time he predicted *"the foreign slave trade . . . would ultimately be revived without restriction"* in the South while *"fugitive slaves . . .would not be surrendered at all"* in the North.[52]

Lincoln, however, did not believe in moral relativism when it came to the moral-sense view of slavery—provided the moral sense was perfected. However, it was not perfected, which was manifest in the different moral-sense views on slavery in the North and South, as he stated in his First Inaugural. Thomas Brown, whose writings Lincoln read,[53] gave "feelings," especially "violent passion," as a reason for lack of perfection of the moral sense or, more accurately, as a reason why the moral sense did not function when the mind was completely under the influence of such "feelings" or "passion":

> The temporary influence of every feeling that completely occupies the mind, especially of every violent passion, which blinds us at the moment to moral distinctions,—that is to say, prevents, by its own vividness, the rise of the less vivid feelings of approbation or disapprobation [of the conscience or moral sense]; in the same manner as, in similar circumstances, it would blind to the discernment even of the universal truths of science,—that is to say, would not allow us to perceive for the time the amplest and least mutable of all relations,—the proportions of number and quality.[54]

Slavery was of course the basis of the agricultural economy of the South. It was, therefore, vital to Southern interests. Because "violent passion" is aroused when vital interests are threatened, such "passion" overrode or obscured the less intense moral feelings born of the moral sense or conscience on the evil of slavery in many Southerners as well as in Northerners who had an interest in that institution when the continued existence of that institution was threatened. This Brownian explanation of how slavery adversely impacted the moral sense of many was very much a part of Lincoln, as we shall see.

## THE DOCTRINE OF NECESSITY

The fourth similarity between Lincoln's ideas and those of Kames was the "Doctrine of Necessity," described by Lincoln in his 1846 handbill written in response to rumors that he was "an open scoffer at Christianity"—rumors that threatened his political career.[55] His carefully worded handbill was designed to convince his Christian constituency that the rumors were false. However, if scrutinized, what he stated was not a denial of the rumors. After candidly admitting he was "not a member of any Christian Church," he stated that "I have never denied the truth of the Scriptures" or "spoken with intentional disrespect of religion in general" or "of any denomination of Christians in particular." Yet even though Lincoln did not intentionally speak disrespectfully of "religion in general," or of any particular "denomination of Christians," he had "spoken with intentional disrespect" about a particular religion—the Christian religion—when he referred to Jesus as a "bastard" to James H. Matheny, as has been mentioned. With his careful choice of words in his handbill, however, he was able to satisfy most of the faithful in his constituency that he was not "an open" or public "scoffer at Christianity" yet simultaneously to adhere to truth in the light of his past comments. However, although Lincoln had not openly or publicly scoffed at Christianity, he certainly did so privately among friends.

Lincoln went on to state in his handbill: "In early life I was inclined to believe in what I understand is called the 'Doctrine of Necessity'—that is, that the human mind is impelled to action, or held in rest by some power over which the mind itself has no control."[56] Several scholars have "connected Lincoln's belief in the Doctrine of Necessity to the Calvinist notion of predestination," as James Tackach pointed out.[57] Yet as was stated in the last chapter, Lincoln rejected predestination with his ideas of universal salvation since predestination condemns many to eternal damnation. There is, however, an Enlightenment view of the "Doctrine of Necessity" not related to predestination and, therefore, it seems more plausible that this is the "Necessity" Lincoln referred to. The idea that the mind was controlled by factors apart from itself, as Lincoln explained the "Doctrine of Necessity," was held by John Locke in his *Essay concerning Human Understanding* (book 2, chapter 21, "Of Power"), where Locke stated that the will or motivating force of the mind was determined by "uneasiness" or several "uneasinesses," which were anxieties born of unfulfilled desires to relate one's self to some object that gives pleasure outside of one's self or to get away from what gives pain. In other words, the cause of will was in the object of desire external to one's self or what caused pain. Locke maintained that all action or inaction was born of these uneasi-nesses or motivating forces or will, which were beyond the control of the mind, and that our present action was determined by the strongest present uneasiness among several uneasinesses or moti-vating forces in the mind. Kames essentially reiterated Locke's ideas in a chapter titled "Liberty and Necessity" in his *Essays on the Princi-ples of Morality and Natural Religion.* Summing up Locke's ideas on will or motivation determining actions, Kames said:

> Motives being once allowed to have a determining force [on our actions] in any degree, it is easy to suppose the force so augmented by accumulation of motives, as to leave little freedom, or rather none at all. In such instances, there is no denying that we are under *necessity*, to act [my italics].[58]

Like Locke, Kames also stated that we act based on the strongest motive or uneasiness at the time we act.[59] Then, acknowledging that will or motives are not under the control of the mind and empha-sizing that because of this we have no liberty, he said:

> If motives are not under our power or direction, which is confess-edly the fact we can, at bottom, have no liberty. We are so consti-tuted, that we cannot exert a single action but with some view, aim or purpose.[60]

The only sense in which individuals have liberty, according to Kames and Lincoln, which will be discussed in more detail in chapter 5, was if there were no impediments to movements or refraining from movements determined by their will. As Kames put it, once again expressing Lockean ideas contained in *An Essay concerning Human Understanding* in a way that describes the doctrine of necessity:

> In this lies the liberty of our actions, *in being free from constraint* [my italics], and in acting according our inclination and choice is unavoidably caused or occasioned by the prevailing motive; in this lies the *necessity* of our actions, that in such circumstances, it was impossible we could act other ways. In this sense all our actions are equally necessary [my italics].[61]

In his handbill, Lincoln did not state that he no longer believed in the "Doctrine of Necessity." He only said that he no longer argued in favor of it as he admitted he had done previously. In an effort to make "Necessity" more palatable to the faithful of his constituency, he added that he "always understood this same opinion to be held by several of the Christian denominations,"[62] no doubt referring to the idea that God's will, which was of course independent of the human mind, controlled everything as was stated in the Calvinistic Westminster Confession that was followed by many Christian denominations in nineteenth-century America and will be discussed in more detail in chapter 6. Lincoln, however, did not believe in the Westminster Confession, which chapter 6 will make clear.

## ANTISLAVERY USE OF KAMES AND BROWN

In order to strengthen the moral sense of the people on the issue of slavery so it could overcome passions born of interests in that evil institution, Lincoln did three things that were consistent with Kames's and Brown's ideas. First, he used moral arguments against slavery found in literature that exercised and thereby strengthened the moral sense in a Kamesean way. Second, he pointed out that blacks were objects of morality. These were Lincoln's idealistic arguments against slavery. Third, he pointed out objects of selfish interest to whites by showing that slavery was against those interests. These were Lincoln's realistic arguments against slavery.

In pointing out objects of morality and selfish interests, Lincoln was in accord with the ideas of both Kames and Brown. As has been stated, Kames maintained the moral sense with minimal reason could find the moral laws of nature. Yet simultaneously, he maintained that detecting objects of both morality and selfish interests along with methods to relate one's self to those objects often required a considerable amount of reason or rational calculation and restraint. Indeed, both Kames and Brown observed that in complex situations involving either the objects of morality or selfish interests, most humans did not know what those objects were. A principal Kamesean point, however, was that anyone who rationally detected the objects of their selfish interests and then exercised rational restraint and discipline to relate themselves to those objects would also have the necessary discipline to follow the dictates of the moral sense even if their interests conflicted with those dictates. Comparing human reality to a mechanical device, while emphasizing the importance of education and reason, Kames stated:

Man is a complex machine, composed of various principles of motion, which may be conceived as so many springs and weights counteracting and balancing one another. These being accurately adjusted, the movement of life is beautiful, because regular and uniform. But if some springs or weights be withdrawn, those which remain, acting now without opposition from their antagonist forces, will disorder the balance, and derange the whole machine. *Remove those principles of action which operate by reflection [reason], and whose objects are complex and general ideas, and the necessary consequence will be, to double the force of the appetites and passions, pointing at particular objects; which is always the case with those who act by sense, and not reflection. They are tyrannized by passion and appetite, and have no consistent rule of conduct* [my italics]. No wonder, the moral sense is of no sufficient authority to command obedience in such a case. This is the character of savages. We have no reason then to conclude, from the above picture, that even the greatest [of savages] are destitute of the moral sense. *Their defect rather lies in the weakness of their general principles of action, which ter-*

*minate in objects [of interest] too complex for savages readily to compre-
hend. This defect is remedied by education and reflection; and then it is,
that the moral sense, in concert with these general principles, acquires its
full authority, which is openly recognized, and cheerfully submitted to
[my italics].*[63]

Brown, in a statement that carries essentially the same message from
his *Lectures on the Philosophy of the Human Mind*, without comparing
man to a machine, also stressed the importance of "education and
reflection" or reason:

Reason, therefore,—that power by which we discover the various
relations of things, comes to our aid, and pointing out to us all the
probable physical consequences of actions, shows us the good of
what we might have conceived to be evil, the evil of what we might
have conceived to be good, weighing each with each, and calculating the preponderance of either. It thus influences our moral
feelings indirectly,—but it influences them only by presenting to
us *new objects* [my italics], to be admired or hated, and still
addresses itself to a principle which admires or hates. Like a telescope, or microscope, it shows us what was too distant, or too
minute, to come within the sphere of our simple vision; but it does
not alter the nature of vision itself. The best telescope, or the best
microscope, could give no aid to the *blind*. They imply the previous
power of visual discernment, or they are absolutely useless.
Reason, in like manner, supposes in us a discriminating vision of
another kind [conscience or moral sense]. . . . If we did not love
what is for the good of mankind, and love, consequently, those
actions which tend to the good of mankind, it would be vain for
reason to show, that an action was likely to produce good, of
which we were not aware, or evil, of which we were not aware.[64]

Both Kames and Brown in the aforementioned comments imply
or touch upon Locke's idea in book 2, chapter 2, "Of Power" in his
*Essay concerning Human Understanding* that although the will is determined by factors outside the mind, acting on impulses of the will
can often be suspended—at least for a time—during which we can
survey the consequences of acting on the strongest impulse of the

will and then make a judgment on whether or not to act on that impulse or suspend action on it indefinitely and act on another impulse of the will. Indeed, Locke said our nature makes this a necessity: "Man is put under a necessity by his constitution, as an intelligent Being, to be determined in *willing* by his own Thought and Judgement, what is best for him to do."[65] Implied in this statement, which Locke also made explicit, is that yielding to the strongest determined uneasiness or will could, in some instances, cause more pain than pleasure in the long run and, therefore, it should be overruled by "Judgement." For example, the desire for spicy food could give immediate pleasure but more pain through indigestion later. Locke then acknowledged the obvious fact that sane human beings often make wrong judgments that cause a lot of pain even though they seek only pleasure by nature.

One of the main causes of wrong judgments, according to Locke, was ignorance or, as he put it: "He that judges without informing himself to the utmost that he is capable, cannot acquit himself of *judging amiss*."[66] Education, therefore, was important in making correct judgments that have a good overall effect. All of this means human life is not completely foreordained by a will determined by factors outside of one's self. Education could change the determinations of will by presenting new objects of attraction to the mind and making what was once attractive repulsive in the sense that we would now know that relating ourselves to such objects would cause pain. Indeed, altering or changing the will or motivating force through education is a factor that gives liberty in Locke, Kames, and Brown. Brown, in fact, described such education as the function of a "political moralist" in a way that describes what Lincoln did or tried to do in many of his political speeches:

When the political moralist is said to *correct* our moral sentiments, as he unquestionably does often correct our views of particular actions, by pointing out to us general advantages or disadvantages, which flow more or less immediately from certain actions; and when he thus leads us to approve of actions of which we might otherwise have disapproved, to disapprove of actions of which otherwise we should have approved, he does not truly alter the nature of our moral feelings; *he only presents new objects to our moral discrimination* [my italics].[67]

Significantly, Lincoln practiced this view of education not only in politics, as we shall see, but in the way he led his life despite his fatalistic comment to Herndon: "What is to be will be, and no efforts nor prayers of ours can change, alter, modify, or reverse the decree."[68] His education as a young man through reading gave him new objects of desire that motivated him to perform actions that would enable him to relate himself to those objects—objects that would have been unknown to him without education. For example, through education he learned of the legal profession, which became an object of his desire. Then through more education he enabled himself to become a lawyer. To put it another way, the education he attained by his own efforts and resolution changed what he deemed important and thereby the type of actions he performed, which in turn changed the whole course of his life. Lincoln was certainly aware of this, indicating that his comments suggesting a strict fatalism, like the aforementioned one to Herndon, were hyperbole.

## LINCOLN'S IDEALISTIC ARGUMENTS AGAINST SLAVERY

Even before his First Inaugural, Lincoln was painfully aware of the conflicting moral views on slavery in the North and South. This is seen in the aforementioned 6 March 1860 New Haven speech where he said of the North, "Wrong as we think slavery is" and of the South "Holding as they do that slavery is morally right."[69] It was in this speech, however, as well as in others he made during his campaign for the presidency in 1860, that Lincoln presented arguments directed to those who had a "feeling of indifference" or an "absence of moral sense about the question [of slavery]."[70] He was, thereby, seeking to educate such people by pointing out that blacks were objects of morality—the general method of Kames and Brown. He believed that if his educational efforts succeeded, those indifferent to slavery, and even those who favored it, would come to recognize the injustice or harm it did to blacks. Then, in the name of justice and morality born of their moral sense, they would resist slavery's expansion in the territories that was favored by the Stephen Douglas–led Democrats and support his Republican position of restricting slavery to the slave states.

The principal tool Lincoln used in his educational efforts was the Declaration of Independence—a document he believed informed the moral sense or conscience of all Americans. He thereby used the Declaration as literature of the type Kames described that exercised and strengthened the moral sense. Indeed, Lincoln saw the Declaration as uniquely qualified to perform this function, since Americans of the nineteenth century were proud of their recent ancestors' defeat of Great Britain in the Revolutionary War. They were also proud of the Declaration of Independence itself, the Charter of the Revolution, and its universal, all-inclusive, impartial moral idealism of equal rights for all even though most did not practice this idealism. As has been stated, Lincoln was aware that the Declaration's all-inclusive idealistic phraseology "all Men are created equal" included blacks as did its deistic egalitarian, all-inclusive, partial-to-none "Nature's God" of natural theology, as has also been stated.

In fact, Lincoln mentioned in his New Haven speech that virtually everyone believed blacks were included in the Declaration prior to the Kansas-Nebraska Act of 1854 that repealed the Missouri Compromise. After that, the Democratic Party took the position that blacks were excluded from the Declaration by saying they were not men but brutes. Lincoln attacked this revisionist view of the Declaration when he said:

> I venture to defy the whole [Democratic] party to produce one man that ever uttered the belief that the Declaration did not apply to Negroes, before the repeal of the Missouri Compromise! Four or five years ago we all thought negroes were men, and that when "all men" were named, negroes were included. But *the whole Democratic party has deliberately taken negroes from the class of men and put them in the class of brutes.* Turn it as you will, it is simply the truth! Don't be too hasty in saying that the people cannot be brought to this new doctrine, but note that long stride. One more as long com-

pletes the journey, from where negroes are estimated as men to where they are estimated as mere brutes—as rightful property![71]

What Lincoln emphasized at New Haven was that Stephen Douglas and his Democrats were seeking to reinterpret the Declaration because they recognized the problem its universal moral idealism posed to the expansion of slavery in the territories, which they favored. They recognized that although slavery was institutionalized by the Constitution, it was opposed by the Declaration's "All Men were created equal" and "endowed" with the right to "Liberty" regardless of race. If, however, blacks could be defined as brutes, this would exclude them from the human "All Men" category mentioned in the Declaration, thereby removing that document as a moral impediment to slavery's expansion in the territories or anywhere in the United States for that matter.

In opposition to Douglas and the Democrats, Lincoln again and again rejected the idea that blacks were brutes and affirmed that they were included in the Declaration's "all Men are created equal" phrase.[72] By using this approach, he exercised the moral sense of his white audience, who were emotionally attached to the Declaration, as has been mentioned.

In his speech at Hartford on 5 March 1860, Lincoln demonstrated that he was aware of the deistic "Nature's God" natural theology of the Declaration by stating that natural theology's value of "equality" in the Declaration was against slavery:

> The "equality of man" principle which actuated our forefathers in the establishment of the government [the Declaration of Independence] is right; and that slavery, being directly opposed to this, is morally wrong. I think that if anything can be proved by *natural theology* [my italics], it is that slavery is morally wrong. God gave man a mouth to receive bread, hands to feed it, and his hand has a right to carry bread to his mouth without controversy.[73]

In a more elaborate version of the same natural theology argument against slavery, Lincoln used final cause logic. Jefferson, as has been stated, used such logic, which he got from Kames, when he said God intended humans to be sociable and, therefore, He created them with a moral sense of justice not to harm others without which they could not be sociable. In his speech at Cincinnati on 17 September 1859, Lincoln used a similar format, with a touch of humor, in order to prove slavery was against natural theology and God's will, design, or final cause:

> I hold that if there is any one thing that can be proved to be the will of God by external nature around us [natural theology], without reference to revelation [Bible], it is the proposition that whatever any one man earns with his hands and by the sweat of his brow, he shall enjoy in peace. I say that whereas God Almighty has given every man one mouth to be fed, and one pair of hands adapted to furnish food for that mouth, if anything can be proved to be the will of Heaven, it is proved by this fact, that that mouth is to be fed by those hands, without being interfered with by any other man who has also his mouth to feed and his hands to labor with. I hold if the Almighty had ever made a set of men that should do all the eating and none of the work, he would have made them with mouths only and no hands, and if he had ever made another class that he had intended should do all the work and none of the eating, he would he made them without mouths and with all hands. But inasmuch as he has not chosen to make man in that way, if anything is proved, it is that those hands and mouths are to be co-operative through life and not to be interfered with. That they are to go forth and improve their condition as I have been trying to illustrate, is the inherent right given to mankind directly by the Maker.[74]

These natural theology antislavery arguments were made in opposition to the theology of slavery mentioned in the same Cincinnati speech[75] that was based on revelation or scripture developed by Southern Protestant theologians in the 1820s to 1850s in response to Northern abolitionist preachers who had waved their Bibles while arguing that slavery was sinful. Even before this, however, other Christians used Christianity to justify black slavery. Since 1441, the year Antonio Gonsalves "returned to Portugal with ten Africans as gifts for his sovereign," European Catholics said the enslavement of blacks was moral and just, since it gave "them opportunity to cast off their heathenism and embrace the Christian religion."[76] This disposition continued into the eighteenth century.[77] Southern Protestant theologians of the nineteenth century, however, formulated a more elaborate Christian justification of slavery based on scripture.[78] They argued that the word "servant" found throughout the Bible meant "slave." Although this is obviously a self-serving proslavery definition, it is not far from the original biblical meaning of "servant" in the languages of the original biblical texts, according to many modern translators.[79] What this meaning of "servant" did, however, was open the door for interpreting biblical passages like Jesus' parable of the servant in Luke 17:7–10 as favorable to slavery. This is seen when the word "slave" is substituted for the word "servant":

> But which of you, having a servant [slave] plowing or feeding cattle, will say unto him by and by, when he is come from the field, Go and sit down to meat? And will not rather say unto him, Make ready wherewith I may sup, and gird thyself, and serve me, till I have eaten and drunken; and afterward thou shalt eat and drink? Doth he thank that servant [slave] because he did the things that were commanded him? I trow not. So likewise ye, when ye shall have done all those things which are commanded you, say, We are unprofitable servants [slaves]: we have done that which was our duty to do.

Jesus did not specifically condemn or approve of slavery in this statement. Yet the Southern theologians claimed his routine reference to it without condemnation was implicit approval.

Paul's statement from Ephesians 6:58 was also used to justify slavery by the theologians of slavery. Indeed, it provides better justification because it actually instructs slaves to obey their masters:

> Servants [slaves] be obedient to them that are *your* masters, according to the flesh with fear and trembling, in singleness of your heart, as unto Christ; Not with eye-service, as men-pleasers; but as servants [slaves] of Christ, doing the will of Christ from the

heart; with good will doing service as to thy Lord, whether *be he* bond [slave] or free.

Among the Old Testament passages utilized by the theologians of slavery are Leviticus 25:44–46, where Moses set forth God's rules to the Levites:

> Both thy bondsman [slave], and thy bondmaids [slaves], which thou shalt have, *shall be* of the heathen that are round about you; of them shall ye buy bondsmen and bondsmaids [slaves]. Moreover of the children of the strangers that do sojourn among you, of them shall ye buy, and of their families that *are* with you, which they begat in your land: and they shall be your possession. And ye shall take them as an inheritance for your children after you, to inherit *them for* a possession; they shall be your bondmen [slaves] for ever; but over your brethren the children of Israel ye shall not rule one over another with rigour.

Because these verses state that it is proper to enslave "heathen," they were used as justification for slavery by American slave owners who maintained that blacks in America were heathen.

In addition, the Old Testament, according to the Southern theologians of slavery, provided three additional scriptural supports of slavery. First, Abraham, Isaac, Jacob, and Job had slaves or people some translators of the Bible interpreted as slaves.[80] "Hagar," for example, was an African slave bought by Abraham in Egypt and who bore him a child.[81] Second, bondage or slavery was a part of Mosaic Law. Chapter 25 of Leviticus spoke of "buying, selling, holding and bequesting slaves as property."[82] Third, slavery was practiced by the Jewish people, as is stated in Judges 1:28, 30, and 35.[83] According to the theologians of slavery, these scriptural provisions proved that God approved of slavery.

When commenting on the combined effect of proslavery passages from both the Old and New Testaments, Reverend Richard Fuller, a Baptist preacher from South Carolina, stated in 1845: "What God sanctioned in the Old Testament, and permitted in the New, cannot be sin."[84] And, when James Henry Thornwell—editor of the *Southern Presbyterian Review*, president of South Carolina College, and professor of theology at Columbia Theological Seminary—asked the rhetorical question, "Has the Bible, anywhere, either directly or indirectly, condemned the relation of master and servant as incompatible with the will of God?" he answered his own question in a way that sounded like Reverend Fuller:

> Where the Scriptures are silent [the Church] must be silent too. What the Scriptures have not made essential to a Christian profession, she [the Church] does not undertake to make so. *What the Scriptures have sanctioned, she [the Church] does not condemn* [my italics].[85]

That Lincoln was aware of how the partial God of the Bible, who treated people differently due to His partiality, could be used to support slavery by the theologians of slavery because that God maintained some people shall be slaves and others free—as is stated in the previously quoted Leviticus 25:44–46—is seen in his ridicule of the theology of slavery:

> The sum of pro-slavery theology seems to be this: "Slavery is not universally *right*, nor yet universally *wrong*; it is better for some people to be slaves: and, in such cases, it is the will of God that they be such." . . . Slavery is good for some people!!! As a *good* thing, slavery is strikingly peculiar in this, that it is the only good thing which no man ever seeks the good of *for himself*.[86]

## LINCOLN'S REALISTIC ARGUMENTS AGAINST SLAVERY

In his New Haven speech, as well as in others, Lincoln undertook to educate his audience on the objects of their realistic interests, in addition to educating them on the objects of their moral sense. This, as has been mentioned, was consistent with the ideas of Kames and Brown. His assumption, like that of both men, was that most humans have not rationally calculated what these objects are. Or even worse, when it comes to realistic interests, most humans have not rationally calculated what actions work for or against their interests. Or if they have made such calculations, they have not been able to rationally discipline themselves to act accordingly.

The principal thrust of Lincoln's educational effort on objects of selfish interests in connection with slavery was that black slave labor, or any slave labor for that matter, damaged the interests of white labor that worked for wages. "We think," he said when talking of black slave labor, "that species of labor an injury to free white men."[87] He elaborated by stating that black slave labor will not only "underwork you," but will also "degrade you."[88] In other words, slavery would deprive free labor of employment leading to degrading poverty. Lincoln's solution to this degradation was a free labor for wages system open to everyone, whites and blacks, as he stated when praising the labor for wages system of the North:

> I am glad to see that a system of labor prevails in New England under which laborers CAN strike when they want to [Cheers,] where they are not obliged to work under all circumstances, and are not tied down and obliged to labor whether you pay them or not! [Cheers]. I like the system which lets a man quit when he wants to and wish it might prevail everywhere. [Tremendous applause.][89]

This statement was critical of slavery because it praised the fact that in New England "a man" can "quit when he wants to" and that men are not "obliged to labor whether you pay them or not!" It implicitly stated that Lincoln was against slavery because he expressed the wish that the free labor system "might prevail everywhere." The great applause and cheers for these comments indicate that Lincoln's educational efforts to strengthen rational calculations of the damage done by black slavery to the selfish interests of free whites were succeeding despite the fact that many whites in the North were against blacks gaining freedom in the North as well as in the South. Indeed, Lincoln was so convincing that few listening to him at this point in his New Haven speech were indifferent to slavery, and indifference was an extensive problem in the North, according to Lincoln. Having largely eliminated indifference in his New Haven audience, Lincoln proceeded to argue against slavery by advocating an individualistic, self-interested, self-improvement-oriented, capitalistic system linked to property accumulation with free labor. To put it another way, Lincoln argued that slavery was opposed to capitalism, which was based on free labor:

> One of the reasons I am opposed to Slavery is just here. What is the true condition of the laborer? I take it that it is best for *all* [my italics] to leave each man free to acquire property as fast as he can. Some will get wealthy. I don't believe in a law to prevent a man from getting rich; it would do more harm than good. So while we do not propose any war upon capital, we do wish to allow the humblest man an equal chance to get rich with everybody else [Applause]. When one starts poor, as most do in the race of life, free society is such that he knows he can better his condition; he knows that there is no fixed condition of labor, for his whole life. I am not ashamed to confess that twenty-five years ago I was a hired laborer, mauling rails, at work on a flat boat—just what might happen to a poor man's son! [Applause]. I want every man to have the chance—and I believe a black man is entitled to it—in which he *can* better his condition—when he may look forward and hope to be a hired laborer this year and the next, work for himself afterward, and finally hire men to work for him! That is the true system.[90]

In what may be interpreted as a contradiction to this praise of labor-based, selfish, self-interested capitalism, Lincoln made a statement in his short speech to the German immigrants at Cincinnati, Ohio, in February of 1861, which sounded like Jeremy Bentham's Utilitarian statement "the greatest happiness of the greatest number":

> I hold that while man exists, it is his duty to improve not only his own condition, but to assist in ameliorating mankind; without entering upon the details of the question, I will simply say that I am for those means which will give *the greatest good to the greatest number* [my italics].[91]

Bentham's Utilitarianism, however, even though it gave lip service to noninterference in economic matters, implies a method of leveling wealth among the people since this, according to some Utilitarians, provides the greatest good for the greatest number. Yet Lincoln did not specify any wealth-leveling programs in his speech to the Germans. In fact, that speech specified just two actions for "ameliorating mankind." The first was "cutting up wild [government-owned] lands into parcels, so that every poor man may have a home" under the "Homestead Law." The second was his assurance that government would refrain from "heaping upon" the people "greater burdens."[92] It seems clear, therefore, that even in his speech to the Germans, utilitarian devices to increase the happiness of all mankind, such as leveling wealth, were not in Lincoln's thinking as his New Haven comments "I don't believe in a law to prevent a man from getting rich; it would do more harm than good" and "We do not propose any war on capital" clearly state. He made similar comments in other speeches. For example, in his annual message to Congress of 31 December 1861, in which he reiterated his New Haven advocacy of a capitalistic possessive individualism system linked to the accumulation of wealth with free labor, he said: "This is the just, and generous, and prosperous system, which opens the way to *all*—gives hope to *all*, and consequently energy, and progress, and improvement of condition to *all* [my italics]."[93] The fact that Lincoln said the free labor capitalistic system of acquiring wealth was best for *all* in both his New Haven speech and 1861 message to Congress made after his speech to the Germans demonstrates his commitment to capitalism. It was, therefore, capitalism that would bring "the greatest good to the greatest number," according to Lincoln. Indeed, it was by extending to "All Men" the opportunity to accumulate and enjoy the fruits of their own labor and then, using their own enterprise, start their own businesses and employ other men that Lincoln sought to "assist in ameliorating mankind."[94]

At New Haven, however, Lincoln did not argue that slavery should be completely abolished immediately. That would have been political suicide because a large portion of public opinion, even in the North, was opposed to immediate emancipation. Yet he in effect stated in that speech that at some point abolition should be complete when he said: "I believe a black man is entitled to it [the opportunity to rise economically with his own free labor]." Significantly, this remark was greeted with silence, not applause, indicating Lincoln was pushing his audience beyond what their bias would accept.

The main thrust of his New Haven realistic arguments against slavery, however, and those in other speeches as well, was that the expansion of slavery into US territories not designated as states was not in the rationally calculated interests of whites. To clarify his point, he used an analogy in which slavery was compared to a "venomous snake," whites to "children," and "bed" to the area in which the children lived:

> If I saw a venomous snake crawling in the road, any man would say I might seize the nearest stick and kill it; but if I found that snake in bed with my children [whites], that would be another question [Laughter]. I might hurt the children more than the snake, and it might bite them [Applause]. Much more, if I found it in bed with my neighbor's children [the slave states], and I bound myself by a solemn compact [the Constitution] not to meddle with his children under any circumstances, it would become men to let that particular mode of getting rid of the gentleman alone [Great laughter]. But if there was a bed newly made up [the territories], to which the children were to be taken and it was proposed to take a batch of young snakes and put them there with them, I take it no man would say there was any question how I ought to decide! [Prolonged applause and cheers.][95]

This statement takes into account the fear of many whites, in the North as well as in the South, that if slavery were abolished blacks might riot and kill or injure whites. As Lincoln put it, killing the snake or ending slavery "might hurt the children [whites] more than the snake, and it might bite them"—a comment that received applause. It is reminiscent of Jefferson's comment on slavery, which Lincoln quoted when he eulogized Henry Clay in 1852: "We have a wolf [slavery] by the ears and we can neither hold him, nor safely let him go. Justice is in one scale, and self-preservation in the other."[96] Indeed, Lincoln's snake analogy, and Jefferson's comment as well, contains the Kamesean idea that the moral-sense duty of justice not to harm others is suspended when self-preservation is at stake, an idea held by many early modern political thinkers, including Thomas Hobbes and John Locke. Lincoln made this clear by stating the "snake" or slavery should not be killed (abolished) where it existed in slave states even though this harmed black slaves by depriving them of freedom and was, therefore, unjust. Lincoln's snake analogy thereby showed concern for the self-preservation of whites and an implicit concern for that of blacks as well. If blacks were freed and violence occurred on the part of either whites or blacks, that would very likely have precipitated more violence that would have threatened the continued existence of either blacks or whites in the area where violence erupted. These concerns were no doubt reasons why Lincoln clung to the notion held by many abolitionists of the eighteenth and nineteenth centuries, including Thomas Jefferson and Henry Clay, that blacks, as part of any abolition plan, should be expatriated or colonized in another country or territory. In fact, Jefferson's influence on Lincoln as well as that of Clay in this area can be seen in Lincoln's quote in his eulogy on Clay from Jefferson's prophetic 1820 letter criticizing the Missouri Compromise, which made slavery legal south of 36 degrees 30 minutes north latitude and illegal north of that line:

> A geographical line, co-inciding with a marked principle, moral and political, once conceived, and held up to the angry passions of men, will never be obliterated; and every irritation will mark it deeper and deeper. I can say, with conscious truth, that there is not a man on earth who would sacrifice more than I would to relieve us from this heavy reproach [slavery], in any *practicable* way. The cession of that kind of property, for so it is misnamed, is a bagatelle which would not cost me a second thought, if, in that way, a general emancipation, and *expatriation* could be effected; and, gradually, and with due sacrifices I think it might be. But as it is, *we have the wolf by the ears and we can neither hold him, nor safely let him go. Justice is in one scale, and self-preservation in the other* [my italics].[97]

Change of circumstances, like the use of blacks as Union soldiers in the Civil War in exchange for their freedom as well as pressure from radical abolitionists to free the slaves without deportation or colonization, no doubt caused Lincoln to see that his deportation or colonization plans in conjunction with abolition were not moral or feasible.

Lincoln's snake analogy in his New Haven speech also took into account that the Constitution protected the "snake" or slavery in states where it existed and his commitment not to disrupt that protection if he were elected president. "I bound myself," he said, "to a solemn compact [the Constitution] not to meddle with his [the slave states'] children under any circumstances." Nonetheless, the "venomous snake" or slavery posed a major threat to the interests of free white labor wherever it existed, according to Lincoln. This was especially true in the territories, which Lincoln emphasized with the snake in his analogy in a way that could not help but appeal to the interests of his white audience:

> I desire that if you get too thick [in population] here, and find it hard to better your condition on this soil, you may have a chance to strike and go some where else, where you may not be degraded, nor have your family corrupted by forced rivalry with negro slaves. I want you to have a clean bed, and no snakes in it! [Cheers.] Then you can better your condition. . . .[98]

The cheers tell us Lincoln's realistic rational arguments against the expansion of slavery into the territories received an extremely favorable response.


## EMANCIPATION PROCLAMATION

Whether or not Lincoln knew of Kames's ideas on the uniform and universal common standard of morality born of the "internal" constitution of the human species that gave rise to laws from which "the most universal and the most lasting from among the polite [or civilized] nations" were selected as the measure of that standard, he was aware of a similar standard. On the international scene, he was subjected to moral pressure from "polite [or civilized] nations," especially England, to bring American law in accord with their law and the moral sense of the English people. Since 1809, Great Britain had laws against slavery supported by British public opinion that slavery was morally wrong, even though England had previously been extensively involved in slave trade with the colonies that established slavery in America. Therefore, as long as the Union had not declared opposition to slavery, which it had not during the Civil War until the Emancipation Proclamation of 1 January 1863, public opinion in England had no moral or idealistic reason to support the Union. In fact, realists in England had two selfish reasons to support the Confederacy. First, a Union victory could have disrupted the flow of Southern grown cotton produced by slave labor, which was a cornerstone of the British textile industry. Second, it was in England's interest to split the United States in half. Once divided, each part could be manipulated against the other by England or other European powers, rendering both parts impotent. Consistent with this second reason, Austria actually sided with the Confederacy and Napoleon III of France started a European coalition for the purpose of intervening against the Union in the first part of the Civil War. In this context, a foreign affairs reason for the Emancipation Proclamation was to gain the pro-Union support of English public opinion, which was opposed to slavery. This would make it difficult for realists in the British government to support the Confederacy. If they did, they would find themselves in the awkward position of advocating the birth of a slave nation in opposition to British public opinion. The Emancipation Proclamation, when it was finally declared, did in fact send a surge of public opinion in favor of the Union in England and thereby put a check on English realists. These circumstances made Lincoln very much aware of a Kamesean-like common standard of morality found in the laws of "polite [or civilized] nations" of the world that were founded upon and supported by the moral sense of the people of those nations. [99]

Despite efforts to obtain a common standard of morality, there remained a subjective element in moral-sense determinations of morality, which resulted in different and conflicting views of right and wrong. Lincoln was acutely aware of this as he stated in his New Haven speech and First Inaugural, as has been mentioned. He was also acutely aware that inner feelings of right and wrong aided by reason had a habit of corresponding with and morally justifying what was in a particular individual's or group of individuals' selfish interests even when pursuing those interests gave rise to harmful and unjust acts. To put it another way, interests could give rise to delusional or wrong views of what was right and wrong. Although Lincoln denied original sin and the idea that every person inherited a depraved or semidepraved nature, he recognized early in life that interests interfered with natural inclinations to do right. As he stated in a speech to the Illinois legislature in 1837: "I believe it is universally understood and acknowledged that all men will act correct unless they have a motive to do otherwise."[100] Selfish interests supplied that motive. Indeed, to Lincoln, selfish interests were a principal cause of human subjectivity and error when it came to determining what was moral.

This subjective element in moral determinations was what caused Lincoln on one occasion to sound like John Locke, who late in life became an advocate of scripture as the principal source of morality. After his inability to formulate the moral laws of nature with demonstrative reason became clear, Locke, in *The Reasonableness of Christianity*, said that morals were "best . . . left to the Precepts and Principles of the Gospel."[101] Lincoln's similar comment was made to the loyal colored people of Baltimore and Washington, DC, in September of 1864 after they presented him with a Bible. As he put it when he thanked them: "All the good the Saviour gave to the world was communicated through this book. *But for it we could not know right from wrong* [my italics]."[102] Praise indeed for Jesus' moral teachings and injunctions in the Gospels! Yet Lincoln knew that even Jesus' morality in the Bible could be rendered obscure, confusing, and even conflicting. It could be twisted to serve selfish interests as the Southern theologians of slavery had done. Moreover, Lincoln, as a lawyer, was thoroughly familiar with how attorneys could interpret the law so it would support their clients' interests. He was, as a result, aware that reason could be used to justify almost anything. Feelings of morality, however, were not as easily altered. To Lincoln, therefore, his own inner feeling or moral sense was ultimately the most reliable factor in determining the immorality of slavery. This is no doubt why he went by his own moral-sense feelings on slavery. As he wrote in his 1864 letter to Albert Hodges: "I am naturally antislavery. If slavery is not wrong, nothing is wrong. I cannot remember when I did not so think, and *feel* [my italics]."[103]

## MORAL SENSE AND DEMOCRACY

From a political perspective, it was the moral sense in humans that made them self-governing, according to Jefferson. He maintained that this sense was what enabled the individuals of the populace to provide moral direction not only to their own lives but also to the state. On the other hand, he maintained that those who fervently believed in the original sin concept of humankind—which held that everyone was infected with depravity, semidepravity, or moral taint—also believed humans and the state were dependent on an extrahuman or a divine source of morality such as a Christian king anointed or deputized by God via the church, the church itself, or scripture for which the church was custodian. This line of thought was what caused medieval politics to be dominated by monarchs and/or the church, as has been stated. Jefferson mentioned how these different and conflicting views of human moral capacity resulted in different and conflicting approaches to politics when he said of the Continental Congress that approved of the Declaration of Independence: "*We believed . . . that man was a rational animal, endowed by nature with rights, and with an innate sense of justice*; and that he could be restrained from wrong and protected in right, by moderate powers, confided to persons of his own choice, and held to their duties by dependence on his own will [my italics]." Of Europeans imbued with the original sin concept of humanity, he said: "The doctrines of Europe were, that men in numerous associations cannot be restrained within the limits of order and justice, but by forces physical and moral, wielded over them by authorities independent of their will. Hence their organization of Kings, hereditary nobles, and priests."[104]

Lincoln succinctly expressed similar human self-government capacity implications in politics, as Jefferson did in the first of these aforementioned comments, to the Minister Resident from Sweden and Norway in November 1861 when he said: "This country, Sir, maintains, and means to maintain, the rights of human nature and the capacity of man for self-government."[105] Two years later the same thought was immortalized in the last phrase of the Gettysburg Address where he resolved that the "government of the people, by the people, for the people, shall not perish from the earth."[106] Humans should govern themselves, not God, His church, His scripture, His clergy, or His king. This was Lincoln's commitment as it was Jefferson's. And he, like Jefferson, held a moral-sense view of human nature that deemed humans were morally competent to govern themselves rather than the morally tainted or morally incompetent view of human nature due to original sin that was dependent upon extrahuman moral guidance in government.

Lincoln's moral-sense view of human nature as distinct from the original sin view is illustrated in his First Inaugural Address where he changed William Seward's suggested alterations from:

> The mystic chords which, proceeding from so many battle-fields and so many patriot graves, pass through all the hearts and all the heaths in this broad continent of ours, will yet again harmonize in their ancient music when *breathed upon by the guardian angels of the nation* [my italics].

Lincoln's alterations to Seward's suggested alterations, which became the final version of the First Inaugural, were:

> The mystic chords of memory, stretching from every battlefield, and patriot grave, to every living heart and hearthstone, all over this broad land, will yet swell the chorus of the Union, *when again touched, as surely they will be, by the better angels of our nature* [my italics].[107]

While Seward's words "breathed upon by the guardian angels of the nation" amounted to a plea for extrahuman or angelic help, Lincoln's reliance was on "the better angels of our nature." Lincoln thereby affirmed that the very nature of human reality had an angelic or moral-sense side that would eventually prevail and give a uniform view on the immorality of slavery that would resolve the differences between the North and the South on this issue.

*Chapter 4*

# THE DECLARATION'S
# ADVOCATE

*I*n 1854, Abraham Lincoln emerged as a major figure in the ide-ological war raging in nineteenth-century America between aboli-tionists and those who favored slavery—a conflict that finally erupted into civil war. That was the year of the Kansas-Nebraska Act, which made Lincoln aware that slavery's pro-expansionist move-ment was making rapid progress toward legalizing slavery in the ter-ritories. Lincoln's biggest fear was that the momentum of this move-ment could lead to legalized slavery throughout the nation—a fear that grew after the Dred Scott decision in 1857. That decision put Lincoln on a collision course with the Supreme Court and Chief Jus-tice Roger Taney, who Lincoln perceived as pro-expansionist. Lin-coln believed that the expansionists' attacks on the Declaration of Independence made a huge contribution to their gains. When describing these attacks, he said they "denied, and evaded, with no small show of success" that the right of *"liberty"* was given by the Declaration's God to "all men."[1] Black men, according to the expan-sionists, were excluded. To Lincoln, this was not only a gross distor-tion of the Declaration's universal moral idealism but also a cor-rupting influence on the morality of the American people, which he believed had deteriorated substantially from what it was in 1776. As he stated in his 1855 letter to George Robinson:

On the question of liberty, as a principle, we are not what we have
been. When we were the political slaves of King George [III], and
we wanted to be free, we called the maxim that "all men are created equal" a self evident truth; but now when we have grown fat,
and have lost all dread of being slaves ourselves, we have become
so greedy to be masters that we call the same maxim "a self-evident
lie[.]" . . . The Autocrat of all the Russians will resign his crown,
and proclaim his subjects free republicans sooner than will our
American masters voluntarily give up their slaves.[2]

Lincoln then added with bitter sarcasm: "The fourth of July has not
quite dwindled away; it is still a great day—for burning fire-
crackers!!!" To Lincoln the stakes were high in the ideological war
over the meaning of the Declaration of Independence. If blacks'
God-given right of "liberty" could be challenged, so could that of
any individual or group, which could lead to the "extinction of liberty" for everyone.[3]

It was Senator John Pettit of Indiana who made the "self-evident
lie" comment in the Senate while arguing for the Kansas-Nebraska
Act passed in 1854, as Lincoln stated in his speech on that act delivered the same year. At that time, Lincoln maintained that the disposition of the American people had changed so much from the Revolutionary period that if Pettit had stated his "self-evident lie"
opinion on the steps of Independence Hall during the Revolutionary War, "the very door keeper would have throttled the man,
and thrust him into the street."[4] Lincoln further maintained that if
Pettit's view "had been said to the men who captured Andre [the
British spy involved in Benedict Arnold's treason], the man who said
it, would probably have been hung sooner than Andre was."[5] The
Senate's apathetic reaction to Pettit's "self-evident lie" comment was
a study in contrast that demonstrated the moral decline of the
people since the Revolution. As Lincoln described that reaction: "Of
the forty odd Nebraska Senators who sat present and heard Pettit,
no one rebuked him."[6] Yet Lincoln believed he needed to be
rebuked. More fundamentally, the idealism of the Declaration of
Independence needed to be defended against men like Pettit, and
Lincoln undertook that task.

Apathy toward the Declaration, however, was not the only sign of moral deterioration in America. Lincoln maintained throughout the 1850s that the "fathers of this Government" had placed slavery "in the course of ultimate extinction." Indeed, he believed "the public mind" rested in that "belief" despite the fact that people were beginning to change their minds.[7] Lincoln's opinion was based on three factors, which he summed up in the last of his debates with Stephen Douglas—debates, which Damon Wells stated, "covered very little new ground."[8] First, the Constitution provided that "the African slave trade—should be cut off at the end of twenty years."[9] Second, the Northwest Ordinance of 1787 provided "that in all the new territory [apart from the States] that we owned at that time[,] slavery should be forever inhibited."[10] Lincoln argued that to "stop" the "spread" of slavery "in one direction and cut off its source in another" clearly demonstrated that the "fathers" had intended to place slavery "in the course of ultimate extinction."[11] Third, "the institution of slavery is only mentioned in the Constitution of the United States two or three times." Yet nowhere does that document use "the word 'slavery' or 'negro race.'"[12] Rather, as Lincoln stated, "covert language is used."[13] He cited as an example the constitutional provision that protected the African slave trade until 1808: "The migration or importation of such persons as any of the States now existing shall think proper to admit, shall not be prohibited by the Congress prior the year one thousand eight hundred and eight."[14] No mention of slavery or blacks here. He also cited as another example the infamous clause that allowed three-fifths of each black slave to be included in computing congressional representation, even though blacks could not vote: "Representatives and direct taxes shall be apportioned among the several States which may be included within this Union, according to their respective numbers, which shall be determined by adding to the whole number of free persons, including those bound to service for a term of years, and excluding Indians not taxed—three fifths of all other persons."[15] Black slaves of course were included in the phrase "three fifths of all other persons" but there was no specific mention of slavery or blacks. Finally, Lincoln cited the obligation to return fugitive slaves provision: "No person held to service or labor in one State under the laws thereof escaping into another, shall in consequence of any law or regulation therein, be discharged from such service or labor, but shall be delivered up, on the claim of the party to whom such service or labor may be due."[16] Once again, no mention of slavery or blacks. Lincoln argued that the reason for only "covert" references to blacks and slavery was that those who drafted the Constitution—which they "hoped . . . will endure forever"—wanted "nothing on the face of the great charter of liberty suggesting that such a thing as negro slavery had ever existed" when it was "read by intelligent and patriotic men, after the institution of slavery had passed from among us."[17] Here Lincoln was not only stating that the Constitution makers "intended" that slavery would "come to an end" but also in effect that they were ashamed of that evil institution.[18] That shame, however, was not shared by many Americans in Lincoln's time, according to Lincoln, who maintained that acceptance of slavery had increased among the populace since the Revolution, a sure sign of moral decline.

Despite the fact that he always "hated slavery," Lincoln was "quiet" about it "until," as he stated, "this new era of the introduction of the Nebraska Bill [Kansas-Nebraska Act of 1854] began."[19] That bill repealed the Missouri Compromise of 1820 that confined slavery in the Louisiana Territory to land south of 36 degrees 30 minutes north latitude. It was Illinois Senator Stephen Douglas who introduced the Kansas-Nebraska Bill, which made it law that the white people of the Kansas and Nebraska Territories—part of the Louisiana Purchase and North of the Missouri Compromise line—could decide for themselves whether or not they would have slavery. Douglas called this "Popular Sovereignty." When the bill passed it shocked Lincoln and "convinced" him that "either I had been resting in a delusion [that slavery was on a course of ultimate extinction] or that the institution was being placed on a new basis—a basis for making it perpetual, national and universal."[20] He quickly concluded that he was deluded and that slavery was in fact being placed on a new basis because of organized efforts to expand and perpetuate it nationwide—another sign of moral deterioration since Revolutionary times.

## RESISTING THE KANSAS-NEBRASKA ACT

Having served as a representative in the Illinois legislature and two years in the same capacity in the US Congress, Lincoln had substantial political influence in Illinois even though from 1849 to 1854 he had devoted "almost his entire time to his legal profession."[21] However, when the Kansas-Nebraska Act passed in 1854, which he vehemently opposed, he used his political influence to resist the act and its architect, Illinois senator and judge Stephen Douglas, by criticizing both in a speech delivered 16 October of that year at Peoria, Illinois. There he invoked the moral idealism of the Declaration of Independence as he did in most of his major political speeches from then on. He thereby sought to educate and arouse the moral sense of his audiences on slavery, as was stated in chapter 3, and simultaneously prevent the Declaration's moral principles from being "denied and evaded," as he said they were by Douglas and his faction. To Lincoln, the Kansas-Nebraska Act with its potential to increase slavery was an example of the effects of such denial and evasion.

In his 1854 speech criticizing that act, a principal target of his criticism was "Popular Sovereignty," which Douglas described as the "sacred right of self government."[22] Lincoln argued that Douglas's "Popular Sovereignty" was "a total violation" of the "sacred right of self-government" principle. Then, affirming that "the doctrine of self-government is right—absolutely and eternally right," Lincoln simultaneously stated that genuine "Popular Sovereignty" was in the "consent of the governed" political theory of the Declaration of Independence. Unlike Douglas's version, where the majority of white men in the territories would decide whether or not there would be black slavery without the consent of those enslaved, Lincoln explained and quoted the Declaration's version, which of course had not been put into practice as respects black slaves:

No man is good enough to govern another man, *without that other's consent.* I say this is the leading principle—the sheet anchor of American republicanism. Our Declaration of Independence says:

"We hold these truths to be self evident: that all men are created equal; that they are endowed by their Creator with certain inalienable rights; that among these are life, liberty and the pursuit of happiness. That to secure these rights, governments are instituted among men, DERIVING THEIR JUST POWERS FROM THE CONSENT OF THE GOVERNED."

I have quoted so much at this time merely to show that according to *our ancient faith* [my italics], the just powers of governments are derived from the consent of the governed. Now the relation of masters and slaves is, PRO TANTO, a total violation of this principle. The master not only governs the slave without his consent; but he governs him by a set of rules altogether different from those which he prescribes for himself. *Allow ALL the governed an equal voice in the government, and that, and that only is self government* [my italics].[23]

Here Lincoln in effect admitted that Douglas's accusation against him and his faction for believing "the white people of Nebraska are good enough to govern themselves, *but they are not good enough to govern a few miserable negroes*" was true.[24] Yet, he also stated that the idea that no man was good enough to govern others without their consent was a "principle" of the Declaration of Independence used at the time of the Revolutionary War when many Englishmen believed the colonists were not good enough to govern themselves and should therefore be governed by Great Britain. The philosopher David Hume, when commenting on the thirteen Atlantic colonies and Benjamin Franklin, stated as much: "The colonies are no longer in their infancy. But yet I say to you, they are still in their nonage, and Dr. Franklin wishes to emancipate them too soon from their mother country."[25] However, what Lincoln was in effect arguing here was that there should be some consistency in American behavior. He was stating that whites governing blacks without their consent in the territories, or anywhere for that matter, were treating blacks the same way—indeed in a much worse way—than the British treated their colonial citizens in America, which caused the Revolutionary War.

Consistent with the "consent of the governed" theme of the Declaration, Lincoln argued in his 1854 speech that as the Declaration defined King George III as a "despot" for governing the colonists without their consent, white slave owners were also despots for governing black slaves without their consent:

> When the white man governs himself that is self-government; but when he governs himself, and also governs *another* man, that is *more* than self-government—that is despotism. If the negro is a *man*, why then *my ancient faith* [my italics] teaches me that "all men are created equal"; and that there can be no moral right in connection with one man's making a slave of another.[26]

According to Lincoln in this 1854 analysis and quotation of the political theory part of the Declaration of Independence, the Declaration itself morally condemned slavery. As he put it, the Declaration "teaches me that 'all men are created equal,' and that there can be no moral right in connection with one man's making a slave of another."

Twice in the aforementioned quotations from his 1854 speech, Lincoln described the Declaration as "ancient faith." First, he said it was "our ancient faith" or the faith of the American people. Then, a few sentences later, he called it "my ancient faith." Either way, these references to the 1776 Declaration make no sense if Lincoln was referring to the written document itself because in 1854, when he made these statements, the Declaration was only seventy-eight years old. Yet these statements did make sense if Lincoln was referring to the Declaration's deistic "Nature's God" and natural theology of that God that created "all men" equal. Both "Nature's God" and natural theology were truly "ancient" because both were revealed at the time of creation by the creation itself and knowledge of them was born of observing or "reading" God's works or creation. To put it another way, the scripture of that "ancient faith" was not the Bible or revealed word of God that came long after creation. It was the creation itself in the form of the universe, or, as Thomas Paine described it, the "scripture called the *Creation*," or, as Theodore Parker described it, "the Universe is the only scripture of God," as was stated in chapter 2. As was also stated in that chapter, Lincoln read Paine's deistic *Age of Reason* that contained the words "scripture called the *Creation*" as well as Theodore Parker's works that contained "the Universe is the only scripture of God."[27]

Some might argue that Lincoln was referring to Old or New Testament faith with his "ancient faith" description of the Declaration of Independence. However, both of these scriptures and their resultant religions had proslavery statements used by proslavery theologians who morally justified slavery, which Lincoln knew, as was stated in the last chapter. Therefore, in pointing out that the "ancient faith" of the Declaration was morally opposed to slavery in his 1854 speech, Lincoln could not have been referring to either the Old or New Testament faiths. Rather, he was referring to the deism of the Declaration of Independence described in chapter 1 with its universal morality that extended equally to individuals of both sexes, all races as well as those of all religious (theistic), irreligious (agnostic), or nonreligious (atheistic) beliefs.

Significantly, Lincoln never morally condemned the South or Southerners for being predominantly proslavery.[28] Nor did he praise the morality of the North or Northerners because most antislavery advocates were found in the North. He maintained that both North and South had small numbers of just and freedom-loving individuals and similar numbers of slavery-loving despots in his 1854 speech on the Kansas-Nebraska Act: "We know that some southern men do free their slaves, go north, and become tip-top abolitionists; while some northern ones go south, and become most cruel slavemasters."[29] Apart from these extremes, Lincoln believed it was different circumstances that gave the majority of Southerners and Northerners different and conflicting dispositions toward slavery. That evil institution was in the vital interests of the South because its economy, land, and agricultural system were based on slavery.[30] And, since interests dominated most humans, according to Lincoln, it was natural that most Southerners would defend slavery, as has been stated. Northerners, on the other hand, could afford to speak in lofty, virtuous, moral terms about the abolition of slavery because abolition was not opposed to their interests. Indeed, it favored their interests—as Lincoln would point out in 1860 as was mentioned in chapter 3—since slavery worked against the Northern capitalistic free labor system even though most Northerners did not perceive slavery as a threat to their interests in the mid-1850s.

Lincoln also maintained in his 1854 speech that the South was no more responsible for slavery than the North since Northern ship owners had participated in transporting slaves to America and thereby profited handsomely. Then, affirming his belief that Northerners would not react any differently to slavery than Southerners if placed in similar circumstances and acknowledging that abolition was a difficult and complex issue, he said:

> When the southern people tell us they are no more responsible for the origin of slavery, than we; I acknowledge the fact. When it is said that the institution exists; and that it is very difficult to get rid of it, in any satisfactory way, I can understand and appreciate the saying. I surely will not blame them for not doing what I should not know how to do myself. If all earthly power were given me, I should not know what to do, as to the existing institution. My first impulse would be to free all the slaves, and send them to Liberia,—to their own native land. But a moment's reflection would convince me, that whatever of high hope, (as I think there is) there may be in this, in the long run, its sudden execution is impossible. If they were all landed there in a day, they would all perish in the next ten days; and there are not surplus shipping and surplus money enough in the world to carry them there in many times ten days. What then? Free them all, and keep them among us as underlings? Is it quite certain that this betters their condition? I think I would not hold one in slavery, at any rate; yet the point is not clear enough for me to denounce people upon. What next? *Free them, and make them politically and socially our equals? My own feelings will not admit of this; and if mine would, we well know that those of the great mass of people will not. Whether this feeling accords with justice and sound judgment, is not the sole question. . . . A universal feeling, whether well or ill-founded, can not safely be disregarded. We can not, then, make them equals.* It does seem to me that systems of gradual emancipation might be adopted; but for their tardiness in this, I will not undertake to judge our brethren of the south [my italics].[31]

Lincoln spoke from the perspective of a complete abolitionist in this statement, one who favored expatriation along with emancipation. Yet he tempered his remarks with concern for the safety of blacks, the difficulties in any immediate mass expatriation plan, plus a candid evaluation of his own feelings and those of the white masses, which were against giving freed slaves political and social equality if they remained in the United States. Moreover, with his comment that "a universal feeling whether well or ill-founded can not be safely disregarded," he demonstrated his awareness, as did Jefferson, that in a democratic republic, the feelings of the majority limited any course of action that was contrary to those feelings—even a just course of action like emancipation.

With his ideas on withholding political equality from blacks, which entails the vote, even if blacks were emancipated, Lincoln was at odds with his previously mentioned arguments taken from the Declaration of Independence: "Allow ALL the governed an equal voice in the government . . . , that only is self government," plus those who govern others without their "consent" are despots. In other words, political equality or "an equal voice in the government" is based on "consent of the governed" according to the Declaration, and the ballot is what provides that political equality or "equal voice." Yet Lincoln was against black suffrage as he stated in his fourth debate with Douglas in 1858 where he reiterated his views against black social and political equality stated in his speech on the Kansas-Nebraska Act of 1854:

> I am not nor have ever been in favor of making voters or jurors of negroes, nor of qualifying them to hold office, nor to intermarry with white people; and I will say in addition to this that there is a physical difference between the white and the black races which I believe will forever forbid the two races living together on terms of social and political equality. And inasmuch as they cannot so live, while they do remain together there must be the position of superior and inferior, and I as much as any other man am in favor of having the superior position assigned to the white race. . . . [Cheers.][32]

The cheers for these unegalitarian, racist comments demonstrate their popularity, at least in Charleston, Illinois, where they were made, which is in the southern half of the state. Douglas, however, questioned whether Lincoln's comments were sincere by calling attention to Lincoln's conflicting egalitarian comments made in other parts of Illinois. He thereby suggested that Lincoln was altering his remarks to cater to the more proslavery bias of southern Illinois and the more antislavery bias of northern Illinois in order to win votes[33]—a charge that Lincoln refuted by calling attention to his unegalitarian comments made in northern Illinois a month prior to his Charleston comments.[34] When it came to black suffrage, however, Lincoln while president was pressured by radical Republicans to publicly endorse black suffrage—pressure he resisted until his speech of 11 April 1865—just four days before his death. Yet even then, Lincoln hedged by limiting his endorsement of voting rights to blacks to "the very intelligent, and on those who serve our cause as soldiers."[35] This lengthy resistance to, and finally limited endorsement of, black suffrage indicates Lincoln meant his racist comments despite his idealistic commitment to emancipation.

## THE DRED SCOTT DECISION

Not only the Kansas-Nebraska Act and "the forty odd" senators who stood by without protest while Senator Pettit called the Declaration of Independence a "self-evident lie" were the cause of Lincoln's belief that the moral idealism of that document was being undermined along with the moral fiber of the American people. In 1857, the Supreme Court of the United States made its infamous Dred Scott decision that not only excluded blacks from the "all men are created equal" and "consent of the governed" provisions of the Declaration, it also smashed Douglas's version of "Popular Sovereignty"—made lawful by the Kansas-Nebraska Act—that whites in US territories north of 36 degrees 30 minutes north latitude could choose whether or not to have slavery. *Dred Scott* eliminated the right of any territorial legislature, as well as the Congress of the

United States, to make slavery either legal or illegal by making slave ownership a constitutionally guaranteed right in any territory whether north or south of 36 degrees 30 seconds north latitude. That decision was so alien to the "consent of the governed" principle of the Declaration of Independence that Lincoln became a dedicated opponent of those who maintained the Court had the sole power to judge on constitutional questions and could overrule the legislative and executive branches of government, as we shall see.

Scott was a slave who was taken by his master to a free state and then a free territory.[36] Subsequently, he brought suit in a US Circuit Court in the District of Missouri arguing that he was free because he had lived in areas where slavery was outlawed. He lost his case when the Supreme Court, which finally decided it, ruled he was not a citizen and that "neither *Congress* nor a *Territorial Legislature* can exclude slavery from any United States Territory."[37] This was total defiance of any form of "consent of the governed" as respects territorial slavery, which caused Lincoln to perceive the Court as a threat to republican democratic government in the territories. Moreover, Lincoln maintained that *Dred Scott* flagrantly usurped the legislative power of the federal government by going against a long-standing congressional act—the Northwest Ordinance of 1787—that stated the US legislature could regulate territorial slavery, thereby making the Court a threat to republican democratic government on the federal level. In addition, despite the intentional equal division of power among the three branches of government under the Constitution—the Congress, the president, and the Supreme Court—the Court ruled in effect in *Dred Scott* that it was above the other two branches when deciding what was the law of the land.

The decision was not unanimous and Chief Justice Roger B. Taney wrote the majority opinion from which Lincoln quoted Taney's interpretation of the Declaration's "All Men are created equal" phrase: "The general words above quoted would seem to include the whole human family [including blacks], and if they were used in a similar instrument at this day, would be so understood."[38] The implication was clear. Taney did not believe the all-inclusive language of the Declaration was meant to include blacks in 1776 but would if it were written in 1857. With this comment, Taney, according to Lincoln, "plainly assumes, as a fact, that the public estimate of the black man is more favorable *now* than it was in the days of the Revolution."[39] In his 1857 speech criticizing *Dred Scott*, Lincoln rejected Taney's view and elaborated on the moral deterioration of America compared to Revolutionary times by claiming Taney's

> assumption is a mistake. In some trifling particulars, the condition of that race [blacks] has been ameliorated; but, as a whole, in this country, the change between then and now is decidedly the other way; and their ultimate destiny has never appeared so hopeless as in the last three or four years [beginning with the Kansas-Nebraska Act].[40]

Lincoln gave several reasons for this view. First, he pointed out that "the five states . . . that gave the free negro the right of voting" during the Revolution have since taken it away or curtailed it. "New Jersey and North Carolina," for example, had taken it away while New York had "greatly abridged" it. Lincoln went on to state that although "the number of States has more than doubled" from the original thirteen, to his knowledge none of the added states gave suffrage to free blacks.[41] Second, subsequent to the Revolutionary period, several states added legal restraints and conditions that prevented masters from emancipating their slaves "at their own pleasure," restraints and conditions that Lincoln said amounted "almost to prohibition" of emancipation.[42] Garry Wills described some of these legal restraints in Jefferson's Virginia in *Inventing America*.[43] Third, state "legislatures held the unquestioned power to abolish slavery" in Revolutionary times. Yet "now," Lincoln complained, "it is becoming quite fashionable for State Constitutions to withhold that power."[44] Fourth, "by common consent, the spread of the blackman's bondage to new countries [territories] was prohibited [in the Northwest Ordinance of 1787]; but now, Congress decides that it *will* not continue the prohibition."[45] Lincoln was of course referring to the Kansas-Nebraska Act that allowed territories north of 36 degrees 30 minutes to choose whether or not to have slavery. Fifth, "the Supreme Court [in *Dred Scott*] decides" that any congress, whether federal or territorial, "*could* not" prohibit slavery in the territories even "if it would."[46] The sixth reason was his recurring theme—the change of attitude toward the Declaration of Independence that in Revolutionary times

> was held sacred by all, and thought to include all; but now, to aid in making the bondage of the negro universal and eternal, it is assailed, and sneered at, and construed, and hawked at, and torn, till if its framers could rise from their graves, they could not at all recognize it.[47]

The seventh reason was money. Slaves were now more valuable because supply had decreased since 1808 when the foreign slave trade was outlawed by the Constitution and demand had increased since slavery was legalized in the territories due to *Dred Scott.*[48] This was a principal reason that Lincoln said, "It is grossly incorrect to say or assume, that the public estimate of the Negro is more favorable now than it was at the origin of the government."[49] To Lincoln, the rising monetary value of slaves caused "all the powers of the earth" to be "rapidly combining against" the slave, making him more hopelessly enslaved than ever. As he put it:

> Mammon is after him; ambition follows, and philosophy follows, and the Theology of the day [the theology of slavery] is fast joining the cry. They have him in his prison house; they have searched his person, and left no prying instrument with him. One after another they have closed the heavy iron doors upon him, and now they have him, as it were, bolted in with a lock of a hundred keys, which can never be unlocked without the concurrence of every key; the keys in the hands of a hundred different men, and they have scattered to a hundred different and distant places; and they stand musing as to what invention, in all dominions of mind and matter, can be produced to make the impossibility of his escape more complete than it is.[50]

As a result of *Dred Scott,* when it came to "consent of the governed" and slavery, Lincoln perceived the enormous irony in this principle of the Declaration of Independence in the way it applied to the British government in colonial America prior to 1776 and the US government after the 1857 Dred Scott decision. The Supreme Court in that decision had become the equivalent of the British Board of Trade in colonial times because both deprived the people of self-government or "consent of the governed" when it came to slavery. Moreover, both forced slavery on the people against their "consent" when they had legislated or wanted to legislate against it. As was mentioned in chapter 1, Jefferson listed such force as a grievance against King George III in his anti–slave trade, antislavery passage of the Declaration because the king did not veto the Board of Trade's veto of colonial legislation outlawing the slave trade, which the king had the power to do. As was also mentioned, even though Jefferson's antislavery passage was deleted by the Continental Congress and did not appear in the final approved copy, Lincoln knew this passage was included in Jefferson's original draft of the Declaration since he read and quoted from Jefferson's *Autobiography*, which contained a copy of Jefferson's original draft.[51] Lincoln also knew of Henry Clay's description of a colonial grievance against Great Britain that was identical to the one in Jefferson's deleted provision (Clay no doubt got his ideas from Jefferson's rough draft). When putting his knowledge of Jefferson's deleted passage to work in his arguments against *Dred Scott*, Lincoln pointed out the similarity between what the British government with its Board of Trade had done to the people of the colonies and their legislatures and what the government of the United States with its Supreme Court via the Dred Scott decision was now doing to the people of the territories and their legislatures as well as to the people of the United States and their Congress:

> It has now been decided that *slavery cannot be kept out of our new territories by any legal means*. In what does our new territories now differ in this respect, from the old colonies when slavery was first planted within them? It was planted as Mr. Clay once declared, and as history proves to be true, by individual men in spite of the wishes of the people; the mother government refusing to prohibit it, and withholding from the people of the colonies the authority to prohibit it for themselves. Mr. Clay says this was one of the great and just causes of the complaint against Great Britain by the colonies, and the best apology we can now make for having the institution among us. *In that precise condition our Nebraska politi-*

*cians have at last succeeded in placing our own new territories; the gov-*
*ernment will not prohibit slavery within them, nor allow the people to*
*prohibit it* [my italics].

I defy any man to find any difference between the policy which
originally put slavery in these colonies and that policy which now
prevails in our own new Territories.[52]


## LINCOLN'S CONSPIRACY THEORY

When Lincoln mentioned that with *Dred Scott* "slavery cannot be
kept out of our new territories by any legal means" and "in that precise condition *our Nebraska politicians have at last succeeded in placing
our own new territories* [my italics]," he was referring to his conspiracy
theory that involved the "Nebraska politicians." In his famous
"House Divided" speech in 1858, he maintained that circumstances
surrounding the Kansas-Nebraska Act, when considered with some
surrounding the Dred Scott decision, demonstrated there was collusion between Stephen Douglas, the architect of the Kansas-Nebraska
Act, Roger Taney, the chief justice of the Supreme Court, and James
Buchanan, who was elected president in 1856.[53] He argued that
these "Nebraska politicians," who supported the Kansas-Nebraska
Act, especially Douglas, did not genuinely favor the "Popular Sovereignty" principle of the act as they claimed. They simply wanted to
expand slavery, and "Popular Sovereignty" was an expedient method
to accomplish this until a better one came along, which it did in
*Dred Scott*. Indeed, according to Lincoln, Douglas and his supporters
revealed their expedient commitment to "Popular Sovereignty" even
in 1854 when the Kansas-Nebraska Act was pending in Congress. At
that time, the act's opponents proposed an amendment, which said
that "the people of the territory *may* exclude slavery."[54] However, this
authority of the people of the territories was already included in the
language of the act itself. And, Lincoln quoted that language: "It
being the true intent and meaning of this act not to legislate slavery
into any Territory or state, nor to exclude it therefrom; but to leave

the people thereof perfectly free to form and regulate their domestic institutions in their own way, *subject only to the Constitution of the United States* [my italics]."[55] Although the "Nebraska politicians," including Douglas, voted for the act itself, which passed, they did not vote for the amendment, which did not pass. This made no sense to Lincoln because the proposed amendment only clarified what was generally stated in the 1854 act.

In his effort to explain this seemingly contradictory vote, Lincoln pointed out in his "House Divided" speech—delivered after being nominated to run for US senator against the incumbent Douglas—that Dred Scott filed his lawsuit in 1854, about the same time Douglas introduced the Kansas-Nebraska Bill in Congress.[56] This raised the question, could Douglas and his supporters have anticipated that the Dred Scott decision might nullify the "Popular Sovereignty" principle of the act, which it subsequently did, by ruling that slavery in the territories was guaranteed by the Constitution and, therefore, any legislation outlawing slavery in the territories passed by either Congress or territorial legislatures was unconstitutional? Lincoln believed that Douglas and his Nebraska politicians "did look forward to such a decision, or had it in contemplation, that such a decision . . . would or might be made," as he stated in his second debate with Douglas.[57] To Lincoln, this anticipation explained why the clarifying amendment was voted down and also why the phrase "subject only to the Constitution of the United States" was inserted in the bill. That left, as he stated, "an exactly fitted *N i c h e*, for the Dred Scott decision" in the Kansas-Nebraska Act.[58] If the amendment had passed, *Dred Scott* would have put the Court in the position of overruling a very specific constitutional law, which would very likely have precipitated a congressional movement to curtail the Court's powers.

Lincoln also found it curious that the Court delayed announcing the Dred Scott decision until after the election and inauguration of President Buchanan in early 1857, even though they had reached their decision before the election.[59] He explained the delay by pointing out that Buchanan had made "Popular Sovereignty" or the "freedom" of the people of a territory to decide on slavery a major issue in his campaign and indeed won the election because he supported "Popular Sovereignty." If the Court had promptly announced its decision, Buchanan's campaign would have been ruined. As Lincoln put it: "Speaking out *then* [before or during the election] would have damaged the *'perfectly free'* argument upon which the election was carried."[60] Although Lincoln's evidence for his conspiracy theory was circumstantial, it sounded plausible. Therefore, he used it as campaign rhetoric against Douglas and the Democrats throughout the 1858 debates. An indication that there was substance to Lincoln's conspiracy theory was provided by historian Don E. Fehrenbacher, who confirmed that Buchanan was in contact with the Supreme Court during the election and governed his statements in anticipation of its delayed announcement of the Dred Scott decision.[61]

## LINCOLN VERSUS THE SUPREME COURT

What especially concerned Lincoln about Dred Scott was that it would cause the growth of slavery in the territories after a few slave owners initially settled there. This in turn would cause the people of the territories to develop a vested interest in slavery, causing them to cling to it and then legalize it when they formed states.[62] A similar pattern had unfolded in states that arose from colonies where slavery thrived after beginning on a small scale. Therefore, Lincoln maintained Dred Scott would lead to the expansion of slavery and more slave states. Moreover, it obliterated the "consent of the governed" principle of the Declaration of Independence not only for blacks but for whites as well, as has been mentioned. These were the reasons Lincoln vehemently resisted the Dred Scott decision and the Supreme Court that made it. He invoked the ideas of Andrew Jackson and especially those of Thomas Jefferson in his resistance in order to counter Stephen Douglas's statement "Whoever resists the final decision of the highest judicial tribunal, aims a deadly blow to our whole Republican system of government—a blow, which if successful would place all our rights and liberties at the mercy of passion, anarchy and violence."[63] Jackson, and particularly Jefferson, had argued it was the other way around. If the Supreme Court became excessive and those excesses were not successfully resisted, the Court itself would lead to the destruction of republican government and the rights and liberties of the people. In his resistance to *Dred Scott*, however, Lincoln never said anything as extreme as President Jackson's alleged defiance of Chief Justice John Marshall and his Court: "Well, John Marshall has made his decision, now let him enforce it."[64] What Lincoln advocated, however, amounted to virtually the same thing because he stressed Jackson's view that the president or Congress could make their own interpretations of the Constitution independent of the Court and act accordingly. In other words, the Court was not above the president or Congress but rather their coequal when it came to interpreting the Constitution. In support of this view, Lincoln quoted President Jackson's opinion that rejected a Supreme Court decision that a national bank was constitutional and explained his veto of a "re-charter" bill for such a bank. Jackson's rationale was based partly on precedent and "partly on constitutional" grounds:

> It is maintained by the advocates of the bank, that its constitutionality, in all its features, ought to be considered as settled by precedent, and by the decision of the Supreme Court. To this conclusion, I cannot consent. Mere precedent is a dangerous source of authority, and should not be regarded as deciding questions of constitutional power, except where the acquiescence of the people of the States can be considered as well settled. So far from this being the case on this subject, an argument against the bank might be based on precedent. One Congress in 1791, decided in favor of a bank; another in 1811, decided against it. One congress in 1815 decided against a bank; another in 1816 decided in favor. Prior to the present Congress, therefore the precedents drawn from that source were equal. If we resort to the States, the expressions of legislative, judicial and executive opinions against the bank have been probably to those in its favor as four to one. There is nothing in precedent, therefore, which if its authority were admitted, ought to weigh in favor of the act before me. . . .
>
> If the opinion of the Supreme Court covered the whole ground of this act, it ought not to control the co-ordinate authorities of this Government. The Congress, the executive and the court, must

each for itself be guided by its own opinion of the Constitution. Each public officer, who takes an oath to support the Constitution, swears that he will support it as he understands it, and not as it is understood by others.[65]

Jefferson had more nuances in his ideas on the Court but a virtually identical opinion on its authority, which probably informed Jackson. He argued that if justices of the Supreme Court were the "ultimate arbiters" as to what was constitutional in every situation, then republican government established by the Constitution was no longer republican but an "oligarchy" where five out of nine justices could and eventually would become despots. Jefferson maintained—in a way consistent with the "consent of the governed" principle of the Declaration—that "I know no safe depository of the ultimate powers of society but the people themselves; and if we think them not enlightened enough to exercise their control with a wholesome discretion, the remedy is not to take it from them, but to inform their discretion by education."[66] To make Supreme Court justices the "ultimate arbiters" in constitutional questions was in effect to take away the "ultimate powers of society" from "the people themselves," in Jefferson's view. Consistent with this view, Jefferson argued that Supreme Court justices appointed by the president *for life*, according to the Constitution, was a major flaw in that document if it was interpreted as giving the Court "ultimate" authority in all "Constitutional questions." Yet to Jefferson this was an erroneous interpretation. He maintained that the Constitution made the three branches of government—the executive, the legislative, and the judiciary—"co-equal and co-sovereign within themselves," which implies Jackson's aforementioned view that each branch can decide for itself what is constitutional and act on that decision within the scope of its constitutionally limited powers.[67] Jefferson also pointed out that, according to the Constitution, "when the legislative or executive functionaries act unconstitutionally, they are responsible to the people in their elective capacity," which places "the ultimate powers of society" with "the people themselves."[68] In other words, the people judge whether or not presidents, senators, and congressmen violate the Constitution and vote against them if their judgments are adverse. This was not the case with Supreme Court justices. Once appointed and confirmed by the Senate, they are answerable to no one. This is not to say that Jefferson did not recognize the need for an independent judiciary; he did. To him, however, there were degrees of independence and no official of a republican government, including a judge, should be completely independent of the people or their elected officials for life. That would be antithetical to a republic. It turned a republic into what Jefferson described as "the despotism of an oligarchy."[69]

Realizing the difficulty in amending the Constitution in order to give the people more control over the Supreme Court, Jefferson emphasized that the Court had no constitutional power to order either the president or the individual members of Congress or the Congress itself to perform what the Court judged to be their constitutional duties because of the "co-equal and co-sovereign" status of all three branches. He argued that the principal function of the Court involved constitutional questions concerning "the laws of meum and tuum and of criminal action" and not those concerning the other branches of government. These ideas are contained in Jefferson's 1820 letter to William Charles Jarvis where he discussed Jarvis's manuscript "Republican," which he hoped would "lead our youth to the practice of thinking on such subjects and for themselves."[70] Lincoln quoted the following portion of that letter in a speech delivered at Springfield on 17 July 1858:

> That it [the "Republican"] will have this tendency [to lead our youth to think for themselves] may be expected, and for that reason I feel an urgency to note what I deem an error in it, the more requiring notice as your opinion is strengthened by that of many others. You seem, in pages 84 and 148, to consider the judges as the ultimate arbiters of all constitutional questions—a very dangerous doctrine indeed and one which would place us under *the despotism of an oligarchy* [my italics]. Our judges are as honest as other men, and not more so. They have, with others, the same passions for party, for power, and the privilege of their corps. Their maxim is "boni judicis est ampliare jurisdictionem [good judges enlarge their jurisdictions]"; and their power is more dangerous as they are in office for life, and not responsible, as the other functionaries are,

to elective control. The Constitution has erected no such tribunal, knowing that to whatever hands confided, with the corruptions of time and party, its members would become despots. It has more wisely made all the departments [legislative, executive, and judicial] co-equal and co-sovereign within themselves.[71]

Lincoln commented on this statement from Jefferson when he said: "Thus we see that the power claimed by the Supreme Court by Judge Douglas"—that it has ultimate authority in all constitutional questions and should not be resisted—"Mr. Jefferson holds, would reduce us to *the despotism of an oligarchy* [my italics]."[72] Lincoln added that when Jackson decided "not to be bound to hold a national bank to be constitutional, even though the Court had decided it to be so," he "fell in precisely with the view of Mr. Jefferson, and acted upon it under his official oath, in vetoing a charter for a national bank."[73] In his fifth debate with Douglas on 7 October 1858, Lincoln repeated Jefferson's statement "Judges are as honest as other men, and not more so" taken from Jefferson's letter to Charles Jarvis that he quoted on 17 July. He then summarized the substance of Jefferson's letter to Jarvis: "Whenever a free people should give up in absolute submission to any department of government, retaining for themselves no appeal from it, their liberties were gone."[74]

With knowledge of these ideas of Presidents Jefferson and Jackson, it becomes understandable why Lincoln, when president, did not hesitate to make his own interpretation of the Constitution when suspending the right of habeas corpus, which is authorized under the Constitution in times of rebellion and invasion, without a decision by the Supreme Court. It also becomes understandable why he overruled lower court orders demanding a writ of habeas corpus for those arrested after that right was suspended. Indeed, he used the military to enforce his overruling because he believed he was acting within the scope of his presidential powers as prescribed by the Constitution.[75] In fact, Lincoln completely defied the Supreme Court on habeas corpus. Shortly after the attack on Fort Sumter, Lincoln suspended habeas corpus. John Merryman, a Maryland secessionist accused of "sabotage and treason," was promptly arrested without any writ of habeas corpus. Supreme Court Chief

Justice Roger Taney immediately challenged Lincoln by issuing a writ for Merryman. However, the Union general in command of the area where Merryman lived refused to honor it because Lincoln had suspended habeas corpus. Taney then ordered the general to be arrested by a federal marshal for contempt of court. However, when the marshal arrived at the gate of Fort McHenry to make the arrest, he was turned away. Taney then instructed Lincoln to enforce the Court's orders and told Lincoln this was his duty under the Constitution. Lincoln responded by ignoring Taney and the Supreme Court while simultaneously justifying his position to Congress.[76] In 1863, Congress backed up Lincoln's position by passing a Habeas Corpus Act that specifically gave him the power to suspend habeas corpus.[77] In such instances, according to historian William Gienapp, Lincoln, "with remarkable deftness" traversed the "line between failing to respond vigorously and the abuse of power." And, although he had "unprecedented power," it did not corrupt him or cause him to view it "as an end in itself."[78]

Lincoln's position on the Dred Scott decision, however, was far from proposing that the people themselves, "as a mob," should disregard it, as Douglas suggested. Lincoln explained his position by stating:

We do not propose that, when any other one, or one thousand, shall be decided by that court to be slaves, we will in any violent way disturb the rights of property thus settled; but we nevertheless do oppose that decision as a political rule which shall be binding on the voter, to vote for nobody who thinks it wrong, which shall be binding on the members of Congress or the President to favor no measure that does not actually concur with the principles of that decision. We do not propose to be bound by it as a political rule in any way, because we think it lays the foundation not merely of enlarging and spreading out of what we consider an evil, but it lays the foundation of spreading that evil into the States themselves. *We propose so resisting it as to have it reversed if we can, and a new judicial rule established upon this subject* [my italics].[79]

The people, according to this statement, are not coequal with the Court. They are subject to it. The president and the Congress, on the other hand, are both coequal with the Court. As a result, they could interpret the Constitution independently and differently and go against the Court. The only thing the people could do if they disagreed with a Supreme Court decision, as Lincoln implicitly suggests here, was vote for representatives, senators, and presidents who shared their views. Since the president appoints new Supreme Court justices, which are confirmed by the Senate, the people's influence could eventually be felt and the Court's unpopular decisions reversed when older justices were replaced with new ones sympathetic to the people's views. This of course could take a long time, especially if there were no vacancies on the Court for several years. Less time-consuming would be for an elected Congress and president sympathetic to the people's adverse view of a Supreme Court decision to sponsor and pass legislation that would increase the number of Supreme Court justices. The president could then legally "pack" the Court with justices who would override the Court's former unpopular decision with a new one.

The president, however, had a more immediate but also more limited power—the power of pardon—which in some situations could be used to nullify the effects of law he deemed unconstitutional, including law resulting from Supreme Court decisions. Jefferson had used this power to remedy the unconstitutional Sedition Act of 1798, which violated First Amendment protections of freedom of speech and freedom of the press. That act, signed into law by President John Adams, provided that citizens could be fined and imprisoned for criticizing the government and its officials—exactly what you find in the most repressive dictatorships. Jefferson, after resisting the Sedition Act—as quietly and indirectly as possible, otherwise he would have been jailed—pardoned all of its imprisoned victims immediately after he became president in 1801.[80]

The power of pardon, however, would not help in alleviating the effects of *Dred Scott*, which, in Lincoln's opinion, was clearly unconstitutional. In support of his opinion, he quoted a clause from Chief Justice Taney's majority opinion on *Dred Scott*, "*the right of property in a slave is distinctly and expressly affirmed in the Constitution.*"[81] This statement, however, is erroneous. As Lincoln pointed out, nowhere in the Constitution was the right of slave ownership "distinctly and expressly affirmed." On the contrary, the terms "slave" and even "negro" were not mentioned at all in the Constitution, let alone "distinctly and expressly," as has been mentioned. This is the reason Lincoln said, "I believe that the Supreme Court and the advocates of that decision [Dred Scott] may search in vain for the place in the Constitution where the right of property in a slave is distinctly and expressly affirmed" and is why Lincoln believed *Dred Scott* was unconstitutional.[82] Yet as long as Taney and his supporters sat as Supreme Court justices, Lincoln was aware that the Dred Scott decision would stand. Therefore, he considered "packing" the Court, since it was the least time-consuming and most effective way of reversing *Dred Scott*.

Lincoln did not specifically mention that the Constitution of the United States provided the people with the power to "pack" the Supreme Court and thereby reverse its decisions. Yet he knew it provided this power, as did the Constitution of the state of Illinois where its supreme court had already been packed. Indeed, in his first debate with Douglas, he explained that this was the way Douglas "got his title of Judge" and that there was an account of it in "Ford's *History of Illinois*."[83] According to Lincoln's description of that account, Douglas and his party were displeased with an Illinois Supreme Court decision that the governor could not remove "a Secretary of State."[84] They sought to overturn "that decision." Their method was "adding five new Judges, so as to vote down" the court's previous majority decision.[85] Their efforts resulted in Douglas's appointment as a judge and his *"sitting down on that very bench* [Illinois Supreme Court] as one of the five new Judges."[86] An indication that the packing method of dealing with the federal supreme court was in Lincoln's mind is seen in his previously quoted comment on *Dred Scott*, "We [Republicans] propose . . . to have it [*Dred Scott*] reversed if we can, and a new judicial rule established upon this subject"[87] Without packing the Court, however, this statement makes little sense. There was no reasonable expectation for reversing *Dred Scott* in the lifetime of any Republican president, even if he wanted to reverse it, since waiting for existing justices to retire or die and be replaced could take several years.

With the outbreak of the Civil War, reversing *Dred Scott* was no longer an issue with Lincoln. As president, his main concern was holding the Union together by military force. Yet Lincoln packed the Court anyway—not to reverse *Dred Scott* but to secure the loyalty of California to the Union by appointing a Californian as justice of the Supreme Court. This is why he urged Congress to pass legislation increasing the size of the Court from nine to ten justices. Congress accommodated him and on 6 March 1863, Lincoln appointed Stephen J. Field, a California jurist, as a Supreme Court justice. Field's abolitionist brother, David Dudley Field, who had influence with the Lincoln administration, no doubt helped secure his brother's appointment.[88]

## "THE NEW DRED SCOTT DECISION"

Electing representatives, senators, and a president opposed to *Dred Scott* in the forthcoming elections, thereby providing power to pack the Court, was not only the means to reverse *Dred Scott*. It was also the means to prevent what Lincoln dreaded—a "new Dred Scott decision" that would make slavery legal throughout the nation. Lincoln maintained "a new Dred Scott decision" was implied in *Dred Scott*. He quoted Taney's statement "The right of property in a slave is distinctly and expressly affirmed in the Constitution" from Taney's majority opinion on *Dred Scott*, along with the following second clause of the sixth article of the federal constitution to support his view of what was implied:

> This Constitution and the laws of the United States which shall be made in pursuance thereof; and all treaties made or which shall be made under the authority of the United States, shall be the supreme law of the land; and the judges in every State shall be bound thereby anything in the Constitution or laws of any State to the contrary notwithstanding.[89]

Lincoln then composed a syllogism using elements of this constitutional provision and Taney's majority opinion to demonstrate that

*Dred Scott* implied all state- and federal-legislated law outlawing slavery was unconstitutional and, therefore, the right to own slaves in any state was guaranteed by the federal constitution. As Lincoln stated that syllogism in his fifth debate with Douglas:

> Nothing in the Constitution or laws of any State can destroy a right distinctly and expressly affirmed in the Constitution of the United States.
>
> The right of property in a slave is distinctly and expressly affirmed in the Constitution of the United States;
>
> Therefore, nothing in the Constitution or laws of any State can destroy the right of property in a slave.[90]

Although the second premise of this syllogism was clearly erroneous, because the words "slave" or "slavery" are nowhere "distinctly" expressed in the Constitution, Lincoln believed this syllogism's logic was unassailable. Therefore, he argued that all the Supreme Court had to do to nationalize slavery was make another decision explicitly ruling what was implicit in *Dred Scott.* Jean Baker tells us that Lincoln saw the "*Lemmon v. the People* case making its way through the [court] system" as giving the Taney Court an opportunity "to apply the principles of Dred Scott more precisely to northern states."[91] Moreover, Lincoln maintained that if the pro-expansion-of-slavery Democrats won enough seats in the Congress as well as the presidency in the forthcoming election, the Court would be able to make a "new Dred Scott decision" without any possibility of effective resistance such as packing the Court. In fact, he maintained that the Dred Scott decision would have never been made or sustained without an overwhelming majority of Democrats in Congress, which had been the case for many years. As he put it in his fifth debate with Douglas:

> It is my opinion that the Dred Scott decision, as it is, never would have been made in its present form if the party that made it [Democrats] had not been sustained previously [in office as they had been for most of the last fifty years] by the elections. My own opinion is, that *the new Dred Scott decision* [ my italics], deciding against the right of the people of the States to exclude

slavery, will never be made, if that party is not sustained [in office] by the elections.[92]

This was campaign rhetoric to be sure. It reeks of "Vote for me and the Republicans and a new Dred Scott decision will never be made." Yet it is not without an element of truth. There was an ideological war going on to capture the heart and soul of America between the pro-expansion-of-slavery Democrats, led by Stephen Douglas, and procontainment-of-slavery Republicans, led by Abraham Lincoln, who believed containment would ultimately end in complete emancipation.[93] This was plainly apparent in the Illinois elections of 1858 as well as in the national election of 1860. And, as both Jefferson and Lincoln knew, as has been stated, the majority opinion of the populace could not be ignored in a democratic republic like the United States, since it would ultimately prevail even over the Supreme Court. This was the reason these elections were crucial. They would determine the majority opinion and even the Supreme Court would be subject to it, as Lincoln in effect said in the aforementioned statement, especially in the context of "packing" the Court.

## THE DECLARATION OF INDEPENDENCE AND EQUALITY

The principal issue in the nineteenth-century ideological war was of course slavery. Yet, as Lincoln stated in his letter to H. L. Pierce, the moral "principles of Jefferson" specified in the Declaration of Independence—which were not being observed as much as in Revolutionary times—were also at issue because they were linked to slavery. Lincoln compared those principles to the "simpler propositions of Euclid," which being simple were easy to understand and, therefore, easily taught to any "sane child."[94] Yet if those simple, easily understood "propositions" were "denied" by any child, then all efforts to teach that child geometry were undermined and would "fail utterly" because those "simpler propositions" were the basis of geometry.[95] In like manner, if the "simpler propositions" or "the principles of Jefferson" in the Declaration were "denied" and "evaded," the entire structure of a free government and free society was undermined and would, therefore, fail because those "principles of Jefferson" were the basis of free society or, as Lincoln stated, they were the "definitions and axioms of free society." Yet this was exactly what the advocates of slavery were doing. It was by them, according to Lincoln in his letter to Pierce, that the "principles of Jefferson" or the Declaration of Independence were

> denied, and evaded, with no small show of success. One dashingly calls them "glittering generalities"; another bluntly calls them "self-evident lies"; and still others insidiously argue that they apply only to "superior races."
>
> These expressions, differing in form, are identical in object and effect—the supplanting the principles of free government [stated in the Declaration of Independence], and restoring those of classification, caste, and legitimacy. They would delight a convocation of crowned heads, plotting against the people. They are the vanguard—*the miners, and sappers*—of returning despotism [my italics]. We must repulse them or they will subjugate us.[96]

Lincoln's recurring theme in his letter to Pierce and other individuals was that the principles of the Declaration could not be denied by applying them to so-called superior races while excluding so-called inferiors without adversely effecting a free society—as Douglas had said they could by excluding "the negro, the savage Indians, the Fejee, the Malay, or any other inferior and degraded race."[97] This exclusive or selective approach to freedom was the basis of all tyranny and "despotism," all systems of "classification, caste, and legitimacy," as Lincoln stated to Pierce. Moreover, if blacks could be excluded from the Declaration's principles now, because some claimed they were inferior, how could any group be sure they would not receive similar treatment in the future and thereby become victims of tyranny and despotism. As Lincoln put it, "I should like to know if taking this old Declaration of Independence, which declares that all men are equal upon principle and making exceptions to it[,] where will it stop. If one man says it does not mean a negro, why not another say it does not mean some other man?"[98]

Lincoln condemned excluding anyone from the egalitarian principles of the Declaration as despotism in his 1855 letter to Joshua Speed, in what constituted another of his arguments that the morality of the Declaration was not being observed as much as it was in Revolutionary times. Ranting against the American or Know-Nothing Party, which maintained that not only blacks but also foreigners and Catholics should be excluded from the principles of the Declaration, Lincoln said:

> I am not a Know-Nothing. That is certain. How could I be? How can any one who abhors the oppression of negroes, be in favor of degrading classes of white people? Our progress in degeneracy appears to me to be pretty rapid. As a nation, we began by declaring that *"all men are created equal."* We now practically read it "all men are created equal, *except negroes.* When the Know Nothings get control, it will read "all men are created equal, except negroes, *and foreigners, and catholics."* When it comes to this I should prefer emigrating to some country where they make no pretence of loving liberty—to Russia, for instance, where despotism can be taken pure, and without the base alloy of hypocracy.[99]

With this statement, Lincoln made it clear that not only all races were included in the "principles" of the Declaration but also all religious persuasions with his mention of Catholics, which is consistent with his deistic tolerance and alien to nineteenth-century bias against Catholics in America. Yet despite Lincoln's private denunciation of Know-Nothings to his friend Speed, Lincoln prudently avoided similar denunciations in public in 1860 of the then defunct party because he believed he would need the votes of former Know-Nothings when running for president.[100]

Jews as well as Catholics were victims of nineteenth-century bias in America, and Lincoln's deistic tolerance and respect for the rights of all citizens regardless of their religious views was manifest in his treatment of Jews. When it was called to his attention that no rabbis were serving as military chaplains, despite the fact that many Jews were fighting for the Union, Lincoln found there was a law preventing the appointment of Jewish chaplains.[101] He immediately sought a new law from Congress that remedied this injustice, and on 12 May 1862 Jewish chaplains became a reality. In addition, upon hearing of General Ulysses S. Grant's infamous order expelling Jews from the Department of Tennessee, Lincoln immediately had it revoked.[102] As Rabbi Philip Joachimsen said of Lincoln, "His mind was not subject to the vulgar clamor against Jews."[103]

Lincoln was careful not to disrupt separation of church and state even though ministers in areas occupied by Union armies often encouraged sympathy for the South. One such minister was the Reverend Doctor Samuel B. McPheeters of the Pine Street Presbyterian Church in St. Louis. His actions caused an officer under the command of General Samuel P. Curtis to order McPheeters's church closed. When McPheeters complained to Lincoln in person and presented the president with a copy of the order, Lincoln, by telegraph, immediately suspended the order. He then wrote a letter to General Curtis with the following instruction:

> The U.S. government must not, as by this order, undertake to run the churches. When an individual, in a church or out it, becomes dangerous to the public interest, he must be checked; but let the churches, as such take care of themselves.[104]

In his aforementioned letter to Pierce, Lincoln referred to "the miners, and sappers—of returning despotism," a comment aimed at pro-expansion-of-slavery men like Judge Douglas and Supreme Court Justice Taney. By excluding blacks from the principles of freedom of the Declaration of Independence, these two men and their supporters were undermining those principles and therefore had become "miners, and sappers—of returning despotism." Lincoln's use of the military term "sappers" or engineers and specialists in military fortifications in his Pierce letter, as well as "miners" or those who laid minefields, was appropriate in describing opponents in the ideological war against slavery. Jefferson himself had used these terms in his *Autobiography* of 1821, where he described Supreme Court justices, and he used them again in his 1820 letter to William Charles Jarvis, from which Lincoln quoted the passage "It is the office of a good judge to enlarge his jurisdiction," as has been mentioned.[105] As was also mentioned, Lincoln was familiar with Jefferson's *Autobiography* because he had read and quoted from it.[106]

Of all the "miners" and "sappers," according to Lincoln, Douglas was doing more of what "prepares the public mind to take the next [Dred Scott] decision [which would nationalize slavery] when it comes, without any inquiry."[107] Then he stated exactly what the articulate and persuasive Douglas was doing. First, he stated that Douglas was arguing: "All of us who stand by the [Dred Scott] decision of the Supreme Court are friends of the Constitution; and all you fellows that dare question it in any way, are enemies of the Constitution."[108] If the majority of people accepted this, they would quietly accept a "new Dred Scott decision." Second, Lincoln stated that when Douglas argued that "he don't care whether Slavery is voted up or down"[109]—the "Popular Sovereignty" idea that the people of each territory could decide whether or not to have slavery—Douglas was preparing people to accept slavery in any state provided the people in that state favored it. Indeed, Douglas's second argument fostered the disposition, "We should not interfere in the affairs of any territory or another state as they should not interfere in ours," a disposition that stultified moral indignation against slavery. Indeed, it led to indifference toward that evil. Third, Douglas was arguing that the territories had "a right to have it [slavery]," which was of course the ruling in *Dred Scott*.[110] Fourth, he was arguing that "upon the principles of equality it [slavery] should be allowed to go everywhere."[111] This argument was premised upon the idea that people owning slaves should not be barred from the territories any more than people owning cattle. Property is property whether slaves or cattle and all property owners should be treated equally. If, however, the people accepted this argument in principle, they would not object to slave owners bringing their slave property to any state. Fifth, Douglas argued that "there is no inconsistency between free and slave institutions,"[112] an argument based on Douglas's second argument of not caring whether slavery is voted up or down. As long as the people supported either slavery or freedom, there was no inconsistency in the sense that the people in either case made the choice. In Lincoln's view, this put slavery on an equal footing with freedom.

Lincoln emphasized in his letter to Pierce that if Douglas and his supporters were successful in their campaign to extend and nationalize slavery, freedom in America would not last long for anyone. Using logic based on justice and echoing Jefferson's statement from *Notes on the State of Virginia*, "I tremble for my country when I remember that God is just" regarding slavery, which Lincoln quoted, as was stated in chapter 1, Lincoln said: "This is a world of compensations; and he who would *be* no slave, must consent to *have* no slave. Those who deny freedom to others, deserve it not for themselves; and, under a just God, can not long retain it."[113] Retaining "freedom" was one of the main reasons why Lincoln fought to promote the "simpler propositions" or "principles of Jefferson" in the Declaration of Independence for *all* humans. Those "principles" were the foundation of everyone's freedom. Consistent with this view, Lincoln argued that the "simpler propositions" or "principles" of the Declaration were "the father of all moral principle" in patriotic Americans. The fundamental precept of that "moral principle" was that no human being's freedom should be taken away or abused. Lincoln saw the "principles of Jefferson" or the Declaration as a cohesive force that bound all humans together because they applied to everyone. This was the reason they struck a spiritual or "electric cord" in the "hearts" of "patriotic and freedom loving" Americans—an "electric cord" that "links" them together as a people. Moreover, anyone who cherished the "principles" of the Declaration and thereby identified with them could claim the Declaration as their own just as if they were blood relatives of its authors. As Lincoln stated of "German, Irish, French and Scandinavian" Americans—and all those who emigrated to the United States after the Revolutionary War:

> When they look through that old Declaration of Independence they find that those old men say that "We hold these truths to be self-evident, that all men are created equal," and then they feel that moral sentiment taught in that day evidences their relation to those men, that is the father of all moral principle in them, and that they have a right to claim it [the Declaration] as though they were blood of the blood, and flesh of the flesh of the men who

wrote the Declaration, [loud and long continued applause] and so they are. That is the electric cord in the Declaration that links the hearts of patriotic and liberty-loving men together, that will link those patriotic hearts as long as the love of freedom exists in the minds of men throughout the world. [Applause.][114]

Lincoln knew that most Americans were aware that their recent ancestors had experienced the tyranny of kings, who, as he stated, were "always bestride the necks of the people." Moreover, he maintained those kings were so puffed up with arrogance born of their feelings of superiority that they believed "the people were better off for being ridden" by them.[115] Yet the white supremacist advocates of black slavery had the same puffed-up superiority complex toward blacks, which manifested itself in similar arrogance. Douglas himself provided an example of this arrogance when he said:

> It does not follow by any means because a negro is not your equal or mine that hence he may necessarily be a slave. On the contrary, it does follow that we ought to extend to the negro every right, every privilege, every immunity *which he is capable of enjoying consistent with the good of society* [my italics].[116]

Douglas also said, "I do not believe that the Almighty made the negro capable of self-government."[117] Therefore he left it to whites to judge what "right" or "privilege" or "immunity" blacks were "capable of enjoying consistent with the good of society." Whites, as Douglas perceived them, thereby assumed a position similar to king and church in medieval politics when both maintained that humankind was incapable of self-government because of its morally tainted or depraved nature. This resulted in king and church doling out what rights, privileges, and immunities they deemed the people "capable of enjoying consistent with the good of society," which, in many instances, turned out to be few or none, especially when it came to the right of religious freedom which was nonexistent in governments dominated by Christianity. That Lincoln, unlike Douglas, saw clearly how feelings of superiority and denial of human capacity for self-government produced similar moralizations and rationalizations in either kings or slavery advocates for depriving those they regarded inferior of their rights and exploiting or abusing them is seen when he described them in his 1858 speech at Chicago as

> the same old serpent that says you work and I eat, you toil and I will enjoy the fruits of it. Turn in whatever way you will—whether it come from the mouth of a *King* [my italics], an excuse for enslaving the people of his country, or from the mouth of men of one race as a reason for enslaving the men of another race, it is the same old serpent.[118]

Lincoln's reference to the "serpent," a principal cause of sin in the Bible, enabled him to emphasize to his predominantly Christian audience that white slave owners were just as sinful as kings who were condemned by Americans as evil despots in the Declaration of Independence. Moreover, his statement that kings were enslavers of their subjects, just as slave owners were of their human property, was calculated to make whites—whose memory of kingly despotism and political slavery in colonial times was still vivid—have guilt feelings as well as sympathy for blacks who were still experiencing the despotism of slavery at their hands. To put it another way, Lincoln was saying that whites were doing the very same things to blacks that caused their ancestors to rise up in bloody revolution.

Indeed, Lincoln maintained that as the Declaration's idea of equality or the equal rights of "all men" erected an obstacle to kingly despotism born of feelings of superiority, it also erected an obstacle to any form of despotism born of anyone's feelings of superiority. No one, according to the principles of Declaration, just because they felt and claimed superiority, or even were superior in some respect, could take away the equal rights of others. Jefferson himself stated this principle in his letter to Henri Gregoire, an accomplished black man, when he wrote: "Because Sir Isaac Newton was superior to others in understanding, he was not therefore lord of the person or property of others."[119] Lincoln maintained that this liberating principle of equal rights in the Declaration, even though that document's specific purpose was to declare "national independence" from Great Britain, was placed there by Jefferson as an ideological

barrier to any form of tyranny or despotism based on claims of superiority "applicable to all men and all times." This is why Lincoln
paid tribute to Jefferson in his letter to Pierce and others by stating:

> All honor to Jefferson—to the man who, in the concrete pressure
> of a struggle for national independence by a single people, had the
> coolness, forecast, and capacity to introduce into a merely revolu-
> tionary document, an abstract truth, *applicable to all men and all
> times* [my italics], and so to embalm it there, that to-day, and in all
> coming days, it shall be a rebuke and a stumbling-block to the very
> harbingers of re-appearing tyranny and oppression.[120]

Harry Jaffa laments the "widespread notion . . . among political
scientists" that "the principles of the Declaration are more to be considered an expression of 'the thought of the time'" of the Revolution
"than a serious teaching about man and his nature."[121] Yet to Lincoln in this statement, the principles of the Declaration were "applicable to all men and all times." Moreover, they were a major "rebuke
and stumbling block" to slavery because they were irreconcilable
with slavery. Therefore, Lincoln reasoned, either the Declaration had
to go or slavery had to go—either abandon the Declaration's principles as untrue, as Senator John Pettit had done by calling them "a
self-evident lie," or, ultimately abandon slavery. In his speech at
Chicago in 1858, Lincoln, relying on Americans' love for the Declaration of Independence, made this point dramatically in a dialogue
with his audience:

> If that declaration [of Independence] is not the truth, let us get the
> Statute book, in which we find it and tear it out! Who is bold
> enough to do it! [Voices—"me" "no one," &c.] If it is not true let
> us tear it out! [Cries of "no, no"] let us stick to it then, [cheers] let
> us stand firmly by it then. [Applause.][122]

To "stick to" the Declaration and "stand firmly by it," however, mandated total abolition of slavery. Lincoln was keenly aware of this, as
was Jefferson, as has been stated, and because of Lincoln's efforts the
populace were becoming aware of it too. As Damon Wells said of
Lincoln, "He had succeeded in arousing the conscience of a

nation."[123] However, what Wells did not mention was that the principal instrument Lincoln used to arouse that conscience was the moral idealism of the Declaration of Independence, which he defended from the negative and corrupting revisionist onslaughts of slavery advocates. Indeed to Lincoln, the Declaration of Independence was the source of *the conscience of a nation.* Without that conscience, he believed the United States would degenerate into another despotism—one among many that had existed throughout history—as he would state in his Gettysburg Address in which he once again utilized the idealism of the Declaration of Independence that he called "our ancient faith" and "my ancient faith" in his 1854 speech on the Kansas-Nebraska Act.

# Chapter 5

# THE GETTYSBURG ADDRESS

𝒯he Gettysburg Address is a succinct version of ideas Lincoln expressed as an advocate of the Declaration of Independence and the Union in previous speeches during and after the ideological wars of the 1850s that finally erupted into civil war. The stage for his famous address was set on the first three days of July in 1863 when a major battle of that war was fought near Gettysburg, Pennsylvania. Over fifty thousand men died in that battle—twenty-three thousand Union soldiers and twenty-eight thousand Confederates. After three days of intense fighting in summer heat and humidity, both sides were exhausted and stunned by their losses, especially the South. As a result, on 4 July General Robert E. Lee withdrew what remained of his Confederate forces and began the long march back to Southern territory. General George Meade, commander of the Union army, did not pursue. If he had, he could have attacked Lee and his army when they were confined to a poor defensive position for several days by a flooded river, which Lee did not cross until 14 July—ten days after he disengaged his troops at Gettysburg.[1] In a letter to Meade that was never sent, Lincoln maintained that an aggressive and prompt attack by Meade would "have ended the War."[2] Lincoln was probably right and he never forgave Meade for his omission, especially because, as Gerald J. Prokopowicz stated, Lincoln wanted the Army of the Potomac "to follow" Lee, "attack him, cut him off from his base, and destroy him," ever since Lee had marched his army "north into Maryland" and finally into Pennsylvania in June of 1863.[3]

Apart from Meade's egregious mistake, Lincoln was highly pleased with the battle. It gave the North a key victory that kept Confederate troops from invading Washington. The crowd that serenaded the White House on 7 July in celebration of that victory was also pleased. In a brief speech addressing the crowd, Lincoln once again referred to the principles of the Declaration of Independence in a way that gave a hint of what was to come in his Gettysburg Address a few months later:

> How long ago is it?—eighty odd years—since on the fourth of July for the first time in the history of the world a nation by its representatives, assembled and declared as a self-evident truth that "all men are created equal." [Cheers] That was the birthday of the United States of America.[4]

He went on to point out that on the "Fourth of July just passed," those in "Rebellion," whose purpose was to "overthrow the principle that all men were created equal," had "'turned tail' and run." This, he concluded, "is a glorious theme, and the occasion for a speech, but I am not prepared to make one worthy of the occasion."[5]

For the next four and a half months Lincoln had time to prepare a speech that was more than "worthy of the occasion." He delivered it at Gettysburg on 19 November in a ceremony commemorating those who died there in early July. Ironically, even though that speech became enshrined in America, Lincoln was not the principal speaker at Gettysburg. That honor went to Edward Everett, the distinguished senator, abolitionist, minister, scholar, and president of Harvard University. Lincoln was invited to make a few remarks after Everett, who spoke for nearly two hours, which was expected in those days. An accomplished orator, Everett performed magnificently. He received a tremendous ovation. In stark contrast, Lincoln delivered his comments—only two hundred and seventy-two words —in less than three minutes. The crowd gave light and scattered applause.[6] Lincoln interpreted this as disapproval and "is reported to have whispered" that his speech had failed as he walked away "from the edge of the platform."[7] However, it was Lincoln, not Everett, who captured the significance of the battle, the civil war, and indeed the nation itself with his brief address. Yet despite his sage remarks, one of them—"The world will little note nor long remember what we say here"—completely missed the mark. Although this comment applies to Everett's oration, Lincoln's speech became immortal in the annals of America. It has been memorized by generations of schoolchildren and is firmly embedded in the American mind.

The emotional impact of the Gettysburg Address on Americans is enormous. It still brings tears to the eyes of many. Yet the ideas contained in that speech were so succinctly expressed that it is not always clear exactly what they were. Therefore, in order to fully understand Lincoln's famous address, some of its statements need to be considered in the light of his more elaborate comments made previously on the same subjects. Indeed, the Gettysburg Address without such clarification contains contradictions. It mentions the values of Freedom and Equality by quoting the word "Liberty" and the phrase "all men are created equal" from the Declaration of Independence. These two values, however, can conflict with each other depending on their meaning. In addition, the statement "this nation *under God* [my italics] shall have a new birth of freedom" can be contradictory to the idea of "government of the people, by the people, for the people." A nation "under God" is often interpreted as a theocracy where people are ruled by God, His agents, or His revealed law contained in scripture. "Government of the people, by the people, for the people," on the other hand, is democracy or rule by humans and human-made law. The questions then arise, what did Lincoln mean by these phrases? Was he oblivious to their possible conflict or were they reconciled by the meaning he ascribed to them? Moreover, apart from these questions, Lincoln's references to "a new nation" and "testing whether that nation . . . can long endure" need to be considered in order to determine what he meant by them. It also needs to be determined whether some of the basic ideas and "values" of American civilization were "created by the Gettysburg Address," as Garry Wills maintains, or whether those ideas and values came from Jefferson in the Declaration of Independence.[8]

## LIBERTY AND EQUALITY

Many early modern English political thinkers defined "Liberty" in terms of what must be absent in order to have it, which is a negative definition of "Liberty." John Locke, for example, who was a major influence on Jefferson and the Declaration, used this approach in defining "Liberty" both implicitly and explicitly.[9] In his *Essay concerning Human Understanding* (book 2, chapter 21, "Of Power") he wrote that "*Liberty* . . . is the power a Man has to do or forbear doing any particular Action, according as its doing or forbearance has the actual preference in the Mind, which is the same thing as to say, according as he himself *wills* it."[10] This implies that if there is no external restraint or compulsion as well as physical incapacity obstructing one's power to perform an act such as moving or not moving one's hand as one wills, then one has liberty to move that hand. Locke stated this explicitly when he said, "Our *Idea* of Liberty reaches as far as that Power [to move one's hand], and no farther. For wherever restraint comes to check that Power, or compulsion takes [it] away . . . Ability on either side to act, or to forbear acting, there *liberty*, and our Notion of it, presently ceases."[11] Of the absence of physical disability being necessary to have "Liberty" or "Power" to move one's hand, Locke said: "If during the rest of my Hand, it be seized by a sudden Palsy, . . . that operative Power [to move the hand] is gone, and with it my Liberty."[12] With these statements, Locke specified exactly what must be absent in order to have "Liberty," which is a negative definition of "Liberty."

Jefferson himself used this Lockean definition of "Liberty" when he said, "Liberty is 'unobstructed action according to our will.'"[13] He went on to make a distinction between "Liberty" in this negative sense and "rightful Liberty," which he defined as the "'unobstructed action according to our will, within the limits drawn around us by the equal rights of others.'"[14] To put it another way, "rightful Liberty" is liberty that respects the right of "Liberty" in others while simultaneously being free from obstructions. Locke placed a similar moral restriction on "Liberty" in his *Second Treatise on Government*, which Jefferson read carefully and used extensively in the Declaration of

Independence,[15] where he said "Liberty" is the freedom "to follow my own Will in all things, where the Rule prescribes not; and not to be subject to the inconstant uncertain, unknown, Arbitrary Will of another Man."[16] The "Rule" Locke referred to is the moral law of nature, and he maintained that law made by the "legislative Power" of government had to be in accord with the moral law of nature to be legitimate.[17] Thus both natural and legislated law put humans under moral restraints in Locke.

Lincoln expressed similar ideas on negative "Liberty" in the "rightful" sense in terms of slavery when he defined democracy: "As I would not be a *slave*, so I would not be a *master*. This expresses my idea of democracy. Whatever differs from this, to the extent of the difference, is not democracy."[18] Implied in this definition of democracy is the idea that the antithesis of slavery, which is liberty, is contingent upon everyone not making a slave of any other human because slavery is compelling someone to move their bodies or refrain from moving them according to someone else's will. Therefore, Lincoln's definition of democracy is in effect a negative definition of Liberty since it says being a master or slave is what must be absent before you can have "Liberty" and true democracy in the sense of everyone having the unimpeded power to move according to their will. Considering Lincoln's definition of liberty and democracy, the Gettysburg Address—with its last sentence reference to "government of the people by the people, for the people" or democracy and its first sentence reference to a nation or government "conceived in Liberty"—is clearly antislavery without mentioning slavery. Lincoln made no specific reference to slavery at Gettysburg because, as Barry Schwartz put it, "Lincoln knew" that "Americans did not feel strongly enough about slavery to sacrifice their children's lives" in order to end it. Therefore, he was not about to state explicitly that he was against slavery or that the war was against slavery, as he did subsequently in his Second Inaugural Address, as we shall see in the next chapter, especially when among those whose loved ones and friends had recently died at Gettysburg.[19]

Having given a negative definition of "Liberty," the question arises, what is "Liberty" in the positive sense? Isaiah Berlin says it is self-realization or self-actualization,[20] meaning the use of "Liberty" or power to move or act in a way that realizes or actualizes one's aspirations and human faculties—faculties that can be used to attain one's aspirations. That Lincoln had this positive definition of "Liberty" is seen in his speech to the troops of the 166th Ohio Regiment in 1864:

> I am a living witness that any one of your children may look to come here [to the presidency] as my father's child has. It is in order that each of you may have through this free government which we have enjoyed, an open field and a fair chance for your industry, enterprise and intelligence; that you may all have equal privileges in the race of life, with all its desirable human aspirations. It is for this the struggle should be maintained. . . . The nation is worth fighting for, to secure such an inestimable jewel.[21]

In other words, "Liberty" meant any child could dream what he or she would like to be—such as the president of the United States— and then use their "industry, enterprise and intelligence" to actualize or develop these faculties and then use them to guide their "Liberty" or "Power" to move or act in a manner that would realize their dream. Lincoln himself, as he stated, was an example of this. From youth, he was ambitious and dreamed of being important.[22] He educated himself, became a lawyer, and entered the political arena in order to realize his dream. Of course, all are not equal in "industry, enterprise and intelligence" or physical strength. Yet "all," as Lincoln stated here, should "have equal privileges in the race of life." In other words, "all" should have equal "Liberty" or opportunity in the system of law prescribed by the Constitution to attain their dreams "or desirable human aspirations" subject to their own limited abilities or powers to act or move in an intelligent effective way. With his reference to "free government," Lincoln was in effect stating that no human's movements should be obstructed or compelled by government or any humans or human institutions, for that matter, thereby robbing them of their "Liberty" or "birthright" to pursue their human "aspirations" according to their own will and abilities. Lincoln's reference to the "race of life" demonstrates his awareness that people have unequal power or ability to move effectively even when they enjoy freedom from restraints, compulsions, and physical disabilities, which is obvious in any competitive "race" such as a running race.

Jefferson, too, had this positive self-actualization or self-realization concept of "Liberty" as is seen in his *Notes on the State of Virginia* when commenting on the purpose of public education that he proposed for his state in 1779:

> The first stage of this education . . . wherein the great mass of the people will receive their instruction, the principal foundations of future order will be laid. . . . Their memories may here be stored with the most useful facts from Grecian, Roman, European and American history. The first elements of morality too may be instilled unto their minds; such as, when further developed as their judgments advance in strength, may teach them how to work out their own greatest happiness, by shewing that it does not depend on the condition of life in which chance has placed them, but is always the result of a good conscience, good health, occupation, and freedom in all just pursuits.[23]

With education, according to this statement, a human being can "work out their own greatest happiness" resulting from their "freedom" to choose from among "all just pursuits" plus their "Liberty" or power to move in a way that would enable them to attain what they chose. In other words, with education and "Liberty" individuals can dream what they want to be and then use their reason, "as their judgments advance in strength," and their freedom of movement to actualize their dream, subject of course to their limited power to move in a rational way. Indeed, Jefferson—like Lincoln, who said that men, according to the Declaration of Independence, are not equal in "color, size, intellect, moral developments, or social capacity"[24]—acknowledged unequal capacities of intelligence and power in humans, which resulted in unequal ability to move effectively.[25]

What Lincoln's definition of democracy and statement to the troops of the 166th Ohio Regiment in 1864 did, however, was to state that he believed the "Liberty" and "all men are created equal" or equality phrase of the Declaration of Independence, which he quoted at Gettysburg, meant that "all men" were equally created with the *right* of "Liberty" or "Power" of movement. Yet simultaneously, they were subject to their own unequal limitations of that "Power" plus moral restraints born of their obligation to respect the right of "Liberty" in others. His ideas on "Liberty," and Equality therefore, were in accord with those of Locke, Jefferson, and the Declaration. Gabor Boritt maintains that Lincoln's "central idea" of equality emphasized "equality of opportunity to get ahead (economically with one's own labor and industry) in life" and that this "meaning he gave to Jefferson's words [in the Declaration] was scarcely identical with Jefferson's own."[26] It seems clear, however, that Jefferson's meaning of equality also includes "equality of opportunity to get ahead in life." Jefferson said as much in his Second Inaugural Address when he wished—and hoped that all Americans wished—that "equality of rights be maintained" as well as "the state of property, equal or unequal, which results to every man from his own industry."[27] There is little doubt that Lincoln had read Jefferson's Inaugural Addresses.[28]

Lincoln made a statement containing similar ideas on "Liberty" and Equality in a speech delivered at Chicago in 1858 that says much about his views on religion, morality, and the Declaration of Independence:

> My friend has said to me that I am a poor hand to quote Scripture. I will try it again, however. It is said in one of the admonitions of the Lord, "As your Father in Heaven is perfect, be ye also perfect." The Savior, I suppose, did not expect that any human creature could be perfect as the Father in Heaven; but . . . He set up that as a standard, and he who did most towards reaching that standard, attained the highest degree of moral perfection. So I say in relation to the principle that *all men are created equal* [my italics], let it be as nearly reached as we can. If we cannot give *freedom* [my italics] to every creature, let us do nothing that will impose slavery upon any other creature. [Applause.][29]

Here, in addition to the values of "freedom" or Liberty and "all men are created equal" or Equality, Lincoln mentions two methods of attaining as much moral perfection as possible. The first is by following Jesus' instruction "As your Father in heaven is perfect, be ye also perfect," emphasized by Theodore Parker, as was mentioned in chapter 2. Although we cannot be as perfect as the "Father," according to Lincoln, those who work hard to be like the "Father" will attain the "the highest degree of moral perfection." The second method of attaining as much moral perfection as possible that Lincoln mentioned in this speech is to apply the same hard work ethic and dedication that one would apply to being "perfect" like the "Father" to the "principle that *all men are created equal* [my italics]" of the Declaration of Independence by extending "Liberty" or "freedom" to "every creature" as much "as we can." After this statement, Lincoln explained how we can do as much "as we can" by giving a negative definition of Liberty, or what must be absent before you can have it, similar to the one he used in his definition of democracy by stating: "Let us do nothing that will impose slavery on any other creature."

The effect of Lincoln's 1858 statement at Chicago was to put the methods of acquiring as much moral perfection "as we can" of both Jesus and the Declaration of Independence on equal terms. This is because the same moral effects can be attained by observing Jesus' moral commandments or respecting the rights of "Life, Liberty and the Pursuit of Happiness" of others. Indeed, Jesus' norms: "Thou shalt do no murder, Thou shalt not commit adultery, Thou shalt not steal, Thou shalt not bear false witness [Matthew 19:18]" is a negative definition of "Liberty" or what must be absent before you can have it. This is because the enjoyment of one's right of "Liberty" in the positive sense of power to move according to one's own will that would actualize one's faculties and realize one's aspirations is difficult or impossible if one is constantly in the presence of those who violate Jesus' moral norms by killing, committing adultery, stealing, and bearing false witness. One must, under such circumstance, constantly protect one's self and one's possessions, leaving little or no time to consider or perform actions that would actualize one's human faculties and realize one's aspirations. To put it another way, an effect of observing these Judeo-Christian moral norms is to respect the rights of "Life, Liberty and the Pursuit of Happiness" of others. Conversely, respecting those rights necessarily involves abiding by the aforementioned Judeo-Christian norms. Therefore, the moral methods of Jesus and the Declaration of Independence are similar or equal in that they lead to similar effects.

Although Lincoln's use of "Be ye perfect as your Father in Heaven" is Christian in the sense that it comes from Jesus, it is opposed to the original sin view of human nature of orthodox Christian doctrine both Protestant and Catholic. According to original sin, all humans are miserable sinners or morally tainted beings. Moreover, that tainted nature, which is inclined to sin, does not change, according to prominent Christian theologians both Protestant and Catholic.[30] Jesus dying on the cross merely atones or satisfies God's anger at all humans for the culpability they inherit from Adam and Eve because of their disobedience in the Garden of Eden. The moral flaws in human nature, however, that are caused by original sin remain, thereby making the attainment of moral perfection or even getting close to it by human effort alone without God's help impossible, as has been stated. Therefore, Lincoln's use of "Be ye perfect as your Father in Heaven" in Chicago, which says in effect that humans by their own efforts can attain a great deal of moral perfection, is alien to the doctrine of original sin held by eminent Christian theologians Catholic and Protestant. It harkens back to Pelagius,[31] who opposed Augustine's original sin view of human nature in the fourth century, and is completely in tune with the theology of Thomas Paine and Theodore Parker, who influenced Lincoln and rejected the doctrine of original sin. Indeed, Lincoln with his use of "Be ye perfect as your Father in Heaven," like Paine, Jefferson, and other deists as well as Parker, believed a high degree of moral perfection by human effort alone without any help from God is attainable. And, like most deists, Lincoln, Paine, Parker, and Jefferson made a distinction between much of what Jesus taught, such as "Be ye perfect as your Father in Heaven," and the doctrine that most Christians believed, such as original sin.

## "Under God" and "Of the People"

In the light of Lincoln's deistic religious views discussed in chapter 2, when he stated at Gettysburg "that this nation *under God* [my italics] shall have a new birth of freedom," he was referring to the deistic God of reason and freedom.[32] That God, as has been mentioned, allows individuals complete freedom or liberty to believe or disbelieve what they want in religion based on their own rational calculations and still attain salvation, since salvation is based on moral action, not grace and belief. In contrast, God in the form of Lord Jesus Christ, the second person of the Trinity, according to Christian orthodoxy both Catholic and Protestant, says everyone must believe a certain way and follow a certain path—His way and His path—to be saved. As Jesus said in John 14:6: "I am the way, the truth, and the life; no man cometh unto the Father, but by me," which Jefferson deleted when he edited the Gospels to bring them into accord with deism, as has been mentioned. Consistent with this one-way approach to salvation, Paul called himself "the slave of Jesus Christ" in the sense of being bound by Jesus' teachings and doctrines.[33] Indeed, the collar worn by many modern Christian clergymen, both Catholic and Protestant, is patterned after the Roman slave collar. It is symbolic of the slave relationship between Christ and His loyal followers or servants.

Being "under" a one-way "God" and a slave of God, however, is alien to "Liberty," both religious and political, as well as the "new birth of freedom" for the American "nation" that Lincoln referred to at Gettysburg. The deistic God, on the other hand, is a Transcendental Being in the sense that He is completely above and beyond humans who are "under" Him in this sense and not in the sense of being "under" His terrestrial jurisdiction and governance through His agents in the form of church, scripture, clergy, or an anointed king. Nor are humans, according to deism, "under" a rigid requirement that everyone must subscribe to a particular doctrinal belief system in order to be saved because the God of deism does not prescribe or insist that humans follow any doctrinal belief system, as has been mentioned. This interpretation of "under God" is not only consistent with the "Liberty" and the "new birth of freedom" that Lincoln mentioned at Gettysburg, but also his heterodox, deistic religious views, derived from reading Thomas Paine and Theodore Parker, as stated in chapter 2. Moreover, it is consistent with his democratic statement at Gettysburg "that the government of the people, by the people, for the people, shall not perish from the earth," a statement scholars have attributed to the influence of Parker, who used it or similar language several times in his writings.[34] Whether or not this phrase came from Parker, however, it can make sense only if "under God" meant the deistic God and not the God of orthodox Christianity, because the deistic God left humans alone to govern themselves once He created them. Indeed, the phrase "Government of the people, by the people, for the people" is opposed to Christian God-based political systems as a supporter of Charles I of England stated when he said God "hath expressed in Scripture that both Soveraignty and the person clothed with Soveraignty are *of him, by him and from him* immediately [my italics]."[35] The scriptural source of the Christian *of God, by God and from God* as the only source of governmental power is Jesus' comment to Pilate: "Thou couldest have no power *at all* against me, except were it given thee from above [John 19:11]" and Paul's statement, "There is no power but of God: the powers that be are ordained of God [Romans 13:1]."[36]

## "A NEW NATION"

When Lincoln stated in the first sentence of his Gettysburg Address: "Four score and seven years ago our fathers brought forth on this continent *a new nation* conceived in *Liberty* and dedicated the proposition that *all men are created equal* [my italics]," he was not just referring to a newly formed nation. He was referring to a "new" kind of nation based on the "Liberty" and "all men are created equal" or Equality—the ideals or values of his "ancient faith" or deism contained in the 1776 Declaration of Independence. Deism of course was ancient. It was as old as creation itself. Yet never before had any nation been founded on its egalitarian theology, a theology in which

God gave humans the freedom to govern themselves. It was in this sense that America was a "new nation" in 1776. The "new nation" idea of the Gettysburg Address was also expressed by Lincoln in his aforementioned statement to his White House serenaders on 7 July, a few months before his address at Gettysburg, when he stated that never before had any nation "in the history of the world" been formed by "representatives" of the people who "assembled and declared as a *self-evident* truth 'that *all men are created equal* [my italics].'" In other words, the God-given egalitarian values of the Declaration, the fact that the people's "representatives" "assembled and declared" those values, and the Declaration's idea that "governments are instituted among men" in order to "secure" the right of "Liberty" of each individual were what made the "new nation" new in the sense of a different kind of nation. This was the reason Lincoln said at Gettysburg that the power of government in this "new nation" was "of the people" and "by the people" and not of God or by God, either totally or partially, through His agents in the form of kings, magistrates, or clergymen or His revealed words and laws, as were other governments in the West in 1776.

Not only the Declaration of Independence and the Gettysburg Address specified a government that is founded and controlled by the people. The same idea is found in the preamble to the Constitution: "We, the people . . . do ordain and establish this Constitution for the United States of America." It is difficult to conceive just how radical these ideas were in 1776 or even in Lincoln's time. Yet the American Republic established in Revolutionary times was one of a kind then as it was in Lincoln's era. It was based on the principle that government derived its authority solely and wholly from the people. It was the power of the people below that could make or break their leaders via the ballot, not God, who many believed designated them from above. Lincoln was acutely aware of this distinction. He lived in close time proximity to the American Revolution, which enabled him to fully appreciate just how radical the theory and practice of American government was compared to other nations in the West that clung to values of class and privilege by birth—including hereditary monarchs who were ordained by God via the church and claimed to rule by His grace.

Because of the values of Liberty and Equality in the Declaration of Independence that were made part of the Constitution by adding the Bill of Rights, in Jefferson's and especially Lincoln's time there was little caste and privilege by birth in America compared to Europe, apart from slavery. This attracted millions of European immigrants to the United States who were more than happy with "Liberty" in the sense of an equal chance to move by their own will subject to their own unequal power or ability to do so effectively. They were relieved to have comparatively little or no obstruction to their "Liberty" or power of movement from either an entrenched aristocracy or government. The huge liberating impact this concept and practice of "Liberty" had in Lincoln's time is often minimized today because many are inclined to think of "Liberty" as conflicting with "Equality" because of the inability of some to move effectively.[37]

## "TESTING WHETHER THAT NATION . . . CAN LONG ENDURE"

To Lincoln, the Civil War was fought primarily to preserve the Union or nation from disintegration, at least at the war's inception. The eradication of slavery, at that time, could not be expressed as Lincoln's goal since it was protected by the Constitution he had sworn to uphold. His antislavery references during the war, therefore, were for the most part implicit. For example, he continued to invoke the antislavery "ancient faith" of the Declaration of Independence. Yet he did so without specifically stating that the Declaration was antislavery as he had in the 1850s. This is seen in the first two sentences of the Gettysburg Address where he stated that the war was being fought to preserve the Union or nation on the basis of the moral idealism of the Declaration. Indeed, he stated that the war was "testing whether that nation" based on the idealism of the Declaration of Independence could survive or "long endure." Using biblical language to express time, the Gettysburg Address echoed the comments Lincoln made to his serenaders four and a half months earlier when he said the birthday of the United States was 4 July 1776:

Four score and seven years ago, our fathers brought forth on this continent a new nation, conceived in *Liberty*, and dedicated to the proposition that *all men are created equal*.

Now we are engaged in a great civil war, *testing whether that nation, or any nation so conceived and so dedicated, can long endure* [my italics].[38]

From the beginning of the war Lincoln maintained that the Confederate States had abandoned the Declaration's principles of Liberty and Equality and the Constitution's "We, the people" principle of democratic government by adopting and acting on the doctrine of state sovereignty. Those who subscribed to this doctrine argued that the people did not form the federal government. Rather, it was the result of a compact between individual sovereign states. This doctrine maintains that each state, because of its sovereignty, can withdraw from the Union and thereby break the compact forming the federal government without the consent of the people, the other states party to the compact, or the federal government itself.

Senator Daniel Webster of Massachusetts had argued against state sovereignty doctrine in his response to Senator Robert Hayne of South Carolina in their famous debate in 1830. Lincoln considered that response one of the greatest speeches ever made.[39] There, Webster maintained that the federal government was based on the authority of the people, not a compact between the states. He further maintained that any disputes between the states and the federal government, according to the Constitution, would be judged by the federal government. As he put it in the style of the nineteenth-century orator that he was:

The People, then, Sir, erected this Government. They gave it a Constitution, and in that Constitution they have enumerated the powers which they bestow on it. They have made it a limited Government. They have defined its authority. They have restrained it to the exercise of such powers as are granted; and all others, they declare, are reserved to the States or the People. But, sir, they have not stopped here. . . . No definition can be so clear, as to avoid possibility of doubt; no limitation so precise, as to exclude all uncertainty. Who, then, shall construe this grant of the People? Who shall interpret their will, where it may be supposed they have left it doubtful? With whom do they repose this ultimate right of deciding on the powers of the Government? Sir, they have settled all this in the fullest manner. They have left it, with the Government itself, in its appropriate branches [Webster subsequently quoted the constitutional provision *"that the Judicial power shall extend to all cases under the Constitution and Laws of the united states"* to prove this point]. Sir, the very chief end, the main design, for which the whole Constitution was framed and adopted, was to establish a Government that should not be obliged to act through State agency, or depend on State opinion and State discretion. The People had had quite enough of that kind of Government, under the Confederacy [Articles of Confederation]. Under that system, the legal action— the application of law to individuals, belonged exclusively to the States. Congress could only recommend—their acts were not of binding force, till the States had adopted and sanctioned them. Are we in that condition still? Are we yet at the mercy of State discretion, and State construction? Sir, if we are, then vain will be our attempt to maintain the Constitution under which we sit.[40]

That Lincoln subscribed to Webster's idea that the federal government was based on the people's authority is seen in many of his speeches. In his First Inaugural, for example, he referred to "my rightful masters, the American People."[41] Then, in his special message to Congress of 4 July 1861, he stated that the Southern states, by acting on the state sovereignty principle as opposed to the people-based principle of the federal government, had regressed to an aristocratic oligarchy where a few, who deemed themselves superior to others, governed. He did this by asking a series of rhetorical questions in which his commitment to the people-based arguments of Webster was obvious:

Our adversaries have adopted some Declaration of Independence; in which, unlike the good old one, penned by Jefferson, they omit the words "all men are created equal." Why? They have adopted a temporary national constitution, in the preamble of which, unlike our good old one, signed by Washington, they omit "We, the People," and substitute "We, the deputies of the sovereign and independent States." Why? Why this deliberate pressing out of view, the rights of men, and the authority of the people?[42]

To Lincoln, this undemocratic, aristocratic, and even despotic element introduced by the Confederate government made the war "essentially a People's contest" with the Union on the side of the "People" fighting to maintain "in the world, that form, and substance of government, whose leading object is, to elevate the condition of men . . .—to clear the paths of laudable pursuit for all—to afford all . . . a fair chance, in the race of life."[43] In other words, the North was fighting for "Liberty" or the enjoyment of the unobstructed right of movement for all individuals subject only to their limited power to move and their refraining from acts that interfere with the "Liberty" of others. The South on the other hand was fighting for privilege, caste, and despotism where many people, because of slavery, did not get "a fair chance" to compete in life or even compete at all because they were denied the power to move according to their own will. Therefore, a principal issue of the war or one thing it was "testing," as Lincoln stated at Gettysburg, was whether the American continent would have a republican democracy in accordance with the Declaration of Independence or an aristocratic despotism, which would have been the case with the South if the South had won the war, in Lincoln's view.

Related to this issue and at the heart of the "testing" aspect of the war, according to Lincoln, was whether or not republican governments like America's were too weak and thereby flawed to "long endure," as he mentioned at Gettysburg. He maintained that the Union began with the Continental Congress in 1774—two years before the nation began with the Declaration of Independence.[44] The Constitution of 1789, therefore, did not give birth to the Union. Its purpose was "to form a more perfect Union" and to "secure the blessings of liberty" as its preamble states and thereby give all "a fair chance, in the race of life." Apart from the Bill of Rights, the Constitution accomplished this by distributing political power equally among three branches of government—the legislative, executive, and judiciary. In addition, it left considerable power with each of the states. This division of political power was designed to prevent the rise of tyrants with a monopoly of political power, or "absolute Despotic" power, as Jefferson described it in the Declaration of Independence, because experience in Europe and colonial America demonstrated such power was sooner or later used to take away the "Liberty" of the people.

The outbreak of the Civil War, however, made it obvious that this arrangement of power left the federal government too weak to hold a nation of individual states together, especially if it was interpreted as giving any state or several of them together the sovereign power to leave the nation. In fact, according to Lincoln, this interpretation cast a huge shadow of doubt not only on the continued existence of the American Republic but on any republic. As he put it in his 4 July 1861 special message to Congress, this was an issue that

> presents to the whole family of man, the question, whether a constitutional republic, or democracy—a government of the people, by the same people—can, or cannot, maintain its territorial integrity, against its own domestic foes. It presents the question, whether discontented individuals, too few in numbers to control administration, according to organic law, in any case, can always, upon the pretences made in this case, or on any other pretences, or arbitrarily, without any pretence, break up their Government, and thus practically put an end to free government upon the earth. It forces us to ask: "Is there, in all republics, this inherent, and fatal weakness?" Must a government, of necessity, be too *strong* for the liberties of its own people, or too *weak* to maintain its own existence?[45]

To Lincoln, as he implied here, the Confederacy of states was led by a minority of "discontented individuals, too few in number to control administration" of the federal government with the ballot. Many of these individuals were in South Carolina and had vehemently opposed Lincoln in the election of 1860. Moreover, they were the ones responsible for the attack on Fort Sumter that started the war. Their purpose was of course to split the Union.[46] And, if the South won the war, reasoned Lincoln, it would encourage other "discontented" individuals to act similarly in the future and thereby make a lasting nation based on the principles of the Declaration of Independence and the majority principle of "We, the people" in the federal constitution impossible. Implicitly echoing Webster's constitutionally based "Popular Government, founded in popular election" theme,[47] Lincoln expressed ideas similar to these in his 4 July 1861 speech to Congress:

> Ballots are the rightful, and peaceful, successors of bullets; and . . . when ballots have fairly, and constitutionally, decided, there can be no successful appeal, back to bullets; there can be no successful appeal, except to ballots themselves, at succeeding elections. Such will be a great lesson of peace [brought about by a Union victory in the war]; teaching men that what they cannot take by an election, neither can they take by war.[48]

In his First Inaugural, Lincoln had argued in much the same way by describing the behavior of the seceding states as a recipe for anarchy on one hand or despotism on the other—anarchy, because it made a mockery of federal governmental power by encouraging minority factions to go their own way if they disagreed with the majority, and despotism, since it tended to make minorities insist on their own way against the majority, which, if carried to extremes, could lead to a powerful minority or even a powerful individual dictating to everyone else. To avoid either anarchy or despotism, Lincoln, echoing Webster,[49] argued that logic dictated that the only "true sovereign" in a republic of "free people," or more specifically the republic of the United States, was the majority of the American people:

> The central idea of secession [by any of the states], is the essence of anarchy. A majority, held in restraint by constitutional checks, and limitations, and always changing easily, with deliberate changes of popular opinions and sentiments, is the only true sovereign of a free people. Whoever rejects it, does, of necessity, fly to anarchy or to despotism. Unanimity is impossible; the rule of a minority, as a permanent arrangement, is wholly inadmissible; so that, rejecting the majority principle, anarchy, or despotism in some form, is all that is left.[50]

Again echoing Webster,[51] Lincoln argued in his First Inaugural that even if the Confederacy won the war, by establishing a precedent with minority-led secession, it would have sown the seeds of its own destruction:

> If a minority . . . will secede rather than acquiesce [to the majority], they make a precedent which, in turn, will divide and ruin them; for a minority of their own will secede from them, whenever a majority refuses to be controlled by such minority. For instance, why may not any portion of a new confederacy, a year or two hence, arbitrarily secede again, precisely as portions of the present Union now claim to secede from it. All who cherish disunion sentiments, are now being educated to the exact temper of doing this. Is there such perfect identity of interests among the [Confederate] States to compose a new Union, as to produce harmony only, and prevent renewed secession?[52]

## CALHOUN AND THE TESTER'S IDEOLOGY

The Confederate States, which were "testing whether" the "nation" would "long endure" with war, got their state sovereignty ideology from John C. Calhoun, who Ross Lence described as the "foremost intellectual spokesman of the South" right up to "the outbreak of the Civil War."[53] Born in 1782 of Scots-Irish parents, Calhoun became South Carolina's leading politician and a major figure in national politics. After serving in the state legislature, he was elected US congressman in 1810. He then became secretary of war to President James Monroe, where he served from 1817 to 1825; then vice president under John Quincy Adams and Andrew Jackson from 1825 to 1832, when he resigned to take Robert Hayne's seat in the Senate where he served from 1832 to 1844; then secretary of state to President John Tyler from 1844 to 1845; then senator again from 1845 until he died in 1850. He was also a presidential candidate in 1821 and remained a contender for that office in all elections up to and including the 1848 election.[54]

In 1828, while vice president under Adams, Calhoun anonymously wrote his *Exposition and Protest* for South Carolina that justified and explained the doctrine of interposition or nullification of federal law by a state and even its secession from the Union. The *Exposition* was written in protest of the federal government's Abominable Tariff laws. Southerners hated those laws because they protected Northern manufacturing interests at the expense of Southern farming interests by increasing the cost of European goods, which Southerners purchased in substantial quantities. Although it was rumored that Calhoun himself had written the *Exposition*, that rumor was not confirmed until 1832. This discovery infuriated Jackson, who aggressively opposed nullification and secession and therefore saw as betrayal his vice president's anonymous and sometimes not so anonymous opposition to his own views and policy. This fury, when added to the fact that Jackson had discovered that Calhoun, while serving as Monroe's secretary of war, had advocated disciplinary action against Jackson for invading Florida without authorization, led to Calhoun's resignation. After that Calhoun became a dedicated and outspoken opponent of "King Andy."[55]

Ironically, Calhoun's ideas on nullification and secession came from New England Federalists, who had been traditional advocates of strong central government. However, many Federalists became disgruntled after the election of 1800 in which the opposition party, led by Thomas Jefferson, won the presidency. The Federalists despised Jefferson and his ideas on limited government and separation of church and state.[56] Some were so disgruntled that they began to manifest a "small-town, localist, anti-national sentiment, combined with skepticism of numerical majorities." These ideas had become "popular in certain parts of New England" and, as Lence stated, "Yale University had become the intellectual center for these ideas."[57] These ideas culminated in a New England Federalist movement to secede from the Union, led by Governor Timothy Pickering of Massachusetts. The movement was strengthened by the trade embargo of 1807 and War of 1812, which disrupted New England's trading interests. Prominent Federalists John Quincy Adams, Josiah Quincy, Fisher Ames, Joseph Story, George Cabot, and Elbridge Gerry supported the movement.[58]

Calhoun graduated Phi Beta Kappa from Yale in 1804 and then studied law at Litchfield, Connecticut. Staunch Federalist Timothy Dwight, then president of Yale, was an enormous influence on Calhoun, as were two Federalists from Litchfield, Judges Tappin Reeve and James Gould. All three men condemned the principle of majority rule in Jeffersonian politics.[59] Their impact on Calhoun is seen in his *Disquisitions on Government*, a work on political theory published posthumously in 1852 that explains his idea of "concurrent majority," which holds that a majority of states could not pass law binding on any state without the concurrence of that state. However, Calhoun expressed similar ideas long before his *Disquisitions* in his speeches and writings—especially in his *Exposition* of 1828. Those ideas became the basis of South Carolinian Robert Hayne's arguments in his famous 1830 debate in the Senate with Massachusetts' Daniel Webster.[60] As vice president at that time, Calhoun could not participate in the debate because of his obligation to preside over the Senate. Later, however, when senator, he did debate Webster and, according to August Spain, "gave the great orator the forensic lacing of his life."[61]

The *Exposition*'s condemnation of majority rule is found where Calhoun stated that the nation was divided into two sections— North and South—with the North dominating, indeed tyrannizing the South with its majority:

> In a word, . . . the country is divided and organized into two great parties—the one sovereign and the other subject—bearing towards each other all the attributes which must ever accompany that relation, under whatever form it may exist. That our industry is controlled by many, instead of one—by a majority in Congress, *elected* by a majority in the community having a opposing interest, instead of *hereditary* rulers—forms not the slightest mitigation of the evil. In fact, instead of mitigating, it aggravates.[62]

The "evil" Calhoun referred to where the stronger would tyrannize the weaker was anarchy, which he claimed was caused by majority rule, and he cited a passage from Alexander Hamilton's *Federalist* 51 to support his claim.[63]

Calhoun did acknowledge that the US government provided some protection of the minority against the majority by dividing governmental power among the three branches of the government, thereby limiting governmental power. The limited powers of each branch were specifically delegated to it by the people under the Constitution. The powers not delegated were reserved to either the individual states or to the people themselves. Moreover, and more important to Calhoun and the South, Calhoun claimed that the federal and state governments had an obligation not to infringe on each other's powers.[64]

The problem was, however, which of the two governments, federal or state, had the right to judge whether the powers of either had been exceeded. The federal or general government claimed its Supreme Court had this right exclusively. If that were true, argued Calhoun, the individual states had no sovereignty: "The right of judging, in such cases, is an essential attribute of Sovereignty—of which the states cannot be divested without losing their sovereignty itself—and being reduced to a subordinate corporate condition."[65] Supreme judicial power in the federal government would in effect establish "a great consolidated government with unlimited powers," according to Calhoun. He maintained that with such power, the government would sooner or later "divest the States, in reality, of all their rights."[66] This is the reason Calhoun argued that individual states, as sovereign powers, had the right to judge whether or not the general government had exceeded its constitutionally designated powers as well as the right to veto or nullify any action judged to exceed those powers.[67]

In support of this interpretation, Calhoun quoted James Madison's and Thomas Jefferson's Virginia and Kentucky Resolutions written or sponsored by them in order to counter the repressive Alien and Sedition Acts of 1798 passed by Federalists in Congress and signed into law by President John Adams. Among other things, the Alien and Sedition Acts provided for jailing and or fining those who criticized the government. Madison, in the Virginia Resolutions, said that the Constitution of the United States was established by the individual sovereign states that ratified it. Therefore, these states, as sovereigns, had no tribunal "above their authority" to make ultimate judgments as to whether the Constitution was "violated" by the federal government. Jefferson, in the Kentucky Resolutions, argued similarly.[68]

The Abominable Tariff Acts, however, passed under John Quincy Adams's administration that caused Calhoun to write his *Exposition*, were not the primary issue with him and the South. Slavery was, and the conclusions of the *Exposition* were applied to maintain that evil institution, which was, little by little, becoming morally offensive to more and more Northerners and some Southerners too, thanks in no small part to Lincoln's efforts, as was seen in the last chapter. Although the majority of Northerners had not yet condemned slavery, Northern public opinion was gradually moving in that direction. Calhoun and slavery advocates in the South feared this trend because the North was more populous than the South and its majority threatened the institution of slavery, which was the basis of the South's agrarian economy.

To Calhoun, the principal cause of moral condemnation of slavery was the "error" that Thomas Jefferson placed in the Declaration of Independence, contained in the phrase "all men are created equal" and "endowed by their creator with certain unalienable rights, among which are Life, Liberty, and the Pursuit of Happiness." In his speech on the Oregon Bill of 1848, Calhoun described Jefferson's "error" and its impact:

> We now begin to experience the danger of admitting so great an error to have a place in the declaration of our independence. For a long time it lay dormant; but in the process of time it began to germinate, and produce its poisonous fruits. It had a strong hold on the mind of Mr. Jefferson, the author of that document, which caused him to take an utterly false view of the subordinate relation of the black to the white race in the South; and to hold, in consequence, that the former, though utterly unqualified to possess liberty, were as fully entitled to both liberty and equality as the latter; and that to deprive them of it was unjust and immoral. To this error, his proposition to exclude slavery from the territory northwest of the Ohio may be traced, and to that the Ordinance of '87 and through it the deep and dangerous agitation which now threatens to ingulf, and will certainly ingulf, if not speedily settled, our political institutions, and involve the country in countless woes.[69]

In his argument that the "all men are created equal" phrase of the Declaration was Jefferson's "error," Calhoun referred to the creationist theory of the Bible by stating: "All men are not created" let alone created equal. He pointed out that "according to the Bible, only two, a man and woman [Adam and Eve], ever were [created], and of these one [the woman] was pronounced subordinate to the other."[70] Everyone else "came into the world by being born, and in no sense . . . [were] either free or equal."[71] Infants, he argued, were "destitute alike of the capacity of thinking and acting, without which there can be no freedom."[72] And, when it came to human equality, Calhoun said, "They [humans] are not so in any sense," especially when it came to liberty, which he argued, "must necessarily be very unequal among different people, according to their different conditions."[73] If, for example, humans were "ignorant, stupid, debased, corrupt, exposed to violence from within and danger from without," these conditions required that government have more power and the people "less and less" liberty. Indeed, if the people suffered from these conditions in the extreme, according to Calhoun, this would necessarily result in "absolute and despotic power . . . on the part of government, and [make] individual liberty extinct."[74] Therefore, Calhoun concluded: "liberty and equality" are not individual rights but "high prizes to be won"—prizes "that can be bestowed on our race."[75] With these arguments and reference to "our race," Calhoun excluded blacks from having liberty and equality, the exact opposite of what Jefferson did in his anti–slave trade, antislavery passages of the Declaration of Independence deleted by the Continental Congress, where he wrote that blacks have "the most sacred rights of life & liberty" equally with whites, as was mentioned in chapter 1.

By stating that blacks were "utterly unqualified to possess liberty" and that only the white race could win or earn it, Calhoun established a basis for concluding that black slavery was not "an evil," as the abolitionists claimed, but "far otherwise."[76] It was, in fact, "a good" thing because, as he rationalized:

Never before has the black race of Central Africa, from the dawn of history to the present day, attained a condition so civilized and so improved, not only physically, but morally and intellectually. It came to us in a low, degraded, and savage condition, and in the course of a few generations it has grown up under the fostering care of our institutions [slavery], as reviled as they have been, to its present comparatively civilized condition.[77]

Here Calhoun unintentionally offered an argument for abolition. If freedom had to be earned and was not a God-given right, as he claimed in his efforts to refute the Declaration of Independence and Jefferson, had not blacks by their rapid improvement while slaves now earned their "liberty"?

What caused many if not most Southern whites to cling to black slavery was the perception that their very existence would be threatened without that institution. Calhoun cited two reasons for this perception. First, if slavery were abolished, he maintained that a race war would ensue, causing the genocide of either blacks or whites, or, as he put it, the "drenching of the country in blood, and extirpating one or the other of the races."[78] Second, he stated: "Be it [slavery] good or bad, it has grown up with our society and institutions, and is so interwoven with them, that to destroy it would be to destroy us as a people."[79] Both of these ideas were deep-seated in the minds of many Southern whites. They resulted in Southern determination to resist the rising ground swell of abolition sentiment in the North even to the extent of breaking the Union. Calhoun summed up this mind-set when he said, "Abolition and the Union can not coexist" and "We of the South will not, cannot, surrender our institutions [slavery]."[80] These statements were not dissimilar to those of Lincoln, who said the nation could not "endure, permanently half *slave* and half *free*" and "A house divided against itself cannot stand" in his famous "House Divided" speech of 1858. Yet Lincoln also believed that ultimately slavery had to be abolished and the Union preserved, which put his ideas on a collision course with those of Calhoun.[81]

Public opinion against slavery in the North, however, kept rising, and the South increasingly felt itself a tyrannized minority dominated by the free-state majority in the federal government it claimed was going beyond the limited delegated powers specified in the Constitution. In a statement of his view that federal and state governmental power would prevent each other from encroaching on one another, Calhoun emphasized that states could veto or nullify law passed by the federal government. However, that veto could then be nullified by an amendment to the federal constitution requiring ratification by "three fourths of the states." Yet even if it went that far, Calhoun maintained that individual states, as sovereign entities, could refuse to go along with the ratified amendment. Moreover, he maintained that such refusal would dissolve or sever ties with the Union, which was what gave individual states the "ultimate and highest power" over the federal government—the power to withdraw from the Union.[82]

Daniel Webster pointed out what would happen if either his ideas, which influenced Lincoln, or the opposing views of Calhoun, which influenced Hayne, prevailed when he said: "One of two things is true; either the laws of the Union are beyond the discretion, and beyond the control of the States; or else we have no Constitution of General Government, and are thrust back again to the days of the Confederacy [Articles of Confederation]."[83] In his First Inaugural Address, Lincoln echoed Webster:

> In 1787, one of the declared objects for ordaining and establishing the Constitution, was "*to form a more perfect union.*" But if destruction of the Union, by one, or by a part only, of the States, be lawfully possible, the Union is *less* perfect than before the Constitution, having lost the vital element of perpetuity. It follows from these views that no State, upon its own mere motion, can lawfully get out of the Union.[84]

Only a Union victory in the war, according to Lincoln, would resolve the dispute between these conflicting views of sovereignty and the meaning of the Declaration of Independence held by himself and most Northerners on the one hand and Calhoun and his followers in the South on the other hand and thereby save the Union and the Declaration's universal, none-are-excluded idealism. To put it another way, the "testing" of these different views of sovereignty and the Declaration was the Civil War, as Lincoln stated in the first lines he uttered at Gettysburg: "Four score and seven years ago our fathers brought forth on this continent, a new nation, conceived in Liberty and dedicated to the proposition that all men are created equal. Now we are engaged in a great civil war, *testing whether that nation, or any nation so conceived and so dedicated can long endure* [my italics]." Because the Union won the war, it settled the sovereignty issue permanently, and because the war contributed to the rising tide of abolition sentiment in the North that finally resulted in the Thirteenth Amendment to the Constitution that abolished slavery, it also settled the dispute over the meaning of the principles of the Declaration of Independence in favor of Jefferson's and Lincoln's all-inclusive meaning that extended to blacks rather than Calhoun's whites-only meaning.[85]

At the time of the Gettysburg Address, however, Union victory in the war was far from certain, largely because public support for the war was weakening in the Union due to the ever-increasing battle casualties like those at Gettysburg. Therefore, Lincoln needed to exhort the people to sustain their support and attain victory in the war. His forthcoming address at Gettysburg presented an opportunity to do just that and Lincoln took full advantage of that opportunity.

## Self-evident Truths, Propositions, and Axioms

Before analyzing Lincoln's exhortation at Gettysburg, the meaning of "self-evident" "truths," "propositions," and "axioms" needs to be clarified because Lincoln used these terms and there are conflicting views on their significance. Allen Guelzo argues that Lincoln had doubts regarding the Declaration's "self-evident" "truths" or principles of "Liberty" and Equality. This, however, does not seem plausible because if Lincoln had questioned the "truths" of the Declaration it would have placed him in a similar position to that of Calhoun and others who denied the "self-evident" truth "that all men are created equal" and "endowed by their Creator with" the "unalienable" right of "Liberty" in order to justify slavery. Lincoln was aware of Calhoun's attack on the Declaration and criticized him as the first to make such an attack.[86] Indeed, Lincoln was critical of anyone who questioned or denied the truth of the principles of the Declaration as is evidenced by his denunciation of Indiana Senator John Pettit for calling the Declaration a "self-evident lie," as was mentioned in the last chapter. Guelzo, in support of his argument, makes much of the fact that Lincoln used the word "proposition" at Gettysburg in referring to the "all men are created equal" phrase he quoted from the Declaration rather than the Lockean "self-evident" "truths" language Jefferson used in that document. Yet Lincoln used "self-evident truths" when referring to "all men are created equal" just four months earlier in his speech to his serenaders, as has been mentioned. This suggests that Lincoln used "self-evident" and "proposition" synonymously when referring to the principles of the Declaration. Morever, Guelzo seems to assume that all propositions have to be proved, which is not the case with "simpler propositions." In the last chapter it was pointed out that Lincoln, in his letter to Pierce and others, referred to "the principles of Jefferson" in the Declaration as the "simpler propositions of Euclid" that any "sane child" could "understand." Thus Lincoln stated that the propositions of the Declaration could be easily understood, which made them very much like or even the equivalent of Locke's "self-evident" truths, which, as Locke stated, "the Mind is at no pains of proving or examining, but perceives" as "Truth, as the Eye does light, only by being directed toward it."[87]

Lincoln went on to state in his letter to Pierce and others that since the "simpler propositions of Euclid" and the "principles" of Jefferson in the Declaration were the basis of Euclidean geometry and the morality of the Declaration of Independence respectively, a willful denial of those easily understood "propositions" and "principles" would make Euclidean geometry incomprehensible and the universal morality of the Declaration ineffective. With this analysis, as has been mentioned in the last chapter, Lincoln sounded like John Locke in his *Essay concerning Human Understanding*, where he said that one of the enemies of truth was the "Want of Will" to accept something that was true. Locke explained that if any truth did not "best suit" our "Prejudices, Lives and Designs" or interests, we often willfully deny it by turning our head away from it. To Locke as to Lincoln, in cases of such willful denial, the problem was not the inability to perceive a truth but rather a deliberate refusal to acknowledge it or something that proved it.[88]

Glen Thurow argues that Lincoln changed equality, one of the founding principles of the nation contained in the Declaration of Independence, from the category of "definitions and axioms," as he called them in his letter to Pierce and others, to that of propositions or a "proposition," as he stated in the Gettysburg Address. However, since a definition of the word "axiom" is "a proposition regarded as self-evident truth," Lincoln's change from axiom to proposition is of little or no significance. Thurow went on to state that Lincoln's change made equality "an end as well as the beginning" of the United States, which was something new to America. However, the Declaration itself makes equality an end because it states that "to secure" the individual "Rights" that "all men are created" equally with is one of the "ends" of government.[89]

## THE EXHORTATION AT GETTYSBURG

The Gettysburg Address in a fundamental respect was the culmination of Lincoln's many speeches invoking the values of the Declaration of Independence in the ideological war that took place in nineteenth-century America. Many who followed those speeches were, by the time of the Gettysburg Address, familiar with what Lincoln meant by the succinct terminology he used at Gettysburg because he had, in those speeches, elaborated on the ideas conveyed by that terminology. Therefore, at Gettysburg, Lincoln could concentrate on the organization and presentation of those ideas rather than on elaborating on what he meant. Indeed, the way he rationally organized, presented, and linked those ideas together, both implicitly and explicitly, is one of the principal factors contributing to the effectiveness of his famous address.

Lincoln had long maintained that the Union began with the Continental Congress in 1774, as has been mentioned. It was the Declaration of Independence of 1776, however, that gave birth to the nation and its principal values of Liberty and Equality. Lincoln made this clear in the opening lines of the Gettysburg Address delivered in November of 1863 where he quoted the "Liberty" and "all men are created equal" words of the Declaration: "Four score and seven years ago our fathers brought forth on this continent, a new nation conceived in *Liberty* and dedicated to the proposition that *all men are created equal* [my italics]." Therefore, the values of "Liberty" and Equality mentioned by Lincoln at Gettysburg were not, as Garry Wills asserts, "values created by the Gettysburg Address."[90] They were the values of the Declaration of Independence. Moreover, it is obvious that Lincoln's famous address was not made to create either the nation or its values. A principal reason it was made was to exhort the people to win the war in order to preserve the nation and the Declaration's values, as Lincoln succinctly and implicitly stated at Gettysburg with the second sentence he uttered there: "Now we are engaged in a great civil war testing whether that nation or any nation so conceived and so dedicated can long endure." These words were challenging the people to respond to the test. It was they who were being tested by the war, and Lincoln's challenge and exhortation of them to respond favorably to the test would become clear in his two-hundred-and-seventy-two-word speech.

Apart from the creation and preservation difference between the Declaration of Independence and the Gettysburg Address, they have four similarities. First, both were written in moments of crisis. Second, both are reasoned expressions of idealistic political philosophy. Third, and probably most important at the time they were written, both were justifications for war. Fourth, both were, and still are, manifestos or public declarations of national intentions, motives, and worldviews—a principal reason they have made such a huge and lasting impact on the American mind. Indeed, both have been and continue to be referred to again and again in order to clarify what the United States of America is, or should be.

The crisis in June and July of 1776, when the Declaration of

Independence was written, was of course the Revolutionary War between the thirteen British Atlantic colonies and England. That war began in the fall of 1775 with skirmishes at Lexington and Concord. After several months, Americans were in desperate need of foreign support. However, since there had been no formal pronouncement of separation from Great Britain by the colonies, the conflict was technically a civil war, making foreign support for the colonies amount to meddling in England's internal affairs. The Declaration of Independence removed that technicality. It announced to the world that all ties with the British government were severed by the colonies, indeed, that they were no longer colonies but a nation because of alleged injustices inflicted on colonial Americans enumerated in the Declaration. Therefore, it was the Declaration that formed the new American nation. Indeed, the Declaration marked the first time the name "UNITED STATES OF AMERICA" was officially used for the new nation.[91] As has been mentioned, this was the reason the Declaration of Independence was "the birthday of the United States of America," as Lincoln stated in his speech to his serenaders on 7 July 1863. Moreover, the Declaration announced that the American people would establish their own self-government in order "to secure" the God-given unalienable natural rights of individuals.[92] This was the idealistic political philosophy of the Declaration that claimed humankind was capable of self-government—a totally different worldview than the one prevailing in the West at the time, as has also been mentioned. In doing all of this, the Declaration provided a publicly stated manifesto or declaration of national intention, motive, and worldview.

The Declaration was also a justification for war in which Jefferson used the ideas of John Locke, who argued against "*Despotical Power*" or "Absolute, Arbitrary Power" because its absolute and arbitrary nature could be used to "take away" the lives of those subject to that "Power."[93] Despotic power is, therefore, opposed to self-preservation, which, as Locke stated, is "*the fundamental Law of Nature.*"[94] Locke maintained that, because this "Law" was the "Will of God," each person was duty "*bound to preserve himself*, and not to quit his Station willfully."[95] In other words, don't allow yourself to come under despotic power. When applying these ideas to would-be absolute sovereigns, Locke stated: "It being out of a Man's power so to submit himself to another, as to give him a liberty to destroy him; God and Nature never allowing a Man so to abandon himself, as to neglect his own preservation: And since a man cannot take away his own Life, neither can he give another power to take it."[96] To put it another way, to submit to an absolute sovereign has suicidal implications and suicide is against God's will. Therefore, everyone should continuously scrutinize their government, according to Locke, and if by "a long train of Abuses" or "*a long Train of Actings*" and "Pretences of one Kind, and Actions of another" it demonstrated that it was moving toward despotic power, the people had a duty to get rid of it—by force if necessary—and form a new one with safeguards against despotism for their future security.[97] The effect of these Lockean arguments in the *Second Treatise* was to justify preemptive war.[98]

These ideas are seen in the Declaration of Independence where Jefferson wrote: "But when a long Train of Abuses and usurpations, pursuing invariably the same Object, evinces a Design to reduce them [the people] under Absolute Despotism, it is their Right, it is their duty to *throw off* such Government, and to provide new Guards for their future security [my italics]."[99] Jefferson's use of "Design" or purpose to describe the British government's despotic intentions was in effect saying that Americans were not yet under "Absolute Despotism." Yet they still had a duty to "throw off" the British government because of the several actions listed in the Declaration committed by king and Parliament that were leading toward despotism. Lincoln's knowledge of the Declaration made him aware of its "throw off" provision. This is seen in his special message to Congress of 4 July 1861, where he stated "the Union *threw off* their old dependence [my italics]" on England,[100] thereby expressing himself in the unique "throw off" way Jefferson did in the Declaration.

The Gettysburg Address, like the Declaration, was also written at a crisis point in American history, but a crisis point that was quite different from the one in 1776. While the Declaration referred to the United States of America as a union of states or nation and justified preemptive war to establish that nation, the Gettysburg Address was written when several states had seceded from that nation in order to justify a war to keep that nation intact by preventing their secession. There is a touch of irony here. In the Civil War, the nation or union was in a similar position to England in 1776 when it fought to keep the colonies from forming a separate nation. However, there was also a huge difference in those positions. The colonies were subject to British rule without representation—one of the offenses listed in the Declaration. The white secessionists of the Southern slave states, however, not only had representation in Congress before they seceded but even more than the whites in the Northern free states that remained in the Union. The Constitution provided that slave states could count their nonvoting slave population in determining their number of representatives in Congress. This is the infamous provision that counted three-fifths of each slave as one white. Exactly how this favored white voters in the slave states of the South was explained by Lincoln in his Kansas-Nebraska Act speech of 1854:

> By the constitution, each State has two Senators—each has a number of Representatives; in proportion to the number of its people. . . . But in ascertaining the number of the people, for this purpose, five slaves are counted as being equal to three whites. The slaves do not vote; they are only counted and so used, as to swell the influence of the white people's votes. The practical effect of this is more aptly shown by a comparison of the States of South Carolina and Maine. South Carolina has six representatives, and so has Maine. . . . Thus in the control of the government, the two States are equals precisely. But are they in the number of their white people? Maine has 581,813—while South Carolina has 274,567. Maine has twice as many as South Carolina, and 32,679 over. Thus each white man in South Carolina is more than the double of any man in Maine. This is because South Carolina, besides her free people, has 384,984 slaves. The South Carolinian has precisely the same advantage over the white man in every other free State, as well as in Maine. . . . The same advantage, but not to the same extent, is held by all the citizens of the slave States, over those of the free. . . .[101]

An implication of this disparity of white representation between free and slave states was that if slavery was allowed to expand in the territories, which in turn became slave states, it would enable those slave states to attain a larger number of seats in the House compared to free states with equal white population. Moreover, if the slave population expanded rapidly in the territories that became states and the white population decreased, it is possible that the slave states could have eventually dominated the House of Representatives in the Congress of the United States with a minority of the white population—an injustice to the white population of the free states apart from the obvious injustice to blacks. Lincoln in effect pointed this out in his Kansas-Nebraska Act speech.

When arguing against secession, one of Lincoln's arguments was that each of the thirteen original states of the United States owed their existence as self-governing entities to the Union—the entity that fought and won the Revolutionary War. No individual state could have accomplished this by themselves, which Lincoln made clear in his 4 July 1861 message to Congress.[102] He also argued that if the Confederacy, which included several of the thirteen original states, had its way and withdrew from the Union, the Union itself that brought the Confederate states into being would disintegrate—another injustice according to Lincoln. It was of course the disintegration of the Union that was the crisis the nation and Lincoln, as its chief executive, faced with the outbreak of the Civil War. It was in the midst of this war brought on by this crisis that Lincoln gave his manifesto or public declaration at Gettysburg of the nation's intention, motive, and worldview. He did this succinctly with well-reasoned statements that included the nation's idealistic political philosophy contained in the Declaration of Independence and a justification for war, thereby paralleling at Gettysburg what Jefferson had done in the Declaration of Independence. As Lincoln put it in his immortal two hundred and seventy-two words delivered at Gettysburg:

> Four score and seven years ago our fathers brought forth on this continent, a new nation, conceived in Liberty, and dedicated to the proposition that all men are created equal.

Now we are engaged in a great civil war, testing whether that nation, or any nation so conceived and so dedicated, can long endure. We are met on a great battle-field of that war. We have come to dedicate a portion of that field, as a final resting place for those who here gave their lives that that nation might live. It is altogether fitting and proper that we should do this.

But, in a larger sense, we cannot dedicate—we cannot conse-crate—we cannot hallow—this ground. The brave men, living and dead, who struggled here, have consecrated it, far above our poor power to add or detract. The world will little note, nor long remember what we say here, but it can never forget what they did here. It is for us the living, rather, to be dedicated here to the unfin-ished work which they who fought here have thus far so nobly advanced. It is rather for us to be here dedicated to the great task remaining before us—that from these honored dead we take increased devotion to that cause for which they gave the last full measure of devotion—that we here highly resolve that these dead shall not have died in vain—that this nation, under God, shall have a new birth of freedom—and that government of the people, by the people, for the people shall not perish from the earth.[103]

The first paragraph, containing Lincoln's reference to the ide-alism of the Declaration of Independence, was one sentence, as was the first paragraph of the Declaration. In this paragraph-sentence, Lincoln described the "new nation" as "conceived" in or conceptu-alized in the minds of "our fathers" in the Declaration, especially Jefferson's mind, since Lincoln stated that Jefferson was the author of the Declaration, as was previously mentioned. Lincoln also spec-ified that "Liberty" or freedom to move without any impediment was a principle the "new nation" was "conceived in." He then used the word "dedicated" in reference to the Declaration's "proposition" that "all men are created equal," which was "simple" and "easily understood," as he described that proposition in his aforemen-tioned letter to Pierce and others.

The second paragraph, which elaborates on the first, consists of four sentences. In the first, Lincoln mentioned that the Civil War was a "testing" or survival test for the "new nation" or union as it was "conceived" and "dedicated." In other words, if the Confederacy won the war, the nation in its present form, governmental as well as territorial, would cease to exist. The surviving nations—the Union and the Confederacy if the Confederacy won the war—would continue to break apart every time any of their states had an agenda at odds with the majority of the Union or the Confederacy, according to Lincoln, as has been mentioned. Then, Lincoln again referred to dedication in his second paragraph, as he did in the first, but this time he was speaking of dedicating the graves of those who died at Gettysburg "that that nation might live."[104] Significantly, the Confederate dead were excluded in this statement because they were not fighting "that that nation might live." They were fighting to destroy "that nation" or union. Yet by not specifically excluding the Confederate dead, Lincoln gave the impression of standing above the conflict—transcending it—which was not the case. He was for Union victory because, in his view, only victory would preserve the Union and its unique form of government described by the Declaration of Independence referred to in the first paragraph.

Moving from the first to the second paragraph, there is a sequence of ideas linked by dedication. In fact, dedication is a principal theme of the Gettysburg Address. The opening lines of the first paragraph state that the nation was conceived in and dedicated to the Declaration's idealism. Then, in the second paragraph, Lincoln stated the Civil War was "testing" whether "any nation" could "long endure" the way the American nation was "conceived" and "dedicated." This was followed by stating the purpose of the commemoration ceremony at Gettysburg—the dedication of the graves of those who died to maintain the nation. Such a dedication was the appropriate or "fitting and proper" thing to do as Lincoln said at the end of the second paragraph.

Then, in the third and final paragraph, consisting of five sentences, Lincoln continued the dedication theme. There he argued that no living person or persons could appropriately dedicate "a portion" of the battlefield at Gettysburg "for those who here gave their lives that that nation might live." His reasoning was that those who fought for the Union at Gettysburg on the first three days of July in 1863 had already dedicated the ground at Gettysburg "far" more than anyone living could possibly do. With these lines, Lincoln de-emphasized the dedication ceremony at Gettysburg and simultaneously exalted those who died there. He thereby laid the foundation for what he really wanted to say at Gettysburg, which was what the living should be dedicated to. The living, he maintained, should be dedicated to "the unfinished work" in the war to preserve the Union according to the principles of the Declaration of Independence that those who died at Gettysburg had "thus far so nobly advanced." In other words, the living should now be as dedicated to fighting and winning the war as those who died at Gettysburg had been. Such dedication would give hope "that that nation," based on the principles of the Declaration of Independence, "might live."

Implicit in the words Lincoln uttered in his first sentence at Gettysburg—"our fathers who brought forth on this continent, a new nation"—is that those "fathers" brought that nation "forth" by fighting a long and bloody war—the Revolutionary War. More important, "our fathers" won that war and thereby established the nation. Without their victory there never would have been the "new nation" Lincoln mentioned in his first sentence at Gettysburg. With these words, Lincoln implicitly invoked the achievements of the Revolutionary warriors as examples to the living as he was invoking the achievements of the Union warriors who died at Gettysburg in the second and third paragraphs of his address. He was saying in effect that now it was up to the "living" to attain victory in the Civil War as the Revolutionaries had done in the Revolutionary War and the Union soldiers had done in the battle at Gettysburg in order that the "nation might live" or continue to exist. Victory alone could accomplish this. The attainment of victory by the living, therefore, was the "great task remaining before us," according to Lincoln at Gettysburg.

Lincoln then mentioned devotion in the third paragraph. As he put it, "from these honored dead" soldiers who died fighting to save the "new nation" at Gettysburg and thereby gave their "last full measure of devotion" to accomplish this, "we take increased devotion to that cause for which they gave the last full measure of devotion." Here, the "devotion" of the dead was being used by Lincoln to inspire similar "devotion" in the living. In all of these arguments, Lincoln was justifying the war. Indeed, he was doing more. He was exhorting the people in the Union to attain victory in the war.

Lincoln then moved from devotion to the "cause" of winning the war to save the Union to "resolve" to win that war when he said "we here highly resolve" that those Union soldiers who died at Gettysburg "shall not have died in vain," which they would have if the Union lost the war and thereby ceased to exist. Victory, therefore, was the only thing acceptable in the light of the sacrifice paid by those who died to save the Union at Gettysburg. What Lincoln did at Gettysburg, therefore, was effectively ratchet up his rhetoric from dedication to the "cause" of winning the war, to "devotion" to that "cause," and finally "resolve" in that "cause." Moreover, his call for "resolve," implicitly extended to abolition of slavery with his statement of resolve that "this nation, under God, shall have a new birth of freedom." Abolishing slavery would give that "new birth" and thereby bring America more in line with the deistic God-given principles of "Liberty" and Equality that extended to "all men" contained in "our ancient faith" or "my ancient faith," as Lincoln called the Declaration of Independence, because slavery so flagrantly violated those principles.

Significantly, Lincoln's last utterance at Gettysburg was yet another resolution to win the war, this time to ensure that the unique "government of the people, by the people, for the people"—described as "consent of the Governed" in the Declaration—"shall not perish from the earth." If the Confederacy had won the war and the Union was thereby split in two, it would have continued to split, in Lincoln's view, as he stated in his First Inaugural, as has been mentioned. This would have caused the nation's unique "of the people, by the people, for the people" form of government to "perish from the earth" because the parts that split off, all weakened as a result, would have been taken over or become puppets of the superior imperial powers of Europe. And, with his emphasis on the "people" with his "of the people, by the people, for the people" in his last words spoken at Gettysburg, Lincoln alluded to the Constitution and its "We, the people" principle of the preamble. His resolve, therefore, extended to upholding the Constitution—properly revised of course to exclude slavery. Indeed, his expression of resolve or resolution was intense as is seen in his phrase "We here *highly resolve* [my italics]," preceding all that was resolved.

Despite his use of "We" in the phrase "We here highly resolve," what Lincoln did at Gettysburg was to express his own resolve, intention, purpose, and objective for the Union, which he believed should be adopted by the nation. The Gettysburg Address was therefore his manifesto or declaration of national purpose and intention. It called for the sacrifice of blood and treasure in order to win the war and thereby preserve the nation as well as uphold and extend the principles of the Declaration of Independence. Yet in the months after he made his famous address, Lincoln became pessimistic about the war's outcome for two reasons. First, he became convinced that most people in the Union were not willing to make the sacrifices necessary to win the war. Second, and because of the first, he also became convinced that he and his agenda or manifesto calling for sacrifices, which was succinctly stated at Gettysburg, would be rejected when he ran for reelection in 1864 by his defeat in that election. He was wrong of course on both counts, and the Gettysburg Address that stated his agenda became an immortal manifesto of the nation enshrined alongside the Declaration of Independence, the original American manifesto, which contains the foundational "truths," principles, and values that Lincoln used so effectively at Gettysburg and throughout his struggle against slavery.

# Chapter 6

# THE SECOND INAUGURAL ADDRESS

*T*he main theme of Abraham Lincoln's Second Inaugural Address, delivered in March of 1865, was that God's will started the civil war as punishment for the injustice of slavery and would continue the war until there was total abolition of that evil institution. In this way, Lincoln used fear of God or vengeance of God theology to motivate abolition. This, along with the sermonlike characteristics of the Second Inaugural, has caused many to conclude that by the time Lincoln delivered that address he had become a mainstream Christian who believed in "providence" or "God is ordering human affairs" according to His will theology.[1] However, the providence theology that predominated in nineteenth-century America has theocratic implications opposed to democracy or "government of the people, by the people, for the people" that Lincoln championed at Gettysburg, as we shall see. Lincoln would have known this. He was able and willing to analyze theology and religions critically, having cultivated this capacity by reading and discussing Thomas Paine's and Theodore Parker's critical religious writings. In addition, he had great "love and capacity for analysis," according to Joseph Gillespie, his friend from the Black Hawk War in 1832 and longtime colleague in law and politics.[2] Considering his knowledge of the theocratic implications of providence theology as a result of his "capacity for analysis," the questions arise, especially since he was committed to democracy: did Lincoln really believe the theology he

227

placed in the Second Inaugural Address? Or did he merely use that theology pragmatically in order to convince God-fearing Christian people in the North, and the South as well, to abolish slavery? To answer these questions, Lincoln's previous use of such theology as well as the Second Inaugural Address need to be examined.

Before the Civil War, Lincoln used vengeance-of-God theology to oppose Stephen Douglas and Douglas's pet doctrine popular sovereignty, according to which the people of a US territory could accept or reject slavery in that territory. At that time, Lincoln was influenced by Thomas Jefferson's book *Notes on the State of Virginia*. He quoted Jefferson's comment on slavery from *Notes* ("I tremble for my country when I remember God is just") in an 1859 speech in which he maintained that popular sovereignty would lead to slavery's expansion in the territories. Moreover, he maintained that Douglas knew popular sovereignty would have this effect. Therefore, concluded Lincoln, Douglas had to believe that slavery was not immoral. Otherwise, he would have resisted its expansion in the territories instead of fostering it with popular sovereignty. Lincoln stated these views in a way that assumed humans are free moral agents accountable for their actions and subject to punishment by a just God for their moral transgressions:

> He [Judge Douglas] ought to remember that there was once in this country a man by the name of Thomas Jefferson, supposed to be a Democrat—a man whose principles and policy are not very prevalent amongst Democrats to-day, it is true; but that man did not take exactly this view of the [moral] insignificance of the element of slavery which our friend Judge Douglas does. In contemplation of this thing [slavery], we all know he [Jefferson] was led to exclaim, *"I tremble for my country when I remember that God is just* [my italics]." We know how he looked upon it when he thus expressed himself. There was danger to this country—the danger of the avenging justice of God in that little unimportant popular sovereignty question of Judge Douglas. He supposed there was a question of God's eternal justice wrapped up in the enslaving of any race of men, or any man, and those that did so braved the arm of Jehovah—that when a nation thus dared the Almighty every friend of the nation had cause to dread His wrath. Choose ye between Jef-

ferson and Douglas as to what is the true view of this element among us [applause].[3]

Significantly, since he would do something similar but even more emphatic in the Second Inaugural, Lincoln made it clear here that the vengeance-of-God ideas he expressed were not his. In this case they were Jefferson's.

Immediately after becoming president, Lincoln was still thinking of God's vengeance over slavery. This is seen in his First Inaugural Address delivered in March of 1861. Although he did not specifically mention will-of-God vengeance in that address, he did mention the will of God, albeit implicitly, in a way that set the stage for his use of vengeance theology as a weapon against slavery in the Second Inaugural. After describing the only significant dispute between the South and the North with "one section of our country believes slavery is *right*, and ought to be extended, while the other believes it is *wrong*, and ought not to be extended,"[4] the First Inaugural stated each side had "faith" that it was morally right. Because God is moral, this implied that each side believed God's will was on its side. Lincoln then stated implicitly that this North versus South moral dispute would ultimately be settled by God's will—meaning the side that was in accord with His will, His truth, His justice, and His morality would prevail. In so stating, Lincoln implied that God's justice and morality would prevail even if neither side were in accord with God.

Despite this noncommittal approach to exactly what the will of God was as respects slavery, the First Inaugural expressed confidence in the *"ultimate"* judgment capacity of the "American people" to determine what God's will, truth, justice, and morality were on slavery. To put it another way, the "American people," which to Lincoln meant all the people in both the North and the South, would *ultimately* come to God's single judgment on what His will, truth, justice, and morality were on slavery. Obviously, God could not have conflicting judgments on the justice and morality of slavery. Yet this is what the North and the South in effect maintained because the South claimed God was in accord with its view that slavery was "right" and should be expanded, while the North claimed God favored its view that slavery was "wrong" and should be restricted in the territories yet supported in the slave states under the Constitution. As Lincoln expressed these ideas in the First Inaugural:

> Why should there not be a *patient confidence* in the *ultimate justice* of the people [my italics]? Is there any better, or equal hope in the world? In our present differences is either party without faith of being in the right? If the Almighty Ruler of nations, with his eternal truth and justice, be on your side of the North, or on yours of the South, that truth, and that justice, will surely prevail, by the judgment of this great tribunal, the American people.[5]

The will of God as the "Ruler" of all is included in Lincoln's reference to "the Almighty Ruler of nations" in the First Inaugural, which made him sound like a mainstream Protestant Christian. Yet his *"patient confidence"* in the *"ultimate justice"* judgments of the people as to what God's will, truth, justice, and morality were on slavery is opposed to the original sin or morally tainted view of human nature because morally tainted judgments of justice and morality are not to be trusted according to Christian theology, which was discussed in the first three chapters. Indeed, at the end of chapter 3 it was discussed how Lincoln's alterations of Seward's suggested changes to the conclusion of the First Inaugural brought that address in accord with Lincoln's moral-sense view of human nature, which is opposed to the original sin or morally tainted view. This de facto denial of original sin in the First Inaugural makes Lincoln unorthodox at the time he wrote that address.

However, while Lincoln trusted the people's *ultimate justice* judgments on slavery in the First Inaugural, he did not trust their immediate justice judgments. He did not trust the South's judgment that slavery was "right" and should be expanded. Nor did he trust the North's judgment that slavery was "wrong" and therefore should be restricted in the territories while simultaneously supported in the slave states under the Constitution. He in effect said this when he stated: *"If* [my italics] the Almighty Ruler of nations, with his eternal truth and justice, be on yours of the North, or on yours of the South, that truth and justice, will surely prevail." His use of "If" indicates that he doubted the immediate justice and morality judgments of both sides and, in addition, considered the possibility that both were wrong. And, if both *were* wrong, God would not support either side. However, the First Inaugural in 1861 was not the time to mention this possibility because both sides were passionately committed to the righteousness of their conflicting views and, as a result, neither was disposed to consider they might be wrong. After four long years of bloody war, the situation had changed. The passion of both sides had diminished due to the suffering inflicted by war. It was therefore an appropriate time to argue—as Lincoln did in the Second Inaugural in 1865—that God's will, truth, justice, and morality were opposed to both the North's and the South's conflicting views on slavery. Despite the diminishment of passion, however, Lincoln knew these conflicting views persisted and he feared that they would continue to divide the nation and thereby make it difficult to attain and maintain a lasting peace.

Therefore, one of Lincoln's objectives in the Second Inaugural was to convince "the great tribunal" of the entire "American people" in both the North and the South, as he described them in the First Inaugural, to agree on what constitutes God's will, truth, justice, and morality on slavery as he said they ultimately would in the First Inaugural. The Second Inaugural was therefore Lincoln's elaboration on ideas that were in his mind at the time of the First Inaugural. To accomplish this objective of the Second Inaugural, Lincoln, after arguing that neither side was in accord with God, suggested what was in accord with God by appealing to the Christian will of God that governs all aspects of existence or, as Mark Noll put it, "the traditional Christian opinion that God ruled over all events."[6] Yet simultaneously Lincoln, in the Second Inaugural, did not acknowledge belief in the religious and theological views he expressed there, as he also did when quoting Jefferson in his aforementioned 1859 speech. In fact, in the Second Inaugural Lincoln subtly stated that he did not believe the religious and theological views he expressed in that address, as we shall see.

Between his First and Second Inaugurals, however, Lincoln continued to contemplate on vengeance of God over slavery. In August of 1862, the disastrous defeat of the Union army in the Second

Battle of Bull Run stimulated that contemplation. The result was Lincoln's September of 1862 expression of vengeance-of-God ideas, only this time they were privately and not publicly expressed. That was when he wrote his "Meditation on the Divine Will," as his secretary John Hay called it, which contained ideas that could be used in any speech to rationalize the failures of the Union military by blaming them on God—failures that were extremely disturbing to Lincoln and the North. The Meditation suggested implicitly that God's providence willed or caused "the contest" or civil war, as well as the Union's military failures that prolonged the war in order to punish the South and the North for allowing slavery to persist—the same theme explicitly expressed in the Second Inaugural. To put it another way, the war was God's vengeance against the South for practicing and seeking to expand slavery as well as against the North for protecting it in the slave states while simultaneously seeking to restrict it in the territories. Both sides thereby supported slavery, albeit in different ways. As Lincoln put it in his 1862 Meditation:

> The will of God prevails. In great contests each party claims to act in accordance with the will of God. Both *may* be, and one *must* be wrong. God can not be *for*, and *against* the same thing at the same time. In the present civil war it is quite possible that God's purpose is something different from the purpose of either party—and yet the human instrumentalities, working just as they do, are of the best adaptation to effect His purpose. I am almost ready to say this is probably true—that God wills this contest, and wills that it shall not end yet. By his mere quiet power, on the minds of the now contestants, He could have either saved or *destroyed* the Union without a human contest. Yet the contest began. And having begun He could give the final victory to either side any day. Yet the contest proceeds.[7]

Lincoln's reference to the "human instrumentalities" of God in his Meditation suggests that God directs and controls human actions according to His will. This makes humans puppets and God the puppeteer. Although this is consistent with nineteenth-century Protestant will of God that governs all human actions and aspects of existence theology, which is specifically stated in the Westminster Confession of Faith that Lincoln was familiar with, it makes God responsible for slavery because God's will controlled the "human instrumentalities" that initiated and perpetuated slavery.[8] Moreover, if God's will governs all human actions, humans are not free moral agents accountable for their actions and, therefore, subject to punishment by a *just* God, as Lincoln's aforementioned 1859 statement quoting Jefferson in effect says. Indeed, if God punishes humans for actions He Himself directs and controls, as the Meditation suggests, He is not just. Lincoln was aware of this because of his ability to critically analyze theology as a result of reading Thomas Paine and Theodore Parker, as has been mentioned.

Significantly, the Westminster Confession of Faith, the basis of Old School Presbyterian churches that Lincoln attended for several years, which gave him knowledge of the Confession,[9] asserts that God governs all human actions and events and simultaneously asserts that humans are free moral agents.[10] Logically, however, this cannot be, which the Confession ignores. If God governs all human actions and events, humans are not free. And, if humans *are* free, God does not govern all human actions and events. Phineas Densmore Gurley, minister of the New York Avenue Presbyterian Church in Washington where Lincoln worshiped, did not ignore this contradiction of Old School Presbyterian theology. On the contrary, he "heightened" it in sermons Lincoln attended.[11] Considering Lincoln's logical, legally trained mind as well as his ability and willingness to critically analyze theology, he would have deemed this contradiction absurd, making it difficult for him to subscribe to the Westminster Confession.

The Meditation's implications of God's injustice are also found in the Second Inaugural. Therefore, even though Lincoln had a logical, legal mind[12] and the ability to critically analyze theology, the question arises: Between the First and Second Inaugurals did he come to believe the Westminster Confession, which states that God "doth uphold, direct, dispose, and govern all creatures, actions, and things, from the greatest even to the least" or any other similar Confession or Catechism[13] and thereby become an orthodox Protestant

Christian, as some have in effect stated?[14] To answer this question, it is necessary to consider statements that Lincoln made in the Second Inaugural as well as in his Meditation.

## GOD'S WAR

A theme of the Second Inaugural Address, like the Gettysburg Address, is justification for war. However, the rationale for justification is different. At Gettysburg, Lincoln said the Civil War was being fought for two reasons: first, to preserve the Union; and second, to preserve it in accordance with the principles of the Declaration of Independence. The Declaration's "consent of the Governed" or people-based government was emphasized at Gettysburg when Lincoln said: "We here highly resolve . . . that the government of the people, by the people, for the people shall not perish from the earth." Consistent with this people-based theme, Lincoln described the Civil War as "essentially a People's contest" in his 4 July 1861 speech to Congress.[15] In contrast to that speech and the Gettysburg Address, the Second Inaugural emphasized God by stating that the Civil War was essentially God's contest because God started and prolonged it as punishment for the evil of slavery. As Lewis Perry points out, some Christian abolitionists took this position because they opposed human violence as anti-Christian and if God was responsible for starting and continuing the war, it enabled them "to portray the war not as the fighting of individuals but a purifying act of God" and therefore they could support the war.[16]

Before Lincoln mentioned justification for war in the Second Inaugural, however, he stated that slavery was "the cause of the war"—something he avoided or did implicitly after becoming president. As he put it:

> One eighth of the whole population were colored slaves, not distributed generally over the Union, but localized in the Southern part of it. These slaves constituted a peculiar and powerful interest. All knew that this interest was, somehow, the cause of the war. To

strengthen, perpetuate, and extend this interest was the object for which the insurgents would rend the Union, even by war; while the government claimed no right to do more than restrict the territorial enlargement of it.[17]

The justification of war as the will-of-God provision that followed this statement began with Jesus' words in Matthew 18:7, "Woe unto the world because of offenses! for it must needs be that offenses come; but woe to that man by whom the offense cometh!"[18] followed by:

> If we shall suppose that American Slavery is one of those offenses which, in the *providence* [my italics] of God, must needs come, but which, having continued through His appointed time, He now wills to remove, and that He gives both North and South, this terrible war, as the woe due to those by whom the offense came, shall we discern therein any departure from those divine attributes which the believers in a Living God always ascribe to Him? Fondly do we hope—fervently do we pray—that this mighty scourge of war may speedily pass away. Yet, if God wills that it continue, until all the wealth piled by the bond-man's two hundred and fifty years of unrequited toil shall be sunk, and every drop of blood drawn with the lash, shall be paid by another drawn with the sword, as was said three thousand years ago, so still it must be said "the judgments of the Lord, are true and righteous altogether."[19]

The similarity of what was said here to Lincoln's comments in his Meditation is striking even though the Meditation did not explicitly link slavery to the war, as the Second Inaugural did. In addition, both the Meditation and the Second Inaugural contain an element typical of Lincoln. Neither commits to a definite conclusion about the will of God. In the Meditation, Lincoln prefaced his comments on God's will with: "I am almost ready to say this is probably true" and in the Second Inaugural with "If we shall suppose." What the Second Inaugural makes explicit, however, which the Meditation only implies, is that God's "providence" or power to determine destiny according to His will explains three things:

1. The "offense" of "American slavery," which "must needs come."
2. The abolition of slavery after its "appointed time" was up.
3. "This terrible war, as the woe [punishment] due to those by whom the offense came."[20]

No doubt Lincoln knew that the providence theology mentioned in his Second Inaugural, which was commonplace in nineteenth-century America, put the blame on God for slavery, since it was caused by His will. As Leonard Swett put it, Lincoln "judged of Providence by the same system of great generalization as of every thing else" just as Thomas Paine and Theodore Parker, who Lincoln read extensively, had done.[21]

Despite the Second Inaugural's statement that God's will caused slavery, it invoked the idea that exact retribution or punishment in the form of civil war was meted out by God to those who caused and perpetuated slavery—even though those who caused and perpetuated that evil were God's instruments directed and controlled by His will. To put it another way, God was punishing His puppets for actions that He, as puppeteer, directed and controlled. This unjust retribution of God idea is found in the aforementioned quotation from the Second Inaugural, which states: God's will caused slavery; God's will caused and sustained the war as punishment for slavery; and God's will would cause the war to continue until all the wealth accumulated by slavery was spent on the war and all the blood spilled in the war was equal to that "drawn" from slaves "by the lash." Lincoln seemed to support this injustice on the part of God with his statement that "the judgments of the Lord, are true and righteous altogether"—a phrase he borrowed from Psalm 19:9, which was written, as he stated, "three thousand years ago." Stewart Winger pointed out that every "system of determinism" denying human "free will" faces the "problem of whether people, individually or collectively, can be held morally responsible for their actions." Winger then maintained that Lincoln's reflections in the Second Inaugural were on a "predetermined providential world," yet despite this Lincoln "simply asserted," albeit implicitly in his famous address, that people were responsible for their actions anyway.[22] The same assertion was made by the Puritan movement, which consisted "primarily of Presbyterians, Congregational and Baptist groups" that, for the most part, "represented a vital Calvinist tradition," according to John Dillenberger and Claude Welch. That "tradition" believed in "Providence" or "God's continual sustenance and ordering activity" as well as "Predestination" or "the governance of human destiny," both of which "were virtually identified as the determination of all things by God." Yet God was not "accountable" for "sin" even though it "could not be excluded from God's providential activity." It was humans who were responsible for sin because of original sin, according to the Calvinistic Puritan movement.[23] And it was "historic Calvinism" with its providence theology that "had profoundly shaped most of Northern Protestantism," according to Richard Carwardine.[24] Southern Protestantism, however, also had a tradition of providence theology, which was not confined to Presbyterians and Baptists. Anglicanism, the major denomination in the South before the Revolution, had a tradition of providence, as Quentin Skinner tells us.[25] Therefore, when colonial Anglicans became Episcopalians during Revolutionary times, providence theology was no stranger to them.

Considering, however, Lincoln's aforementioned comments in the Second Inaugural, there is no question that he sounded like an orthodox fundamentalist Protestant—indeed like a preacher. The effect of his address was to suggest powerfully, if not logically, with his reference to providence, God's will and scripture—like a preacher would—that slavery "should cease" or be totally eradicated in America in order to avoid God's extending the war He started and controlled as punishment for slavery that He also started.[26] This abolition thrust of the Second Inaugural departed from the First Inaugural where Lincoln stated slavery should not be interfered with in the slave states, since the Constitution protected it there. As he put it in 1861: "I have no purpose, directly or indirectly, to interfere with the institution of slavery in the States where it exists. I believe I have no lawful right to do so, and I have no inclination to do so."[27] At that time, Lincoln's priority was the preservation of the Constitution, which to him meant not only the document itself that made slavery lawful but also the territorial limits of the nation or Union prior to the war that were governed by the Constitution. The only way this could be accomplished, after the Confederate States used military force to secede from the Union, according to Lincoln, was Union military force. This entailed doing nothing to weaken the Union's military and everything to strengthen it while simultaneously doing everything to weaken the Confederacy's military and nothing to strengthen it. In explaining his efforts to do just that, Lincoln made another statement that has been used to demonstrate he became a believer in the will-of-God-governs-all aspects of human-existence theology like that contained in the Westminster Confession. That statement was made in his extraordinary 4 April 1864 letter to Albert Hodges, a Kentucky newspaper editor:

> I claim not to have controlled events, but confess plainly that events have controlled me. Now, at the end of three years struggle the nation's condition is not what either party, or any man devised, or expected. God alone can claim it. Whither it is tending seems plain. If God now wills the removal of a great wrong [slavery], and wills also that we of the North as well as you of the South, shall pay fairly [with war] for our complicity in that wrong, impartial history will find therein new cause to attest and revere the justice and goodness of God.[28]

However, circumstances that caused Lincoln to write Hodges along with the overall thrust of the letter need to be considered in order to understand and interpret this will-of-God comment to Hodges.

## COMPENSATED ABOLITION, REASON OF STATE, AND GOD'S WILL

Unlike Lincoln's priority of preserving the Union, newspaper editor Horace Greeley's priority was an immediate and complete Emancipation Proclamation that applied to all slaves. Greeley—a self-righteous "lofty philosopher, reformer of everything from diet to the position of women in a democratic society"—believed his emancipation priority would strengthen the Union's cause.[29] He further believed that emancipation was called for under the recently passed Confiscation Act.[30] Therefore he criticized Lincoln's priority in an open letter addressed to the president titled "The Prayer of Twenty Millions" that was never mailed but was published in his *New York Tribune*.[31] Lincoln's candid response to Greeley left no doubt about his priorities. They were the result of his *"official* duty" born of his oath to preserve the Constitution. And Lincoln's response, like Greeley's letter, was never mailed but was published in the *New York Tribune*. It gave a hint of Lincoln's *reason of state* or breaking-the-law method to save the nation and Constitution if this became necessary, despite his claim that he would stay "under the Constitution":

> As to the policy I "seem to be pursuing" as you say, I have not meant to leave any one in doubt.
>
> I would save the Union. I would save it the shortest way under the Constitution. The sooner the national authority can be restored; the nearer the Union will be "the Union as it was." If there be those who would not save the Union, unless they could at the same time *save* slavery, I do not agree with them. If there be those who would not save the Union unless they could at the same time destroy slavery, I do not agree with them. My paramount object in this struggle is to save the Union, and is *not* either to save or to destroy slavery. If I could save the Union without freeing *any* slave I would do it, and if I could save it by freeing *all* the slaves I would do it; and if I could save it by freeing some and leaving others alone I would also do that. What I do about slavery, and the colored race, I do because I believe it helps save the Union; and what I forbear, I forbear because I do *not* believe it would help to save the Union. I shall do *less* whenever I shall believe what I am doing hurts the cause, and I shall do *more* whenever I shall believe doing more will help the cause. I shall try to correct errors when shown to be errors; and I shall adopt new views so fast as they shall appear to be true views.
>
> I have here stated my purpose according to my view of *official* duty; and I intend no modification of my oft-expressed *personal* wish that all men every where could be free.[32]

Later, Lincoln told Greeley's *Tribune* that an immediate Emancipation Proclamation that applied to all slaves as advocated by Greeley would cost the Union at least twenty thousand troops from Kentucky, a slave state that remained in the Union. Lincoln explained that Kentucky's troops, after such a proclamation, would either lay down their arms or defect to the Confederacy because they favored slavery, which would of course weaken the Union's military and strengthen the Confederacy's.[33] This was no doubt one reason why the final Emancipation Proclamation of 1 January 1863 applied only to slave states in the Confederacy and not to those in the Union. This fact drew criticism from a British labor newspaper: "Lincoln offers freedom to the Negroes over whom he has no control and keeps in slavery those other Negroes within his power. Thus he associates his Government with slavery by making slaveholding the reward to the planters rejoining the old Union."[34] Richard Hofstadter's famous, more recent comment on the Emancipation Proclamation—that it had "all the moral grandeur of a bill of lading"—carries a similar thrust.[35] In defense of Lincoln's position, he had no constitutional authority to abolish slavery everywhere in the Union since it was legally protected under the Constitution he was sworn to uphold. Yet as commander in chief of the military during war, he believed he had authority to declare emancipation in the Confederacy and did so because this would weaken their military by causing their slaves, whose labor supported their military, to escape to the Union, which was an effect of the Emancipation Proclamation.[36]

Lincoln, however, was not neutral or passive on slavery as his Greeley letter and even the limitations of the Emancipation Proclamation might suggest. He had a plan for abolition—compensated abolition—which he believed would help preserve the Union.[37] He described this plan in his 1 December 1862 annual message to Congress. It called for an amendment to the Constitution to authorize the federal government to pay slave owners for emancipating their slaves in a manner similar to plans in effect in some states.[38] It also called for an amendment that would have compensated slave owners loyal to the Union whose slaves escaped to "Union lines" and another that would have funded colonization—voluntary colo-nization—of freed blacks.[39] The plan was aimed at slave states that remained in the Union—like Delaware, Maryland, Kentucky, and Missouri—as an inducement to keep them in the Union, since the Confederacy believed they could and likely would defect to the Con-federacy to protect their slave assets, which the Confederacy main-tained were endangered by the federal government. The plan, how-ever, would be costly, as Lincoln stated. Yet he also said that it "would shorten the war, perpetuate peace, insure this increase in population, and proportionately the wealth of the country."[40] The projected increase in national population was the cornerstone of Lincoln's plan. In 1900, the population would be 103 million, according to projections, as compared to 31 million when Lincoln proposed his plan.[41] In order to take advantage of this increase, the plan called for interest payments only on moneys spent to compen-sate slave owners until the year 1900, at which time principal pay-ments would begin.[42] If adopted, Lincoln maintained that the plan would not only shorten the war and thereby save lives and money, it would also make it easier to pay off debt incurred under the plan than debt incurred by the war. This was because the huge projected increase in population by the time principal payments were made under the plan would help pay the debt it incurred. In contrast, the method of paying war debt called for earlier payments on principal as well as continuing interest payments that would be paid by a much smaller population. As Lincoln described his plan:

> The great advantage of a policy by which we shall not have to pay until we number a hundred millions, what, by a different policy, we would have to pay now, when we number but thirty-one mil-lions [is obvious]. In a word, it shows that a dollar will be much harder to pay for the war, than will be a dollar for emancipation on the proposed plan. And then the latter will cost no blood, no precious life.[43]

The Civil War's toll on "precious life" and limb was devastating. Gabor Boritt tells us the war cost 1.5 million casualties at a time when the American population was 31 million. Boritt put these figures in a contemporary perspective by stating this would be the equivalent of 13 million casualties based on the population of 275 million in the year 2000.[44]

Lincoln concluded his annual message to Congress in which he explained his compensated abolition plan with an exhortation to adopt it:

> We know how to save the union. The world knows we do know how to save it. We—even *we here*—hold the power, and bear the responsibility. In *giving* freedom to the *slave*, we *assure* freedom to the free—honorable alike in what we give, and what we preserve. We shall nobly save, or meanly lose, the last best, hope of earth. Other means may succeed; this could not fail. The way is plain, peaceful, generous, just—a way which, if followed, the world will forever applaud, and God must forever bless.[45]

By promising applause from the "world" and blessings from "God" in the last sentence of this statement if his plan were adopted, Lincoln was offering a "carrot" to motivate adoption. It did not work. The plan was rejected—even by slave states remaining in the Union that would have been principal beneficiaries under the plan. This rankled Lincoln, and in his Second Inaugural the "carrot" was abandoned for the "stick" by suggesting that God's will or providence would prolong the horrendous civil war if the evil of slavery—the cause of the war and "offense" to God—were not completely abolished. This was a major shift in Lincoln's public disposition toward slavery from the First Inaugural where he stated slavery would not be interfered with because it was lawful under the Constitution that he had sworn to uphold.

Lincoln explained the reasons for his shift in emphasis and policy that took place before the Second Inaugural to Kentucky editor Albert Hodges of the *Frankfort Commonwealth* in his aforementioned letter of 4 April 1864. There he reiterated his comments to former Kentucky senator Archibald Dixon and Governor Thomas Bramlette, who along with Hodges had called on Lincoln 26 March 1864 to express "dissatisfaction" over emancipated slaves being used in the Union military.[46] The black soldiers and sailors were the result of the Emancipation Proclamation of 1 January 1863 in which Lincoln stated they were "an act of justice, warranted by the Constitution, upon *military necessity* [my italics]."[47] However, before the Emancipation Proclamation, Lincoln had revoked Major General David Hunter's order in Florida, Georgia, and South Carolina declaring all slaves in those states to be "forever free" after imposing martial law. Lincoln explained this revocation, which took place just four months before the preliminary Emancipation Proclamation in September of 1862, by stating that only he, as commander in chief of the military, had the authority to free the slaves and only if this was "indispensable to the maintenance of the government" in times of war.[48] Because a principal reason why Lincoln decided black combatants were a "military necessity" by the time of the Emancipation Proclamation was the rejection of his compensated emancipation plan, Lincoln welcomed an opportunity to explain himself to the three prominent Kentuckians because their state was among those that rejected the plan. Consistent with his save-the-union-at-all-costs policy stated in his aforementioned letter to Greeley, he wrote Hodges an extraordinary letter in which he admitted using *reason of state* or breaking-the-law methods to save the Union and explained in detail his reasons for doing this:

> I am naturally anti-slavery. If slavery is not wrong, nothing is wrong. I can not remember when I did not so think, and feel. And yet I have never understood that the Presidency conferred upon me an unrestricted right to act officially upon this judgment and feeling. It was in the oath I took that I would, to the best of my ability, preserve, protect, and defend the Constitution of the United States. I could not take the office without taking the oath. Nor was it in my view that I might take an oath to get power, and break the oath in using the power. I understood, too, that in ordinary civil administration this oath even forbade me to practically indulge my primary abstract judgment on the moral question of slavery. I had publicly declared this many times, and in many ways. And I aver that, to this day, I have done no official act in mere deference to my abstract judgment and feeling on slavery. I did understand however, that my oath to preserve the constitution to the best of my ability, imposed upon me the duty of preserving, by

every indispensable means, that government—that nation—of which that constitution was the organic law. Was it possible to lose the nation, and yet preserve the constitution? By general law life *and* limb must be protected; yet often a limb must be amputated to save a life; but a life is never wisely given to save a limb. *I felt that measures, otherwise unconstitutional, might become lawful, by becoming indispensable to the preservation of the constitution, through the preservation of the nation. Right or wrong, I assumed this ground, and now avow it.* I could not feel that, to the best of my ability, I had even tried to preserve the constitution, if, to save slavery, or any minor matter, I should permit the wreck of government, country, and Constitution all together. When, early in the war, Gen. Fremont attempted military emancipation, I forbade it, because I did not then think it an *indispensable necessity*. When a little later, Gen. Cameron, then Secretary of War, suggested the arming of the blacks, I objected, because I did not yet think it an *indispensable necessity*. When, still later, Gen. Hunter attempted military emancipation, I again forbade it, because I did not yet think the *indispensable necessity* had come. When, in March, and May, and July 1862 I made earnest, and successive appeals to the border states [of which Kentucky was one] to favor compensated emancipation, I believed the *indispensable necessity* for military emancipation, and arming the blacks would come, unless averted by that measure. They declined the proposition; and I was, in my best judgment, driven to the alternative of either surrendering the Union, and with it, the Constitution, or of laying strong hand upon the colored element. I chose the latter. In choosing it, I hoped for greater gain than loss; but of this, I was not entirely confident. More than a year of trial now shows no loss by it in our foreign relations, none in our home popular sentiment, none in our white military force,—no loss by it in any how or any where. On the contrary, it shows a gain of quite a hundred and thirty thousand [black] soldiers, seamen, and laborers. These are palpable facts, about which, as facts, there can be no cavilling. We have the men; and we could not have had them without the measure.[49] (My italics)

The admission of using measures "otherwise unconstitutional" or unlawful when they were an "indispensable necessity"—a phrase Lincoln used four times in this passage—to preserve "the constitution, through the preservation of the nation" makes Lincoln a practitioner of *reason of state*. Moreover, it gives testimony to his prudence when it came to saving the Constitution and the nation. He was against breaking the law, as he emphasized in his Lyceum speech in 1838, as has been stated. Yet, by his own admission in his letter to Hodges, he would do just that to save the Union and the Constitution. However, as Lincoln's letter shows and Allen Guelzo points out, Lincoln tried to adhere to the specific provisions of the Constitution before using prudent *reason-of-state* methods.[50] Indeed, before he used those methods, he familiarized himself with the writings of legal scholars who explained and defended the use of his presidential war powers as commander in chief of the military. Among those writings was *The War Powers of the President*, written by his solicitor general, William Whiting, who argued that emancipating slaves was within Lincoln's war powers.[51] The issue, however, was not clearly stated in law, as is the case with many legal issues. And, as Lincoln made clear to Hodges, he had "assumed this ground" or the use of methods "otherwise unconstitutional" or unlawful when they were "indispensable" to the "preservation of the nation," which is exactly what constitutes "reason of state."

An essential element of reason-of-state methods is prudence, provided those methods were used to save or preserve the state and not to further the self-interests of a ruler.[52] Lincoln's *reason of state* or raison d'etat was the prudent variety and could well have been the result of Jefferson's influence.[53] In his letter to Dr. James Brown in 1808, Jefferson wrote:

> Should we have ever gained our Revolution, if we had bound our hands by manacles of the law, not only in the beginning, but in any part of the revolutionary conflict? There are extreme cases where the laws become inadequate even to their own preservation, and where the universal resource is a dictator, or martial law.[54]

In an 1810 letter to J. B. Colvin, Jefferson wrote similarly:

> A strict observance of the written laws is doubtless *one* of the high duties of a good citizen, but it is not the highest. The laws of neces-

sity, of self-preservation, of saving our country when in danger, are of higher obligation. To lose our country by a scrupulous adherence to written law, would be to lose the law itself, with life, liberty, property and all those who are enjoying them with us; thus absurdly sacrificing the end to the means.[55]

As harming others is permissible if necessary to preserve one's self, suspending, going beyond, or even breaking the law is permissible in order to preserve the state or nation in "reason of state." Lincoln applied this logic to the "unarmed foes to the North" that "might be as dangerous to the union as the armed enemy to the South" with his suspension of the right of "habeas corpus" on Confederate "sympathizers" that might be intent on damaging the North—a suspension allowed by the Constitution in times of rebellion or attack.[56] Lincoln, however, as has been mentioned, defied the courts when suspending habeas corpus, which allowed the arrest and indefinite jailing of those suspected of being "dangerous to the union" without specific charges being formally brought against them or giving them a court trial based on those charges. Lincoln justified such action by stating:

> Nothing is better known to history than that courts of justice are utterly incompetent to such cases. Civil Courts are organized chiefly for trials of individuals, or, at most, a few individuals acting in concert; and this in quiet times, and on charges of crimes well defined in the law. Even in times of peace, bands of horse-thieves and robbers frequently grow too numerous and powerful for the ordinary courts of justice. But what comparison, in numbers, have such bands ever borne to the insurgent [Southern] sympathizers even in many of the loyal states? Again, a jury too frequently have at least one member, more ready to hang the panel than to hang the traitor.[57]

In his letter to Hodges, however, Lincoln's detailed explanation of his rational calculations and actions that finally caused him to use *reason-of-state* methods demonstrates that he believed in cause and effect and that his own actions caused effects that aided the Union— like the "gain of quite a hundred and thirty thousand [black] soldiers, seaman, and laborers" he mentioned in that letter. In other words, it was human action that determined human conditions, not God. Therefore, Lincoln's letter to Hodges—that is, the greatest part of it—echoed a theme of Constantin Volney's *The Ruins or a Survey of the Revolutions of Empires.* Volney was a deist and natural theologian scholar of late eighteenth- and early nineteenth-century France,[58] and his book made a profound impression on Lincoln, according to Abner Y. Ellis and Elliot B. Herndon, William Herndon's brother.[59]

*The Ruins* is a critical historical account of civilizations in the Middle East and the religions of Judaism, Christianity, and Islam as well as Zoroastrianism, Hinduism, and Buddhism. As Volney expressed his theme that humans and not God are responsible for human conditions—a theme diametrically opposed to the God's-will-governs-all-vengeance theology of the Second Inaugural:

> Is it the arm of God that has introduced the sword into the city, and set fire to the country, murdered the people, burned the harvests, rooted up the trees, and ravaged the pastures? or is it the arm of man? And when, after this devastation, famine has started up, is it the vengeance of God that has sent it, or the mad fury of mortals? When, during the famine, the people are fed with unwholesome provision, and pestilence ensues, is it inflicted by the anger of heaven, or brought about by human *imprudence* [my italics]? When war, famine, and pestilence united, have swept away the inhabitants, and the land is become a desert, is it God who has depopulated it? Is it his rapacity that plunders the labourer, ravages the productive fields, and lays waste the country; or the rapacity of those who govern? Is it his pride that creates murderous wars; or the pride of kings and their ministers? Is it the venality of his decisions that overthrows the fortune of families, or the venality of the organs of the laws? Are they his passions that, under a thousand forms, torment individuals and nations; or the passions of human beings? And if, in the anguish of their misfortunes, they perceive not the remedies, is it the ignorance of God that is in fault, or their own ignorance? Cease, then, to accuse the decrees of Fate or the judgments of Heaven? If God is good, will he be the author of your punishment? If he is just, will he be the accomplice of your crimes?

No, no: the caprice of which man complains, is not the caprice of
destiny; the darkness that misleads his reason, is not the darkness
of God; the source of his calamities, is not in the distant heavens,
but near to him upon the earth; it is not concealed in the bosom
of the Divinity; it resides in himself, man bears it in his heart.[60]

Yet despite Lincoln's detailed description in his Hodges letter that
demonstrates he believed human actions are the cause of human
conditions, the last paragraph of that letter previously quoted
abruptly turned to the will-of-God-governs-human-actions theology
similar to what Lincoln mentioned in the aforementioned Meditation as well as the Second Inaugural. As has been mentioned, that
paragraph has been perceived as support for the claim that Lincoln
had come to believe that God's will controls the actions of individual human beings as well as human events.

What Lincoln expressed in that paragraph, however, especially
because it came after a detailed rational explanation of the human
actions that caused him to choose his own actions and the positive
effects of his actions, is more a politically astute disclaimer of any
blame for the use of blacks as soldiers and sailors that the three
prominent Kentuckians were protesting than an expression of his
religious or theological beliefs. As he put it to Hodges, "God alone
can claim it." In other words the will of "God alone" was directing
the course of the war and events, not Abraham Lincoln as president
of the United States. Thus Lincoln blamed God for blacks in the military. Blaming God this way was sound strategy to use on the three
prominent Kentuckians. They could argue with President Lincoln's
rationale in the first part of his letter, but as good Christians they
could not argue with God, who most Christians in America at that
time believed controlled all events.[61]

Lincoln used the same strategy in letters to Eliza P. Gurney, a
Quaker minister from Philadelphia. Gurney held a prayer meeting
for Lincoln on 26 September 1862 after waiting two days with three
friends to see the president. On 26 October 1862, Lincoln wrote
Gurney thanking her for the "sympathy and prayers" expressed at
the meeting. He also stated that if he "had been allowed" his "way,"
the "war would never have been commenced," and if he had been

allowed his way after the war commenced, it "would have been ended before this." Lincoln failed to have his way because God had done things His way. As Lincoln explained to Gurney: "He [God] who made the world still governs it" and governs it "according to his *will* [my italics]," meaning God alone was directing the course of the war and events, not Abraham Lincoln, president of the United States—the same message he delivered to editor Hodges. Gurney wrote Lincoln 8 August 1863 thanking him for his letter. Lincoln's response of 4 September 1864, almost two years from the prayer meeting, again spoke of the will of God or "purposes of the Almighty." Those "purposes," he said: "Are perfect, and must prevail, though we erring mortals may fail to accurately perceive them in advance. We hoped for a happy termination of this terrible war long before this; but God knows best, and has ruled otherwise." Once again, Lincoln stated it was God who determines the events of the war, not Abraham Lincoln, a sound strategy that good Christians, even if they were critical of Lincoln as many Quakers were because they opposed war, would find difficult to refute.[62]

Similar strategy to that used in the Hodges and Gurney letters was used in the Second Inaugural when Lincoln addressed all the people of the nation on the issue of slavery, only this time Lincoln used God's will not merely as a defensive weapon to shield himself from blame for events in the war. He also used it as an offensive weapon to blame the entire nation, both North and South, which of course included himself, for the war. His method was to state in effect that God's will was antislavery and therefore against both sides because one believed slavery was right and wanted to expand it while the other believed it was wrong but allowed it to continue in the slave states under the Constitution. If God's will had supported either side, argued Lincoln, they would have long since won the war. However, because this had not happened after four agonizing years of war, God's will must be antislavery and God was, therefore, punishing both sides with continuous war for their roles in perpetuating that evil institution. The underlying message of these arguments in the Second Inaugural was: Get rid of slavery and God, who governed all actions and events according to His will, would end the war. With these arguments, good Christian people in both the North and the South would find it difficult to argue against abolition because it was God's will—or at least Lincoln hoped the Second Inaugural would have this effect and thereby bring a unified judgment against slavery that would support the Thirteenth Amendment.[63]

In 1864, the Thirteenth Amendment abolishing slavery was introduced before Congress partly because Lincoln insisted that abolition be part of his reelection platform. It passed with the required two-thirds majority in early 1865 thanks in no small measure to Lincoln's efforts.[64] At the time of the Second Inaugural, however, it still had not been completely ratified by 75 percent of the states, the required number in order to become law. Therefore, in that famous address, delivered 4 March 1865, Lincoln spoke in favor of the Thirteenth Amendment, albeit implicitly in that sermonlike speech by denouncing slavery as an evil or an "offence" against God that should be abolished to avoid further punishment by God to both the North and the South with war.[65] Lincoln, however, did not believe the theology he invoked in the Second Inaugural, as he made very clear in his famous address even though it had sermonlike characteristics. Indeed, in a fundamental respect, Lincoln departed from nineteenth-century sermon format in the Second Inaugural.

## THE LANGUAGE OF SKEPTICISM

In nineteenth-century America, preachers dealt in certainty when they preached. They were not tentative or hypothetical. They were certain they knew God's truth. They were certain they knew His will. They maintained they were God's spokespersons on earth and they projected their certitude in their sermons. They carried God's book containing His word and His certain Truth, which they quoted to support their claims of certainty. In his Second Inaugural, Lincoln abandoned this approach. Although he quoted scripture to support views expressed in his address, as a preacher would, he was unpreacherlike in that he was both tentative and hypothetical in his statements about God's will—the antithesis of certainty. This is seen in his "If we shall suppose" preface to his idea that three events were caused or to be caused by God's "providence" or will, which were: that slavery "must needs come," that it must be removed after exceeding its "appointed time," and "this terrible war" as punishment to both North and South as the offenders in slavery. His use of both "if" and "suppose" or "supposition" were anathema to a preacher. No one wanted to listen to an iffy preacher. People wanted certainty from a preacher in matters of God, salvation, and God's will. "If" was alien to certainty. For the same reason, no one wanted to listen to supposition about God from a preacher. Supposition implies something hypothetical, something doubtful. To be hypothetical or doubtful about God's will, as Lincoln was with his "If we shall suppose," is far removed from the method of the preacher that used faith and certainty born of faith.

The question then arises, why would Lincoln use "If we shall suppose" as a preface to the theological content of the Second Inaugural? The fact that he had used "if" previously when he wanted to put ideas before the public without stating that he subscribed to them provides an answer to this question. This is seen in the first paragraph of his response to Horace Greeley's aforementioned letter where Greeley criticized his single-minded policy to save the Union:

> I have just read yours of the 19th addressed to myself through the New York Tribune. *If* there be in it any statements, or assumptions of fact, which I may know to be erroneous, I do not, now and here, controvert them. If there be in it any inferences which I may believe to be falsely drawn, I do not now and here, argue against them. If there be perceptible in it an impatient and dictatorial tone, I waive it in deference to an old friend, whose heart I have always supposed to be right [my italics].[66]

The use of "if" here allowed Lincoln to suggest that Greeley was guilty of three things: erroneous "statements, or assumptions of fact"; "falsely drawn" inferences; and "an impatient and dictatorial tone." More important, it allowed him to do this without actually stating that he believed Greeley was guilty of any of these things.

In like manner, by using "If we shall suppose" as a preface to his "God's will" and "providence" theological comments in the Second Inaugural, Lincoln was able to deliver a stern warning to his mostly Christian audience without stating that these theological comments were true or held by him. It enabled him to deliver the idea that civil war was sent by God as punishment to the nation for slavery and that this punishment could well continue until it caused as much grief to whites as slavery had to blacks unless that evil institution was completely abolished. Moreover, this idea was delivered in Christian theological terms familiar to his audience because most in that audience believed in providence or God's will theology, as has been stated. However, because Lincoln distanced himself from belief in the theology he used with his "if we shall suppose" phrase, his arguments in the Second Inaugural were a pragmatic use of theology for political purposes similar to what he had done in his aforementioned 1859 Columbus, Ohio, speech critical of his Democratic opponent Douglas that contained Jefferson's but not necessarily his views on a just God. They were also similar to his pragmatic use of theology in the last paragraph of his letter to Hodges disclaiming any blame for the use of blacks in the military. It should be emphasized, however, that the "If we shall suppose" phrase Lincoln used put the God's-will-governs-all theology of the Second Inaugural in the tentative category of maybe or perhaps—a very unchristian thing to do. "If we shall suppose" is the language of a philosopher or a skeptic, not a true believer or person of faith.

Moreover, after citing the three hypothetical "if we shall suppose" events caused or to be caused by divine providence or God's will—that slavery "must needs come," that it must be removed after exceeding its "appointed time," and "this terrible war" as punishment to both North and South as the offenders in slavery—Lincoln asked rhetorically: "Shall we discern therein any departure from those divine attributes which the believers in a Living God always ascribe to Him?" When he referred to the "attributes" of the "Living God," Lincoln was referring to the "one only living and true God" theological language of the Westminster Confession, according to Ronald White.[67] I concur with White. For many years, Lincoln attended Old School Presbyterian churches that subscribed to the

Westminster Confession, as has been mentioned.[68] This gave him repeated exposure to that Confession, which maintains that God governs or determines all events in His creation thereby making God in effect the puppeteer and humans puppets, as has also been mentioned.[69] This aspect of the theology of the Westminster Confession—as well as similar confessions like the London Baptist Confession of 1689, known in America as the "Philadelphia Confession"—makes any political system, including democracy, de facto theocracy because God governs or determines the actions of all humans.[70] If Lincoln actually subscribed to the Westminster Confession, there was no such thing as "government of the people, by the people, for the people" he championed at Gettysburg, which he would have known because of his ability and willingness to critically analyze theology as a result of reading Thomas Paine, Theodore Parker, and Constantin Volney. What Lincoln's rhetorical question in his Second Inaugural pointed out, however, was that the three events he hypothetically attributed to God with his "If we shall suppose" phrase—the coming of slavery, that it must be removed after exceeding its "appointed time," and "this terrible war" as punishment to both North and South as the offenders in slavery—were in accord with the God-controls-all-events "attributes" of the "Living God" theology of the Westminster Confession that "the believers" in that theology "always ascribe to Him."

Yet Lincoln was not among "the believers" in the Westminster Confession as his rhetorical question from his Second Inaugural, "Shall *we discern* therein any departure from those divine attributes which *the believers* in a living God always ascribe to Him?" clearly shows. The italics are mine since I wish to call attention to Lincoln's sudden shift from *"we"* discerners to *"the believers* in a Living God" in these phrases from the same sentence and ask: How can this shift be explained if Lincoln believed in the "Living God" theology of the Westminster Confession, which maintains that God governs all events in His creation? In fact, Lincoln's shift from *"we"* discerners to *"the believers"* makes a distinction between *"we"* as discerners, which includes Lincoln, and *"the believers,"* which excludes Lincoln. Thus he stated he did not count himself among "the believers" in the

"Living God" theology of the Westminster Confession, otherwise he would have said *"we believers"* instead of *"the believers."*[71] This may be seen as giving too much importance to particular words and phrases of the Second Inaugural. Yet, as both Ronald White and Garry Wills emphasize, Lincoln was extraordinarily discriminating in his choice of words not only to convey a particular meaning but also for aesthetic and emotional appeal because this was crucial in persuading his audience to accept his point of view.[72]

Arthur Goodhart suggests that Lincoln's meticulousness when it came to precise language was born of his legal training. To support his view, Goodhart quoted Lincoln's hyperbole on a judge whose punishments he regarded excessive but who he respected for demanding precise language: "He would hang a man for blowing his nose in the street but he would quash the indictment if it failed to specify what hand he blew it with."[73] Helen Nicolay, daughter of Lincoln's personal secretary John Nicolay, based on material her father meant to incorporate in a book coauthored with Lincoln's other secretary, John Hay, held views similar to Goodhart's. As she put it: "His lawyer's training is visible in everything he wrote, down to the smallest scrap, in a clearness of expression which leaves no chance for misunderstanding either the fact stated or his own motive."[74]

Other language in the Second Inaugural tells us that Lincoln did not subscribe to the "Living God" theology of the Westminster Confession, which maintains that faith and predestinating saving grace are granted by God to certain souls while in the womb while "others" are "foreordained to everlasting death."[75] This is found where Lincoln said each side in the war prayed to God for "His aid against the other."[76] Because the South was fighting "to strengthen, perpetuate, and extend" their "interest" in slavery, their prayers were in effect, as Lincoln stated, "for a just God's assistance in wringing their bread from the sweat of other men's faces."[77] This was the Second Inaugural's reference to Genesis 3:19: "In the sweat of thy face shalt thou eat bread"—the punishment of hard labor in order to get food that God inflicted on Adam for his role in original sin inherited by all males. Three months earlier, however, Lincoln made a similar reference to Genesis 3:19 in a way that sheds light on his interpretation of this biblical passage as well as his religious views. At that time, two women from Tennessee called on him to plead for the freedom of their husbands who were Confederate soldiers and prisoners of war. One of the women mentioned that her "husband was a religious man." Lincoln immediately responded:

> Tell him when you meet him, that I say I am not much of a judge of religion, but that, in my opinion, the religion that sets men to rebel and fight against their government, because, as they think, that government does not sufficiently help *some* men to eat their bread on the sweat of *other* men's faces, is not the sort of religion upon which people can get to heaven.[78]

Here Lincoln said in effect that slavery or living off of slave labor was a moral transgression that would prevent the attainment of salvation and heaven, which is also stating in effect that moral action is the means of attaining heaven. In other words, Lincoln said good works earn salvation and humans are capable of performing such works. This belief of what constitutes religion, salvation, and human moral capacity is a denial of original sin or the morally tainted view of human nature and belief that salvation is predestined by God's grace and not earned by good works, as the Westminster Confession states.[79]

Predestination is also antithetical to Lincoln's belief in universal salvation for everyone as mentioned in chapter 2.[80] If God did not grant a person predestinating saving grace when they were in their mother's womb—which He did not to many, according to the doctrine of predestination—then that person "shall be cast into eternal torments," as the Westminster Confession states. It also states of those predestined: "Their number is so certain and definite, that it cannot be either increased or diminished."[81] This predestinator God was not the kind of God that Lincoln worshiped. It was the kind that Theodore Parker claimed "creates millions of men only for the pleasure of squelching them down in a bottomless, and eternal hell."[82] Predestination is also at odds with the idea that "all men are created equal" that Lincoln subscribed to and emphasized in his Gettysburg Address. Indeed, Calvin, the great champion of predestination, whose influence pervades the Westminster Confession, stated that "all men are not created in equal condition; eternal life is foreordained for some, eternal damnation for others," as was mentioned in chapter 1.[83]

While it is true that Lincoln attended Old School Presbyterian churches that subscribed to the Westminster Confession, it is also true that he never became a member of those churches or any church. The reason for this, as he explained to Congressman Henry Deming a year before he was assassinated, was that he had difficulty "in giving his assent, without mental reservation, to the long complicated statements of Christian doctrine, which characterize their Articles of belief and Confessions of Faith"[84]—like the one contained in the Westminster Confession of Faith formulated in 1646 as the basis of Presbyterian religion.[85] By not compromising his "mental reservation" and private judgment on religion and "doctrine"—and by not joining any church—Lincoln followed the lead of Thomas Paine. As Paine famously described his own views on organized religion, doctrine, and churches in the *Age of Reason* that Lincoln read as a young man, which was quoted in chapter 2: "I do not believe in the creed professed by the Jewish church, by the Roman church, by the Greek church, by the Turkish [Islamic] church, by the Protestant church, nor by any church that I know of. *My own mind is my own church* [my italics]." Lincoln's lack of doctrinal commitment also placed him in conformity with Theodore Parker, who said that real Christianity "makes us outgrow any form of doctrines," as was mentioned in chapter 2.

Certainly, there was no Augustinian "wrath of God" against all humanity because of original sin, as the Westminster Confession states of Christian theology, in Lincoln's universal deistic God.[86] The deistic God includes all humans in His love and benevolence regardless of what they believe or disbelieve in religion or what their race or gender is, as was explained in chapters 1 and 2. This all-inclusive love with wrath toward none idea is seen in the last paragraph of the Second Inaugural:

> With malice toward none; with charity for all [my italics]; with firmness in the right, as God gives us to see the right, let us strive on to

finish the work we are in; to bind up the nation's wounds; to care for him who shall have born the battle, and for his widow, and his orphan—to do all which may achieve and cherish a just, and a lasting peace, among ourselves, and with all nations.[87]

When Lincoln said, "Let us strive to finish the work we are in," he no doubt meant winning the war. He also referred to doing "all which may achieve and cherish a just, and a lasting peace." He had, as has been mentioned, again and again referred to the injustice of slavery. Since there could be no guaranteed complete abolition of slavery and therefore "a just, and a lasting peace" in both the North and the South without winning the war, victory was the key to "a just, and a lasting peace" along with the passage of the Thirteenth Amendment abolishing slavery. Thus in the last phrases of the Second Inaugural, Lincoln was implicitly admonishing the Union to win the war and the states to ratify the Thirteenth Amendment.[88] Some might ask why Lincoln did not make this admonition explicit. An explicit call for victory would have been blatantly partisan. Therefore, it could have aroused do-or-die resistance in the proud Southerners. And, since Lincoln's address was directed to all the American people, in both the North and the South, his strategy was not to offend his Southern brethren with blatantly partisan statements, but to win their hearts and minds. If he was successful in doing this with his God's-will-is-antislavery argument, they would favor the Thirteenth Amendment and have little reason to continue the war.

## LINCOLN'S PERSISTENT HETERODOXY

There is, however, testimony that Lincoln became a devout and orthodox Christian who believed in the literal meaning of the Bible late in life despite testimony to the contrary mentioned in chapter 2. Joshua F. Speed, Lincoln's close friend from his early adulthood, wrote a book published in 1884 titled *Reminiscences of Abraham Lincoln and Notes of a Visit to California*. There Speed gave an account of a meeting with Lincoln in the summer of 1864 at the soldiers' home a few miles north of Washington. The home was the Lincoln family's retreat for relief from the miserable summer heat and humidity of the low-lying tidewater area of the White House.[89] When Speed arrived for the meeting, Lincoln was reading the Bible and Speed commented: "I am glad to see you profitably engaged." Lincoln responded: "Yes, I am profitably engaged." Speed, who recalled Lincoln's early religious skepticism, then said: "Well, If you have recovered from your skepticism, I am sorry to say that I have not," to which Lincoln replied: "You are wrong, Speed. Take all of this book upon reason that you can, and the balance on faith, and you will live and die a happier and better man."[90] Although this statement can be interpreted as Lincoln's affirmation that the Bible is completely true, he does not say this. He merely says that if Speed would take what was reasonable in the Bible as true and the rest "on faith," he would "live and die a happier and better man." This statement can also be interpreted as Lincoln's effort to convince himself to take the position he advised Speed to take on the Bible because it would enable him to "live and die a happier and better man." It would give him a certainty about religion and salvation that he never had. An indication this interpretation is correct is found in Speed's statement that after Lincoln "was elected President, he *sought* to become a believer [my italics]."[91]

Speed also described a conversation he heard between Lincoln and "a real dignified lady" while waiting to see his old friend at the White House about two weeks before Lincoln's death. That conversation demonstrates Lincoln never became "a believer" despite his efforts to do so. The "lady," according to Speed, "walked up to L." and "taking one of his hands in both of hers . . . said—Mr L I thank you[.] I never shall see you again—I hope to meet you in heaven— L then took her hands in his—. . . & said—I don't know that I will eve[r] get to heaven."[92] With such doubt and skepticism, Lincoln himself would certainly have lived and died "a happier" man if he could have convinced himself to believe in the Bible like an orthodox Christian, as he urged Speed to do. Significantly, Lincoln lamented the fact that he was not "a more devout" or believing man in front of his minister, Phineas Gurley, and the Baltimore Presbyterian Synod on 24 October 1863 at the White House, when he said:

"I have often wished that I was a more devout man than I am."[93] Of course to Gurley and that synod, the only truly "devout man" was one who professed belief in the doctrines of their church, which Lincoln never did with their church or any church.

Other testimony of Lincoln's conversion to orthodoxy came from Ninian W. Edwards, Lincoln's brother-in-law, who married Mary Todd Lincoln's older sister Elizabeth. Edwards claimed that Lincoln told him he was "convinced of the truth of the Christian religion" after reading a book, or at least portions of it, written by Reverend James Smith, minister of the First Presbyterian Church in Springfield where the Lincolns attended services in the 1850s after Mary became a member. Smith's book was titled *The Christian's Defense, Containing a Fair Statement, and Impartial Examination of the Leading Objections Urged by Infidels Against the Antiquity, Genuineness, Credibility, and Inspiration of the Holy Scriptures*. In 1841, Smith debated skeptic Charles G. Olmstead, after which he wrote his book reiterating his arguments against Olmstead's challenge to the truth content of the Bible.[94] Edwards's testimony that Lincoln was "convinced of the truth of the Christian religion," however, does not mean much when considered in the light of Theodore Parker's influence on Lincoln. As was stated in chapter 2, Parker maintained that all versions of Christianity contained part of the truth of Christian religion—even heterodox versions like deism that did not believe that much of what was contained in the Bible was true. Imbued with Parker's ideas, Lincoln could be a deist or heterodox Christian and say that he was "convinced of the truth of the Christian religion" while simultaneously rejecting a few or even many biblical passages as well as orthodox versions of Christianity as untrue because this would, according to Parker, be one of the many facets of the truth of Christian religion.

## GOD'S WILL IS MY WILL

During his first term as president, Lincoln never had majority support. In fact, the majority did not elect him. He received less than 40 percent of the vote due to a split between four candidates: himself; Democrat Douglas; John Bell of the National Union Party, which was "more or less a reincarnation of the Whig and American parties"; and John Breckinridge, who the Southern Democrats nominated after the Democratic Party split in June of 1860.[95] Then, after the election, numerous Confederate battle victories eroded the minority support Lincoln had when elected. As a result, in the summer of 1862, according to George W. Julian, leader in the Free Soil Party and congressman during as well as after Lincoln's administration: "The popular hostility to the president at this time cannot be described, and was wholly without precedent and the opposition to him in Congress was even more intense."[96] Only after extraordinary Union military success that included Sherman's taking Atlanta and Sheridan's victory in the Shenandoah Valley in 1864 did public opinion rise in favor of Lincoln. It continued to rise and finally gave him and the Republicans a huge victory over General George B. McClellan and the Democrats in the election of 1864. McClellan carried only three states.[97] The final electoral vote was 212 for Lincoln and 21 for McClellan.[98] It was a sweet moment for Lincoln. For the first time he had political security, which he used in the Second Inaugural to publicly criticize in a major speech the common practice of claiming to know God's will, which Volney in *The Ruins* criticized by stating that people "have said that he [God] is incomprehensible" and yet "they have undertaken to be interpreters of his will."[99] Even before the Second Inaugural, however, Lincoln criticized the practice of claiming to know God's will. In his 13 September 1862 response to resolutions for emancipation made by Chicago ministers of various denominations that were presented him by a delegation led by William Patton and John Dempster, he stated in the critical style of Thomas Paine, Theodore Parker, and Constantin Volney:

> I am approached with the most opposite opinions and advise [on whether to make an Emancipation Proclamation], and that by religious men, who are equally certain that they represent the Divine will. . . . I hope it will not be irreverent for me to say that if it is probable that God would reveal his will to others, on a point so

connected with my duty, it might be supposed he would reveal it directly to me; for, unless I am more deceived in my self than I often am, it is my earnest desire to know the will of Providence in this matter. *And, if I can learn what it is I will do it!* These are not, however, the days of miracles, and I suppose it will be granted that I am not to expect a direct revelation.[100]

Lincoln with this good-natured ridicule of "religious men" made it clear that he did not expect any revelations from God on what Providence or God's will wanted him to do. Moreover, he made it equally clear that he did not believe those "religious men" who claimed knowledge of what God willed him to do had such knowledge or revelations of such knowledge because they had so many conflicting views on God's will. This was a thoroughgoing criticism of the concept of Providence or God's will as a guide to human action because Lincoln was saying in effect that no one could know "the will of Providence" or will of God despite claims to the contrary because of the many views on what it was. These were not, as Lincoln stated, "the days of miracles" or miraculous revelations that gave such knowledge. Lincoln thereby echoed Volney's skepticism of claims of knowledge of God's will. With the will of Providence or God thus unknowable, Lincoln described what he deemed the best alternative guide to action: "I must study the plain physical facts of the case, ascertain what is possible and learn what appears to be wise and right."[101] No willful Romantic element or religious certainty born of faith here—just observation and analysis of facts as the means of finding "what appears to be" the most "wise and right" course of action, which was the Enlightenment method. Significantly, in the Second Inaugural, Lincoln echoed this "what appears to be wise and right" or tentative method in the last paragraph when he said: "With firmness in the right, as God gives us to see the right," meaning that God does not give us infallible knowledge of the "right" course of action but we must find that course as best we can with the powers of perception that "God gives us to see the right" and then persist in that course with "firmness."

What particularly bothered Lincoln, however, was that what people claimed was God's will was almost always the same as their own will. Moreover, this confusion of human with divine will almost always corresponded with the interests of people who then prayed that God enforce their claims of what constitutes His will against those who opposed their claims. In other words, their prayers were in effect for the enforcement of what was in their interests in the name of God's will. This of course was what both the North and the South had done with their conflicting interpretations of God's will during the war that corresponded to their respective wills. As Lincoln said in his Second Inaugural, echoing the First Inaugural, the South's will or purpose was "to strengthen, perpetuate, and extend" slavery while the North's was "to restrict the territorial enlargement of it," as has been mentioned.[102] Then he stated that both sides invoked "His [God's] aid against the other [in order to attain their will]" by praying that God grant them victory despite the fact that, as Lincoln put it, "Both read the same Bible, and pray to the same God."[103] Obviously, God could not answer the conflicting prayers of both sides, since only one could be victorious, which Lincoln stated with "the prayers of both could not be answered."[104]

Lincoln's crucial point in the Second Inaugural, however, which was not mentioned in his First Inaugural, was that "neither [side] anticipated that the *cause* of the conflict [which was slavery] might cease with, or even before, the conflict itself *should* cease [my italics]." This suggested that "the Almighty has his own purposes" or will, which was that slavery "*should*" be completely abolished before the War "*should* cease" or would cease.[105] Lincoln was in effect stating, as has been mentioned, that both the South and the North were opposing God's will because both supported slavery, which was against God's will. Their only disagreement, as has also been mentioned, was whether slavery should be expanded or restricted.

To say, however, to devout, self-righteous Christians in the North, who claimed they were doing God's will by seeking to restrict slavery in the territories while allowing it in the slave states under the Constitution, that they were opposing God's will was bound to offend them. In like manner, to say to devout, self-righteous Christians in the South, who claimed they were doing God's will by seeking to expand slavery, that they were opposing God's will was bound to offend them. Despite this offensive opposing-God element of the Second Inaugural, however, devout Christians in the North or the South would have difficulty refuting the idea that God was opposed to both sides because of their religious beliefs. After all, the war had gone on four long years despite fervent prayers by both sides for victory, as Lincoln pointed out. This was a strong indication that God's will did not favor the will of either side or He would have long since granted victory to the side He favored. It was also an indication that God was punishing both sides with war for allowing slavery, which was against His will, to persist. These arguments would make sense to good Christians in both the North and the South in the nineteenth century unless they were willing to abandon the idea that God's will governs the world, which they could not and remain good mainline Christians. When describing this aspect of his Second Inaugural in a letter to Thurlow Weed, Lincoln said he expected his address would

> wear as well as—perhaps better than—any thing I have produced; but I believe it is not immediately popular. Men are not flattered by being shown that there has been a difference of purpose between the Almighty and them. To deny it, however, in this case, is to deny that there is a God governing the world![106]

Significantly, Lincoln's expression of pride here in his famous address is in the way he cleverly linked its unpopular opposing-God's-will element to the popular Christian belief that "there is a God governing the world" in order to support the goal of abolition.

## THE PRAGMATIC USE OF THEOLOGY IN THE SECOND INAUGURAL

From the time of his Emancipation Proclamation in January 1863, Richard Carwardine says that Lincoln addressed "issues from the standpoint of both religious conviction and hard-nosed pragmatism."[107] Certainly his will-of-God statements, which began before the Emancipation Proclamation, have a pragmatic element as we have seen. Moreover, he had "conviction" about those statements. But it was not the "religious conviction" they were true. Rather, it was quite the opposite. This is especially true of his Second Inaugural Address where he used vengeance of God theology—while simultaneously denying belief in that theology—to influence public opinion against slavery and thereby help bring constitutional law and "government of the people, by the people, for the people" more in line with the equal rights moral idealism of the Declaration of Independence. To put it another way, the Second Inaugural was Lincoln's way of using the people's fear of God to aid in the acceptance and approval of the Thirteenth Amendment abolishing slavery by threatening them with more war unless that amendment was adopted. Although he sounded like a preacher by invoking terror and fear of a vengeful God in his famous address in order to persuade his audience, he was also doing something he could have learned from Thomas Brown—the Scottish moral philosopher he read as a young man who wrote on the use of education, persuasion, and eloquence when appealing to the individual minds in one's audience. As Brown put it:

> It is not merely *with* the mind that we operate; the subject of our operations is also often the *mind [of others] itself*. In education, in criticism, in poetry, in eloquence, the mind has to act upon mind, to produce in it either emotions that are *temporary*, or affections and opinions that are *permanent*. We have to instruct it,—to convince it,—to persuade it,—to delight it,—to soften it with pity,—*to agitate it with terror* [my italics] or indignation.[108]

A cursory look at Lincoln's numerous speeches demonstrates that he knew how "to convince . . . to persuade . . . to delight . . . to soften . . . with pity" the minds of his fellow Americans with his own mind. In the Second Inaugural, however, the time was right for Lincoln—especially since he had political security, and the passionate conviction of each side that it was right was diminished by four years of war—"to agitate . . . with terror," to use Brown's words, the minds of his God-fearing fellow Americans when it came to slavery with a sermonlike speech threatening more war as God's punishment for the "offense" of slavery unless it was abolished. Yet simultaneously, Lincoln disclaimed any belief in the theology he preached in the Second Inaugural with his "If we shall suppose" and "*the* believers" instead of "*we* believers" phraseology.

It took sophistication to use religion this way, which Lincoln had in abundance, according to Leonard Swett, who Douglas Wilson and Rodney Davis described as "one of the most astute and sought after lawyers" in Illinois and "a close legal and political associate of AL."[109] As Swett described Lincoln:

> One great public mistake of his character is generally received and acquiesced in:—he is considered by the people of this country as a frank, guileless, unsophisticated man. There was never a greater mistake. Beneath a smooth surface of candor and an apparent declaration of all his thoughts and feelings, he exercised the most exalted tact and wisest discrimination. He handled and moved man *remotely* as we do pieces upon a chessboard. . . . This was not by cunning, or intrigue in the low acceptation of the term, but by far seeing, reason and discernment. He always told enough only, of his plans and purposes, to induce the belief that he had communicated all; yet he reserved enough, in fact, to have communicated nothing. He told all that was unimportant with a gushing frankness; yet no man ever kept his real purposes more closely, or penetrated the future further with his deep designs.[110]

In order to exercise "the most exalted tact and wisest discrimination," move men "*remotely* as we do pieces upon a chessboard," keep "his real purposes more closely," and penetrate "the future further with his deep designs," Lincoln needed self-control, which he had in abundance. As John Nicolay, his secretary while president, put it:

> His self control was simply wonderful. During more than four years the writer had opportunities almost daily and nightly to witness his bearing under most trying conditions and circumstances, and during the whole time never saw him manifest any extraordinary excitement beyond that of an eager interest to acquire infor-

mation, or indulge in any violence of speech or action beyond that of impressive emphasis, either in comment or command: while on the other hand he was never phlegmatic or indifferent even when annoyed by the most trivial requests, or patiently enduring the waste of precious time by the most wearisome of bores.[111]

Not only does Lincoln's use of theology and religion in the Second Inaugural accord with Brown's ideas and the "astute" Swett's description of Lincoln, it also accords with Edward Gibbon's statement in *The Decline and Fall of the Roman Empire*: "The various modes of worship which prevailed in the Roman world were all considered by the people as equally true; by the philosophers as equally false; and by the magistrate as equally useful."[112] Lincoln must have read this passage for he "read" "Gibbon's histories," according to his lifelong friend William G. Greene, who stated that he "loaned them" to Lincoln when they were young men.[113] What the people considered as "true" in religion, however, and what "philosophers" and even Lincoln regarded as "false," Lincoln as a "magistrate" found "useful," which is manifest in his Second Inaugural Address.

Lincoln's use of orthodox Christian theology pragmatically for political purposes without believing it gives rise to the question: Would he mislead people as to his true religious beliefs in this manner, especially since he had the reputation of being "honest Abe"?[114] James H. Matheny, Lincoln's friend from early manhood, said he would. In an interview with Herndon, Matheny said "that Lincoln played a sharp game here [Springfield prior to the presidency] on the Religious world" because "knowing that the old infidel, if not Atheistic charge would be made & proved against him"—which would destroy his political career—Lincoln said in effect to the "Religious world," "Come and Convert me." This caused "the Elders—lower & higher members of the churches, including Ministers" to flock "around him" so that he "appeared openly to the world as a seeker . . . after salvation &c in the Lord." This led to the view "that Lincoln was soon to be a changed man &c and thus it was that he [Lincoln] used the Revd Jas Smith."[115] Douglas Wilson and Rodney Davis tell us that although "Matheny embarrassed" Herndon in 1872 "by publicly recanting . . . some things he had

once told WHH [Herndon] about AL's early religious beliefs,"
Matheny had recanted "under pressure," no doubt political pressure,
because he sought an elected judgeship and some of the things he
said about Lincoln's religious views—such as that Lincoln referred to
Jesus as a bastard—were bound to offend the predominantly Protestant community where Matheny was finally elected to the bench in
1873.[116] When not "under pressure," however, Matheny said that
Lincoln did not hesitate to play a "sharp game" or mislead the "Religious world" about his religious beliefs. Late in life, just eighteen
months before his death, Lincoln in effect admitted apologetically
that he had done just that since his Springfield days with Reverend
Smith. As has been mentioned, on 24 October 1863 he stated before
his Washington minister Phineas Gurley and the Baltimore Synod,
"I have often wished that I was a more devout man than I am." This
statement makes it clear that Lincoln still had not become a
"changed man" or converted man in the mainstream Christian sense
as he led the "Religious world" to believe he "was soon" to become
in Springfield. This was because, according to Phineas Gurley and
the Baltimore Synod of the Presbyterian Church to whom Lincoln
made this statement, only a man who professed belief in doctrines
was a truly "devout man," which Lincoln never did with their
church, as they no doubt hoped he would, or with any church.

Despite his lack of belief in doctrine, however, Lincoln did not
hesitate to mislead the "Religious world" in his Second Inaugural
Address. He did this by pragmatically using mainstream Christian
belief for political purposes and in the process sounded mainstream
Christian. Simultaneously, however, in a very subtle and sophisti-
cated way, he renounced the mainstream Christian beliefs he used.
Therefore, it was not the Gettysburg Address in which Lincoln
accomplished an "open-air sleight-of-hand" or the public had its
"intellectual pocket picked," as Garry Wills maintains.[117] It was the
Second Inaugural. In addition, six factors indicate that Lincoln
maintained a consistent skepticism of mainstream Christian belief
from his Springfield days until his death, all of which have been
mentioned. First, he in effect denied original sin in the First Inaugural. Second, in October 1863 he admitted to Phineas Gurley, minister of the church he attended in Washington, of a long-term lack of

being "a more devout" or believing "man." Third, he stated to Congressman Deming one year before his death that he could never bring himself to believe in the doctrines of any church. Fourth, he in effect denied original sin in the Second Inaugural just six weeks before his death. Fifth, he pragmatically used mainstream providence or God's-will theology in the Second Inaugural while simultaneously stating that he did not believe that theology. Sixth, he made skeptical comments to the "real dignified lady" witnessed by Speed two weeks before his death. Considering his consistent skepticism, all Lincoln's public biblical and religious references indicating mainstream Christian belief should not be considered his beliefs. Rather, they should be considered as his consistent pragmatic use of mainstream Christianity for political purposes. Moreover, it should be emphasized that with Lincoln's denial of original sin in the First and Second Inaugurals, he would also have denied the doctrine of atonement and satisfaction or God sending his only begotten innocent son Jesus Christ to die on the cross to atone and give God satisfaction for the guilt that each human inherits from Adam and Eve as a result of original sin. Lincoln knew that without original sin there was no reason for atonement and satisfaction, as was stated in chapter 2.

To these arguments, some may point out that in early September of 1862, Lincoln made a covenant with God indicating that he had come to believe God's will was a governing factor in human affairs and that he had come to know that will. That was when General Robert E. Lee and his Confederate army invaded Maryland, thereby threatening Pennsylvania and nearby Washington with invasion. A successful invasion of either would have been devastating to the Union and could have ended the war with a Confederate victory. Therefore, a victory in battle that would drive Lee's army from Maryland was desperately needed. According to Secretary of the Treasury Salmon P. Chase and Secretary of the Navy Gideon Welles, in the cabinet meeting of September 22—the day Lincoln made his preliminary Emancipation Proclamation—Lincoln stated that he made his covenant after Lee invaded Maryland in early September by promising God and himself that he would make an emancipation proclamation and consider it "divine will" that it be made if the Union military was successful in driving Lee from Maryland. After the bloody battle of Antietam on September 17, in which more casualties were inflicted in a single day than on any other day in American history, Lee did withdraw from Maryland and Lincoln kept his promise with the September 22 preliminary Emancipation Proclamation that culminated in the final version of 1 January 1863. These factors give rise to the appearance that Lincoln did come to believe in God's will as a governing factor in human affairs and that he had come to know that will. If Lincoln held such belief, however, it was extremely short-lived. On September 13, just a few days after he made his promise to God, Lincoln told the Chicago ministers— some of whom were urging him to make the Emancipation Proclamation because it was God's will—that no one could know God's will, as has been mentioned. In addition, he told them that he would "study the plain physical facts of the case" in order to "ascertain what is possible and learn what appears to be" the "wise and right" course of action and act accordingly, as has also been mentioned. The effect of these statements was to denounce action based on claims of knowledge of God's will and simultaneously emphasize action based on rational analysis of facts. Moreover, since these statements came just a few days after Lincoln's covenant or promise, they indicate that he began to think that his arbitrarily making success by the Union army in driving Lee from Maryland a sign it was "divine will" that emancipation be made was absurd because it was an effort to govern by God's unknowable will. A statement Lincoln made in the September 22 cabinet meeting supports this view. According to Gideon Welles, Lincoln told the cabinet that his covenant method of deciding the emancipation issue "might be thought strange." Consistent with the view that Lincoln thought his method "might be thought strange" or absurd, he never mentioned Antietam in his aforementioned April 1864 letter to Kentucky editor Hodges that gave a detailed account of events that led him to make the Emancipation Proclamation. This indicates Antietam held no special sign-from-God-of-His-will significance to Lincoln.[118]

It should be emphasized that at the moment Lincoln made his

covenant the potential invasion of Pennsylvania or Washington was a desperate crisis for the Union and Lincoln. In such desperate wartime moments, men often do and say things contrary to their prevailing beliefs. As Ernie Pyle, the famous frontline war correspondent in World War II who shared many a foxhole with soldiers while in desperate circumstances under enemy fire, put it: "I never met an atheist in a foxhole." It seems that Lincoln's covenant fell in this desperate wartime moment category, especially in the light of his skeptical comments on human ability to know God's will and emphasis on a fact-based rational approach in dealing with wartime crises, a few days after he made his covenant.

Despite his lack of mainstream Christian doctrinal belief, however, we have ample testimony that Lincoln was a profoundly religious man in a profoundly heterodox way, as was mentioned in chapter 2. That testimony shows that his ideas on God and religion were similar to Theodore Parker's, as has also been mentioned. And, because of his lack of doctrinal belief, Lincoln can be described as "post-Protestant, even post-Christian," to use Mark Noll's terminology. Noll, however, did not use this phrase in connection with Parker's nondoctrinal Christianity and God, which it describes perfectly, since Parker's Christianity transcends Christian doctrinal belief systems to the extent that most mainstream Christians would call it non-Christian. To Parker, however, and Lincoln as well as Jefferson, the ecumenical, nondoctrinal deistic God was the real Christian God, not orthodoxy's partial God who favored followers of certain doctrinal beliefs and condemned others. And, as we have seen, it was this deistic ecumenical God that Jefferson made the foundational truth of the Declaration of Independence, which Lincoln described as "my ancient faith."[119]

# Conclusion

*H*aving read Thomas Paine and Theodore Parker as well as Constantin Volney's *The Ruins*, where Volney wrote on the history of morality, Lincoln was aware that Jews, Christians, and Muslims had killed nonbelievers in the name of God and at His command.[1] Moreover, he was aware that fear of being put to death for nonbelief of religious doctrine or creed had been used by these religions to maintain and expand belief in their religions even though God in the Old and New Testament commanded, "Thou shalt not kill" and in the Qur'an, "You shall not kill any man."[2] To Volney, the cause of violence in these religions was the emphasis of belief over morality, which he said fostered the "spirit of intolerance and exclusivism" that "destroys the whole basis of morals in society."[3] Emphasis on belief over morals made religious morality limited, partial, and dependent on belief rather than universal, impartial, and independent of belief. Not only was Lincoln aware of this limitation of Jewish, Christian, and Islamic morality, he was aware that when it came to the morality of slavery, Judeo-Christian religion was ambiguous, since the Old and New Testaments can be used, and indeed were used, to justify slavery, as we have seen in the theology of slavery.

## THE DECLARATION'S UNIVERSAL MORALITY

Unlike Judaic, Christian, and Islamic morality, the deistic morality of the Declaration of Independence—expressed in the phrase "all men are created equal" in the sense that each human being has the God-given "unalienable rights" of "Life, Liberty, and the Pursuit of Happiness" that are made "secure" or protected by government—extends to people of all races, both sexes, and all religious beliefs, as we have seen in chapter 1. Moreover, as we have also seen, this universal, none-are-excluded morality originates from a universal none-are-favored or -excluded deistic God who prescribes no belief system. In addition, the deistic God is not jealous. Therefore, He is not revengeful if you don't believe in Him or follow another god. It is this God—the deistic God rather than the jealous, angry, revengeful God of Judeo-Christian orthodoxy—who created each and every human being with the equal rights of "Life" and "Liberty," thereby undermining all ideologies, religions, theologies, and philosophies, including racist philosophies, that have been used to justify violence and immoral treatment of others. Moreover, it is the Declaration's concept of government protection of God-given individual rights, when put into practice, that prevents any person, group of persons, religion, philosophy, or ideology from using physical force against the rights of those holding conflicting beliefs or who are different or regarded as inferior. No one was more aware of this element of the Declaration than Abraham Lincoln. Stephen Douglas and John C. Calhoun had the same awareness. Yet because they supported slavery, they attacked the universal equal rights morality of the Declaration by stating it was false, or, a "self-evident lie," as Indiana Senator John Pettit called it. Lincoln, on the other hand, as an abolitionist, staunchly defended the Declaration's universal moral idealism. In 1858, he said the Declaration's statement: "We hold these truths to be self-evident, that all men are created equal," in the sense of each person having equal rights given them by the deistic God of the Declaration, "is the father of all moral principle" in Americans, as has been mentioned.[4] He also called the Declaration with its deistic theological foundation "my ancient faith" in his 1854 speech on the Kansas-Nebraska Act, as has also been mentioned. As a result of Lincoln's stress on the universal morality of the Declaration of Independence rather than on Christian morality as "the father of all moral principle" in Americans, John Diggins's statement that Lincoln reintroduced "into political discourse the Christian moralism that Machiavelli had purged from his theory of statecraft" is unjustified.[5] Not that Lincoln was against Christian morality. He simply emphasized a different source of morality because he was aware of the damaging impact doctrinal belief had on Christian morality as well as the fact that Judeo-Christian scripture was used to support slavery.

What Lincoln saw and emphasized was that when the Declaration stated "governments are instituted among men" in order "to secure" the rights of "Life, Liberty, and the Pursuit of Happiness" that "Nature's God" gave equally to each human being, it stated that moral action toward everyone should and must be practiced by each individual respecting the rights of everyone else regardless of their race, gender, or religious, philosophical, and political beliefs. Jefferson saw and said essentially the same thing, not only in the Declaration but also in his comment to Isaac Tiffany: "Liberty is 'unobstructed action according to our will; but rightful Liberty is the unobstructed action according to our will, within the limits drawn around us by the equal rights of others.'"[6] It was the Constitution of the United States, ratified in 1789, and the Bill of Rights, ratified in 1791, that actualized the Declaration's ideology of government protection of individual rights. Black slavery, which was protected by constitutional law, was, of course, a blatant violation of the Declaration's universal moral idealism. Therefore, when the Thirteenth Amendment finally abolished slavery, it was a major step toward bringing American law in accord with the nonselective, universal moral idealism of the Declaration of Independence.

It should be clear by now that the Declaration's theory of nonselective, universal morality through respecting and protecting the God-given rights of "Life, Liberty, and the Pursuit of Happiness" of everyone was never flawed from the time it was first institutionalized in America on 4 July 1776 in the sense that it applied universally to all human beings, as was stated in chapter 1. What was flawed was the practice of Equality or the application of the Declaration's moral theory to everyone. Lincoln was painfully aware of this, as was Jefferson, as we have seen. Indeed, in a fundamental respect, the story of America since 1776 has been the struggle to extend the principles of the Declaration to everyone so no one would be deprived of their God-given rights.[7] Abraham Lincoln was in the forefront of this struggle. His enormous contribution was his successful effort to have the Constitution altered to protect the rights of blacks with the Thirteenth Amendment when circumstances finally became favorable.

Lincoln's statement that the Declaration with its God-given equal rights idealism is "the father of all moral principle" in Americans was in effect echoed recently by Sean Hannity in a way that captures what the Declaration has meant and continues to mean to Americans and American civilization:

> America is a superior society *not* because Americans are superior human beings, but because our culture was founded on a recognition of our God-given natural rights—the "unalienable rights" referred to in the Declaration of Independence. From that awareness flows a basic, shared respect for humanity, individual liberty, limited government, and the rule of law.[8]

Because Hannity is American, many non-Americans will probably consider this statement self-praise. However, Karl Jaspers, the German philosopher, made a similar statement. After quoting Winston Churchill's description of democracy as "the worst form of government except for all the others," Jaspers said, "the American one is farthest from being the worst." He added that despite the presence of evils like the "Ku Klux Klan, juvenile delinquents, unsafe streets, deteriorating cities" found in America, the American people are "not blind" to these and other evils. Indeed, they make "giant efforts to fight" them. Finally, Jaspers stated that "more than anywhere else in the world, it seems that righteousness, decency, trustworthiness, reason, and helpfulness are facts in that nation of emigrants from almost all nations" of the world that make up "the American people."[9]

It should be emphasized that it was not Augustine's "compel them to come in" God of Christian orthodoxy that granted all human beings their "God-given natural rights" in the Declaration of Independence, which Hannity referred to, but rather the deistic "Nature's God" of natural theology. In fact, the Christian "compel them to come in" God and Christian nations did not respect the "rights" of all "humanity" and "individual liberty" prior to the

American Bill of Rights—especially the right of religious liberty or freedom of belief according to the conscience of each individual—as did Jefferson's, Lincoln's, and the Declaration's "Nature's God." Historically, many human beings were compelled to become and remain Christian against their will and persecuted if they did not by institutionalized Christianity and law.[10] Law had been used this way in all countries in the West since the fourth century under the Roman emperor Theodosius. Such law was still on the books in most of the colonies prior to the Revolution. In contrast, respect by the tolerant God of deism for every human being's right and ability to determine and believe what they deem religious truth or untruth with their own reason became protected under American law thanks largely to the efforts of Thomas Jefferson and James Madison. The effects of such law, as Jefferson commented when speaking of the Virginia Statute for Religious Freedom that he authored, was to protect "the Jew and the Gentile, the Christian and Mahometan, the Hindoo, and Infidel of every denomination."[11] Jefferson said much the same thing about the religious freedom provision of the First Amendment of the Bill of Rights that he insisted his friend Madison add to the Constitution, as has been mentioned, when he told an American Jew that

> your sect by its sufferings has furnished a remarkable proof of the universal spirit of religious intolerance inherent in every sect, disclaimed by all while feeble and practiced by all while in power. Our laws have applied the only antidote to this vice, protecting our religions, as they do our civil rights by putting all on equal footing.[12]

In 1800, Dennis Driscol, editor of the American deistic paper *The Temple of Reason*, sounded much like Jefferson when he wrote: "Fortunately for the peace and prosperity of America, *Mohometism* is as much *established by law*, here, as Christianity."[13] Driscol could have said the same thing about any religion or religious belief. This is because the legal equality or "equal footing" of all religions means all religions and all views on religion, whether for or against it, are legally protected from the use of violence and force against them by those of different religious views and thereby "established by law" in America. Such equal legal establishment, however, is not to be confused with an established religion in the sense of a single government-protected and enforced religion outlawed by the First Amendment of the Bill of Rights.[14]

It should also be emphasized that the legal equality or the "equal footing" of all religious views is antithetical to Judaism, Christianity, and Islam, each of which claims it is superior to any other religion, as has been mentioned. Yet this legal equality, the gift of the Founding Fathers, is what has provided religious freedom and peace in America often lacking in other nations throughout history. As Jefferson put it: "We have experienced the quiet as well as the comfort which results from leaving every one to profess freely and openly those principles of religion which are the inductions of his own reason, and the serious convictions of his own enquiries."[15] And Abraham Lincoln, as was mentioned in the introduction, praised the Founding Fathers' gift of religious freedom in his Lyceum speech.

When considering Hannity's aforementioned comment, it needs to be clarified that the Declaration's "natural rights," a part of natural law or the "Laws of Nature" of the Declaration, are not orthodox Christianity's version of moral natural law. Christianity put individually, rationally determined "laws of nature" or natural law under the authority of church in Catholicism and scripture in Protestantism. As a result, individual determinations of natural law are valid only if they agree with those of church or scripture.[16] This scholastic version of moral natural law was Thomas Aquinas's contribution to Christianity.[17] Its effect was to put the moral direction of the state under the authority of church and scripture in Christian countries rather than under the people, which was destructive to democracy. On the other hand, Jefferson maintained, as did Kames who influenced him, which was pointed out in chapters 1 and 3, that each human being could easily find the moral "Laws of Nature" and individuals were not under church or scriptural authority for final determinations of such law. This individual approach to natural law is what enabled the people—not a Christian king or a church or a scripture or the clergy—to supply moral direction to the state and thereby govern themselves in a democratic republic, as was pointed out in chapters 1 and 3.

Like Thomas Jefferson, Abraham Lincoln, as a result of his heterodox views on religion, was aware that individual moral autonomy was the bedrock of "government of the people, by the people, for the people" or democracy that he championed in his Gettysburg Address. Individual moral autonomy, as has been mentioned, was also the bedrock of the democratic political theory of the Declaration of Independence, which Lincoln described as "my ancient faith." He also described the Declaration as "our ancient faith" because all Americans regardless of belief, race, or gender were equally included in its universal morality and equally bound by that morality to respect the rights of others and the laws of their government that enforced that morality. Hence the Declaration was "the father of all moral principle" in Americans as Lincoln stated.

## THE PRUDENCE OF LINCOLN AND THE FOUNDERS

Abraham Lincoln was a firm believer in cause and effect. As he stated to William Herndon:

> There are no accidents in my philosophy. Every effect must have its cause. The past is the cause of the present, and the present will be the cause of the future. All these are links in the endless chain stretching from the finite to the infinite.[18]

This statement does not mean Lincoln was a fatalist in the sense that he believed his life and actions were totally and completely the effects of causes over which he had no control, even though he made fatalistic comments that might suggest this on several occasions. Simultaneously, however, there is no doubt that many of the causes and effects in his life were beyond his control, which is true of any human being. However, what gives any person freedom, according to Lincoln if you judge by his actions, was the ability to initiate new action in the "present" that would cause different effects—desired effects. Lincoln was a master of initiating such action. Few Americans ever started in more humble, poverty-ridden circumstances than Lincoln.[19] And certainly no American ever rose to greater heights than he did by initiating new causes in his life through his own actions that had positive effects. In fact, Lincoln is the epitome of the self-made man and regarded himself as such.[20] He took the same activist approach in his efforts to win the Civil War, which at first went badly for the Union due to circumstances beyond his control. Yet he was in a unique position to initiate new causes that would change the course of the war. He took advantage of this if you judge by his actions and not his fatalistic remarks to friends or comments calculated to silence or tame his critics, like those in his aforementioned letter to editor Hodges of Kentucky, or those he made to motivate a religious audience in a political speech like his Second Inaugural. In this sense, Lincoln was an activist and a very effective one even though David Herbert Donald perceives him as passive.[21]

Judging from his actions, it is clear that Lincoln was an extremely prudent man, and prudent men often appear passive because they are cautious and careful before they act. In fact, sometimes they will not act at all if circumstances are not favorable to attaining their objectives because action in such circumstances is often counterproductive. Prudent men wait for circumstances to become more favorable, which gives the appearance of being passive. Or, sometimes they systematically perform actions that result in more favorable circumstances if they deem this feasible, which Lincoln often did.[22] More important, prudent men seek knowledge of cause and effect before they act so they can calculate the effects of a proposed action before they act. The fact that Lincoln valued knowledge, which is vital to effective action, is seen in the importance he placed on education as was pointed out in chapter 1.

The link between prudence and knowledge is emphasized in Volney's *The Ruins* in a quotation from that work placed in the last chapter where Volney, in a series of rhetorical questions, makes it clear that human "imprudence" and "ignorance," not the will of God, is what leads to human misery.[23] Volney, however, gave a detailed analysis of the interdependence of knowledge and prudence in a short work titled *The Law of Nature or Principles of Morality Deduced from the Physical Constitution of Mankind and the Universe,* which Lincoln probably read because it was included in many editions of *The Ruins*. There, Volney stated that knowledge was necessary for self-preservation—which was part of the law of nature—and self-actualization or the actualization of one's human faculties. As he put it, with emphasis on gaining knowledge of cause and effect:

> The man who is acquainted with the causes and effects of things, provides in a very extensive and certain manner for *his own preservation* [my italics] and the development of his faculties [self-actualization]. Knowledge is for him, as it were, light acting upon its appropriate organ, making him discern all the objects which surround him, and in the midst of which he moves with precision and clearness. And for this reason, we used to say an *enlightened* man, to designate a wise and well informed man.[24]

But knowledge of cause and effect, although necessary, was not sufficient for self-preservation and self-actualization, according to Volney. Prudence was equally important, which he defined as:

> An anticipated view, a foresight of effects, and the consequences of every event: a foresight by which a man avoids dangers which threaten him, and seizes and raises up opportunities which are favourable: whence it appears, that he provides, on a large and sure scale, for his present and future conservation; while the *imprudent man*, who neither calculates his progress nor his conduct, the efforts required, nor the resistances to overcome, falls every moment into a thousand difficulties and dangers, which, more or less, slowly destroy his faculties and his being [my italics].[25]

The Age of Enlightenment values of knowledge, self-preservation, and progress are all included in this statement—values that were the foundation of Lincoln's successful life. Therefore, it seems clear that the principal influence on Abraham Lincoln's mind was the Enlightenment as a result of reading men like Benjamin Franklin, Thomas Paine, Theodore Parker, Thomas Brown, Constantin Volney, and, of course, Thomas Jefferson and not from reading Romantic idealists, as Garry Wills maintains.

The self-educated Lincoln had a high level of knowledge—more than enough to compete on an equal footing with his formally educated colleagues in law and politics. Where Lincoln shone, however, was his prudence or ability to put his knowledge to effective use—an ability often lacking even in extremely knowledgeable and intelligent people. He had "foresight of effects, and the consequences" caused by his own and others' actions, to use Volney's definition of prudence, and he used that "foresight" to "avoid dangers which threatened him" and take advantage of "opportunities" that were "favourable," as Volney stated a prudent man would. Lincoln did this in his political life with great skill. He positioned himself to be a candidate for US senator from Illinois in 1856 and 1858. He lost both times. Yet his debates with the well-known Douglas, his opponent in the Senate election of 1858, made him a highly regarded national figure because they were published in newspapers throughout the land. Although his ideas on slavery were unpopular in the South and in parts of Illinois, they were well received in the politically powerful Northeast and started a movement there to make him the Republican candidate for president in 1860. There seems little doubt that Lincoln, shrewd and prudent politician that he was, knew his ideas would win him favor outside Illinois and a chance to become president.[26]

Lincoln's prudence was also manifest in "avoiding dangers which threatened" the nation and war effort and in taking advantage of "opportunities" that were "favourable" to winning the war, despite adverse circumstances that included inept military commanders, hostile cabinet members, Copperhead Democrats against the war, and radical Republican abolitionists who wanted the immediate abolition of slavery, which would have alienated support for the war, since a large portion of Union public opinion was against abolition until late in the war.[27] Lincoln struck a moderate, prudent course in this context that kept "a fractious coalition of Radical Republicans, moderates, War Democrats and border-state Unionists who supported the war" from collapsing.[28] This bought him time until competent military commanders like Grant and Sherman emerged. Then, when the Union military achieved major victories in battle, public opinion altered from lukewarm to overwhelming support for the war. Those victories also caused public support for abolition to rise. At that time, Lincoln saw that circumstances were favorable to abolition so he actively supported the complete eradication of slavery and thereby sought to expand the practice of "Liberty"—a right belonging "all Men," according to the Declaration of Independence. This was Lincoln's long-held goal, according to Joseph Gillespie, his "legal and political" friend for over thirty years, which means Lincoln was an abolitionist at heart from his early adulthood.[29] Lincoln, however, would never have sought complete abolition at the expense of damaging the Constitution and the Union he was sworn to uphold. Yet to the prudent Lincoln, keeping the Union intact was essential in order to abolish slavery in the entire nation, both the North and the South. He was aware that splitting the Union would have not only destroyed the integrity of the nation, it would also have perpetuated slavery in the South. Moreover, it would have made both the North and the South, weakened as a result of the split, relatively impotent to resist being taken over by European powers or becoming their satellites.[30] Therefore, if the South had won the war, both sides would have lost and the abolitionists would have lost out completely in the South. Some idealistic abolitionists and Republicans, who "favored peaceable separation" of the seceding states "as a policy of good riddance to slavery," seemed oblivious to this.[31] Lincoln, however, unlike many idealists, was not "the imprudent man, who neither calculates" the "effects" of his actions, "the efforts required" to attain his goals, or "the resistances" to attaining them that needed to be "overcome," to use Volney's words. He was the prudent antithesis of these things that enabled him to keep the nation intact and then contribute to the eradication of slavery nationwide by arguing in favor of the Thirteenth Amendment—which he helped initiate—when circumstances finally became favorable. He thereby used prudent realism to expand the idealism of the Declaration of Independence—his "loadstone" or guide, as Charles Black stated.[32] Significantly, the Declaration of Independence that profoundly influenced Lincoln contains the value of prudence: "Prudence, indeed, will dictate that Governments long established should not be changed for light and transient causes." Just as significantly, in a letter discussing the Greek philosopher Epicurus, Jefferson defined "Prudence" in terms of its opposite, which he called "Folly."[33] Consistent with this definition, Lincoln was no fool because he, like Jefferson, was "an adherent of classical Western prudence," and more importantly, its effective practicioner.[34]

Lincoln's knowledge of American history no doubt gave him knowledge of the Founding Fathers' prudence. Indeed, when it came to slavery, Lincoln's prudent civil war policy parallels that of the Founders in the Revolutionary period. The prudence of the Continental Congress is seen in its deletion of Jefferson's anti–slave trade, antislavery paragraph of his original draft of the Declaration of Independence mentioned in chapter 1. This paragraph was repugnant to delegates from South Carolina and Georgia. Therefore, to ensure their support for the Declaration and the Revolution, the Congress prudently deleted this paragraph, much to Jefferson's disgust, as has been mentioned. In this instance, however, it was Jefferson who was being imprudent because without deleting this paragraph South Carolina and Georgia very likely would have withheld support for the Revolution and remained colonies in order to protect the institution of slavery. As British colonies, with harbors at Charleston and Savannah, which would no doubt have been used as British military bases, they would have been important British assets and crucial American liabilities. Such assets could well have enabled England to win the war, and an English victory would have meant a short-lived United States and the preservation of slavery and the slave trade in the colonies because in 1776 England supported colonial slavery and the slave trade, as has been mentioned. Therefore, insistence on Jefferson's antislavery provision of the Declaration in 1776 would have served neither abolition nor Revolution. Indeed, it would have worked against both.

Similar prudential compromise that legalized slavery was made in the Constitution of the United States, ratified in 1789, in order to induce ratification by the slave states. Without their ratification, the nation would have split in two at its inception with institutionalized slavery remaining intact in the South and both the North and the South, weakened as a result of the split, subject to domination by European powers. Thus the prudential morality of the Founders on slavery, so harshly condemned by many contemporary "latter-day abolitionist historians," as Harry Jaffa calls them,[35] was of key importance to a successful Revolution and establishment of the nation. In addition, it seems abundantly clear, in the light of the enormous struggle to eradicate slavery in the Civil War, that the imprudent insistence on total abolition at the nation's founding would have failed as well as divisively doomed the establishment of a viable nation.

That prudence—which accommodates a lesser evil if this is necessary to achieve a greater good—was part of Lincoln's thinking from the beginning of his career in national politics is seen in a statement he made in his speech to the US House of Representatives in 1848:

> The true rule, in determining to embrace, or reject any thing, is not whether it have *any* evil in it; but whether it have more of evil, than of good. There are few things *wholly* evil, or *wholly* good. Almost every thing, especially of governmental policy, is an inseparable compound of the two; so that our best judgment of the preponderance between them is continually demanded.[36]

Rational prudential calculations of "the preponderance" of "good" over "evil" in any situation necessitates the use of "cold, calculating, unimpassioned reason" that Lincoln advocated in his Lyceum address in 1838.[37] Such reason is something Lincoln practiced all his adult life and thereby demonstrates his commitment to Enlightenment rather than Romantic values.

## IN PRAISE OF LINCOLN

Lincoln's contributions to the American nation during its civil war crisis were enormous. Those contributions were praised again and again after his assassination and continue to be praised today. Three extraordinary praises made by three extraordinary individuals tell us much about the way Lincoln has been and indeed continues to be seen in the eyes of others. The first was made by General James Longstreet of Gettysburg fame whose praise is especially significant because he was a Confederate, not a Union general. Longstreet said Lincoln was "without doubt the greatest man of rebellion times, the one matchless among forty millions for the peculiar difficulties of the period."[38]

Lincoln's moral courage, his universalism, his tolerance, his knowledge, and his prudence were among the qualities that made him "matchless among forty millions for the difficulties of the period."

The second comment came in 1909 from the aged Russian literary giant Leo Tolstoy, described by Merrill Peterson as "arguably the most famous man in the world" at that time. While Longstreet singled out Lincoln from among forty million Americans during the Civil War, Tolstoy made him stand above all the "heroes and statesmen" of all nations throughout all "history" by stating: "Of all the great national heroes and statesmen of history, Lincoln is the only true giant."[39] Praise indeed from Tolstoy who knew a great deal about history.

The third comment came from Robert Ingersoll—Civil War veteran, lawyer, skeptic, and famed orator:

> He knew no fear except the fear of doing wrong. Hating slavery, pitying the master—seeking to conquer, not persons, but prejudices—he was the embodiment of self-denial, the courage, the hope, and the nobility of a nation. He spoke, not to inflame, not to upbraid, but to convince.[40]

Lincoln did indeed speak "to convince"—to convince Americans that slavery was wrong. His principal method was to preach over and over again the Enlightenment moral idealism or all-inclusive "ancient faith" of the Declaration of Independence. He did this because he, like Jefferson who authored the Declaration, understood that the kind of ideas human beings have in their minds are what determines their worldview and their worldview is what profoundly influences the type of actions they perform. Lincoln, as well as Jefferson and the Enlightenment, saw that those imbued with all-inclusive, universal moral ideas—like the deistic equal rights of all human beings contained in the Declaration—will be large-minded and tolerant human beings. Moreover, Lincoln, as well as Jefferson, saw that without a large-minded, universal, tolerant culture in America, the majority would be bigoted, and because the law would ultimately reflect the will of the majority in the American political system, a bigoted majority would sooner or later infringe on minority rights. In addition, both men were aware that history demonstrated that infringement of rights invariably led to hatred, violence, death, and destruction along with the ensuing miseries they entailed. In fact, both men had witnessed this in their lifetimes and this is why Jefferson, not long after the Revolutionary War, stated: "All the tranquility, the happiness and security of mankind, rest on justice or the obligation to respect the rights of others."[41] This is a succinct statement of the premise that underlies the "ancient faith" of the Declaration of Independence of 1776, "the father of all moral principle" in Americans, as Lincoln described the document he used so effectively in arousing the conscience of the nation in the struggle against slavery.

# *Epilogue*

*I*t would be a happy ending if Abraham Lincoln's efforts and the Civil War had truly eradicated the blight of slavery in America. They did not, however, even though the Thirteenth Amendment was finally ratified seven months after Lincoln's April 1865 assassination. Yes, blacks were legally free as a result of that amendment. De facto, however, they were still slaves due to poverty, lack of education, and lack of "liberty" or opportunity to move effectively as a result of being excluded from living and functioning effectively among the nineteenth-century white population dominated by "racist convictions" that "held sway in the South" and with "most Northerners" as well.[1] As a result of these circumstances, most blacks did not have the means, the knowledge, or the environment to effectively practice their legal freedom. Or, as Carl Sandburg put it: "Black men could now move from where they were miserable to where they were equally miserable."[2] Significantly, color prejudice was not manifest in Lincoln, according to Frederick Douglass, the famed black abolitionist who knew Lincoln.[3] Lincoln thereby differed from most American abolitionists who manifested implicit prejudice against blacks by patronizing them, according to another black abolitionist, William G. Allen.[4]

Even the law was manipulated to deprive blacks of freedom, despite the Thirteenth Amendment. This was especially true of the Fourteenth Amendment even though it was designed to augment the Thirteenth Amendment by nullifying state laws depriving blacks of the "privileges and immunities" they were entitled to as "citizens" as well as their "life, liberty, or property without due process of law," despite the fact that blacks were not specifically mentioned in that amendment ratified in 1868.[5] This is because, as J. R. Pole stated, the Fourteenth Amendment's overall intent was to create "legal equality of all American citizens, state and federal, on the individual basis that lay at the existing foundations of American constitutional law."[6]

Unfortunately, the amendment was quickly rendered ineffective by Lincoln's old nemesis the Supreme Court of the United States in the infamous *Slaughterhouse* case.

In 1869, the Louisiana state legislature passed an act granting a corporation it created the exclusive right to operate slaughterhouses in certain areas that included parts of New Orleans. The act was challenged in the Louisiana courts and ruled valid. The case should have stopped at this level, according to Charles L. Black Jr., since "common sense" as well as "soundness of judicial practice" tells us that state law could be used for reasonable "regulation of the practice of slaughtering" because it was "fraught with danger to the health and comfort of the people unless so located as to minimize these effects."[7] Nonetheless, the US Supreme Court decided to review the Louisiana court's ruling, which it upheld. Simultaneously, however, it interpreted the "privilege and immunities" clause of the Fourteenth Amendment in a way that destroyed the amendment's underlying intent, which, once again, was to nullify state laws depriving blacks of their "privileges and immunities" as citizens and their "life, liberty or property without due process of law."

The court's ruling was based on the second clause of the Fourteenth Amendment, which gave Congress the power to enforce that amendment. That clause could also be construed as giving Congress the power to judge what "privileges and immunities" or "rights" ought to be "enforced."[8] Moreover, it could be construed as giving the courts the right to answer two questions: first, was the source of civil rights federal or state government, and second, which of these two governments should enforce civil rights? The Supreme Court's ruling on these questions severely restricted the amendment's scope, as Justice Samuel Miller, who wrote the majority opinion, stated when he said that the amendment's "privileges and immunities" clause extended solely to those rights derived from "the Federal Government, its National Character, its Constitution, or its laws." Such rights, however, were relatively few, leaving all other rights to be defined and enforced by state law and state courts. This put the protection of rights largely, if not completely, in the hands of the states, which violated the intent if not the letter of the Fourteenth Amendment.[9] In the dissenting Supreme Court minority opinion, Justice Stephen J. Field, Lincoln's appointee from California, wrote that the Court's decision made the Fourteenth Amendment

> a vain and idle enactment, which accomplished nothing, and most unnecessarily excited Congress and the people on its passage. With privileges and immunities thus designated or implied no state could ever have interfered by its laws, and no new constitutional provision was required to inhibit such interference.[10]

John C. Calhoun, long since deceased, would have rejoiced at the Court's decision. His views on state sovereignty, especially the right of judging by individual states, which Lincoln and the Union fought to defeat in the Civil War, were now, to a large extent, upheld by the Supreme Court of the United States. Calhoun would have also rejoiced that the *Slaughterhouse* case gave support to "every sleazy trick concoctable" on the state level "to keep black people in their place," including the absurd separate-but-equal facilities for blacks and whites doctrine. Indeed, those tricks were "blessed by the Court," as Black states, which made blacks de facto slaves even though technically free as a result of the Thirteenth Amendment.[11]

It was not until the 1950s and 1960s that the Supreme Court began to uphold the rights of blacks under the leadership of Chief Justice Earl Warren. The Civil Rights Acts of 1964, 1965, and 1968, inspired by Martin Luther King Jr., another advocate of the Declaration of Independence, made further contributions to improving the status of blacks. This means that blacks finally got help from the law, but only after one hundred years, give or take, had elapsed from the ratification of the Thirteenth and Fourteenth Amendments. That was not only a travesty of justice against blacks but also against soldiers who died fighting for black freedom in the war, as well as Abraham Lincoln, who was assassinated as a result of his efforts to eradicate slavery in America.

Nonetheless, because of the Civil War, Abraham Lincoln, the Thirteenth Amendment, and most of all, the idealism of the Declaration of Independence that Lincoln referred to as "my ancient faith" and "our ancient faith," the repression of blacks became increasingly ugly in the land that values "Life, Liberty, and the Pursuit of Happiness" for "all Men." In fact, it became shamefully ugly, not only to blacks but also to many whites, and not just in the North but also in the South. It was shameful because the conscience of the nation became increasingly against such repression—a conscience shaped by the Declaration of Independence, as Lincoln fully understood. Martin Luther King Jr. also understood this and, like Lincoln, effectively used the Declaration's morality in arguing the cause of blacks to white America in his own efforts to put an end to racial repression in the United States. And like Lincoln's, King's efforts on behalf of blacks caused his assassination.[12]

# Appendix 1

# THE DECLARATION OF INDEPENDENCE

When in the Course of human events, it becomes necessary for one People to dissolve the Political Bands which have connected them with another, and to assume among the Powers of the Earth, the separate and equal Station to which the Laws of Nature and of Nature's God entitle them, a decent Respect to the Opinions of Mankind requires that they should declare the causes which impel them to the Separation.

We hold these Truths to be self-evident, that all Men are created equal, that they are endowed by their Creator with certain unalienable Rights, that among these are Life, Liberty, and the Pursuit of Happiness. That to secure these Rights, Governments are instituted among Men, deriving their just Powers from the Consent of the Governed, that whenever any Form of Government becomes destructive of these Ends, it is the Right of the People to alter or to abolish it, and to institute new Government, laying its Foundation on such Principles and organizing its Powers in such Form, as to Them shall seem most likely to effect their Safety and Happiness. Prudence, indeed, will dictate that Governments long established should not be changed for light and transient Causes; and accordingly all Experience hath shewn, that Mankind are more disposed to suffer, while Evils are sufferable, than to right themselves by abolishing the Forms to which they are accustomed. But when a long Train of Abuses and Usurpations, pursuing invariably the same Object, evinces a design to reduce them under absolute Despotism, it is their Right, it is their Duty, to throw off such Government, and to provide new Guards for their future Security. Such has been the patient Sufferance of these Colonies; and such is now the Necessity which constrains them to alter their former systems of Government. The History of the present King of Great-Britain is a History of repeated Injuries and Usurpations, all having in direct Object the Establishment of an absolute Tyranny over these States. To prove this, let Facts be submitted to a candid World.

He has refused his Assent to Laws, the most wholesome and necessary for the public good.

He has forbidden his Governors to pass Laws of immediate and pressing Importance, unless suspended in their Operation till his Assent should be obtained; and when so suspended, he has utterly neglected to attend to them.

He has refused to pass other Laws for the Accommodation of large Districts of People, unless those People would relinquish the right of Representation in the Legislature, a Right inestimable to them and formidable to Tyrants only.

He has called together Legislative Bodies at Places unusual, uncomfortable, and distant from the Depository of their public Records, of the sole Purpose of fatiguing them into Compliance with his Measures.

He has dissolved Representative Houses repeatedly, for opposing with manly Firmness his Invasions on the Rights of the People.

He has refused for a Long Time, after such Dissolutions, to cause others to be elected; whereby the Legislative Powers, incapable of Annihilation, have returned to the People at large for their exercise; the State remaining in the mean time exposed to all the Dangers of Invasion from without, and Convulsions within.

He has endeavored to prevent the Population of these States; for that Purpose obstructing the Laws for Naturalization of Foreigners; refusing to pass others to encourage their Migrations hither, and raising the Conditions of new Appropriations of Lands.

He has obstructed the Administration of Justice, by refusing his Assent to Laws for establishing Judiciary Powers.

He has made Judges dependent of his Will alone, for the Tenure of their Offices, and the Amount and Payment of their Salaries.

He has erected a Multitude of new Offices, and sent hither Swarms of Officers to harass our People, and eat out their Substance.

He has kept among us, in Times of Peace, Standing Armies, without the Consent of our Legislatures.

He has affected to render the Military independent of and superior to the Civil Power.

He has combined with others to subject us to a Jurisdiction foreign to our Constitution, and unacknowledged by our Laws; giving his Assent to their Acts of pretended Legislation:

For quartering Large Bodies of Armed Troops among us:

For protecting them, by a mock Trial, from Punishment for any Murders which they should commit on the Inhabitants of these States:

For cutting off our Trade with all Parts of the world:

For imposing Taxes on us without our Consent:

For depriving us, in many Cases, of the Benefits of Trial by Jury:

For transporting us beyond Seas to be tried for pretended Offences:

For abolishing the free System of English Laws in a neighboring Province, establishing therein an arbitrary Government, and enlarging its Boundaries, so as to render it at once an Example and fit Instrument for introducing the same absolute Rule into these Colonies:

For taking away our Charters, abolishing our most valuable Laws, and altering fundamentally the Forms of our Governments:

For suspending our own Legislatures, and declaring themselves invested with Power to legislate for us in all Cases whatsoever.

He has abdicated Government here, by declaring us out of his Protection and waging War against us.

He has plundered our Seas, ravaged our Coasts, burnt our Towns, and destroyed the Lives of our People.

He is, at this Time, transporting large Armies of foreign Mercenaries to compleat the Works of Death, Desolation, and Tyranny, already begun with circumstances of Cruelty and Perfidy, scarcely paralleled in the most barbarous Ages, and totally unworthy the Head of a civilized Nation.

He has constrained our fellow Citizens taken Captive on the high Seas to bear Arms against their Country, to become the Executioners of their Friends and Brethren, or to fall themselves by their Hands.

He has excited domestic Insurrections amongst us, and has endeavored to bring on the Inhabitants of our Frontiers, the merciless Indian Savages, whose known Rule of Warfare, is an undistinguished Destruction, of all Ages, Sexes and Conditions.

In every stage of these Oppressions We have Petitioned for Redress in the most humble Terms: Our repeated Petitions have been answered only by repeated Injury. A Prince, whose character is thus marked by every act which may define a Tyrant, is unfit to be the Ruler of a free People.

Nor have We been wanting in Attention to our British Brethren. We have warned them from Time to Time of Attempts by their Legislature to extend an unwarrantable Jurisdiction over us. We have reminded them of the Circumstance of our Emigration and Settlement here. We have appealed to their native Justice and Magnanimity, and we have conjured them by the Ties of our common Kindred to disavow these Usurpations, which, would inevitably interrupt our Connections and Correspondence. They too have been deaf to the Voice of Justice and of Consanguinity. We must, therefore, acquiesce in the Necessity, which denounces our Separation, and hold them, as we hold the rest of Mankind, Enemies in War, in Peace, Friends.

We, therefore, the Representatives of the UNITED STATES OF AMERICA, in GENERAL CONGRESS, Assembled, appealing to the Supreme Judge of the World for the Rectitude of our Intentions, do, in the Name, and by Authority of the good People of these Colonies, solemnly Publish and Declare, That these United Colonies are, and of Right ought to be, FREE AND INDEPENDENT STATES; that they are absolved from all Allegiance to the British Crown, and that all political Connection between them and the State of Great-Britain, is and ought to be totally dissolved; and that as FREE AND INDEPEN-

DENT STATES, they have full Power to levy War, conclude Peace, contract Alliances, establish Commerce, and to do all other Acts and Things which INDEPENDENT STATES may of right do. And for the support of this Declaration, with a firm Reliance on the Protection of divine Providence, we mutually pledge to each other our Lives, our Fortunes, and our sacred Honor.

4 July 1776

# Appendix 2

# LINCOLN'S FIRST INAUGURAL ADDRESS

*F*ellow citizens of the United States:

In compliance with a custom as old as the government itself, I appear before you to address you briefly, and to take, in your presence, the oath prescribed by the Constitution of the United States, to be taken by the President "before he enters on the execution of his office."

I do not consider it necessary, at present, for me to discuss those matters of administration about which there is no special anxiety, or excitement.

Apprehension seems to exist among the people of the Southern States, that by the accession of a Republican Administration, their property, and their peace, and personal security, are to be endangered. There has never been any reasonable cause for such apprehension. Indeed, the most ample evidence to the contrary has all the while existed, and been open to their inspection. It is found in nearly all the published speeches of him who now addresses you. I do but quote from one of those speeches when I declare that "I have no purpose, directly or indirectly, to interfere with the institution of slavery in the States where it exists. I believe I have no lawful right to do so, and I have no inclination to do so." Those who nominated and elected me did so with full knowledge that I have made this, and many similar declarations, and had never recanted them. And more than this, they placed in the platform, for my acceptance, and as a law to themselves, and to me, the clear and emphatic resolution which I now read:

"*Resolved*, That the maintenance inviolate of the rights of the States, and especially the right of each State to order and control its own domestic institutions according to its own judgment exclusively, is essential to that balance of power on which the perfection and endurance of our political fabric depend; and we denounce the lawless invasion by armed force of the soil of any State or Territory, no matter under what pretext, as among the gravest of crimes."

I now reiterate these sentiments: and in doing so, I only press upon the public attention the most conclusive evidence of which the case is susceptible, that the property, peace and security of no section are to be in anywise endangered by the now incoming Administration. I add too, that all the protection which, consistently with the Constitution and the laws, can be given, will be cheerfully given to all the States when lawfully demanded, for whatever cause—as cheerfully to one section, as to another.

There is much controversy about the delivering up of fugitives from service or labor. The clause I now read is as plainly written in the Constitution as any other of its provisions:

"No person held to service or labor in one State, under the laws thereof, escaping into another, shall, in consequence of any law or regulation therein, be discharged from such service or labor, but shall be delivered up on claim of the party to whom such service or labor may be due."

It is scarcely questioned that this provision was intended by those who made it, for the reclaiming of what we call fugitive slaves; and the intention of the law-giver is the law. All members of Congress swear their support to the whole Constitution—to this provision as much as to any other. To the proposition, then, that slaves whose cases come within the terms of this clause, "shall be delivered up," their oaths are unanimous. Now, if they would make the effort in good temper, could they not, with nearly equal unanimity, frame and pass a law, by means of which to keep good that unanimous oath?

There is some difference of opinion whether this clause should be enforced by national or by state authority; but surely that difference is not a very material one. If the slave is to be surrendered, it can be of but little consequence to him, or to others, by which authority it is done. And should any one, in any case, be content that his oath shall go un-kept, on a merely unsubstantial controversy as to *how* it shall be kept?

Again, in any law upon this subject, ought not all the safeguards of liberty known in civilized and humane jurisprudence to be introduced, so that a free man be not, in any case, surrendered as a slave? And might it not be well, at the same time, to provide by law for the enforcement of that clause in the Constitution which guarranties that "The citizens of each State shall be entitled to all privileges and immunities of citizens in the several States?"

I take the official oath to-day, with no mental reservations, and with no purpose to construe the Constitution or laws, by any hyper-critical rules. And while I do not choose now to specify particular acts of Congress as proper to be enforced, I do suggest, that it will be much safer for all, both in official and private stations, to conform to, and abide by, all those acts which stand unrepealed, than to violate any of them, trusting to find impunity in having them held to be unconstitutional.

It is seventy-two years since the first inauguration of a President under our national Constitution. During that period fifteen different and greatly distinguished citizens, have, in succession, administered the executive branch of the government. They have conducted it through many perils; and, generally, with great success. Yet, with all this scope for precedent, I now enter upon the same task for the brief constitutional term of four years, under great and peculiar difficulty. A disruption of the Federal Union heretofore only menaced, is now formidably attempted.

I hold, that in contemplation of universal law, and of the Constitution, the Union of these States is perpetual. Perpetuity is implied, if not expressed, in the fundamental law of all national governments. It is safe to assert that no government proper, ever had a provision in its organic law for its own termination. Continue to execute all the express provisions of our national Constitution, and the Union will endure forever—it being impossible to destroy it, except by some action not provided for in the instrument itself.

Again, if the United States be not a government proper, but an association of States in the nature of contract merely, can it, as a contract, be peaceably unmade, by less than all the parties who made it? One party to a contract may violate it—break it, so to speak; but does it not require all to lawfully rescind it?

Descending from these general principles, we find the proposition that, in legal contemplation, the Union is perpetual, confirmed by the history of the Union itself. The Union is much older than the Constitution. It was formed in fact, by the Articles of Association in 1774. It was matured and continued by the Declaration of Independence in 1776. It was further matured and the faith of all the then thirteen States expressly plighted and engaged that it should be perpetual, by the Articles of Confederation in 1778. And finally, in 1787, one of the declared objects for ordaining and establishing the Constitution, was *"to form a more perfect union."*

But if destruction of the Union, by one, or by a part only, of the States, be lawfully possible, the Union is *less* perfect than before the Constitution, having lost the vital element of perpetuity.

It follows from these views that no State, upon its own mere motion, can lawfully get out of the Union,—that *resolves* and *ordinances* to that effect are legally void; and that acts of violence, within any State or States, against the authority of the United States, are insurrectionary or revolutionary, according to circumstances.

I therefore consider that, in view of the Constitution and the laws, the Union is unbroken, and, to the extent of my ability, I shall take care, as the Constitution itself expressly enjoins upon me, that the laws of the Union be faithfully executed in all the States. Doing this I deem to be only a simple duty on my part; and I shall perform it, so far as practicable, unless my rightful masters, the American people, shall withhold the requisite means, or, in some authoritative manner, direct the contrary. I trust this will not be regarded as a menace, but only as the declared purpose of the Union that it *will* constitutionally defend, and maintain itself.

In doing this there needs to be no bloodshed or violence; and there shall be none, unless it be forced upon the national authority. The power confided to me, will be used to hold, occupy, and possess the property, and places belonging to the government, and to collect the duties and imposts; but beyond what may be necessary for these objects, there will be no invasion—no using of force against, or among the people anywhere. Where hostility to the United States, in any interior locality, shall be so great and so universal, as to prevent competent resident citizens from holding the Federal offices, there will be no attempt to force obnoxious strangers among the people for that object. While the strict legal right may exist in the government to enforce the exercise of these offices, the attempt to do so would be so irritating, and so nearly impracticable with all, that I deem it better to forego, for the time, the uses of such offices.

The mails, unless repelled, will continue to be furnished in all parts of the Union. So far as possible, the people everywhere shall have that sense of perfect security which is most favorable to calm thought and reflection. The course here indicated will be followed, unless current events, and experience, shall show a modification, or change, to be proper; and in every case and exigency, my best discretion will be exercised, according to circumstances actually existing, and with a view and a hope of a peaceful solution of the national troubles, and the restoration of fraternal sympathies and affections.

That there are persons in one section, or another who seek to destroy the Union at all events, and are glad of any pretext to do it, I will neither affirm or deny; but if there be such, I need address no word to them. To those, however, who really love the Union, may I not speak?

Before entering upon so grave a matter as the destruction of our national fabric, with all its benefits, its memories, and its hopes, would it not be wise to ascertain precisely why we do it? Will you hazard so desperate a step, while there is any possibility that any portion of the ills you fly from, have no real existence? Will you, while the certain ills you fly to, are greater than all the real ones you fly from? Will you risk the commission of so fearful a mistake?

All profess to be content in the Union, if all constitutional rights can be maintained. Is it true, then, that any right, plainly written in the Constitution, has been denied? I think not. Happily the human mind is so constituted, that no party can reach to the audacity of doing this. Think, if you can, of a single instance in which a plainly written provision of the Constitution has ever been denied. If, by the mere force of numbers, a majority should deprive a minority of any clearly written constitutional right, it might, in a moral point of view, justify revolution—certainly would, if such right were a vital one. But such is not our case. All the vital rights of minorities, and of individuals, are so plainly assured to them, by affirmations and negations, guarranties and prohibitions, in the Constitution, that controversies never arise concerning them. But no organic law can ever be framed with a provision specifically applicable to every question which may occur in practical administration. No foresight can anticipate, nor any document or reasonable length contain express provisions for all possible questions. Shall fugitives from labor be surrendered by national or by State authority? The Constitution does not expressly say. *May* Congress prohibit slavery in the territories? The Constitution does not expressly say. *Must* Congress protect slavery in the territories? The Constitution does not expressly say.

From questions of this class spring all our constitutional controversies, and we divide upon them into majorities and minorities. If the minority will not acquiesce, the majority must, or the government must cease. There is no other alternative; for continuing the government, is acquiescence on one side or the other. If a minority, in such case, will secede rather than acquiesce, they make a precedent which, in turn, will divide and ruin them; for a minority of their own will secede from them, whenever a majority refuses to be controlled by such minority. For instance, why may not any portion of a new confederacy, a year or two hence, arbitrarily secede again, precisely as portions of the present Union now claim to secede from it. All who cherish disunion sentiments, are now being educated to the exact temper of doing this. Is there such perfect identity of interests among the States to compose a new Union, as to produce harmony only, and prevent renewed secession?

Plainly, the central idea of secession, is the essence of anarchy. A majority, held in restraint by constitutional checks, and limitations, and always changing easily, with deliberate changes of popular opinions and sentiments, is the only true sovereign of a free people. Whoever rejects it, does, of necessity, fly to anarchy or to despotism. Unanimity is impossible; the rule of a minority, as a permanent arrangement, is wholly inadmissible; so that, rejecting the majority principle, anarchy, or despotism in some form, is all that is left.

I do not forget the position assumed by some, that constitutional questions are to be decided by the Supreme Court; nor do I deny that such decisions must be binding in any case, upon the parties to a suit, as to the object of that suit, while they are also entitled to very high respect and consideration, in all paralel cases, by all other departments of the government. And while it is obviously possible that such decision may be erroneous in any given case, still the evil effect following it, being limited to that particular case, with the chance that it may be over-ruled, and never become a precedent for other cases, can better be borne than could the evils of a different practice. At the same time the candid citizen must confess that if the policy of the government, upon vital questions, affecting the whole people, is to be irrevocably fixed by decisions of the Supreme Court, the instant they are made, in ordinary litigation between parties, in personal actions, the people will have ceased, to be their own rulers, having, to that extent, practically resigned their government, into the hands of that eminent tribunal. Nor is there, in this view, any assault upon the court, or the judges. It is a duty, from which they may not shrink, to decide cases properly brought before them; and it is no fault of theirs, if others seek to turn their decisions to political purposes.

One section of our country believes slavery is *right*, and ought to be extended, while the other believes it is *wrong*, and ought not to be extended. This is the only substantial dispute. The fugitive slave clause of the Constitution, and the law for the suppression of the foreign slave trade, are each as well enforced, perhaps, as any law can ever be in a community where the moral sense of the people imperfectly supports the law itself. The great body of the people abide by the dry legal obligation in both cases, and a few break over in each. This, I think, cannot be perfectly cured; and it would be worse in both cases *after* the separation of the sections, than before. The foreign slave trade, now imperfectly suppressed, would be ultimately revived without restriction, in one section; while fugitive slave s, now only partially surrendered, would not be surrendered at all, by the other.

Physically speaking, we cannot separate. We cannot remove our respective sections from each other, nor build an impassable wall between them. A husband and wife may be divorced, and go out of the presence, and beyond the reach of each other; but the different parts of our country cannot do this. They cannot but remain face to face; and intercourse, either amicable or hostile, must continue between them. Is it possible then to make that intercourse more advantageous, or more satisfactory, *after* separation than *before*? Can aliens make treaties easier than friends can make laws? Can treaties be more faithfully enforced between aliens, than laws can among friends? Suppose you go to war, you cannot fight always; and when, after much loss on both sides, and no gain on either, you cease fighting, the identical old questions, as to terms of intercourse, are again upon you.

This country, with its institutions, belongs to the people who inhabit it. Whenever they shall grow weary of the existing government, they can exercise their *constitutional* right of amending it, or their *revolutionary* right to dismember, or overthrow it. I can not be ignorant of the fact that many worthy, and patriotic citizens are desirous of having the national constitution amended. While I make no recommendation of amendments, I fully recognize the rightful authority of the people over the whole subject, to be exercised in either of the modes prescribed in the instrument itself; and I should, under existing circumstances, favor, rather than oppose, a fair opportunity being afforded the people to act upon it.

I will venture to add that, to me, the convention mode seems preferable, in that it allows amendments to originate with the people themselves, instead of only permitting them to take, or reject, propositions, originated by others, not especially chosen for the purpose, and which might not be precisely such, as they would wish to either accept or refuse. I understand a proposed amendment to the Constitution—which amendment, however, I have not seen, has passed Congress, to the effect that the federal government, shall never interfere with the domestic institutions of the States, including that of persons held to service. To avoid misconstruction of what I have said, I depart from my purpose not to speak of particular amendments, so far as to say that, holding such a provision to now be implied constitutional law, I have no objection to its being made express, and irrevocable.

The Chief Magistrate derives all his authority from the people, and they have conferred none upon him to fix terms for the separation of the States. The people themselves can do this also if they choose; but the executive, as such, has nothing to do with it. His duty is to administer the present government, as it came to his hands, and to transmit it, unimpaired by him, to his successor.

Why should there not be a patient confidence in the ultimate justice of the people? Is there any better, or equal hope, in the world? In our present differences, is either party without faith of being in the right? If the Almighty Ruler of nations, with his eternal truth and justice, be on your side of the North, or on yours of the South, that truth, and that justice, will surely prevail, by the judgment of this great tribunal, the American people.

By the frame of the government under which we live, this same people have wisely given their public servants but little power for mischief; and have, with equal wisdom, provided for the return of that little to their own hands at very short intervals.

While the people retain their virtue, and vigilence, no administration, by any extreme of wickedness or folly, can very seriously injure the government, in the short space of four years.

My countrymen, one and all, think calmly and *well*, upon this whole subject. Nothing valuable can be lost by taking time. If there be an object to *hurry* any of you, in hot haste, to a step which you would never take *deliberately*, that object will be frustrated by taking time; but no good object can be frustrated by it. Such of you as are now dissatisfied, still have the old Constitution unimpaired, and, on the sensitive point, the laws of your own framing under it; while the new administration will have no immediate power, if it would, to change either. If it were admitted that you who are dissatisfied, hold the right side in the dispute, there still is no single good reason for precipitate action. Intelligence, patriotism, Christianity, and a firm reliance on Him, who has never yet forsaken this favored land, are still competent to adjust, in the best way, all our present difficulty.

In *your* hands, my dissatisfied fellow countrymen, and not in *mine*, is the momentous issue of civil war. The government will not assail *you*. You can have no conflict, without being yourselves the aggressors. *You* have no oath registered in Heaven to destroy the government, while *I* shall have the most solemn one to "preserve, protect and defend" it.

I am loth to close. We are not enemies, but friends. We must not be enemies. Though passion may have strained, it must not break our bonds of affection. The mystic chords of memory, stretching from every battle-field, and patriot grave, to every living heart and hearthstone, all over this broad land, will yet swell the chorus of the Union, when again touched, as surely they will be, by the better angels of our nature.

4 March 1861

# *Appendix 3*

# THE GETTYSBURG ADDRESS

*F*our score and seven years ago our fathers brought forth on this continent, a new nation, conceived in Liberty, and dedicated to the proposition that all men are created equal.

Now we are engaged in a great civil war, testing whether that nation, or any nation so conceived and so dedicated, can long endure. We are met on a great battle-field of that war. We have come to dedicate a portion of that field, as a final resting place for those who here gave their lives that that nation might live. It is altogether fitting and proper that we should do this.

But, in a larger sense, we can not dedicate—we cannot consecrate—we can not hallow—this ground. The brave men, living and dead, who struggled here, have consecrated it, far above our poor power to add or detract. The world will little note, nor long remember what we say here, but it can never forget what they did here. It is for us the living, rather, to be dedicated here to the unfinished work which they who fought here have thus far so nobly advanced. It is rather for us to be here dedicated to the great task remaining before us—that from these honored dead we take increased devotion to that cause for which they gave the last full measure of devotion—that we here highly resolve that these dead shall not have died in vain—that this nation, under God, shall have a new birth of freedom—and that government of the people, by the people, for the people, shall not perish from the earth.

19 November 1863

# *Appendix 4*

# LINCOLN'S SECOND INAUGURAL ADDRESS

*F*ellow Countrymen:

At this second appearing to take the oath of the presidential office, there is less occasion for an extended address than there was at the first. Then a statement, somewhat in detail, of a course to be pursued, seemed fitting and proper. Now, at the expiration of four years, during which public declarations have been constantly called forth on every point and phase of the great contest which still absorbs the attention, and engrosses the energies of the nation, little that is new could be presented. The progress of our arms, upon which all else chiefly depends, is as well known to the public as to myself; and it is, I trust, reasonably satisfactory and encouraging to all. With high hope for the future, no prediction in regard to it is ventured.

On the occasion corresponding to this four years ago, all thoughts were anxiously directed to an impending civil-war. All dreaded it—all sought to avert it. While the inaugural address was being delivered from this place, devoted altogether to *saving* the Union without war, insurgent agents were in the city seeking to *destroy* it without war—seeking to dissolve the Union, and divide effects, by negotiation. Both parties deprecated war; but one of them would *make* war rather than let the nation survive; and the other would *accept* war rather than let it perish. And the war came.

One eighth of the whole population were colored slaves, not distributed generally over the Union, but localized in the Southern part of it. These slaves constituted a peculiar and powerful interest. All knew that this interest was, somehow, the cause of the war. To strengthen, perpetuate, and extend this interest was the object for which the insurgents would rend the Union, even by war; while the government claimed no right to do more than to restrict the territorial enlargement of it. Neither party expected for the war, the magnitude, or the duration, which it has already attained. Neither anticipated that the *cause* of the conflict might cease with, or even before, the conflict itself should cease. Each looked for an easier triumph, and a result less fundamental and astounding. Both read the same Bible, and pray to the same God; and each invokes His aid against the other. It may seem strange that any men should dare to ask a just God's assistance in wringing their bread from the sweat of other men's faces; but let us judge not that we be not judged. The prayers of both could not be answered; that of neither has been answered fully. The Almighty has His own purposes. "Woe unto the world because of offences! for it must needs be that offences come; but woe to that man by whom the offence cometh!" If we shall suppose that American Slavery is one of those offences which, in the providence of God, must needs come, but which, having continued through His appointed time, He now wills to remove, and that He gives to both North and South, this terrible war, as the woe due to those by whom the offence came, shall we discern therein any departure from those divine attributes which the believers in a Living God always ascribe to Him? Fondly do we hope—fervently do we pray—that this mighty scourge of war may speedily pass away. Yet, if God wills that it continue, until all the wealth piled by the bond-man's two hundred and fifty years of unrequited toil shall be sunk, and until every drop of blood drawn with the lash, shall be paid by another drawn with the sword, as was said three thousand years ago, so still it must be said "the judgments of the Lord, are true and righteous altogether."

With malice toward none; with charity for all; with firmness in the right, as God gives us to see the right, let us strive on to finish the work we are in; to bind up the nation's wounds; to care for him who shall have borne the battle, and for his widow, and his orphan—to do all which may achieve and cherish a just, and a lasting peace, among ourselves, and with all nations.

4 March 1865

# Notes

## INTRODUCTION

1. Charles L. Black Jr., *A New Birth of Freedom: Human Rights Named and Unnamed* (New Haven, CT: Yale University Press, 1999), p. 168.

2. Speech on the Kansas-Nebraska Act at Peoria, Illinois, 16 October 1854 and speech at Chicago, 10 July 1858, in Abraham Lincoln, *Speeches and Writings 1832–1858*, ed. Don E. Fehrenbacher (New York: Library of America, 1989), pp. 328, 456.

3. Peter Onuf, "The Scholars' Jefferson," *William and Mary Quarterly*, 3rd ser., 50, no. 4 (October 1993): 675. Onuf's article, pp. 671–99, contains a summary of much of this literature.

4. Frank J. Williams, in "Abraham Lincoln—Our Ever-Present Contemporary," points out a cyclical pattern in the way Americans regard their presidents by wearing them "down [with criticism] while in office" and "then" turning "them into saints in death, only to tear them down again later" and so on (Williams, "Abraham Lincoln—Our Ever-Present Contemporary," in *"We Cannot Escape History": Lincoln and the Last Best Hope of Earth*, ed. James M. McPherson [Urbana: University of Illinois Press, 1995], p. 139).

5. Harry V. Jaffa, in *A New Birth of Freedom: Abraham Lincoln and the Coming of the Civil War* (Lanham, MD: Rowman & Littlefield, 2004), pp. 77 and 504–505, in his criticism of scholars who take this position, was especially critical of William Freehling's *The Road to Disunion: Secessionists at Bay, 1776–1854* (New York: Oxford University Press, 1990) and called Freehling's attempt to minimize Jefferson's role in the founding a "monument to this point of view."

6. Peter Gay, *The Enlightenment: An Interpretation* (London: Weidenfeld and Nicholson, 1966), p. 130, and Ernst Cassirer, *The Philosophy of the Enlightenment*, trans. Fritz C. A. Koelln and James P. Pettegrove (Princeton, NJ: Princeton University Press, 1951), pp. 234, 134.

7. See Jefferson to James Madison, 20 December 1787, in Thomas Jefferson, *Writings*, ed. Merrill D. Peterson (New York: Library of America, 1984), pp. 915–16. According to Leonard Levy, Jefferson "converted Madison to the cause of adding the Bill of Rights to the new Federal Con-

stitution" (Leonard Levy, "Jefferson as a Civil Libertarian," in *Thomas Jefferson: The Man, His World, His Influence*, ed. Lally Weymouth [London: Weidenfeld and Nicholson, 1973], p. 190).

8. Speech at Lewiston, Illinois, 17 August 1858. Abraham Lincoln, *The Collected Works of Abraham Lincoln*, ed. Roy P. Basler, 11 vols. (New Brunswick, NJ: Rutgers University Press, 1953), 2:546.

9. David Thelen, in "Reception of the Declaration of Independence," explains how Europeans imbued with the Enlightenment value of popular control of government maintained that America put that value into practice beginning with the Declaration of Independence (Thelen, "Reception of the Declaration of Independence," in *The Declaration of Independence: Origins and Impact*, ed. Scott Douglas Gerber [Washington, DC: CQ Press, 2002], pp. 144–45).

10. Onuf, "Scholars' Jefferson," p. 675.

11. Henry Steele Commager, *The Empire of Reason: How Europe Imagined and America Realized the Enlightenment* (New York: Anchor Books, 1978), p. xiii.

12. Douglas L. Wilson, *Honor's Voice: The Transformation of Abraham Lincoln* (New York: Alfred A. Knopf, 1998), p. 241.

13. Address to the Young Men's Lyceum of Springfield, Illinois, 27 January 1838, in Lincoln, *Speeches and Writings 1832–1858*, p. 28.

14. Dwight G. Anderson, "Quest for Immortality: A Theory of Abraham Lincoln's Political Psychology," in *The Historian's Lincoln: Pseudohistory, Psychohistory and History*, ed. Gabor S. Boritt (Chicago: University of Illinois Press, 1988), pp. 258–59.

15. Address to the Young Men's Lyceum of Springfield, Illinois, 27 January 1838, in Lincoln, *Speeches and Writings 1832–1858*, pp. 35–36.

16. Ibid., p. 35.

17. To Calleb Russell and Sallie A. Fenton, 5 January 1863, in Lincoln, *Collected Works of Abraham Lincoln*, 6:40.

18. Address to the Young Men's Lyceum of Springfield, Illinois, 27 January 1838, in Lincoln, *Speeches and Writings 1832–1858*, p. 35.

19. Garry Wills, *Lincoln at Gettysburg: The Words That Remade America* (New York: Touchstone, 1992), p. 103.

20. Richard Tarnas, *The Passion of the Western Mind: Understanding the Ideas That Have Shaped Our World View* (New York: Ballantine Books, 1991), p. 367.

21. David Herbert Donald, *Lincoln* (New York: Touchstone, 1996), p. 31.

22. Benjamin Franklin, *The Autobiography* (New York: Vintage Books, Library of America, 1990), p. 37.

23. Joseph Gillespie to William Herndon, 8 December 1866, in *Herndon's Informants: Letters, Interviews, and Statements about Abraham Lincoln,* ed. Douglas L. Wilson and Rodney O. Davis (Urbana: University of Illinois Press, 1998), p. 508.

24. Stewart Winger, *Lincoln, Religion, and Romantic Cultural Politics* (Dekalb: Northern Illinois University Press, 2003), pp. 166–68, 206.

25. Tarnas, *Passion of the Western Mind*, p. 367.

26. Ibid., pp. 366, 367, 371.

27. Ibid., p. 371.

28. Ibid., pp. 377–78.

29. Walt Whitman, "Dear Democracy," in *Reminiscences of Abraham Lincoln by Distinguished Men of His Time*, ed. Allen Thorndyke Rice (New York: Harper & Brothers, 1909), pp. 413, 414, 417.

30. Karl Marx and Friedrich Engels, *Communist Manifesto*, in *The Marx-Engels Reader*, 2nd ed., ed. Robert C. Tucker (New York: W. W. Norton, 1978), p. 469.

31. Adolf Hitler, *Mein Kampf*, trans. Ralph Manheim (New York: Houghton Mifflin, 1971), p. xviii.

32. Dennis Mack Smith, *Mussolini* (London: Paladin Graften Books, 1987), pp. 32, 165.

33. Ibid., pp. 162–65.

34. Moses Maimonides, "Epistle to Yemen," trans. Boaz Cohen, in *Introduction to Contemporary Civilization in the West*, 3rd ed., ed. Columbia College Staff (New York: Columbia University Press, 1960), 1:104.

35. See William Manchester, *A World Lit Only by Fire: The Medieval Mind and the Renaissance: Portrait of an Age* (Boston: Back Bay Books, 1993); Samuel P. Huntington, *The Clash of Civilizations and the Remaking of World Order* (New York: Touchstone, 1997); and Charles Kimball, *When Religion Becomes Evil* (New York: HarperSanFrancisco, 2002). For the similar effects of authoritarian claims of monopoly on either religious or political truth see Charles W. Sutherland, *Disciples of Destruction: The Religious Origins of War and Terrorism* (Amherst, NY: Prometheus Books, 1987), and Eric Hoffer, *The True Believer* (New York: Harper & Row, 1951).

36. As quoted in Allen C. Guelzo, *Abraham Lincoln: Redeemer President* (Grand Rapids, MI: William B. Eerdmans, 1999), p. 4.

37. Lincoln, *Collected Works of Abraham Lincoln*, 2:249.

38. Leonard Swett as quoted in William H. Herndon, *Herndon's Life of Lincoln: The History and Personal Recollections of Abraham Lincoln, as originally*

*written by William H. Herndon and Jesse W. Weik* (New York: Albert & Charles Boni, 1930), p. 431.

39. For a brief historiography on Lincoln's religious ideas and his use of religion in politics see Lucas E. Morel, *Lincoln's Sacred Effort: Defining Religion's Role in American Self-Government* (Lanham, MD: Lexington Books, 2000), pp. 12–17. For a brief bibliography on Lincoln and religion see Guelzo, *Abraham Lincoln*, pp. 465–72.

40. Stephen B. Oates, *Abraham Lincoln: The Man Behind the Myths* (New York: Harper Perennial, 1994), pp. 5–7.

41. Merrill D. Peterson, *Lincoln in American Memory* (New York: Oxford University Press, 1994), p. 218.

42. Glen E. Thurow, *Abraham Lincoln and American Political Religion* (Albany: State University of New York Press, 1976), p. 28.

## Chapter 1: Jefferson, Deism, and the Declaration of Independence

1. Thomas Jefferson, *The Literary Bible of Thomas Jefferson: His Commonplace Book of Philosophers and Poets*, ed. Gilbert Chinard (Baltimore, MD: Johns Hopkins Press, 1928), pp.19–20. This work is hereafter cited as *Literary Commonplace Book* (Chinard).

2. Isaac Kramnick, *Lord Bolingbroke: Historical Writings* (Chicago: University of Chicago Press, 1972), pp. xii–xxi; Isaac Kramnick, *Bolingbroke and His Circle: The Politics of Nostalgia in the Age of Walpole* (Ithaca, NY: Cornell University Press, 1992), p. 14; H. T. Dickenson, *Bolingbroke* (London: Constable, 1970), p. 162; Jeffrey Hart, *Viscount Bolingbroke: Tory Humanist* (London: Routledge and K. Paul, 1965), p. viii.

3. Thomas Jefferson, *Jefferson's Literary Commonplace Book*, ed. Douglas L. Wilson, Papers of Thomas Jefferson, 2nd ser. (Princeton, NJ: Princeton University Press, 1989), p. 156. This work is the same one edited by Chinard (see note 1) and is hereafter cited as *Literary Commonplace Book* (Wilson).

4. Quoted from Dickenson, *Bolingbroke*, p. 298.

5. Jefferson, *Literary Commonplace Book* (Chinard), p. 40.

6. Ibid., p. 66. Peter Byrne tells of the huge "volume of deistic criticism of orthodox Christianity" in *Natural Religion and the Nature of Religion: The Legacy of Deism* (London: Routledge, 1989), p. 79, and gives an account of much of it in that work.

7. Jefferson, *Literary Commonplace Book* (Chinard), p. 52.

8. Ibid., p. 53.

9. Ibid., p. 67.

10. John W. Yolton, *John Locke and the Way of Ideas* (London: Oxford University Press, 1969), pp. 115, 171.

11. Jefferson, *Jefferson's Literary Commonplace Book* (Chinard), p. 41.

12. Ibid., pp. 70–71.

13. Patricia Fara, *Newton: The Making of Genius* (New York: Columbia University Press, 2002), p. 129.

14. Jefferson to John Adams, 11 April 1823, in Thomas Jefferson, *The Writings of Thomas Jefferson*, ed. Andrew A. Lipscomb and Albert Ellery Bergh, 20 vols. (Washington, DC: Thomas Jefferson Memorial Association, 1903), 15:426–27.

15. Jefferson, *Literary Commonplace Book* (Chinard), p. 60.

16. Ibid., p. 67.

17. Ibid., p. 49.

18. Mark Goldie, "The Reception of Hobbes," in *The Cambridge History of Political Thought 1450–1700*, ed. J. H. Burns and Mark Goldie (Cambridge: Cambridge University Press, 1994), pp. 589–90.

19. See Jefferson's letter to John Adams, 11 April 1823, in Jefferson, *Writings of Thomas Jefferson*, 15:429–30, where he translates the first verses of John from their original Greek using reason as the meaning of *logos*.

20. For the effects of original sin see Romans 7:19, 20, and 23 (KJV); Aurelius Augustine, *The Works of Aurelius Augustine Bishop of Hippo*, ed. and trans. Marcus Dods, vols. 1–2 (Edinburgh: T. and T. Clark, 1871), bk. 2, p. 5; Martin Luther, *Luther's Works*, ed. Hilton C. Oswald (St. Louis, MO: Concordia, 1972), 25:299; John Calvin, *Institutes of the Christian Religion*, ed. John T. McNeil, trans. Ford Lewis Battles, Library of Christian Classics (London: SCM Press, 1961), 20:249–51; Huldreich Zwingli, *The Latin Works of Huldreich Zwingli*, ed. Samuel Jackson Macaulay, trans. Henry Preble, Walter Lichenstein, and Lawrence A. McLouth (Philadelphia: American Society of Church History, 1922), 2:6, 10, 26–27; Sydney E. Ahlstrom, *A Religious History of the American People* (London: Yale University Press, 1972), p. 34; and E. J. Bicknell, *A Theological Introduction to the Thirty-nine Articles of the Church of England*, 3rd ed., rev. H. J. Carpenter (London: Longman's, Green and Co., 1955), p. 181.

21. See Genesis 3:16–19.

22. Jefferson, *Literary Commonplace Book* (Chinard), pp. 56–57.

23. Ibid., 57.

24. Ibid.

25. Jefferson to Peter Carr, August 1787, in Jefferson, *Writings of Thomas Jefferson*, 6:257–58.

26. Jefferson described Jesus as "this first of human sages," not God, in his letter to F. A. Van Der Kemp, 25 April 1816, in ibid., 15:3. He also deleted the Virgin Birth and Resurrection from the Gospels when he edited them. See Thomas Jefferson, *Jefferson's Extracts from the Gospels*, ed. Dickenson W. Adams, *Papers of Thomas Jefferson*, 2nd ser. (Princeton, NJ: Princeton University Press, 1989), p. 41.

27. Jefferson, *Literary Commonplace Book* (Chinard).

28. Ibid., pp. 54–55.

29. Luther, *Luther's Works*, 25:371.

30. W. H. C. Frend, *The Rise of Christianity* (London: Darton, Longman and Todd, 1986), pp. 345–51.

31. For belief in predestination see Aurelius Augustine, *The Enchiridion*, in *The Works of Aurelius Augustine, Bishop of Hippo*, ed. Marcus Dods, trans. J. F. Shaw (Edinburgh: T. and T. Clark, 1873), 9:242–43; Thomas Aquinas, *Basic Writings of Saint Thomas Aquinas*, ed. Anton C. Pegis (New York: Random House, 1945), 1:239–44; Ignatius of Loyola, "Spiritual Exercises of Saint Ignatius of Loyola," trans. Charles Seager, in *Middle Ages, Renaissance, and Reformation*, 3rd ed., ed. Karl F. Thompson, Classics of Western Thought (New York: Harcourt Brace Jovanovich, 1980), 2:574–75; Luther, *Luther's Works*, 25:371–74; Calvin, *Institutes of the Christian Religion*, 21:926–27; Zwingli, *Latin Works of Huldreich Zwingli*, 2:20.

32. Jefferson, *Literary Commonplace Book* (Chinard), p. 64.

33. Jefferson to William Short, 4 August 1820, in Jefferson, *Writings of Thomas Jefferson*, 15:260–61.

34. When George Wythe and Jefferson were opposing lawyers in a trial, Wythe challenged the credibility of jurist Sir Humphrey Winch, after Jefferson cited a case reported by Winch, by citing another case Winch reported containing Winch's own eulogy. Jefferson responded by stating: "We might as well endeavor to destroy the authority of the Pentateuch, by observing, that all the chapters thereof were not written by Moses, because in one of them Deut. XXXIV . . . is a eulogy on himself, on occasion of his death" (Edward Dumbauld, *Thomas Jefferson and the Law* [Norman: University of Oklahoma Press, 1978], pp. 98, 100).

35. Jefferson to William Short, 4 August 1820, in Jefferson, *Writings of Thomas Jefferson*, 15:260–61.

36. Bicknell, *A Theological Introduction to the Thirty-nine Articles of the Church of England*, pp. 218–19.

37. Jefferson to John Adams, 11 April 1823, Thomas Jefferson, Abigail Adams, and John Adams, *The Adams-Jefferson Letters: The Complete Correspondence between Thomas Jefferson and Abigail and John Adams*, ed. Lester J. Cappon (Chapel Hill: University of North Carolina Press, 1959), 2:591. Despite Jefferson's commitment to the impartial egalitarian deistic God of Bolingbroke and rejection of Calvin's partial, unegalitarian God, Garrett Ward Sheldon insists that "Jefferson's words in the Declaration of Independence reflect the prevalent Calvinist culture in the North American colonies" (Sheldon, "The Political Theory of the Declaration of Independence," in *The Declaration of Independence: Origins and Impact*, ed. Scott Douglas Gerber [Washington, DC: CQ Press, 2002], p. 23).

38. Jefferson to William Short, 4 August 1820, in Jefferson, *Writings of Thomas Jefferson*, 15:261–62.

39. Jefferson to John Adams, 11 April 1823, in Jefferson, Adams, and Adams, *Adams-Jefferson Letters*, 2:59.

40. Jefferson to Peter Carr, 10 August 1787, in Jefferson, *Writings of Thomas Jefferson*, 6:258–61.

41. Jefferson to Moses Robinson, 23 March 1801, ibid., 10:237.

42. Jefferson to Thomas Whittmore, 5 June 1822, ibid., 15:373–4, and Benjamin Waterhouse, 26 June 1822, ibid., 15:385.

43. See Thomas Jefferson, *The Jefferson Bible: The Life and Morals of Jesus of Nazareth* (Boston: Beacon Press, 1989).

44. John Thomas Flexner, *Washington: The Indispensable Man* (New York: Back Bay Books, Little, Brown, 1969), p. 216. See also Brooke Allen, *Moral Minority: Our Skeptical Founding Fathers* (Chicago: Ivan R. Dee, 2006), pp. 32–34, where she writes that Bishop White, a clergyman at one of the two Episcopalian churches in Philadelphia that Washington attended while he was president, suspected Washington was a deist, while James Abercrombie, the clergyman at the other Episcopalian church, stated that "Washington was a deist."

45. Notes for a speech to Congress, as quoted in Noemie Emery, *Washington: A Biography* (New York: Capricorn Books, G. P. Putnam's Sons, 1976), pp. 308–309.

46. As quoted in ibid., p. 309. See J. M. Robertson, *A History of Freethought: Ancient and Modern to the Period of the French Revolution*, 4th ed. (London: Watts, 1936), 2:747–48, for tolerance as an impact of deistic thought on eighteenth-century English Whiggism after a period of bigotry caused by a prolonged alliance with Puritanism.

47. Jefferson to James Fishbach, 27 September 1809, in Jefferson, *Writings of Thomas Jefferson*, 12:315.

48. George Washington to the Hebrew Congregation in Newport, Rhode Island, August 1790, as quoted in Abraham J. Karp, *From the Ends of the Earth: Judaic Treasures of the Library of Congress* (New York: Rizzoli, 1991), pp. 236–37.

49. Jefferson to Mordecai M. Noah, 28 May 1818, Thomas Jefferson Papers, S1 R50, 37988, Library of Congress.

50. Jefferson to Thomas B. Parker, 15 May 1819, in ibid., S1 R51, 38400.

51. Jefferson to William Canby, 18 September 1813, Jefferson, *Writings of Thomas Jefferson*, 13:377.

52. Jefferson to Miles King, 26 September 1814, in ibid., 14:198.

53. Jefferson, *Literary Commonplace Book* (Chinard), p. 20.

54. Ibid., p. 63.

55. According to Julian Boyd, the language of this paragraph from the first printed copy, approved by the Continental Congress, was probably Jefferson's. Its differences from Jefferson's original rough draft were in Jefferson's handwriting before the draft was submitted to the Congress for final approval. Jefferson later said that none of these differences were among those he credited to Benjamin Franklin or John Adams. Adams himself in a letter to Timothy Pickering, where he stated that Jefferson was the "author" of the Declaration, said that none of these differences were from the drafting committee of five that included himself, Franklin, Roger Sherman, and Robert Livingston, and, of course, Jefferson, whom the committee authorized to write the Declaration. Changes by the Congress then account for the differences from Jefferson's language in the first paragraph, but they did not alter the meaning of Jefferson's language. Those changes were twofold: "advance from that subordination in which they have hitherto remained" was changed to "dissolve the political bands which have connected them with another" and "equal and independent" and "the change" were changed to "separate and equal" and "to like separation" (Julian Boyd, *Declaration of Independence: The Evolution of the Text* [Washington, DC: Library of Congress, 1943], pl. 10, p. 1 of pl. 5, and p. 32, and John Adams, *The Works of John Adams*, ed. Charles Francis Adams [Boston: Little, Brown, 1850], 2:514).

56. Jefferson, *Literary Commonplace Book* (Chinard), p. 60.

57. Jefferson's rough draft reads, "We hold these truths to be sacred and undeniable; that all men are created equal and independent. That from that equal creation they derive rights, inherent & inalienable, among which are the preservation of life, liberty, & the pursuit of happiness; that to secure these ends, governments are instituted among men, deriving their just

powers from the consent of the governed; that whenever any form of government becomes destructive to these ends, it is the right of the people to alter or to abolish it, & to institute new government, laying its foundation on such principles & organising its powers in such form, as to them shall seem most likely to effect their safety & happiness." In Boyd's analysis, Jefferson amended "sacred and undeniable" to "self-evident." With two exceptions, he also made other alterations, which brought the document to its first printing state, as approved by the Continental Congress. Those exceptions were in the rough draft in his handwriting when it was submitted to the Congress for approval. In his letter to Timothy Pickering, John Adams did not attribute either of these exceptions to any of the five members of the drafting committee, which included himself. The two exceptions, which were made by the Congress, were deletion of the words "inherent and" before "rights" and the insertion of "certain" in their place; plus altering "inalienable" to "unalienable." In his letter to James Madison of 30 August 1823, Jefferson maintained that a few alterations were made in the Declaration by Franklin and Adams but described them as "merely verbal" (Boyd, *Declaration of Independence*, pls. 10 and 5, p. 1 and pp. 24–26, 32; Adams, *Works of John Adams*, 2:514 and Jefferson, *Writings of Thomas Jefferson*, 15:461).

58. Calvin, *Institutes of the Christian Religion*, 21:926–27.

59. D. E. Luscombe and G. R. Evans, "The Twelfth-century Renaissance," in *The Cambridge History of Medieval Thought c. 350–c. 1450*, ed. J. H. Burns (Cambridge: Cambridge University Press, 1991), pp. 307–309.

60. Boyd, *Declaration of Independence*, p. 34.

61. Jefferson, *Autobiography*, in *Writings of Thomas Jefferson*, 1:24.

62. See notes 55 and 57.

63. Boyd, *Declaration of Independence*, p. 3 of pl. 5.

64. Herbert Freidenwald, *The Declaration of Independence: An Interpretation and Analysis* (New York: Macmillan, 1904), p. 32.

65. Henry Steele Commager, "The Declaration of Independence," in *Thomas Jefferson: The Man, His World, His Influence*, ed. Lally Weymouth (London: Weidenfeld and Nicolson, 1973), pp. 179–87.

66. Henry Steele Commager, *The Empire of Reason: How Europe Imagined and America Realized the Enlightenment* (New York: Anchor Books, 1978), pp. 222, 346.

67. Bonnie L. Ford tells how the women's movement in 1848 added "and women" to "all men" in their version of the Declaration of Independence (Ford, "Women, Equality, and the Declaration of Independence," in Gerber, *Declaration of Independence*, pp. 178–79).

68. Thomas Jefferson, *Notes on the State of Virginia*, ed. William Peden (New York: Norton, 1972), p. 60. See also Bernard Fabian, "Jefferson's Notes on Virginia: The Genesis of Query XVII, The different religions received into the state?" *William and Mary Quarterly*, 3rd ser., 12 (1955): 125.

69. Thomas Jefferson, *The Papers of Thomas Jefferson*, ed. Julian P. Boyd and Charles Cullen (Princeton, NJ: Princeton University Press, 1950), 1:536, 545–48, 529, and Thomas Jefferson, *The Portable Thomas Jefferson*, ed. Merrill D. Peterson (Kingsport, TN: Penguin, 1981), pp. 251–53.

70. Ibid.

71. Jefferson to Correa de Serra, 25 November 1817, in Thomas Jefferson Papers, S1 R50, 33731, Library of Congress.

72. See Clay Jenkinson's comments on *Thomas Jefferson*, a film by Ken Burns, pt. 1 (PBS Home Video).

73. To John Adams, 28 October 1813, in Thomas Jefferson, *Writings of Thomas Jefferson*, 13:399.

74. Jefferson, *Portable Thomas Jefferson*, pp. 251–53. See also Allen Jayne, *Jefferson's Declaration of Independence: Origins, Philosophy and Theology* (Lexington: University Press of Kentucky, 1998), chap. 7.

75. Leonard Levy, "Jefferson as a Civil Libertarian," in Weymouth, *Thomas* Jefferson, p. 190, and David N. Mayer, *The Constitutional Thought of Thomas Jefferson* (Charlottesville: University Press of Virginia, 1997), pp. 148–55. See also Adrienne Koch, *Jefferson and Madison: The Great Collaboration* (New York: Hill and Wang, 1969), pp. 49, 56, and Gordon Wood, *The Creation of the American Republic, 1776–1787* (Chapel Hill: University of North Carolina Press, 1969), pp. 542–43.

76. Jefferson to James Madison, 20 December 1787, in Thomas Jefferson, *Writings*, ed. Merrill D. Peterson (New York: Library of America, 1984), p. 916.

77. To Charles Clay, 27 January 1790, in Jefferson, *Writings of Thomas Jefferson*, 8:4.

78. Jefferson to Dr. Thomas Cooper, 7 October 1814, in ibid., 14:200.

79. Henry Steele Commager, *Theodore Parker* (Boston: Little, Brown, 1936), pp. 197–98.

80. Stephen S. Foster, "The Brotherhood of Thieves, or, A True Picture of the American Church and Clergy," in *Agitation for Freedom: The Abolitionist Movement*, ed. Donald G. Mathews (New York: John Wiley & Sons, 1972), pp. 79, 90.

81. To Jean Nicholas Demeunier, 26 June 1786, in Jefferson, *Writings*, p. 592.

82. Jefferson, *Notes on the State of Virginia*, p. 163. Lincoln's quote, or I should say misquote because he substituted "remember" for Jefferson's "reflect," is in Abraham Lincoln, *Speeches and Writings 1859–1865*, ed. Don Fehrenbacher (New York: Library of America, 1989), p. 41.

83. Jefferson to Dupont Nemours, 24 April 1816, in Jefferson, *Writings of Thomas Jefferson*, 14:491–92.

84. To Thomas Seymour, 11 February 1807, in ibid., 11:156.

85. Jefferson to George Wythe, 13 August 1786, in ibid., 5:397.

86. Douglas L. Wilson, *Lincoln before Washington: New Perspectives on the Illinois Years* (Urbana: University of Illinois Press, 1997), pp. 1–5.

87. See 11 February 1859 Lecture on Discoveries and Inventions, Jacksonville, Illinois, Lincoln, *Speeches and Writings 1859–1865*, pp. 9–10.

88. Abraham Lincoln, *The Life and Writings of Abraham Lincoln*, ed. Philip Van Doren Stern (New York: Modern Library, 1940), p. 221.

89. To the People of Sangamo County, 9 March 1832, in Abraham Lincoln, *Speeches and Writings 1832–1858*, ed. Don Fehrenbacher (New York: Library of America, 1989), p. 4.

90. Abraham Lincoln, *Recollected Words of Abraham Lincoln*, comp. and ed. Don E. Fehrenbacher and Virginia Fehrenbacher (Stanford, CA: Stanford University Press, 1996), p. 244.

91. Garry Wills, *Lincoln at Gettysburg: The Words That Remade America* (New York: Touchstone, 1992), pp. 101–10.

92. Lincoln, *Speeches and Writings 1832–1858*, p. 398. Michael Zuckert argues that Lincoln's view expressed in this passage that the idealism of the Declaration would never be completely actualized would prevent "immoderate hopes of utopianism" (Zuckert, "Lincoln and the Problem of Civil Religion," in *Law and Philosophy: The Practice of Theory*, ed. John A. Murley, Robert L. Stone, and William T. Braithwaite [Athens: Ohio University Press, 1992], p. 738).

93. In Jefferson, *Writings of Thomas Jefferson*, 16:181–82. Reinhold Niebuhr wrote that "Lincoln had a Jeffersonian belief in the mission of the new nation to initiate, extend, and preserve democratic self-government" (Niebuhr, "The Religion of Abraham Lincoln," in *Lincoln and the Gettysburg Address*, ed. Allan Nevins [Urbana: University of Illinois Press, 1964], p. 78).

## CHAPTER 2: LINCOLN, DEISM, AND THE DECLARATION OF INDEPENDENCE

1. In 1959, William J. Wolf stated: "Lincoln's knowledge of the Bible far exceeded the content-grasp of most present day clergymen" (Wolf, *The Almost Chosen People: A Study of the Religion of Abraham Lincoln* [Garden City, NY: Doubleday, 1959], p. 39).

2. William H. Herndon to Francis E. Abbot, 18 February 1870, as quoted by Douglas L. Wilson in *Honor's Voice: The Transformation of Abraham Lincoln* (New York: Alfred A. Knopf, 1998), p. 81.

3. Ibid., pp. 81–83.

4. Hardin Bale to William H. Herndon (interview), 29 May 1865, in *Herndon's Informants: Letters, Interviews, and Statements about Abraham Lincoln*, ed. Douglas L. Wilson and Rodney O. Davis (Urbana: University of Illinois Press, 1998), p. 13.

5. Isaac Cogdal to William H. Herndon, 1865–66 (interview), in ibid., p. 441.

6. Wilson, *Honor's Voice*, p. 82.

7. James H. Matheny to Herndon (interview), 2 March 1870, in Wilson and Davis, *Herndon's Informants*, p. 577.

8. Ibid., p. 576.

9. James H. Matheny to Herndon (interview), 6 March 1870, in ibid., p. 577.

10. John T. Stuart to Herndon (interview), 2 March 1870, in ibid., p. 576.

11. Isaac Cogdal to Herndon (interview), 1865–66, in ibid., p. 441.

12. Thomas Paine, *The Age of Reason: Being an Investigation of True and Fabulous Theology, Part I*, in *The Complete Religious and Theological Works of Thomas Paine* (New York: Peter Eckler Publishing, 1917), 1:113, 342, 350.

13. William Herndon, *Herndon's Life of Lincoln: The History and Personal Recollections of Abraham Lincoln, as originally written by William H. Herndon and Jesse W. Weik* (New York: Albert & Charles Boni, 1930), p. 355.

14. Paine, *Age of Reason*, p. 6.

15. Ibid., pp. 63–64.

16. Ibid., p. 95.

17. Ibid., p. 99.

18. Ibid.

19. Ibid., p. 89.

20. Ibid.

21. Ibid., pp. 89–90.
22. Ibid., p. 90.
23. Ibid., p. 96.
24. Ibid., pp. 103–104.
25. Ibid., p. 382.
26. Ibid., p. 431.
27. Ibid., p. 57.
28. To James H. Matheny (interview), 2 March 1870, in Wilson and Davis, *Herndon's Informants*, p. 576.
29. See John T. Stuart (interview), 2 March 1870, in ibid., p. 576, for Lincoln as a freethinker.
30. Paine, *Age of Reason*, p. 400.
31. Ibid., pp. 410–11.
32. Ibid., pp. 338–39.
33. Ibid., p. 337.
34. Ibid.
35. Ibid., pp. 410–11.
36. Ibid., p. 337.
37. Ibid., pp. 337–38.
38. Ibid., p. 339.
39. Ibid., p. 402.
40. Ibid., p. 401.
41. Ibid., p. 338.
42. Ibid., p. 403.
43. Ibid., p. 197.
44. Ibid., pp. 197–99.
45. Ibid., pp. 199–207.
46. Ibid., p. 144.
47. Ibid., pp. 143–44.
48. Ibid., p. 148.
49. Ibid., pp. 155–56.
50. Ibid., pp. 156–57.
51. Ibid.
52. Ibid., p. 161.
53. Ibid., p. 386.
54. Ibid., p. 381.
55. Ibid., p. 30.
56. Ibid., p. 301.
57. Ibid.

58. Ibid., pp. 6–9.

59. Ibid., p. 82.

60. Ibid.

61. Ibid., p. 28.

62. Ibid., p. 406.

63. Ibid., p. 379.

64. Ibid., p. 414.

65. Wayne C. Temple, *Abraham Lincoln: From Skeptic to Prophet* (Mahomet, IL: Mayhaven, 1995), p. 67.

66. As quoted by Temple in ibid., p. 68.

67. Mary Todd Lincoln, September 1866 (interview), in Wilson and Davis, *Herndon's Informants*, p. 360.

68. William Herndon, "Lincoln's Characteristics," *Illinois State Journal* (14 February 1874): p. 2, c.c. 3–4.

69. Jesse W. Fell to Ward Hill Lamon, 22 September 1870, in Wilson and Davis, *Herndon's Informants*, pp. 579–80.

70. Henry Steele Commager, *Theodore Parker* (Boston: Little, Brown, 1936), pp. 287–88.

71. John Orr, *English Deism: Its Roots and Its Fruits* (Grand Rapids, MI: Wm. B. Eerdmans, 1934), pp. 219–20.

72. Theodore Parker, "The Function of a Teacher of Religion," in *Parker's Works*, vol. 4, *The Transient and Permanent in Christianity*, ed. George Wills Cooke (Boston: American Unitarian Association, 1908), pp. 303–304.

73. As quoted by John Edward Dirks in *The Critical Theology of Theodore Parker* (New York: Columbia University Press, 1948), p. 115.

74. Ibid., p. 114.

75. Ibid., p. 91.

76. Ibid.

77. Theodore Parker, "Thoughts on Theology," in *The Transient and Permanent in Christianity*, 4:169.

78. Parker, "Function of a Teacher of Religion," 4:301.

79. Dean Grodzins, *American Heretic: Theodore Parker and Transcendentalism* (Chapel Hill: University of North Carolina Press, 2002), p. 115. See also Matthew Tindal, *Christianity as Old as the Creation* (Stuttgart-Bad Cannstatt: Frommann-Holzboog, 1967 [Facsimile of the 1730 edition]).

80. Parker, "Function of a Teacher of Religion," 4:303.

81. As quoted in Dirks, *The Critical Theology of Theodore Parker*, p. 113.

82. Parker, "Thoughts on Theology," 4:160–61.

83. Parker, "Function of a Teacher of Religion," 4:301.

84. Parker, "The Transient and Permanent in Christianity," 4:29–30.

85. Ibid., 4:33.

86. Ibid., 4:31.

87. Ibid., 4:33.

88. Ibid.

89. Ibid., 4:30.

90. Ibid., 4:29.

91. Ibid., 4:23–24.

92. Ibid., 4:29.

93. Ibid., 4:32, 28.

94. Parker, "Function of a Teacher of Religion," 4:316.

95. Ibid., 4:295.

96. Ibid., 4:315.

97. Ibid., 4:316.

98. Parker, "The Transient and Permanent in Christianity," 4:32, 30.

99. Ibid., 4:30.

100. Ibid., 4:32.

101. Henry Champion Deming, *Eulogy of Abraham Lincoln* (Hartford, CT: A. N. Clark, 1865), p. 42.

102. Parker, "The Transient and the Permanent in Christianity," 4:29.

103. William Jayne, *Personal Reminiscences of the Martyred President* (Chicago: Grand Army Hall and Memorial Association, 1908), p. 51.

104. Leonard Swett to William H. Herndon, 17 January 1866, in Wilson and Davis, *Herndon's Informants*, pp. 167–68.

105. Parker, "The Transient and Permanent in Christianity," 4:32.

106. See notes 68 and 69.

107. Paine, *Age of Reason*, p. 390.

108. In his address at the Cooper Institute, New York, 27 February 1860, Lincoln quoted the following passage from Jefferson's *Autobiography*: "It is still in our power to direct the process of emancipation, and deportation, peaceably, and in such slow degrees, as that evil will wear off insensibly; and their places be, *pari passu*, filled up by free white laborers. If, on the contrary, it is left to force itself on, human nature must shudder at the prospect held up" (Abraham Lincoln, *Speeches and Writings 1859–1865*, ed. Don Fehrenbacher [New York: Library of America, 1989], p. 124). For the source of this quote, see Thomas Jefferson, *The Writings of Thomas Jefferson*, ed. Andrew A. Lipscomb and Albert Ellery Bergh (Washington, DC: Thomas Jefferson Memorial Association, 1903), 1:73.

109. Lincoln, *Speeches and Writings 1859–1865*, p. 213.

110. Address to the New Jersey Senate at Trenton, 21 February 1860, in ibid., p. 209.

## CHAPTER 3: MORAL-SENSE THEORY IN JEFFERSON AND LINCOLN

1. The concept of "a sovereign monarchy" is "Roman and Christian in its bases," according to P. D. King, "The Barbarian Kingdoms," in *Cambridge History of Medieval Political Thought c. 350–c. 1450*, ed. J. H. Burns (Cambridge: Cambridge University Press, 1991), p. 127. For Church authority see I. S. Robinson, "Church and Papacy," in ibid., pp. 252–305.

2. Martin Luther and John Calvin, *Luther and Calvin on Secular Authority*, ed. and trans. Harro Höpfl, Cambridge Texts in the History of Political Thought (Cambridge: Cambridge University Press, 1991), pp. 13, 70.

3. John Dunn, *The Political Thought of John Locke* (Cambridge: Cambridge University Press, 1988), pp. 182–83.

4. John Locke, *An Essay concerning Human Understanding*, ed. Peter H. Niddich (Oxford: Clarendon Press, 1984), p. 532.

5. Ibid., p. 549, and Dunn, *Political Thought of John Locke*, p. 192.

6. See Allen Jayne, *Jefferson's Declaration of Independence: Origins, Philosophy and Theology* (Lexington: University Press of Kentucky, 1998), chap. 2.

7. Thomas Jefferson, *The Commonplace Book of Thomas Jefferson: A Repository of His Ideas on Government*, ed. Gilbert Chinard (Baltimore, MD: Johns Hopkins Press, 1926), p. 19.

8. Henry Home, Lord Kames, *Principles of Equity*, 2nd ed. (Edinburgh: A. Kincaid and J. Bell, 1767), pp. 30–31.

9. Arthur E. McGuinness, *Henry Home, Lord Kames* (New York: Twayne, 1970), p. 35.

10. Henry Home, Lord Kames, *Essays on the Principles of Morality and Natural Religion* (Edinburgh: A. Kincaid and A. Donaldson, 1751), pp. 76, 88–90.

11. Ibid., p. 76.

12. Ibid., p. 123.

13. John Marshall, *John Locke: Resistance, Religion, and Responsibility* (Cambridge: Cambridge University Press, 1994), p. 407.

14. Kames, *Essays*, pp. 60–61.

15. Ibid., p. 128.

16. Ibid., pp. 60–61.

17. Ibid., p. 125.

18. Ibid., pp. 64–65.

19. Ibid., pp. 68, 61, and 71. Harry V. Jaffa states that "for Lincoln, egotism and altruism ultimately coincide, inasmuch the greater self-satisfaction is conceived as service to others" while Jefferson in the Declaration stuck to a strict Lockean hedonistic view of morality with its emphasis on enlightened self-interest (Jaffa, "Abraham Lincoln and the Universal Meaning of the Declaration of Independence," in *The Declaration of Independence: Origins and Impact*, ed. Scott Douglas Gerber [Washington, DC: CQ Press, 2002], p. 39). Jefferson, however, in substituting Kamesean morality that synthesizes Hobbesean egotistical selfishness and Shaftesbury's altruism puts Jefferson and Lincoln on the same page. Indeed, Lincoln had a moral-sense view of human morality essentially the same as Kames's and Jefferson's and he was influenced by the Scottish moral-sense thinkers, as will be demonstrated in this chapter.

20. Jefferson to James Monroe, 20 May 1782, in Thomas Jefferson, *The Portable Thomas Jefferson*, ed. Merrill D. Peterson (Kingsport, TN: Penguin, 1981), p. 365.

21. Jefferson to Francis W. Gilmer, 7 June 1816, in Thomas Jefferson, *The Writings of Thomas Jefferson*, ed. Andrew A. Lipscomb and Albert Ellery Bergh (Washington, DC: Thomas Jefferson Memorial Association, 1903), 15:25.

22. Kames, *Essays*, p. 19.

23. Jefferson to Robert Skipwith, 3 August 1771, in Thomas Jefferson, *The Papers of Thomas Jefferson*, ed. Julian P. Boyd and Charles T. Cullen (Princeton, NJ: Princeton University Press, 1950), 1:76–79.

24. Kames, *Essays*, p. 143, and Kames, *Elements of Criticism*, 3rd ed. (Edinburgh: A. Kincaid and J. Bell, 1765), 2:492, 485.

25. Kames, *Essays*, pp. 37–38.

26. Jefferson to Thomas Law, 13 June 1814, in Jefferson, *Writings of Thomas Jefferson*, 14:144.

27. Kames, *Elements of Criticism*, 2:489, 492.

28. Joshua F. Speed (interview), 6 December 1866, in *Herndon's Informants: Letters, Interviews, and Statements about Abraham Lincoln*, ed. Douglas L. Wilson and Rodney O. Davis (Urbana: University of Illinois Press, 1998), pp. 498–99.

29. Thomas Brown, *Lectures on the Philosophy of the Human Mind* (Andover, MA: Mark Newman, 1822), 3:292–93.

30. Ibid., 3:294.

31. Ibid., 1:176.

32. John Locke, *Two Treatises of Government*, ed. Peter Laslett (Cambridge: Cambridge University Press, 1988), pp. 357–58, 360, 363, 426–27.

33. Kames, *Essays*, pp. 124–25.

34. Ibid., p. 123.

35. Speech at New Haven, 6 March 1860, in Abraham Lincoln, *Speeches and Writings 1859–1865*, ed. Don Fehrenbacher (New York: Library of America, 1989), p. 139. William Paley could have been the source of the plank analogy, which is in his *Principles of Moral and Political Philosophy* (Glasgow: Balwyn, 1821), p. 238. Lincoln read Paley, according to Joshua F. Speed's 6 December 1866 letter to William Herndon, Wilson and Davis, *Herndon's Informants*, p. 499.

36. Abraham Lincoln, *A Treasury of Lincoln Quotations*, ed. Fred Kerner (Chicago: Americana House, 1965), p. 84.

37. Dennis F. Hanks to William W. Herndon, March 1866, p. 229; James H. Matheny (interview), 1865–66, p. 470; Joshua F. Speed to Herndon, 6 December 1866, p. 499 and John T. Stuart (interview), 20 December 1866, p. 519, all in Wilson and Davis, *Herndon's Informants*.

38. Abraham Lincoln, *Speeches and Writings 1859–1865*, ed. Don Fehrenbacher (New York: Library of America, 1989), p. 493.

39. Donn Piatt, "Lincoln the Man," in *Reminiscences of Abraham Lincoln by Distinguished Men of His Time*, ed. Allen Thorndyke Rice (New York: Harper & Brothers, 1909), p. 345.

40. William Shakespeare, *Great Books of the Western World*, vol. 26, *The Plays and Sonnets of William Shakespeare*, ed. William George Clark and William Aldis Wright (Chicago: William Benton, 1952), p. 105.

41. Ibid.

42. James M. McPherson, "Lincoln as Commander in Chief," in *The Lincoln Forum: Rediscovering Abraham Lincoln*, ed. John Y. Simon, Harold Holzer, and Dawn Ruark (New York: Fordham University Press, 2002), p. 2.

43. Benjamin P. Thomas, "Lincoln's Humor: An Analysis," in *"Lincoln's Humor" and Other Essays*, ed. Michael Burlingame (Chicago: University of Illinois Press, 2002), p. 12.

44. Keith Warren Jennison, *The Humorous Mr. Lincoln: A Profile in Wit, Courage, and Compassion* (Woodstock, VT: Countryman Press, 1988), p. 46. Harold Holzer, Gabor S. Boritt, and Mark Neely Jr. state that in 1860 Lin-

coln's ugliness was "already legendary" ("The Lincoln Image: Abraham Lincoln and the Popular Print," in *The Historian's Lincoln: Pseudohistory, Psychohistory, and History*, ed. Gabor S. Boritt and Norman O. Forness [Chicago: University of Illinois Press, 1988], p. 54). For Lincoln's use of stories to make a point in an argument see J. G. Holland, *Holland's Life of Abraham Lincoln* (1866; repr., Lincoln: University of Nebraska Press, 1998), pp. 75–77.

45. Shakespeare, *Plays and Sonnets of William Shakespeare*, 26:145.

46. Ibid., 27:573.

47. Ibid., 27:306.

48. Ibid., 27:296.

49. Ibid.

50. Ibid., 27:53.

51. Ibid., 27:53–54.

52. First Inaugural Address, 4 March 1801, in Lincoln, *Speeches and Writings 1859–1865*, p. 221.

53. Joshua E. Speed to William H. Herndon, 6 December 1866, in Wilson and Davis, *Herndon's Informants*, pp. 498–99.

54. Brown, *Lectures on the Philosophy of the Human Mind*, 3:271.

55. Handbill Replying to Charges of Infidelity, 31 July 1846, Lincoln, *Speeches and Writings 1832–1858*, p. 139.

56. Ibid., pp. 139–40.

57. James Tackach, *Lincoln's Moral Vision: The Second Inaugural Address* (Jackson: University Press of Mississippi, 2002), pp. 62–63.

58. Kames, *Essays*, pp. 164–65.

59. Ibid., p. 167.

60. Ibid., pp. 168–69.

61. Ibid., p. 174.

62. Handbill Replying to Charges of Infidelity, 31 July 1846, in Lincoln, *Speeches and Writings 1832–1858*, p. 139.

63. Kames, *Essays*, pp. 140–42.

64. Brown, *Lectures on the Philosophy of the Human Mind*, 3:178–79.

65. Locke, *Essay concerning Human Understanding*, p. 264.

66. Ibid., p. 278.

67. Brown, *Lectures on the Philosophy of the Human Mind*, 3:210.

68. William H. Herndon to Weik, 6 February 1887, in Abraham Lincoln, *Recollected Words of Abraham Lincoln*, comp. and ed. Don E. Fehrenbacher and Virginia Fehrenbacher (Stanford, CA: Stanford University Press, 1996), p. 245.

69. Lincoln, *Speeches and Writings 1859–1865*, pp. 149–50.

70. Ibid., p. 140.

71. Ibid., p. 139.

72. See, for example, speeches at: Springfield, Illinois, 26 June 1857; Springfield, Illinois, 17 July 1858; Lewiston, Illinois, 17 August 1858; in Lincoln, *Treasury of Lincoln Quotations*, pp. 55–76. See also his speech at Columbus, Ohio, 16 September 1859, Lincoln, *Speeches and Writings 1859–1865*, p. 57.

73. Speech at Hartford, Connecticut, March 5, 1860, Abraham Lincoln, *The Collected Works of Abraham Lincoln*, ed. Roy P. Basler (New Brunswick, NJ: Rutgers University Press, 1953), 4:3.

74. Speech at Cincinnati, 17 September 1859, Lincoln, *Speeches and Writings 1859–1865*, p. 85.

75. Ibid., p. 67.

76. Forrest G. Wood, *The Arrogance of Faith: Christianity and Race in America from the Colonial Era to the Twentieth Century* (New York: Alfred A. Knopf, 1990), pp. 43, 36.

77. Ibid., p. 36.

78. Ibid., p. 43.

79. Ibid., p. 44.

80. Ibid., p. 53.

81. Ibid., p. 56.

82. Ibid., p. 53.

83. Ibid., p. 55.

84. As quoted by Wood in ibid., p. 59.

85. As quoted by Wood in ibid. James Henley Thornwell, *The Collected Writings of James Henley Thornwell, D.D., LL.D.*, ed. John B. Adger and John L. Girardeau, 4:382–88. See James Oscar Farmer Jr., *The Metaphysical Confederacy: James Henley Thornwell and the Synthesis of Southern Values* (Macon, GA: Mercer University Press, 1986), pp. 216–33, for a description and analysis of Thornwell's defense of slavery.

86. Fragment on Proslavery Theology, October 1858, in Lincoln, *Treasury of Lincoln Quotations*, p. 267.

87. Speech at New Haven, 6 March 1860, in Lincoln, *Speeches and Writings 1859–1865*, p. 135.

88. Ibid., p. 145.

89. Ibid., p. 144.

90. Ibid.

91. Ibid., p. 203.

92. Ibid., pp. 203–204.

93. Annual Message to Congress, 31 December 1861, in ibid., p. 297.

94. For Lincoln's ideas on economics, see Gabor S. Boritt, "Lincoln and the Economics of the American Dream," in *The Historian's Lincoln: Pseudohistory, Psychohistory, and History*, ed. Gabor S. Boritt and Norman O. Forness (Chicago: University of Illinois Press, 1994), pp. 87–106.

95. Lincoln, *Speeches and Writings 1859–1865*, p. 137.

96. Eulogy on Henry Clay, 6 July 1852, in Lincoln, *Speeches and Writings 1832–1858*, p. 267. See also Jefferson to John Holmes, 22 April 1820, in Jefferson, *Writings of Thomas Jefferson*, 15:249.

97. Eulogy on Henry Clay, 6 July 1852, in Lincoln, *Speeches and Writings 1832–1858*, p. 267.

98. Lincoln, *Speeches and Writings 1859–1865*, p. 145. Lincoln's argument was not original. It was used by Congressman David Wilmot in the 1840s in support of his Wilmot Proviso, a bill he placed before Congress that would have outlawed slavery in all territory acquired by the United States in its war with Mexico (Norman A. Graebner, "The Politicians and Slavery," in *Politics and the Crisis of 1860*, ed. Norman A. Graebner [Urbana: University of Illinois Press, 1961], pp. 12–13).

99. See *Lincoln and His America 1809–1865*, ed. David Plowden (New York: Viking, 1970), p. 218, and J. G. Randall, *Lincoln the Liberal Statesman* (New York: Dodd, Mead, 1947), p. 144.

100. Lincoln, *Treasury of Lincoln Quotations*, p. 133.

101. John Locke, *The Reasonableness of Christianity*, in *The Works of John Locke*, 3 vols. (London: John Churchill and Samuel Manship, 1714), 2:532, 535.

102. Lincoln, *Speeches and Writings 1859–1865*, p. 628.

103. Ibid., p. 585.

104. Jefferson to William Johnson, 12 June 1823, in Jefferson, *Writings of Thomas Jefferson*, 15:440–41.

105. Lincoln, *Treasury of Lincoln Quotations*, p. 59.

106. Lincoln, *Speeches and Writings 1859–1865*, p. 536.

107. Clarence Edward Macartney, *Lincoln and His Cabinet* (New York: Charles Scribner's Sons, 1931), p. 125.

## CHAPTER 4: THE DECLARATION'S ADVOCATE

1. Lincoln to H. L. Pierce and others, 6 April 1859, in Abraham Lincoln, *Speeches and Writings 1859–1865*, ed. Don Fehrenbacher (New York: Library of America, 1989), pp. 18–19.

2. Lincoln to George Robinson, 15 August 1855, in Abraham Lincoln, *Speeches and Writings 1832–1858*, ed. Don Fehrenbacher (New York: Library of America, 1989), pp. 359–60.

3. George B. Forgie, "Lincoln's Tyrants," in *The Historian's Lincoln: Pseudohistory, Psychohistory and History*, ed. Gabor S. Boritt and Norman O. Forness (Chicago: University of Illinois Press, 1988), p. 300.

4. Speech on Kansas-Nebraska Act, 16 October 1854, Lincoln, *Speeches and Writings 1832–1858*, p. 339.

5. Ibid.

6. Ibid.

7. Seventh Debate with Douglas, 15 October 1858, in ibid., p. 800.

8. Damon Wells, *Stephen Douglas: The Last Years, 1857–1861* (Austin: University of Texas Press, 1990), p. 135.

9. Seventh Debate with Douglas, 15 October 1858, Lincoln, *Speeches and Writings 1832–1858*, p. 800.

10. Ibid., pp. 800–801.

11. Ibid., p. 801. Staughton Lynd states that contrary to Lincoln's view, many Founding Fathers—specifically the delegates to the Constitutional Convention from South Carolina and Georgia—did not believe that slavery was put on the path of "ultimate extinction," nor did those from the states of the upper South because every "Southern delegation" opposed "Jefferson's 1784 proposal to prohibit slavery in the West" (Lynd, "The Abolitionist Critique of the United States Constitution," in *The Antislavery Vanguard: New Essays on the Abolitionists*, ed. Martin Duberman [Princeton, NJ: Princeton University Press, 1965], pp. 237–38).

12. Seventh Debate with Douglas, 15 October 1858, Lincoln, *Speeches and Writings 1832–1858*, p. 801.

13. Ibid.

14. Ibid.

15. Ibid.

16. Ibid.

17. Ibid., pp. 801–802.

18. Ibid., p. 802.

19. Speech at Chicago, 10 July 1858, in ibid., p. 447.

20. Speech at Springfield, 17 July 1858, in ibid., p. 471.

21. Ida M. Tarbell, *The Life of Abraham Lincoln: Drawn from Original Sources and Containing Many Speeches, Letters and Telegrams Hitherto Unpublished* (New York: McClure, Phillips, 1902), 1:279–80.

22. Speech on the Kansas-Nebraska Act at Peoria, 16 October 1854, Lincoln, *Speeches and Writings 1832–1858*, p. 327.

23. Ibid., p. 328.

24. Ibid.

25. As quoted in H. W. Brands, *The First American: The Life and Times of Benjamin Franklin* (New York: Doubleday, 2000), pp. 482–83.

26. Speech on the Kansas-Nebraska Act at Peoria, 16 October 1854, in Lincoln, *Speeches and Writings 1832–1858*, p. 328.

27. Thomas Paine, *The Age of Reason: Being an Investigation of True and Fabulous Theology*, Part 1, in *The Complete Religious and Theological Works of Thomas Paine* (New York: Peter Eckler, 1917), p. 301, and Theodore Parker, "The Function of a Teacher of Religion," in *Parker's Works*, vol. 4, *The Transient and Permanent in Christianity*, ed. George Wills Cooke (Boston: American Unitarian Association, 1908), p. 169.

28. Lord Charnwood wrote of the irony of Lincoln's "unrelenting" enmity toward "the project of the Confederacy" because he "had quite purged his heart and mind from hatred or even anger towards his fellow-countrymen of the South" (Lord Charnwood, "Epilogue," in *The Lincoln Reader*, ed. Paul M. Angle [New Brunswick, NJ: Rutgers University Press, 1955], p. 587).

29. Speech on the Kansas-Nebraska Act at Peoria, 16 October 1854, in Lincoln, *Speeches and Writings 1832–1858*, p. 316. Lincoln's ability to moralize against slavery and not sound self-righteous is described by William Lee Miller in *Lincoln's Virtues: An Ethical Biography* (New York: Alfred A. Knopf, 2002), pp. 286–97.

30. John Perry Pritchett compares the South to the "ancient Greek" city-states: both were based on agriculture, both had slavery, and both had a leisured aristocracy (Pritchett, *Calhoun: His Defence of the South* [Poughkeepsie, NY: Printing House of Harmon, 1937], pp. 21–22).

31. Speech on the Kansas-Nebraska Act at Peoria, 16 October 1854, in *Speeches and Writings 1832–1858*, p. 316.

32. Fourth Debate with Douglas, 18 September 1858, in ibid., p. 636.

33. See Fifth Debate with Douglas, 7 October 1858, in ibid., pp. 694–95.

34. See Harry V. Jaffa, *Crisis of the House Divided: An Interpretation of the*

*Issues in the Lincoln-Douglas Debates* (Garden City, NY: Doubleday, 1959), pp. 365–68.

35. Speech on Reconstruction, 11 April 1865, in Lincoln, *Speeches and Writings 1859–1865*, p. 699, and David Herbert Donald, *Lincoln* (New York: Touchstone, 1996), pp. 584–85.

36. "House Divided" speech at Springfield, 16 June 1858, in Lincoln, *Speeches and Writings 1832–1858*, p. 427.

37. Ibid., p. 429.

38. Speech on the Dred Scott decision at Springfield, 26 June 1857, in ibid., p. 396. Mark David Hall writes that Supreme Court justices, in their opinions on particular cases, as well as those pleading cases before the Court, have consistently "invoked the Declaration as a source of rights that are not clearly enumerated in the U.S. Constitution and its amendments, or as a means of interpreting parts of the Constitution" (Hall, "The Declaration of Independence in the Supreme Court," in *The Declaration of Independence: Origins and Impact*, ed. Scott Douglas Gerber [Washington, DC: CQ Press, 2002], p. 142).

39. Speech on the Dred Scott decision at Springfield, 26 June 1857, in Lincoln, *Speeches and Writings 1832–1859*, p. 396.

40. Ibid.

41. Ibid.

42. Ibid.

43. Garry Wills, *Inventing America: Jefferson's Declaration of Independence* (New York: Vintage Books, 1979), p. 296.

44. Speech on the Dred Scott decision, 26 June 1857, in Lincoln, *Speeches and Writings 1832–1859*, p. 396.

45. Ibid.

46. Ibid.

47. Ibid.

48. Garry Wills, *Negro President: Jefferson and the Slave Power* (New York: Houghton Mifflin, 2003), p. 121.

49. Speech on the Dred Scott decision, 26 June 1857, in Lincoln, *Speeches and Writings 1832–1859*, p. 397.

50. Ibid., pp. 396–97.

51. See chapter 2, note 108.

52. Speech at Springfield, 17 July 1858, Lincoln, *Speeches and Writings 1832–1859*, pp. 475–76.

53. "House Divided" speech at Springfield, 16 June 1858, in ibid., p.

431. Damon Wells called Lincoln's collusion accusation a "ludicrous notion" in *Stephen Douglas*, p. 114.

54. Lincoln, *Speeches and Writings 1832–1859*, p. 427.

55. Ibid.

56. Ibid., pp. 427–28.

57. Second Debate with Douglas, 27 August 1858, in ibid., p. 545.

58. "House Divided" speech at Springfield, 16 June 1858, in ibid., p. 430.

59. Ibid., p. 428.

60. Ibid., p. 430.

61. Don E. Fehrenbacher, *The Dred Scott Case: Its Significance in American Law and Politics* (New York: Oxford University Press, 1979), pp. 306–14.

62. Seventh Debate with Douglas, 15 October 1858, Lincoln, *Speeches and Writings 1832–1858*, pp. 806–807.

63. As Lincoln quoted Douglas in his speech on the Dred Scott decision, 26 June 1857, in ibid., p. 393.

64. Jean Edward Smith, *John Marshall* (New York: Henry Holt, 1996), p. 581.

65. Speech on the Dred Scott decision, 26 June 1857, in Lincoln, *Speeches and Writings 1832–1858*, pp. 394–95.

66. Jefferson to William Charles Jarvis, 28 September 1820, in Thomas Jefferson, *The Writings of Thomas Jefferson*, ed. Andrew A. Lipscomb and Albert Ellery Bergh (Washington, DC: Thomas Jefferson Memorial Association, 1903), 15:278.

67. Ibid., 15:277.

68. Ibid., 15:278.

69. Ibid., 15:277.

70. Ibid., 15:276.

71. Speech at Springfield, 17 July 1858, Lincoln, *Speeches and Writings 1832–1859*, pp. 473–74.

72. Ibid., p. 474.

73. Ibid.

74. Ibid., p. 716.

75. Donald, *Lincoln*, pp. 299, 303–304, 441–44, 489.

76. Don E. Fehrenbacher, "Lincoln and the Constitution," in *The Public and Private Lincoln: Contemporary Perspectives*, ed. Cullom Davis, Charles B. Strozier, Rebecca Monroe Veach, and Geoffrey C. Ward (Carbondale: Southern Illinois University Press, 1979), p. 130.

77. Frank J. Williams, "Abraham Lincoln and the Changing Role of

Commander in Chief," in *Lincoln Reshapes the Presidency*, ed. Charles M. Hubbard (Macon, GA: Mercer University Press, 2003), p. 21.

78. William E. Gienapp, "Abraham Lincoln and Presidential Leadership," in *"We Cannot Escape History": Lincoln and the Last Best Hope of Earth*, ed. James M. McPherson (Chicago: University of Illinois Press, 1995), p. 80.

79. Sixth Debate with Douglas, 13 October 1858, in Lincoln, *Speeches and Writings 1832–1859*, p. 741.

80. David McCollough, *John Adams* (New York: Simon & Schuster, 2001), pp. 505–506, 577.

81. Fifth Debate with Douglas, 7 October 1858, Lincoln, *Speeches and Writings 1832–1858*, p. 714.

82. Ibid., pp. 714–15.

83. First Debate with Douglas, 21 August 1858, in ibid., p. 526.

84. Ibid.

85. Ibid.

86. Ibid.

87. Sixth Debate with Douglas, 13 October 1858, in ibid., p. 741.

88. See Lawrence M. Friedman, *A History of American Law* (New York: Simon & Schuster, 1973), p. 330; Paul Kens, introduction to "Personal Reminiscences of Early Days in California with Other Sketches," *Journal of Supreme Court History* 29, no. 1 (2004): 10; Milton H. Shutes, *Lincoln and California* (Stanford, CA: Stanford University Press, 1943), p. 237; and Carl Brent Swisher, *Stephen J. Field: Craftsman of the Law* (Washington, DC: Brookings Institution, 1930), pp. 114–19.

89. Fifth Debate with Douglas, 7 October 1858, in Lincoln, *Speeches and Writings 1832–1858*, pp. 713–14.

90. Ibid., p. 714.

91. Jean H. Baker, "Lincoln's Narrative of American Exceptionalism," in McPherson, *"We Cannot Escape History,"* pp. 39–40.

92. Fifth Debate with Douglas, 7 October 1858, in Lincoln, *Speeches and Writings 1832–1858*, p. 715.

93. For Lincoln's contribution to the rise of the Republican Party, see Don E. Fehrenbacher, *Prelude to Greatness: Lincoln in the 1850s* (Stanford: Stanford University Press, 1962), pp. 19–47.

94. Lincoln to H. L. Pierce and others, 6 April 1859, in Lincoln, *Speeches and Writings 1859–1865*, p. 19.

95. Ibid.

96. Ibid.

97. Third Debate with Douglas, 15 September 1858, in Lincoln, *Speeches and Writings 1832–1859*, p. 598.

98. Speech at Chicago, 10 July 1858, in ibid., p. 457.

99. Lincoln to Joshua F. Speed, 24 August 1855, in ibid., p. 363.

100. See *The Political Thought of Abraham Lincoln,* ed. Richard N. Current (Indianapolis, IN: Bobbs-Merrill, 1967), p. xxvii.

101. Abraham Lincoln, *The Collected Works of Abraham Lincoln,* ed. Roy P. Basler, 11 vols. (New Brunswick, NJ: Rutgers University Press, 1953), 5:69; and Wayne C. Temple, *Abraham Lincoln: From Skeptic to Prophet* (Mahomet, IL: Mayhaven, 1995), pp. 166–67.

102. Jean Edward Smith, *Grant* (New York: Touchstone, Simon & Schuster), pp. 225–27.

103. *Abraham Lincoln: The Tribute of the Synagogue* (New York: Block, 1927), p. 31.

104. Lincoln, *Collected Works of Abraham Lincoln,* 6:34.

105. Jefferson, *Writings of Thomas Jefferson,* 1:121.

106. See chapter 2, note 108.

107. Fifth Debate with Douglas, 7 October 1858, in Lincoln, *Speeches and Writings 1832–1858,* pp. 716–17.

108. Ibid., p. 716.

109. Ibid., p. 717.

110. Ibid.

111. Ibid.

112. Ibid.

113. Lincoln to H. L. Pierce and others, 6 April 1859, in Lincoln, *Speeches and Writings 1859–1865,* p. 19.

114. Speech at Chicago, 10 July 1858, in Lincoln, *Speeches and Writings 1832–1858,* p. 456.

115. Ibid., p. 457.

116. Third debate with Douglas, 15 September 1858, in ibid., p. 599.

117. Ibid.

118. Speech at Chicago, 10 July 1858, in ibid., p. 457.

119. Jefferson to Henri Gregoire, 25 February 1809, in Jefferson, *Writings of Thomas Jefferson,* 12:255.

120. Lincoln to H. L. Pierce and others, 6 April 1859, in Lincoln, *Speeches and Writings 1859–1865,* p. 19.

121. Harry V. Jaffa, *Equality and Liberty: Theory and Practice in American Politics* (New York: Oxford University Press, 1965), pp. vii–viii.

122. Speech at Chicago, 10 July 1858, in Lincoln, *Speeches and Writings 1832–1858,* p. 457.

123. Wells, *Stephen Douglas,* p. 137.

## CHAPTER 5: THE GETTYSBURG ADDRESS

1. Colin R. Ballard, *The Military Genius of Abraham Lincoln* (New York: World Publishing Company, 1952), pp. 169–70.

2. Lincoln to George G. Meade, 14 July 1863, in Abraham Lincoln, *The Collected Works of Abraham Lincoln*, ed. Roy P. Basler, 11 vols. (New Brunswick, NJ: Rutgers University Press, 1953), 6:327–29.

3. Gerald J. Prokopowicz, "'If I Had Gone Up There, I Could Have Whipped Them Myself': Lincoln's Military Fantasies," in *The Lincoln Forum: Rediscovering Abraham Lincoln*, ed. John Y. Simon, Harold Holzer, and Dawn Ruark (New York: Fordham University Press, 2002), pp. 77–78. Robert Todd Lincoln's reminiscences about his father of 5 January 1885 stated that his father's "distress" over Meade allowing Lee to escape from the flooded river was such that he had "tears upon his face" (Abraham Lincoln, *An Oral History of Abraham Lincoln: John J. Nicolay's Interviews and Essays*, ed. Michael Burlingame [Carbondale: Southern Illinois University Press, 1966], p. 88).

4. Response to Serenade, Washington, DC, 7 July 1863, in Abraham Lincoln, *Speeches and Writings 1859–1865*, ed. Don E. Fehrenbacher (New York: Library of America, 1989), pp. 475–76.

5. Ibid., p. 475. Lincoln's refusal to speak when he was not prepared was typical of the mature Lincoln, as Harold Holzer points out in "Avoid Saying 'Foolish Things': The Legacy of Lincoln's Impromptu Oratory," in *"We Cannot Escape History": Lincoln and the Last Best Hope of Earth*, ed. James M. McPherson (Chicago: University of Illinois Press, 1955), pp. 113–14.

6. There are conflicting eyewitness accounts on whether or not there was applause after Lincoln's address, but William E. Barton, despite the conflicting accounts, judges that there was applause but "it certainly was not enthusiastic" (Barton, *Lincoln at Gettysburg: What He Intended to Say; What He Said; What He Was Reported to Have Said; What He Wished He Had Said* [New York: Peter Smith, 1950], pp. 89–90).

7. John Dos Passos, "Lincoln and His Almost Chosen People," in *Lincoln and the Gettysburg Address*, ed. Allan Nevins (Urbana: University of Illinois Press, 1964), p. 20.

8. Garry Wills, *Lincoln at Gettysburg: The Words that Remade America* (New York: Touchstone, 1992), p. 39.

9. See Allen Jayne, *Jefferson's Declaration of Independence: Origins, Philosophy and Theology* (Lexington: University Press of Kentucky, 1998), chap. 3 and pp. 128–38.

10. John Locke, *An Essay concerning Human Understanding*, ed. Peter H. Niddich (Oxford: Clarendon Press, 1984), p. 241.

11. Ibid., p. 238.

12. Ibid., p. 284.

13. Jefferson to Isaac H. Tiffany, 4 April 1819, Thomas Jefferson Papers, S1 R51, 38353, Library of Congress.

14. Ibid.

15. See Jayne, *Jefferson's Declaration of Independence*, chap. 3.

16. John Locke, *Two Treatises of Government*, ed. Peter Laslett (Cambridge: Cambridge University Press, 1988), p. 284.

17. Ibid., pp. 284, 357–58.

18. "On Slavery and Democracy," written in 1858(?), in Abraham Lincoln, *Speeches and Writings 1832–1858*, ed. Don E. Fehrenbacher (New York: Library of America, 1989), p. 484.

19. Barry Schwartz, "The New Gettysburg Address: A Study in Illusion," in Simon, Holzer, and Ruark, *Lincoln Forum*, p. 183.

20. See Isaiah Berlin, *Two Concepts of Liberty: An Inaugural Lecture Delivered before the University of Oxford on 31 October 1958* (Oxford: Oxford University Press, 1958), p. 16, and also p. 9, where Berlin writes of "that minimum development of his [an individual's] natural faculties which alone makes it possible to pursue, and even to conceive, the various ends which men hold good or right or sacred." See also Quentin Skinner, *Liberty before Liberalism* (Cambridge: Cambridge University Press, 1998), p. 114, note 22.

21. Speech to the 166th Ohio Regiment, 22 August 1864, in Lincoln, *Speeches and Writings 1859–1865*, p. 624.

22. Dennis F. Hanks, June 1865 (interview), p. 42, and Nathaniel Grigsby, September 1865 (interview), p. 114, in *Herndon's Informants: Letters, Interviews, and Statements about Abraham Lincoln*, ed. Douglas Wilson and Rodney O. Davis (Urbana: University of Illinois Press, 1998).

23. Thomas Jefferson, *Notes on the State of Virginia*, ed. William Peden (New York: Norton, 1972), p. 147.

24. Speech on the Dred Scott decision, 26 June 1857, in Lincoln, *Speeches and Writings 1832–1858*, p. 398.

25. Jefferson, *Notes on the State of Virginia*, pp. 143–46. See also Jefferson to John Adams, 28 October 1813, and Jefferson to John Jay, 19 November 1788, in Thomas Jefferson, *The Writings of Thomas Jefferson*, ed. Andrew A. Lipscomb and Albert Ellery Bergh, 20 vols. (Washington, DC: Thomas Jefferson Memorial Association, 1903), 13:396 and 7:207.

26. Gabor S. Boritt, "The Right to Rise," in *The Public and the Private Lin-*

coln: *Contemporary Perspectives*, ed. Cullom Davis, Charles B. Strozier, Rebecca Monroe Veach, and Geoffrey C. Ward (Carbondale: Southern Illinois University Press, 1979), p. 64.

27. Jefferson's Second Inaugural Address, 4 March 1805, in Jefferson, *Writings of Thomas Jefferson*, 3:382.

28. Ronald D. Rietveld tells of the profound impact of the Founders on Lincoln that began in his youth and states that "Library of Congress records" show that four volumes of Jefferson's *Writings* were charged to the president in 1861 (Rietveld, "Lincoln's View of the Founding Fathers," in *Abraham Lincoln: Sources and Style of Leadership*, ed. Frank J. Williams, William D. Pederson, and Vincent J. Marsala [Westport, CT: Greenwood, 1994], pp. 17–44).

29. Lincoln, *Speeches and Writings 1832–1858*, p. 458.

30. See chap. 1, note 20, and Jayne, *Jefferson's Declaration of Independence*, pp. 15–17.

31. W. H. C. Frend, *The Rise of Christianity* (London: Darton, Longman and Todd, 1986), pp. 674–75.

32. As would be expected, freethinker Joseph Lewis makes much of the fact that Lincoln did not mention "under God" or God at all in his original draft of the Gettysburg Address or the Emancipation Proclamation in which Salmon Chase inserted "I invoke the considerate judgment of mankind and the gracious favor of Almighty God" (Lewis, *"Lincoln the Atheist* [Austin, TX: American Atheist Press, 1979], pp. 20–21).

33. Janet Nelson, "Kingship and Empire," in *Cambridge History of Medieval Political Thought c. 350–c. 1450*, ed. J. H. Burns (Cambridge: Cambridge University Press, 1991), p. 245.

34. See, for example, Wills, *Lincoln at Gettysburg*, p. 107, and David Herbert Donald, *Lincoln* (New York: Touchstone, 1996), p. 461. Daniel W. Wilder, a Harvard-educated lawyer who Lincoln appointed surveyor-general of Kansas and Nebraska in 1863, wrote William H. Herndon on 24 November 1866 that Lincoln got the idea of "government of the people, by the people and for the people" along with the idea of "self consecration" from Theodore Parker and used both of these ideas in the Gettysburg Address (Wilson and Davis, *Herndon's Informants*, pp. 419–20, 776–77).

35. As quoted by Skinner, *Liberty before Liberalism*, p. 2.

36. See King, "The Barbarian Kingdoms," in Burns, *Cambridge History of Medieval Political Thought c. 350–c. 1450*, p. 128, and D. E. Luscombe and G. R. Evans, "The Twelfth-century Renaissance," in ibid., pp. 316–17.

37. Eric Foner, *The Story of American Freedom* (New York: W. W. Norton,

1999), pp. xxi, 126–29. Scott Douglas Gerber states that Supreme Court Justice Thomas is opposed to affirmative action to any particular group of citizens because it is paternalistic and also diametrically opposed to emphasis in the Declaration of Independence on governmental protection of individual rights (Gerber, "Clarence Thomas, Civil Rights, and the Declaration of Independence," in *The Declaration of Independence: Origins and Impact,* ed. Scott Douglas Gerber (Washington, DC: CQ Press, 2002), pp. 52–53.

38. Lincoln, *Speeches and Writings 1859–1865*, p. 536.

39. See Wills, *Lincoln at Gettysburg,* p. 127.

40. Webster's speech of 26 and 27 January 1830, in *The Webster-Hayne Debate on the Nature of the Union,* ed. Herman Belz (Indianapolis, IN: Liberty Fund, 2000), pp. 136–37.

41. Lincoln, *Speeches and Writings 1859–1865*, p. 218.

42. Message to Congress in Special Session, 4 July 1861, in ibid., p. 259.

43. Ibid.

44. See First Inaugural Address, in ibid., pp. 217–18.

45. Message to Congress in Special Session, 4 July 1861, in ibid., p. 250.

46. Ibid., p. 258.

47. Webster's speech of 26 and 27 January 1830, in Belz, *Webster-Hayne Debate on the Nature of the Union,* pp. 137–41, 153–54.

48. Message to Congress in Special Session, 4 July 1861, in Lincoln, *Speeches and Writings 1859–1865*, p. 260.

49. Webster's speech of 26 and 27 January 1830, in Belz, *Webster-Hayne Debate on the Nature of the Union,* pp. 153–54.

50. First Inaugural Address, 4 March 1861, in Lincoln, *Speeches and Writings 1859–1865*, p. 220.

51. Webster's speech of 26 and 27 January 1830, in Belz, *Webster-Hayne Debate on the Nature of the Union,* p. 128.

52. First Inaugural Address, 4 March 1861, in Lincoln, *Speeches and Writings 1859–1865*, p. 220.

53. John C. Calhoun, *Union and Liberty: The Political Philosophy of John C. Calhoun,* ed. Ross M. Lence (Indianapolis, IN: Liberty Fund, 1992), p. 402.

54. Ibid., p. xii, and August O. Spain, *The Political Theory of John C. Calhoun* (New York: Bookman Associates, 1951), pp. 18–19.

55. Calhoun, *Union and Liberty,* pp. xv–xvii; H. W. Brands, *Andrew*

*Jackson: His Life and Times* (New York: Doubleday, 2005), pp. 339–41, 444, 477–82; and Spain, *Political Theory of John C. Calhoun*, pp. 19–20.

56. Thomas J. DiLorenzo, *The Real Lincoln: A New Look at Abraham Lincoln, His Agenda, and an Unnecessary War* (New York: Three Rivers Press, 2003), pp. 93–94.

57. Calhoun, *Liberty and Union*, p. xiii.

58. DiLorenzo, *The Real Lincoln*, pp. 93–94.

59. Calhoun, *Liberty and Union*, p. xiii.

60. Senator Robert Hayne of South Carolina in his speech on 25 January 1830 referred to Calhoun's *Exposition* during his debate with Senator Daniel Webster of Massachusetts (Belz, *Hayne-Webster Debate on the Nature of the Union*, p. 73).

61. Spain, *Political Theory of John C. Calhoun*, p. 19.

62. Calhoun, *Union and Liberty*, p. 339.

63. In ibid., p. 338, Calhoun's quote of Hamilton's *Federalist* 51 was: "It is of the greatest importance in a republic, not only to guard society against the oppression of its rulers, but to guard one part of society against the injustice of the other part. Different interests necessarily exist in different classes of citizens. If a majority be united by a common interest, the rights of the minority will be insecure." Again—"In a society, under the forms of which the stronger faction can readily unite and oppress the weaker, anarchy may be said as truly to reign, as in a state of nature, where the weaker individual is not secured against the violence of the stronger."

64. Ibid., p. 343.

65. Ibid., p. 348.

66. Ibid.

67. Ibid., pp. 348–49.

68. In ibid., pp. 349–50, Calhoun's quote from Madison's Virginia Resolutions was: "The Constitution of the United States was formed by the sanction of the States, given by each in its sovereign capacity. . . . The States, then, being parties to the constitutional compact, and in their sovereign capacity, it follows of necessity that there can be no tribunal above their authority to decide, in the last resort, whether the compact made by them be violated; and, consequently, as parties to it, they must themselves decide, in the last resort, such questions as may be of sufficient magnitude to require their interposition." Calhoun's quote from Jefferson's Kentucky Resolutions in ibid., p. 350, was: "The Government, created by this compact [the Federal Government created by the Constitution], was not made

the exclusive or final judge of the extent of the powers delegated to itself . . . —but, as in all other cases of compact between parties having no common judge, each party has an equal right to judge for itself, as well of infractions as of the mode and measure of redress."

69. Ibid., pp. 569–70.

70. Ibid., p. 566.

71. Ibid.

72. Ibid., p. 565.

73. Ibid., pp. 566, 568.

74. Ibid., p. 568.

75. Ibid., p. 569.

76. Speech on the Reception of Abolition Petitions, 6 January 1837, in ibid., p. 473.

77. Ibid.

78. Ibid.

79. Ibid.

80. Ibid., p. 472.

81. "House Divided" speech at Springfield, Illinois, 16 June 1858, in Lincoln, *Speeches and Writings 1832–1858*, p. 426.

82. Calhoun, *Union and Liberty*, p. 360. Clyde N. Wilson, as the "custodian of Calhoun's works" for several years, points out the relevance of Calhoun's thought "to the condition of contemporary man" that has been "expressed by historians, political scientists, economists, journalists, and public officials, representing three continents" in his introduction to *The Essential Calhoun: Selections from Writings, Speeches, and Letters*, ed. Clyde N. Wilson (New Brunswick, NJ: Transaction, 1992), p. xv.

83. Belz, *Webster-Hayne Debate on the Nature of the Union*, p. 134.

84. Lincoln, *Speeches and Writings 1859–1865*, p. 218. Avery Craven points out that in 1860 many Northern newspaper editors defended the right of any state to secede from the Union (Craven, "The Fatal Predicament," in *Politics and the Crisis of 1860*, ed. Norman A. Graebner [Urbana: University of Illinois Press, 1961], pp. 134–35).

85. In the last chapter it was mentioned that Lincoln maintained that most people believed blacks were included in the natural rights idealism of the Declaration. Yet simultaneously, he believed that most people did not favor complete abolition and, therefore, avoided publicly advocating complete abolition explicitly while campaigning because it would have been political suicide.

86. See Eulogy on Henry Clay, 6 July 1852, and Seventh Debate with

Stephen Douglas, 15 October 1858, in Lincoln, *Speeches and Writings 1832–1858*, pp. 269, 795.

87. Allen C. Guelzo, *Abraham Lincoln: Redeemer President* (Grand Rapids, MI: William B. Eerdmans, 1999), p. 371. See also Locke, *An Essay concerning Human Understanding*, pp. 530–31.

88. Locke, *Essay concerning Human Understanding*, pp. 706, 710.

89. Glen E. Thurow, *Abraham Lincoln and American Political Religion* (Albany: State University of New York Press, 1976), p. 113.

90. Wills, *Lincoln at Gettysburg*, p. 39.

91. Julian Boyd, *The Declaration of Independence: The Evolution of the Text* (Washington, DC: Library of Congress, 1943), pl. 10.

92. Thomas G. West explains how constitutions both state and federal were made by the Founders to implement and actualize the "principles of the Declaration" and are, therefore, linked to the political theory of the Declaration of Independence (West, "The Declaration of Independence, the U. S. Constitution, and the Bill of Rights," in Gerber, *Declaration of Independence*, pp. 72–95).

93. Locke, *Two Treatises of Government*, p. 382.

94. Ibid., p. 358.

95. Ibid., pp. 358, 271.

96. Ibid., p. 380.

97. Ibid., pp. 415, 405.

98. Ibid., pp. 278–82.

99. The same language was used in the rough draft except for "under Absolute Despotism," which was originally "arbitrary power." Jefferson altered "arbitrary power" to "under absolute despotism" according to Boyd in *The Declaration of Independence*, pp. 25–26, who believes that perhaps Benjamin Franklin changed "power" to "despotism." However, from a Lockean perspective the change does not alter the meaning of the Declaration since despotism or "Despotical Power" is "Absolute, Arbitrary Power." See Locke, *Two Treatises of Government*, pp. 382–83.

100. Special Message to Congress, 4 July 1861, in Lincoln, *Speeches and Writings 1859–1865*, p. 256.

101. Speech on Kansas-Nebraska Act, 16 October 1854, in Lincoln, *Speeches and Writings 1832–1858*, pp. 331–32.

102. Special Message to Congress, 4 July 1861, in Lincoln, *Speeches and Writings 1859–1865*, p. 256.

103. Gettysburg Address, 19 November 1863, in ibid., p. 536.

104. Paul Cartledge tells of an element of happiness and celebration in

addition to commemoration in the Greek funeral oration when an Athenian died fighting for his city because such a death was "the sweetest and most fitting, the best, sort of death for an Athenian citizen" (Cartledge, *The Greeks: A Portrait of Self and Others* [Oxford: Oxford University Press, 1993], pp. 114–15). This element was absent in the Gettysburg Address even though it has been compared to Greek funeral orations.

## CHAPTER 6: THE SECOND INAUGURAL ADDRESS

1. Ronald C. White Jr., *Lincoln's Greatest Speech: The Second Inaugural* (New York: Simon & Schuster, 2003), pp. 146–49. See also William C. Harris, "Toward Appomattox, Toward Unconditional Surrender?" in *The Lincoln Enigma: The Changing Faces of an American Icon*, ed. Gabor Boritt (New York: Oxford University Press, 2002), p. 121. Merrill D. Peterson states that "from the hour of his death Protestant ministers portrayed the Martyr President as an exemplary Christian" (Peterson, *Lincoln in American Memory* [New York: Oxford University Press, 1994], p. 218). Glen E. Thurow writes that "a host of books were written in the late nineteenth and early twentieth centuries seeking to show that Lincoln was a conventional believer of one sort or another" (Thurow, "Abraham Lincoln and American Political Religion," in *The Historian's Lincoln: Pseudohistory, Psychohistory and History*, ed. Gabor S. Boritt and Norman O. Forness [Chicago: University of Illinois Press, 1988], p. 128). Stephen B. Oates in *Abraham Lincoln* states the Josiah Gilbert Holland's *The Life of Lincoln*, first published in 1866, portrayed Lincoln as a "true Christian" while William Herndon's *Herndon's Lincoln*, first published in 1889, portrayed Lincoln as a religious skeptic and that these two books started a "war" of conflicting interpretations of Lincoln's religious views that persists to this day (Oates, *Abraham Lincoln: The Man behind the Myths* [New York: Harper Perennial, 1994], pp. 5–7).

2. Joseph Gillespie to Herndon, 8 December 1866, in *Herndon's Informants: Letters, Interviews, and Statements about Abraham Lincoln*, ed. Douglas Wilson and Rodney O. Davis (Urbana: University of Illinois Press, 1998), pp. 506–507, 749.

3. Speech at Columbus, Ohio, 16 September 1859, in Abraham Lincoln, *Speeches and Writings 1859–1865*, ed. Don Fehrenbacher (New York: Library of America, 1989), pp. 41–42.

4. The First Inaugural Address, 4 March 1861, in Lincoln, *Speeches and Writings 1859–1865*, ed. Don Fehrenbacher (New York: Library of America, 1989), p. 221.

5. Ibid., p. 223.

6. Mark A. Noll, *America's God: From Jonathan Edwards to Abraham Lincoln* (New York: Oxford University Press, 2002), p. 431.

7. Meditation on the Divine Will, 2 September 1862 [?], in Abraham Lincoln, *The Collected Works of Abraham Lincoln*, ed. Roy P. Basler, 11 vols. (New Brunswick, NJ: Rutgers University Press, 1953), 5:403–404.

8. White, *Lincoln's Greatest Speech*, pp. 147–48.

9. Ibid.

10. "God from all eternity did, by the most wise and holy counsel of his own will, freely and unchangeably ordain whatsoever comes to pass: yet so, as thereby neither is God the author of sin, nor is violence offered to the will of the creatures, nor is the liberty or contingency of second causes taken away, but rather established" (G. I. Williamson, *The Westminster Confession of Faith for Study Classes* [Philadelphia: Presbyterian and Reformed Publishing Company, 1964], p. 30). Then, in another chapter, the *Confession* states: "There is but one only living and true God, who is infinite in being and perfection, a most pure spirit, invisible, without body, parts, or passions, immutable, immense, eternal, incomprehensible, almighty, most wise, most holy, most free, most absolute, *working all things according to the counsel of his own immutable and most righteous will, for his own glory* [my italics]" (p. 23). In still another chapter, the *Confession* states that God controls all human actions: "God, the great Creator of all things, doth uphold, direct, dispose, and govern *all* creatures, actions, and things, from the greatest even to the least, by his most wise and holy providence, according to his infallible foreknowledge, and the free and immutable counsel of his own will, to the praise of the glory of his wisdom, power, justice, goodness, and mercy" (p. 46).

11. White, *Lincoln's Greatest Speech*, pp. 138–41.

12. Joseph Gillespie, Lincoln's friend from the Black Hawk War in 1832 and colleague in law and politics, paid tribute to Lincoln's "sledge hammer logic" in an 8 December 1866 letter to Herndon (Wilson and Davis, *Herndon's Informants*, pp. 508, 749).

13. See note 10.

14. White, *Lincoln's Greatest Speech*, pp. 146–49.

15. Message to Congress in Special Session, 4 July 1861, in Lincoln, *Speeches and Writings 1859–1865*, p. 259.

16. Lewis Perry, *Radical Abolitionism: Anarchy and the Government of God in Antislavery Thought* (Ithaca, NY: Cornell University Press, 1973), p. 270

17. The Second Inaugural Address, 4 March 1865, in Lincoln, *Speeches and Writings 1859–1865*, p. 686.

18. Ibid.

19. Ibid.

20. Ibid., p. 687.

21. Leonard Swett to William H. Herndon, 17 January 1866, in Wilson and Davis, *Herndon's Informants*, p. 167.

22. The Second Inaugural Address, 4 March 1865, in Lincoln, *Speeches and Writings 1859–1865*, p. 687. See also Psalm 19:9 (KJV). Stewart Winger, *Lincoln, Religion, and Romantic Cultural Politics* (Dekalb: Northern Illinois University Press, 2003), p. 206.

23. John Dillenberger and Claude Welch, *Protestant Christianity: Interpreted through Its Development* (New York: Macmillan, 1998), pp. 91–93.

24. Richard J. Carwardine, *Lincoln* (Harlow: Pearson Longman, 2003), p. 223.

25. Quentin Skinner, *The Foundations of Modern Political Thought*, 2 vols. (Cambridge: Cambridge University Press, 1978), 2:54–55.

26. The Second Inaugural Address, in Lincoln, *Speeches and Writings 1859–1865*, pp. 686–87. Billy and Ruth Graham state that Lincoln's "second inaugural address sounds like a sermon on the will of God in the life of a nation. Its citations of Scripture are so frequent that" it "must factually be regarded as the most official religious document in American history" (foreword to *Abraham Lincoln: The Man and His Faith*, by G. Frederick Owen [Wheaton, IL: Tyndale House, 1981], p. ix).

27. First Inaugural Address, 4 March 1861, in Lincoln, *Speeches and Writings 1859–1865*, p. 215.

28. To A. G. Hodges, Esq., 4 April 1864, in Lincoln, *Speeches and Writings 1859–1865*, p. 586.

29. Roy Meredith, *Mr. Lincoln's Contemporaries: An Album of Portraits by Mathew B. Brady* (New York: Charles Scribner's Sons, 1951), p. 218, and Raymond Abraham Ross, "Slavery and the New York City Newspapers, 1850–1860" (PhD diss., New York University, 1966), pp. 324, 349.

30. Allen C. Guelzo, *Abraham Lincoln: Redeemer President* (Grand Rapids, MI: William B. Eerdmans, 1999), p. 340.

31. For the text of Greeley's letter, see *And Why Not Every Man? The Story of the Fight against Negro Slavery*, ed. Herbert Aptheker (Berlin: Seven Seas, 1961), pp. 233–35.

32. Lincoln to Horace Greeley, 22 August 1862, in Lincoln, *Speeches and Writings 1859–1865*, p. 358. Duncan Andrew Campbell states that Lincoln's statement to Greeley had an adverse impact on public opinion favorable to the Union in England (Campbell, *English Public Opinion and the American Civil War* [London: Boydell Press, 2003], pp. 129–30).

33. J. P. Usher, "Lincoln and Slavery," in *Reminiscences of Abraham Lincoln by Distinguished Men of His Time*, ed. Allen Thorndyke Rice (New York: Harper & Brothers, 1909), p. 214.

34. Quoted in James M. McPherson, "Introduction: Last Best Hope for What?" in *"We Cannot Escape History": Lincoln and the Last Best Hope of Earth*, ed. James M. McPherson (Chicago: University of Illinois Press, 1995), p. 9.

35. Richard Hofstadter, *The American Political Tradition: And the Men Who Made It* (New York: Vintage Books, 1973), p. 169. Hofstadter's comment was made regarding the Preliminary Emancipation Proclamation of September 1862, but it applies to the final one of 1 January 1863 as well.

36. J. G. Randall and Richard N. Current, *Lincoln the President: Last Full Measure* (New York: Dodd, Mead, 1955), p. 299.

37. Martin Duberman explains that most abolitionists were against compensated abolition because they believed slavery was a sin and one shouldn't "pay a man" "for ceasing to commit a sin," plus the fact that slave owners "had already been paid many times over in labor for which" they "had never given wages" (Duberman, "The Northern Response to Slavery," in *The Antislavery Vanguard: New Essays on the Abolitionists*, ed. Martin Duberman [Princeton, NJ: Princeton University Press, 1965], p. 403).

38. Lincoln, *Speeches and Writings 1859–1865*, pp. 406–407.

39. Philip Shaw Paludan, "Lincoln and Colonization: Policy or Principle?" *Journal of the Abraham Lincoln Association* 25, no. 1 (Winter 2004): 26–27.

40. Message to Congress, December 1, 1862, in Lincoln, *Speeches and Writings 1859–1865*, p. 411.

41. Ibid., p. 410.

42. Ibid., pp. 406–407.

43. Ibid., p. 411.

44. Gabor S. Boritt, "Did He Dream of a Lily-White America? The Voyage to Linconia," in *The Lincoln Enigma: The Changing Faces of an American Icon*, ed. Gabor S. Boritt (New York: Oxford University Press, 2002), p. 12. Using World War II population figures and deaths of American service personnel, which were 405,000, Philip Shaw Paludan estimates that the 623,000 deaths in the Civil War would be the equivalent of 2.5 million in

World War II (Paludan, *"A People's Contest": The Union and Civil War* (New York: Harper & Row, 1988), pp. 316–17.

45. Lincoln, *Speeches and Writings 1859–1865*, p. 415.

46. White, *Lincoln's Greatest Speech*, p. 81.

47. Final Emancipation Proclamation, 1 January 1863, in Lincoln, *Speeches and Writings 1859–1865*, p. 425. LaWanda Cox refutes the revisionist claims that Lincoln should not be known as the great emancipator (Cox, "Lincoln and Black Freedom," in Boritt and Forness, *The Historian's Lincoln*, pp. 175–96).

48. John Y. Simon, "Commander in Chief Lincoln and General Grant," in *The Lincoln Forum: Rediscovering Abraham Lincoln*, ed. John Y. Simon, Harold Holzer, and Dawn Ruark (New York: Fordham University Press, 2002), pp. 20–21.

49. To A. G. Hodges, Esq., 4 April 1864, in Lincoln, *Speeches and Writings 1859–1865*, pp. 585–86. For inconsistencies of Lincoln in matters of civil rights see Mark E. Neeley Jr., *The Last Best Hope of Earth: Abraham Lincoln and the Promise of America* (Cambridge, MA: Harvard University Press, 1995), pp. 130–37.

50. Allen C. Guelzo, "Apple of Gold in a Picture of Silver," in Boritt, *Lincoln Enigma*, pp. 104–107.

51. David Herbert Donald, "Abraham Lincoln and Jefferson Davis as Commanders in Chief," in Boritt, *Lincoln Enigma*, p. 82.

52. Peter Burke, "Tacitism, Skepticism, and Reason of State," in *The Cambridge History of Political Thought, 1450–1700*, ed. J. H. Burns and Mark Goldie (Cambridge: Cambridge University Press, 1994), p. 480. See also Robert W. Tucker and David C. Hendrickson, *Empire of Liberty: The Statecraft of Thomas Jefferson* (New York: Oxford University Press, 1992), p. 259, note 25; Frederich Meinecke, *Machiavellism: The Doctrine of Raison D'Etat and Its Place in Modern History*, trans. Douglas Scott (New Haven, CT: Yale University Press, 1957), pp. 1–2, 212; and Niccolo Machiavelli, *The Discourses*, ed. Bernard Crick, trans. Leslie J. Walker, rev. Brian Richardson (London: Penguin, 1983), pp. 194–96.

53. Ronald Rietveld tells of the profound impact of the Founders on Lincoln that began in his youth and states that "Library of Congress records" show "that four volumes of Jefferson's Writings were charged to the president in 1861" (Rietveld, "Lincoln's View of the Founding Fathers," in *Abraham Lincoln: Sources and Style of Leadership*, ed. Frank J. Williams, William D. Pederson, and Vincent J. Marsala [Westport, CT: Greenwood, 1994], pp. 17–44).

54. Jefferson to Dr. James Brown, 27 October 1808, in Thomas Jefferson, *The Writings of Thomas Jefferson*, ed. Andrew A. Lipscomb and Albert Ellery Bergh, 20 vols. (Washington, DC: Thomas Jefferson Memorial Association, 1903), 12:183.

55. Jefferson to J. B. Colvin, 20 September 1810, in ibid., 12:418.

56. John P. Frank, *Lincoln as a Lawyer* (Urbana: University of Illinois Press, 1961), p. 164.

57. To Erastus Corning and Others, 12 June 1863, in Lincoln, *Collected Works of Abraham Lincoln*, 5:264.

58. Count Daru, "The Life of Volney," in C.-F. Volney, *Volney's Ruins or Meditations on the Revolutions of Empires* (Boston: Joshua P. Medum, n.d.), pp. 9–17.

59. Wilson and Davis, *Herndon's Informants*, pp. 172, 179, 210, 460, 513.

60. C.-F. Volney, *The Ruins, or, A Survey of the Revolutions of Empires*, 4th ed. (Cheapside: Thomas Tegg, 1811), pp. 10–11.

61. Approximately two weeks after his 4 April 1864 letter to Hodges, Lincoln blamed God for changes in slavery and slavery policy in a speech he gave to citizens in Maryland, which, like Hodges's Kentucky, was another slave state that remained in the Union and that had grievances over changes in slavery and slavery policy. In that short speech, however, Lincoln did not recount the cause-and-effect chain that led to these changes as he did with Hodges. He merely stated: "When the war began, three years ago, neither party, nor any man, expected it would last till now. Each looked for the end, in some way, long ere to-day. Neither did any anticipate that domestic slavery would be much affected by the war. But here we are; the war has not ended, and slavery has been much affected—how much needs not now to be recounted. So true is it that man proposes, and God disposes" (Lincoln, *Speeches and Writings 1859–1865*, p. 589).

62. White, *Lincoln's Greatest Speech*, p. 141; letters to Eliza P. Gurney, 26 October 1862 and 8 August 1863, Lincoln, *Collected Works of Abraham Lincoln*, 5:478 and 7:535–36. David Herbert Donald in *Lincoln* (New York: Touchstone, 1996), p. 515, and Gabor S. Boritt in *Lincoln and the Economics of the American Dream* (Urbana: University of Illinois Press, 1994), p. 256, maintain that Lincoln used the argument that God's will determined the events of the war to shift blame for those events from himself.

63. Richard Carwardine in *Lincoln* stated that after the election of 1864, Lincoln used "every legitimate lever to secure its [the Thirteenth Amendment's] passage" (p. 228).

64. For Lincoln's contribution to the passage of the Thirteenth Amendment, see Randall and Current, *Lincoln the President*, pp. 302–13. For Lincoln's effective methods in rallying Congress to support the Thirteenth Amendment see Michael Vorenberg, "A King's Cure, a King's Style: Lincoln, Leadership, and the Thirteenth Amendment," in *Lincoln Reshapes the Presidency*, ed. Charles M. Hubbard (Macon, GA: Mercer University Press, 2003), pp. 163–68.

65. In a 31 October 1864 letter to William Nast of the Methodist Episcopal Church, Lincoln expressed confidence that "the speedy removal" of slavery would take place (Lincoln, *Collected Works of Abraham Lincoln*, 8:85). However, as a realistic lawyer and politician, he realized there was no certainty of this until the Thirteenth Amendment became a fait accompli.

66. To Horace Greeley, 22 August 1862, in Lincoln, *Speeches and Writings 1859–1865*, pp. 357–58.

67. Williamson, *Westminster Confession of Faith*, p. 23, and White, *Lincoln's Greatest Speech*, pp. 146–48.

68. White, *Lincoln's Greatest Speech*, pp. 128–31, 147–48.

69. Williamson, *Westminster Confession of Faith*, pp. 23, 46.

70. Noll, *America's God*, p. 21.

71. White, in *Lincoln's Greatest Speech*, acknowledges that "the believers" could be interpreted as not including Lincoln among "the believers" but argues that Lincoln often spoke in the third person when he referred to himself in order to interpret Lincoln's use of "the believers" as including himself (pp. 146–47). However, White evidently failed to see that in the same sentence that Lincoln used "the believers" he also used "we discerners," thereby making it clear that he included himself among "we" discerners but excluded himself from "the believers."

72. White, *Lincoln's Greatest Speech*, pp. 124, 126, 155–59, 170–71, and Garry Wills, *Lincoln at Gettysburg: The Words that Remade America* (New York: Touchstone, 1992), pp. 148–75.

73. Arthur Lehman Goodhart, "Lincoln and the Law," in *Lincoln and the Gettysburg Address: Commemorative Papers*, ed. Allan Nevins (Urbana: University of Illinois Press, 1964), pp. 54–55. John J. Duff writes that Lincoln's "immortal" speeches and "wonderfully expressive state papers" actually "sprang in large part from his training in law, which gave him the ability to think and write with precision" (Duff, *A. Lincoln: Prairie Lawyer* [New York: Holt, Rinehart and Winston, 1960], p. 369).

74. Helen Nicolay, *Personal Traits of Abraham Lincoln* (New York: Century, 1912), p. 364.

75. Williamson, *Westminster Confession of Faith*, p. 32.

76. Second Inaugural Address, 4 March 1865, in Lincoln, *Speeches and Writings 1859–1865*, p. 687.

77. Ibid.

78. Story Written for Noah Brooks, 6 December 1864, in Lincoln, *Collected Works of Abraham Lincoln*, 8:154–55.

79. Williamson, *Westminster Confession of Faith*, p. 32.

80. See chap. 2, note 11.

81. Williamson, *Westminster Confession of Faith*, pp. 32–33.

82. Theodore Parker, "The Function of a Teacher of Religion," in *Parker's Works*, vol. 4, *The Transient and Permanent in Christianity*, ed. George Wills Cooke (Boston: American Unitarian Association, 1908), p. 295.

83. See chap. 1, note 58.

84. Henry Champion Deming, *Eulogy of Abraham Lincoln* (Hartford, CT: A. N. Clark, 1865), p. 42.

85. J. C. D. Clark, *The Language of Liberty: 1660–1832: Political Discourse and Social Dynamics in the Anglo-American World* (Cambridge: Cambridge University Press, 1994), p. 352.

86. Williamson, *Westminster Confession*, p. 59. See Aurelius Augustine, *The Enchiridion*, in *The Works of Aurelius Augustine, Bishop of Hippo*, vol. 9, ed. Marcus Dods, trans. J. F. Shaw (Edinburgh: T. and T. Clark, 1873), pp. 242–43, for Augustine's view that God had wrath toward all humans at birth because of the effects of original sin.

87. Second Inaugural Address, 4 March 1865, in Lincoln, *Speeches and Writings 1859–1865*, p. 687.

88. Richard Carwardine, in *Lincoln*, stated that after the election of 1864, Lincoln used "every legitimate lever to secure its [the Thirteenth Amendment's] passage" (p. 228).

89. Stephen B. Oates, *With Malice toward None: The Life of Abraham Lincoln* (New York: New American Library, 1978), p. 269.

90. Joshua F. Speed, *Reminiscences of Abraham Lincoln and Notes of a Visit to California* (Louisville, KY: John P. Morgan, 1884), pp. 32–33.

91. Joshua F. Speed to William H. Herndon, 12 January 1866, in Wilson and Davis, *Herndon's Informants*, p. 156.

92. Joshua F. Speed to William H. Herndon (interview), by 10 June 1865[?], in ibid., p. 31.

93. Lincoln, *Collected Works of Abraham Lincoln*, 6:535–36.

94. White, *Lincoln's Greatest Speech*, pp. 130–31, 220.

95. Donald, *Lincoln*, pp. 247, 253, 256.

96. George W. Julian, as quoted in "Lincoln and the Proclamation of Emancipation," in *Reminiscences of Abraham Lincoln by Distinguished Men of His Time*, ed. Allen Thorndyke Rice (New York: Harper & Brothers, 1909), pp. 237–38. Hostility toward Lincoln in the North in 1862 was nothing compared to the bitter hatred many Southerners held for him throughout the war (Michael Davis, *The Image of Lincoln in the South* [Knoxville: University of Tennessee Press, 1971], p. 73).

97. Donald, *Lincoln*, p. 544.

98. John G. Nicolay and John Hay, *Abraham Lincoln: A History* (New York: Century, 1890), 9:377.

99. Volney, *Ruins*, p. 48.

100. Lincoln, *Collected Works of Abraham Lincoln*, 5:419–20.

101. Ibid.

102. The Second Inaugural Address, 4 March 1865, in Lincoln, *Speeches and Writings 1859–1865*, p. 686.

103. Ibid., pp. 686–87.

104. Ibid. The prayers of both sides for victory in war was in effect the prayers of both sides for the slaughter of their enemy's forces, which Volney stated was "Sacrilegious" and, therefore, such prayers should "return to earth from whence ye came" (Volney, *Ruins*, pp. 46–47).

105. The Second Inaugural Address, 4 March 1865, in Lincoln, *Speeches and Writings 1859–1865*, pp. 686–87.

106. To Thurlow Weed, Esq., 15 March 1865, in Lincoln, *Speeches and Writings 1859–1865*, p. 689.

107. Carwardine, *Lincoln*, p. 226.

108. Thomas Brown, *Lectures on the Philosophy of the Human Mind* (Andover, MA: Mark Newman, 1822), 1:44.

109. Wilson and Davis, *Herndon's Informants*, p. 772.

110. Leonard Swett to William H. Herndon, 17 January 1866, in ibid., p. 168.

111. John G. Nicolay, "Lincoln in the Campaign of 1860," in *An Oral History of Abraham Lincoln: John G. Nicolay's Interviews and Essays*, ed. Michael Burlingame (Carbondale: Southern Illinois Press, 1996), pp. 103–104. Michael Burlingame tells of incidents during Lincoln's presidency when he lost his temper, but goes on to state that this seldom happened considering the continuous negative provocations he had to endure as chief executive of the country during its greatest crisis (Burlingame, *The Inner World of Abraham Lincoln* [Urbana: University of Illinois Press, 1994], p. 208).

112. Edward Gibbon, *The Decline and Fall of the Roman Empire*, abridged by D. M. Low (London: Chatto and Windus, 1986), p. 11.

113. William G. Greene, 30 May 1865 (interview), in Wilson and Davis, *Herndon's Informants*, p. 21.

114. Hans L. Trefousse, "Abraham Lincoln's Reputation During His Administration," in *Lincoln Forum: Rediscovering Abraham Lincoln*, ed. John Y. Simon, Harold Holzer, and Dawn Ruark (New York: Fordham University Press, 2002), pp. 188–98.

115. James H. Matheny to William H. Herndon, 6 March 1870, in Wilson and Davis, *Herndon's Informants*, p. 577.

116. Ibid., p. 762.

117. Wills, *Lincoln at Gettysburg*, p. 38.

118. James M. McPherson, *Crossroads of Freedom: Antietam* (New York: Oxford University Press, 2002), pp. 103, 3, 44. Gideon Welles and Salmon P. Chase in Abraham Lincoln, *Recollected Words of Abraham Lincoln*, comp. and ed. Don E. Fehrenbacher and Virginia Fehrenbacher (Stanford, CA: Stanford University Press, 1996), pp. 474, 96.

119. Noll, *America's God*, p. 438.

## CONCLUSION

1. C.-F. Volney, *The Ruins, or, A Survey of the Revolutions of Empires*, 4th ed. (Cheapside: Thomas Tegg, 1811), pp. 174–80, 88.

2. *Koran*, trans. N. J. Dawood (Baltimore, MD: Penguin, 1968), p. 231.

3. Volney, *Ruins*, p. 102.

4. Speech at Chicago, 10 July 1858, in Abraham Lincoln, *Speeches and Writings 1832–1858*, ed. Don Fehrenbacher (New York: Library of America, 1989), p. 456.

5. John Patrick Diggins, *The Lost Soul of American Politics: Virtue, Self-Interest, and the Foundations of Liberalism* (New York: Basic Books, 1984), p. 315.

6. Jefferson to Isaac H. Tiffany, 4 April 1819, in Thomas Jefferson Papers, S1 R51 38353, Library of Congress.

7. See Ralph Barton Perry, *Puritanism and Democracy* (New York: Vanguard, 1944), p. 133.

8. Sean Hannity, *Deliver Us From Evil: Defeating Terrorism, Despotism, and Liberalism* (New York: Regan Books), 2004, p. 11.

9. Karl Jaspers, *The Future of Germany*, trans. and ed. E. B. Ashton (Chicago: University of Chicago Press, 1967), pp. 140–41.

10. See Paul Johnson, *A History of Christianity* (New York: Simon & Schuster, 1995), pp. 87, 97, 104–105, and 170–77, for Roman persecution and imposition of Christianity by force on non-Christians starting in the fourth century; and Prudence Jones and Nigel Pennick, *A History of Pagan Europe* (New York: Routledge, 1997), pp. 121, 135–37, 156, and 167–71, for similar persecutions and impositions in northern and eastern Europe.

11. *Autobiography*, in Thomas Jefferson, *The Writings of Thomas Jefferson*, ed. Andrew A. Lipscomb and Albert Ellery Bergh (Washington, DC: Thomas Jefferson Memorial Association, 1903), 1:66–67. For Jefferson's indebtedness to John Locke for many of the ideas in the Virginia Statute for Religious Freedom, see chapter 6 in Allen Jayne, *Jefferson's Declaration of Independence: Origins, Philosophy and Theology* (Lexington: University Press of Kentucky, 1998).

12. To Mordecai M. Noah, 28 May 1818, in Thomas Jefferson Papers, S1 R50, 37988, Library of Congress.

13. As quoted by G. Adolf Koch, *Religion of the American Enlightenment* (New York: Thomas Y. Crowell, 1968), p. 85.

14. "Congress shall make no law respecting an establishment of religion, or prohibiting the free exercise thereof" is the religious freedom provision of the First Amendment (Neil H. Cogan, ed., *The Complete Bill of Rights: The Drafts, Debates, Sources and Origins* [New York: Oxford University Press, 1997], p. 11).

15. Jefferson to the General Meeting of Correspondence of the Six Baptist Associations, 21 November 1808, in Jefferson, *Writings of Thomas Jefferson*, 16:320–21.

16. John Dillenberger and Claude Welch, *Protestant Christianity: Interpreted through Its Development* (New York: Macmillan, 1998), p. 175.

17. As Thomas Aquinas put it, "The custom of the Church has the greatest authority and it is always to be emulated in all matters" (*The Pocket Aquinas*, ed. Vernon J. Bourke [New York: Washington Square, 1960], p. 252). See also Carl J. Becker, *The Declaration of Independence: A Study in the History of Political Ideas* (New York: Vintage, 1970), pp. 38–39.

18. Herndon to Jesse W. Weik, as quoted in *Recollected Words of Abraham Lincoln*, comp. and ed. Don E. Fehrenbacher and Virginia Fehrenbacher (Stanford, CA: Stanford University Press, 1996), p. 245.

19. J. G. Holland, *Holland's Life of Abraham Lincoln* (1866; repr., Lincoln: University of Nebraska Press, 1998), pp. 17–19.

20. David Herbert Donald, *Lincoln* (New York: Touchstone, 1996), p. 19.

21. Ibid., pp. 14–15. Kenneth M. Stampp argues that Lincoln's statement "We cannot escape history" in his Second Annual Message to Congress was made like a man "who believed" humans did have a hand in choosing and acting in a manner that would effect their own destinies (Stampp, "Lincoln's History," in *"We Cannot Escape History": Lincoln and the Last Best Hope of Earth*, ed. James M. McPherson [Chicago: University of Illinois Press, 1995], p. 30).

22. Lincoln "fashioned and formed circumstances, so far as he could, to virtue, veracity and integrity," according to William H. Herndon, "Lincoln's Characteristics," *Illinois State Journal* (14 February 1874): p. 2, c.c. 2–4.

23. Volney, *Ruins*, pp. 10–11.

24. C.-F. Volney, *The Law of Nature or Principles of Morality Deduced from the Physical Constitution of Mankind and the Universe* (Cheapside: Thomas Tegg, 1811), p. 19.

25. Ibid., p. 21.

26. Christopher N. Breiseth, "Lincoln, Douglas, and Springfield in the 1858 Campaign," in *The Public and the Private Lincoln: Contemporary Perspectives*, ed. Collum Davis, Charles B. Strozier, Rebecca Monroe Veach, and Geoffrey C. Ward (Carbondale: Southern Illinois University Press, 1979), p. 120.

27. Joseph Gillespie stated to William Herndon, 8 December 1866, in *Herndon's Informants: Letters, Interviews, and Statements about Abraham Lincoln*, ed. Douglas Wilson and Rodney O. Davis (Urbana: University of Illinois Press, 1998), p. 507, that Lincoln was radical "so far as *ends* were concerned while he was conservative as to the *means* to be employed to bring about the ends."

28. James M. McPherson, "Abraham Lincoln: 16th President, 1861–1865," in *"To the Best of My Ability": The American Presidents*, ed. James M. McPherson and David Rubel (New York: Dorling Kindersley, 2001), p. 122.

29. Joseph Gillespie to William H. Herndon, 8 December 1866, in Wilson and Davis, *Herndon's Informants*, pp. 507, 749. Allen Guelzo maintains that Lincoln's goal was emancipation from the time he took the presidential oath and "that he would not leave office without some form of legislative emancipation policy in place" (Guelzo, *Lincoln's Emancipation Proclamation: The End of Slavery in America* [New York: Simon & Schuster, 2005], pp. 4–6).

30. James Madison was aware of this possibility in the Revolutionary period and said so in *The Federalist Papers*, number 41: "The fortunes of disunited America will be even more disastrous than those of Europe. The sources of evil in the latter are confined to her own limits. No superior powers of another quarter of the globe intrigue among her rival nations, inflame their mutual animosities, and render them the instruments of foreign ambition, jealousy, and revenge. In America the miseries springing from her internal jealousies, contentions, and wars would form a part only of her lot. A plentiful addition of evils would have their source in that relation in which Europe stands to this quarter of the earth, and which no other quarter of the earth bears to Europe" (Alexander Hamilton, James Madison, and John Jay, *The Federalist Papers*, ed. Clinton Rossiter [New York: Mentor, New American Library, 1961], pp. 258–59).

31. Don E. Fehrenbacher, *Lincoln in Text and Context: Collected Essays* (Stanford, CA: Stanford University Press, 1987), p. 133. Roy Basler points out that disunion abolitionists like Wendell Philips in their desire to purify the North of slavery "by severing relations with the slaveholding South" never did explain how this would benefit the slave (Basler, *The Lincoln Legend: A Study in Changing Conceptions* [Boston: Houghton Mifflin, 1935], pp. 69–70). See James M. McPherson, *The Struggle for Equality: Abolitionists and the Negro in the Civil War and Reconstruction* (Princeton, NJ: Princeton University Press, 1964), pp. 32–37, for the views of radical abolitionists such as William Lloyd Garrison, Frederick Douglass, John Jay, and John Greenleaf Whittier. J. G. Randall stated, "Comments on Lincoln by abolitionists, if assembled at length, would constitute an anthology of abuse" (Randall, *Lincoln and the South* [Baton Rouge: Louisiana State University Press, 1946], p. 84).

32. Charles L. Black Jr., *A New Birth of Freedom: Human Rights Named and Unnamed* (New Haven, CT: Yale University Press, 1999), p. 168. See David Herbert Donald, "Abraham Lincoln and the American Pragmatic Tradition," in *Lincoln Reconsidered: Essays on the Civil War Era* (New York: Vintage Books, 2001), pp. 121–32, for an analysis of Lincoln's pragmatic approach to politics and the war, which is similar to and parallel to prudence in politics and war. Actually, no one had articulated American pragmatism prior to and during Lincoln's time. That came later with Charles Saunders Pearce, William James, and John Dewey.

33. To William Short, 31 October 1819, in Jefferson, *Writings of Thomas Jefferson*, 15:224.

34. Ethan Fishman, "Under the Circumstances: Abraham Lincoln and

Classical Prudence," in *Abraham Lincoln: Sources and Style of Leadership*, ed. Frank J. Williams, William D. Pederson, and Vincent J. Marsala (Westport, CT: Greenwood, 1994), p. 3.

35. Harry V. Jaffa, *A New Birth of Freedom: Abraham Lincoln and the Coming of the Civil War* (Lanham, MD: Rowman & Littlefield, 2004), pp. 77, 504–505.

36. Abraham Lincoln, *The Collected Works of Abraham Lincoln*, ed. Roy P. Basler, 11 vols. (New Brunswick, NJ: Rutgers University Press, 1953), 1:484.

37. Address to the Young Men's Lyceum, 27 January 1838, in Lincoln, *Speeches and Writings 1832–1858*, p. 36.

38. As quoted by J. P. Usher, "Lincoln and Slavery," in *Reminiscences of Abraham Lincoln by Distinguished Men of His Time*, ed. Allen Thorndyke Rice (New York: Harper & Brothers, 1909), p. 203.

39. As quoted by Merrill D. Peterson, "The International Lincoln," in McPherson, *"We Cannot Escape History,"* p. 158.

40. Robert G. Ingersoll, "The Gentlest Memory in the World," in Rice, *Reminiscences of Abraham Lincoln*, p. 203.

41. Jefferson, Opinion on Treaty, 28 April 1793, Jefferson, *Writings of Thomas Jefferson*, 3:239.

## EPILOGUE

1. Robert F. Durden, "Ambiguities in the Antislavery Crusade of the Republican Party," in *The Antislavery Vanguard: New Essays on the Abolitionists*, ed. Martin Duberman (Princeton, NJ: Princeton University Press, 1965), p. 394.

2. Carl Sandburg, *Abraham Lincoln: The Prairie Years and the War Years* (New York: Harcourt, Brace, 1954), p. 734.

3. Frederick Douglass, "Lincoln and the Colored Troops," in *Reminiscences of Abraham Lincoln by Distinguished Men of His Time*, ed. Allen Thorndyke Rice (New York: Harper & Brothers, 1909), p. 323.

4. Leon F. Litwack, "The Emancipation of the Negro Abolitionist," in Duberman, *Antislavery Vanguard*, p. 140.

5. Charles L. Black Jr., *A New Birth of Freedom: Human Rights Named and Unnamed* (New Haven, CT: Yale University Press, 1999), p. 47. Michael Vorenberg writes of abolitionist James McCune Smith's prophesizing

before the ratification of the Thirteenth and Fourteenth Amendments that slavery would be legally abolished but would de facto survive as a result of cunning law (Vorenberg, *Final Freedom: The Civil War, the Abolition of Slavery, and the Thirteenth Amendment* [New York: Cambridge University Press, 2001], p. 83).

6. J. R. Pole, *The Pursuit of Equality in American History*, 2nd ed., rev. ed. (Berkeley: University of California Press, 1993), p. 222.

7. Black, *New Birth of Freedom*, p. 57.

8. Pole, *Pursuit of Equality in American History*, p. 223.

9. Ibid., pp. 223–25.

10. Black, *New Birth of Freedom*, p. 66.

11. Ibid., p. 152. See James M. McPherson, *Abraham Lincoln and the Second American Revolution* (New York: Oxford University Press, 1991), pp. 145–49, for the adverse impact of the *Slaughterhouse* case and subsequent court decisions on black freedom in the South.

12. See King's "I Have a Dream" speech in Martin Luther King Jr., *I Have a Dream: Writings and Speeches that Changed the World*, ed. James Melvin Washington (San Francisco: HarperSanFrancisco, 1992), pp. 102–106, and Keith D. Miller, "Frederick Douglass, Martin Luther King Jr., and Malcolm X Interpret the Declaration of Independence," in *The Declaration of Independence: Origins and Impact*, ed. Scott Douglas Gerber (Washington, DC: CQ Press, 2002), pp. 163–66.

# *Bibliography*

## MANUSCRIPT SOURCES

Jefferson, Thomas. Papers Series 1. Library of Congress, Washington, DC.
Jenkins, Clay. Comments on Thomas Jefferson in *Thomas Jefferson*, a film by Ken Burns, pt. 1 (PBS Home Video).
Ross, Raymond Abraham. "Slavery and the New York City Newspapers, 1850–1860." PhD diss., New York University, 1966.

## PRIMARY SOURCES

Adams, John. *The Works of John Adams*. Edited by Charles Francis Adams. Boston: Little, Brown, 1850.
Aquinas, Thomas. *Basic Writings of Saint Thomas Aquinas*. Vol. 1. Edited by Anton C. Pegis. New York: Random House, 1945.
———. *The Pocket Aquinas*. Edited by Vernon J. Bourke. New York: Washington Square Press, 1960.
Augustine, Aurelius. *The Enchiridion*. In Augustine, *Works of Aurelius Augustine* (1873).
———. *The Works of Aurelius Augustine, Bishop of Hippo*. Vols. 1–2. Translated and edited by Marcus Dods. Edinburgh: T. and T. Clark, 1871.
———. *The Works of Aurelius Augustine, Bishop of Hippo*. Vol. 9. Edited by Marcus Dods and translated by J. F. Shaw. Edinburgh: T. and T. Clark, 1873.
Calhoun, John C. *Union and Liberty: The Political Philosophy of John C. Calhoun*. Edited by Ross M. Lence. Indianapolis, IN: Liberty Fund, 1992.
Calvin, John. *Institutes of the Christian Religion in Two Volumes*. Edited by John T. McNeil. Translated by Ford Lewis Battles. Library of Christian Classics, vols. 20–21. London: SCM Press, 1961.
Cogan, Neil H., ed. *The Complete Bill of Rights: The Drafts, Debates, Sources and Origins*. New York: Oxford University Press, 1997.
Columbia College Staff, eds. *Introduction to Contemporary Civilization in the West*. Vol. 1. 3rd ed. New York: Columbia University Press, 1960.

Ignatius, of Loyola. "Spiritual Exercises of Saint Ignatius of Loyola." Translated by Charles Seager. In Thompson, *Middle Ages, Renaissance, and Reformation*.

Jefferson, Thomas. *The Commonplace Book of Thomas Jefferson: A Repository of His Ideas on Government*. Edited by Gilbert Chinard. Baltimore, MD: Johns Hopkins Press, 1926.

———. *The Jefferson Bible: The Life and Morals of Jesus of Nazareth*. Boston: Beacon Press, 1989.

———. *Jefferson's Extracts from the Gospels*. Edited by Dickenson W. Adams. Papers of Thomas Jefferson, 2nd series. Princeton, NJ: Princeton University Press, 1989.

———. *Jefferson's Literary Commonplace Book*. Edited by Douglas L. Wilson. Papers of Thomas Jefferson, 2nd series. Princeton, NJ: Princeton University Press, 1989.

———. *The Literary Bible of Thomas Jefferson: His Commonplace Book of Philosophers and Poets*. Edited by Gilbert Chinard. Baltimore, MD: Johns Hopkins Press, 1928.

———. *Notes on the State of Virginia*. Edited by William Peden. New York: Norton, 1972.

———. *The Papers of Thomas Jefferson*. Edited by Julian P. Boyd and Charles T. Cullen. 26 vols. Princeton, NJ: Princeton University Press, 1950.

———. *The Portable Thomas Jefferson*. Edited by Merrill D. Peterson. Kingsport, TN: Penguin, 1981.

———. *Writings*. Edited by Merrill D. Peterson. New York: Library of America, 1984.

———. *The Writings of Thomas Jefferson*. 20 vols. Edited by Andrew A. Lipscomb and Albert Ellery Bergh. Washington, DC: Thomas Jefferson Memorial Association, 1903.

Jefferson, Thomas, Abigail Adams, and John Adams. *The Adams Jefferson Letters: The Complete Correspondence between Thomas Jefferson and Abigail and John Adams*. Edited by Lester J. Cappon. 2 vols. Chapel Hill: University of North Carolina Press, 1959.

Kames, Henry Home, Lord. *Elements of Criticism*. 3rd ed. 2 vols. Edinburgh: A. Kincaid and J. Bell, 1765.

———. *Essays on the Principles of Morality and Natural Religion*. Edinburgh: A. Kincaid and A. Donaldson, 1751.

———. *Principles of Equity*. 2nd ed. Edinburgh: A. Kincaid and J. Bell, 1767.

*Koran*. Translated by N. J. Dawood. Baltimore, MD: Penguin, 1968.

Lincoln, Abraham. *The Collected Works of Abraham Lincoln*. Edited by Roy P. Basler. 11 vols. New Brunswick, NJ: Rutgers University Press, 1953.

———. *The Life and Writings of Abraham Lincoln*. Edited by Philip Van Doren Stern. New York: Modern Library, 1940.

———. *An Oral History of Abraham Lincoln: John J. Nicolay's Interviews and Essays*. Edited by Michael Burlingame. Carbondale: Southern Illinois University Press, 1966.

———. *Recollected Words of Abraham Lincoln*. Compiled and edited by Don E. Fehrenbacher and Virginia Fehrenbacher. Stanford, CA: Stanford University Press, 1996.

———. *Speeches and Writings 1832–1858*. Edited by Don Fehrenbacher. New York: Library of America, 1989.

———. *Speeches and Writings 1859–1865*. Edited by Don Fehrenbacher. New York: Library of America, 1989.

———. *A Treasury of Lincoln Quotations*. Edited by Fred Kerner. Chicago: Americana House, 1965.

Locke, John. *An Essay concerning Human Understanding*. Edited by Peter H. Niddich. Oxford: Clarendon Press, 1984.

———. *The Reasonableness of Christianity*. In Locke, *Works of John Locke Esq*.

———. *Two Treatises of Government*. Edited by Peter Laslett. Cambridge: Cambridge University Press, 1988.

———. *The Works of John Locke Esq*. Vol. 2. London: John Churchill and Samuel Manship, 1714.

Luther, Martin. *Luther's Works*. Vol. 25. Edited by Hilton C. Oswald. St. Louis, MO: Concordia, 1972.

Luther, Martin, and John Calvin. *Luther and Calvin on Secular Authority*. Edited and translated by Harro Höpfl. Cambridge Texts in the History of Political Thought. Cambridge: Cambridge University Press, 1991.

Machiavelli, Niccolo. *The Discourses*. Edited by Bernard Crick. Translated by Leslie J. Walker. Revisions by Brian Richardson. London: Penguin, 1983.

Maimonides, Moses. "Epistle to Yemen." Translated by Boaz Cohen. In Columbia College Staff, *Introduction to Contemporary Civilization in the West*.

Marx, Karl, and Friedrich Engels. *Communist Manifesto*. In Tucker, *Marx-Engels Reader*.

Paine, Thomas. *Age of Reason: Being an Investigation of True and Fabulous Theology*. In *Complete Religious and Theological Works of Thomas Paine*.

———. *The Complete Religious and Theological Works of Thomas Paine*. New York: Peter Eckler, 1917.

Paley, William. *The Principles of Moral and Political Philosophy*. Glasgow: Balwyn & Co., 1821.

Parker, Theodore. "The Function of a Teacher of Religion." In Parker, *Parker's Works*, vol. 4, *The Transient and Permanent in Christianity*.

———. *Parker's Works*. Vol. 4, *The Transient and Permanent in Christianity*. Edited by George Wills Cooke. Boston: American Unitarian Association, 1908.

———. "Thoughts on Theology." In Parker, *Parker's Works*, vol. 4, *The Transient and Permanent in Christianity*.

———. "The Transient and Permanent in Christianity." In Parker, *Parker's Works*, vol. 4, *The Transient and Permanent in Christianity*.

Plato. *The Collected Dialogues of Plato*. Edited by Edith Hamilton and Huntington Cairns. New York: Bollingen Foundation, 1964.

Shakespeare, William. *Great Books of the Western World*. Vols. 26–27, *The Plays and Sonnets of William Shakespeare*. Edited by William George Clarke and William Aldis Wright. Chicago: William Benton, 1952.

Thompson, Karl F. *Classics of Western Thought*. 3rd ed. Vol. 2, *Middle Ages, Renaissance, and Reformation*. New York: Harcourt Brace Jovanovich, 1980.

Thornwell, James Henley. *The Writings of James Henley Thornwell, D.D., LL.D.* 4 vols. Edited by John B. Adger and John L. Girardeau. Richmond, VA: Presbyterian Committee of Publication, 1871–73.

Tindal, Matthew. *Christianity as Old as the Creation*. A facsimile of the 1730 edition. Stuttgart-Bad Cannstatt: Frommann-Holzboog, 1967.

Tucker, Robert C., ed. *The Marx-Engels Reader*. 2nd ed. New York: W. W. Norton, 1978.

Zwingli, Huldreich. *The Latin Works of Huldreich Zwingli*. Vol. 2. Edited by Samuel Jackson Macaulay. Translated by Henry Preble, Walter Lichenstein, and Lawrence A. McLouth. Philadelphia: American Society of Church History, 1922.

## SECONDARY SOURCES

Ahlstrom, Sydney E. *A Religious History of the American People*. London: Yale University Press, 1972.

Allen, Brooke. *Moral Minority: Our Skeptical Founding Fathers*. Chicago: Ivan R. Dee, 2006.

Anderson, Dwight G. "Quest for Immortality: A Theory of Abraham Lincoln's Political Psychology." In Boritt and Forness, *Historian's Lincoln*, 253–74.

Angle, Paul M., ed. *The Lincoln Reader*. New Brunswick, NJ: Rutgers University Press, 1955.

Aptheker, Herbert. *And Why Not Every Man? The Story of the Fight against Negro Slavery*. Assembled and edited by Herbert Aptheker. Berlin: Seven Seas Publishers, 1961.

Baker, Jean H. "Lincoln's Narrative of American Exceptionalism." In McPherson, *"We Cannot Escape History,"* 33–44.

Ballard, Colin R. *The Military Genius of Abraham Lincoln*. New York: World, 1952.

Barton, William E. *Lincoln at Gettysburg: What He Intended to Say; What He Said; What He Was Reported to Have Said: What He Wished He Had Said*. New York: Peter Smith, 1950.

———. *The Soul of Abraham Lincoln*. New York: George H. Doran, 1920.

Basler, Roy P. *The Lincoln Legend: A Study in Changing Conceptions*. Boston: Houghton Mifflin, 1935.

Becker, Carl J. *The Declaration of Independence: A Study in the History of Political Ideas*. New York: Vintage Books, 1970.

Belz, Herman, ed. *The Webster-Hayne Debate on the Nature of the Union*. Indianapolis, IN: Liberty Fund, 2000.

Berlin, Isaiah. *Two Concepts of Liberty: An Inaugural Lecture Delivered before the University of Oxford on 31 October 1958*. Oxford: Oxford University Press, 1958.

Bicknell, E. J. *A Theological Introduction to the Thirty-nine Articles of the Church of England*. 3rd ed. London: Longman's, Green, 1955.

Black, Charles L., Jr. *A New Birth of Freedom: Human Rights Named and Unnamed*. New Haven, CT: Yale University Press, 1999.

Boritt, Gabor S. "Did He Dream of a Lily-White America? The Voyage to Linconia." In Boritt, *Lincoln Enigma*, 1–19.

———. "Lincoln and the Economics of the American Dream." In Boritt and Forness, *Historian's Lincoln*, 87–106.

———. *Lincoln and the Economics of the American Dream*. Urbana: University of Illinois Press, 1994.

———. "The Right to Rise." In Davis, Strozier, Veach, and Ward, *Public and the Private Lincoln*, 57–70.

Boritt, Gabor S., ed. *The Lincoln Enigma: The Changing Faces of an American Icon*. New York: Oxford University Press, 2002.

Boritt, Gabor S., and Norman O. Forness, eds. *The Historian's Lincoln: Pseudohistory, Psychohistory, and History*. Chicago: University of Illinois Press, 1988.

Boyd, Julian. *Declaration of Independence: The Evolution of the Text.* Washington, DC: Library of Congress, 1943.

Brands, H. W. *Andrew Jackson: His Life and Times.* New York: Doubleday, 2005.

———. *The First American: The Life and Times of Benjamin Franklin.* New York: Doubleday, 2000.

Breiseth, Christopher N. "Lincoln, Douglas, and Springfield in the 1858 Campaign." In Davis, Strozier, Veach, and Ward, *Public and the Private Lincoln,* 101–20.

Brown, Thomas. *Lectures on the Philosophy of the Human Mind.* 3 vols. Andover, MA: Mark Newman, 1822.

Burke, Peter. "Tacitism, Skepticism, and Reason of State." In Burns and Goldie, *Cambridge History of Political Thought, 1450–1700,* 479–98.

Burlingame, Michael. *The Inner World of Abraham Lincoln.* Urbana: University of Illinois Press, 1994.

Burlingame, Michael, ed. *"Lincoln's Humor" and Other Essays.* Chicago: University of Illinois Press, 2002.

Burns, J. H., ed. *Cambridge History of Medieval Political Thought c. 350–c. 1450.* Cambridge: Cambridge University Press, 1991.

Burns, J. H., and Mark Goldie, eds. *The Cambridge History of Political Thought, 1450–1700.* Cambridge: Cambridge University Press, 1994.

Byrne, Peter. *Natural Religion and the Nature of Religion: The Legacy of Deism.* London: Routledge, 1989.

Campbell, Duncan Andrew. *English Public Opinion and the American Civil War.* London: Boydell Press, 2003.

Cartledge, Paul. *The Greeks: A Portrait of Self and Others.* Oxford: Oxford University Press, 1993.

Carwardine, Richard J. *Lincoln.* Harlow: Pearson Longman, 2003.

Cassirer, Ernst. *The Philosophy of the Enlightenment.* Translated by Fritz C. A. Koelln and James P. Pettegrove. Princeton, NJ: Princeton University Press, 1951.

Charnwood, Lord. Epilogue to Angle, *Lincoln Reader,* 587–88.

Clark, J. C. D. *The Language of Liberty 1660–1632: Political Discourse and Social Dynamics in the Anglo-American World.* Cambridge: Cambridge University Press, 1994.

Commager, Henry Steele. "The Declaration of Independence." In Weymouth, *Thomas Jefferson,* 179–87.

———. *The Empire of Reason: How Europe Imagined and America Realized the Enlightenment.* New York: Anchor Books, 1978.

———. *Theodore Parker*. Boston: Little, Brown, 1936.

Cox, LaWanda. "Lincoln and Black Freedom." In Boritt and Forness, *Historian's Lincoln*, 175–96.

Craven, Avery. "The Fatal Predicament." In Graebner, *Politics and the Crisis of 1860*, 122–41.

Current, Richard N. Introduction to Current, *Political Thought of Abraham Lincoln*, xiii–xxxi.

———, ed. *The Political Thought of Abraham Lincoln*. Indianapolis, IN: Bobbs-Merrill, 1967.

Daru, Count. "The Life of Volney." In Volney, *Volney's Ruins or Meditations on the Revolutions of Empires*, 9–17.

Davis, Cullom, Charles B. Strozier, Rebecca Monroe Veach, and Geoffrey C. Ward, eds. *The Public and the Private Lincoln: Contemporary Perspectives*. Carbondale: Southern Illinois University Press, 1979.

Davis, Michael. *The Image of Lincoln in the South*. Knoxville: University of Tennessee Press, 1971.

Deming, Henry Champion. *Eulogy of Abraham Lincoln*. Hartford, CT: A. N. Clark, 1865.

Dickenson, H. T. *Bolingbroke*. London: Constable, 1970.

Diggins, John Patrick. *The Lost Soul of American Politics: Virtue, Self-Interest, and the Foundations of Liberalism*. New York: Basic Books, 1984.

Dillenberger, John, and Claude Welch. *Protestant Christianity: Interpreted Through Its Development*. New York: Macmillan, 1998.

DiLorenzo, Thomas J. *The Real Lincoln: A New Look at Abraham Lincoln, His Agenda, and an Unnecessary War*. New York: Three Rivers Press, 2003.

Dirks, John Edward. *The Critical Theology of Theodore Parker*. New York: Columbia University Press, 1948.

Donald, David Herbert. "Abraham Lincoln and Jefferson Davis as Commanders in Chief." In Boritt, *Lincoln Enigma*, 72–85.

———. "Abraham Lincoln and the American Pragmatic Tradition." In Donald, *Lincoln Reconsidered*, 121–32.

———. *Lincoln*. New York: Touchstone, 1996.

———. *Lincoln Reconsidered: Essays on the Civil War Era*. New York: Vintage Books, 2001.

———. *"We are Lincoln Men": Abraham Lincoln and His Friends*. New York: Simon & Schuster, 2003.

Dos Passos, John. "Lincoln and His Almost Chosen People." In Nevins, *Lincoln and the Gettysburg Address*, 15–37.

Douglass, Frederick. "Lincoln and the Colored Troops." In Rice, *Reminiscences of Abraham Lincoln by Distinguished Men of His Time*, 315–29.

Duberman, Martin, ed. *The Antislavery Vanguard: New Essays on the Abolitionists*. Princeton, NJ: Princeton University Press, 1965.

———. "The Northern Response to Slavery." In Duberman, *The Antislavery Vanguard*, 295–413.

Duff, John J. *A. Lincoln: Prairie Lawyer*. New York: Holt, Rinehart and Winston, 1960.

Dumbauld, Edward. *Thomas Jefferson and the Law*. Norman: University of Oklahoma Press, 1978.

Dunn, John. *The Political Thought of John Locke*. Cambridge: Cambridge University Press, 1988.

Durden, Robert F. "Ambiguities in the Antislavery Crusade of the Republican Party." In Duberman, *The Antislavery Vanguard*, 362–94.

Emery, Noemie. *Washington: A Biography*. New York: Capricorn Books, G. P. Putnam's Sons, 1976.

Fabian, Bernard. "Jefferson's Notes on Virginia: The Genesis of Query XVII, The Different Religions Received into the State?" *William and Mary Quarterly*, 3rd ser., 12 (1955): 124–38.

Fara, Patricia. *Newton: The Making of Genius*. New York: Columbia University Press, 2002.

Farmer, James Oscar, Jr. *The Metaphysical Confederacy: James Henley Thornwell and the Synthesis of Southern Values*. Macon, GA: Mercer University Press, 1986.

Fehrenbacher, Don E. *The Dred Scott Case: Its Significance in American Law and Politics*. New York: Oxford University Press, 1979.

———. In Davis, Strozier, Veach, and Ward, *Public and the Private Lincoln*, 121–36.

———. *Lincoln in Text and Context: Collected Essays*. Stanford, CA: Stanford University Press, 1987.

———. *Prelude to Greatness: Lincoln in the 1850s*. Stanford, CA: Stanford University Press, 1962.

Fishman, Ethan. "Under the Circumstances: Abraham Lincoln and Classical Prudence." In Williams, Pederson, and Marsala, *Abraham Lincoln*, 3–15.

Flexner, John Thomas. *Washington: The Indispensable Man*. New York: Back Bay Books, Little, Brown, 1969.

Foner, Eric. *The Story of American Freedom*. New York: W. W. Norton, 1999.

Ford, Bonnie L. "Women, Equality, and the Declaration of Independence." In Gerber, *Declaration of Independence*, 174–90.

Forgie, George B. "Lincoln's Tyrants." In Boritt and Forness, *Historian's Lincoln*, 285–310.

Foster, Stephen S. "The Brotherhood of Thieves, or, A True Picture of the American Church and Clergy." In Mathews, *Agitation for Freedom*, 79–92.

Frank, John P. *Lincoln as a Lawyer*. Urbana: University of Illinois Press, 1961.

Franklin, Benjamin. *The Autobiography*. New York: Vintage Books, Library of America, 1990.

Freehling, William W. *The Road to Disunion: Secessionists at Bay, 1776–1854*. New York: Oxford University Press, 1990.

Freidenwald, Herbert. *The Declaration of Independence: An Interpretation and Analysis*. New York: Macmillan, 1904.

Frend, W. H. C. *The Rise of Christianity*. London: Darton, Longman and Todd, 1986.

Friedman, Lawrence M. *A History of American Law*. New York: Simon & Schuster, 1973.

Gay, Peter. *The Enlightenment: An Interpretation*. London: Weidenfeld and Nicholson, 1966.

Gerber, Scott Douglas. "Clarence Thomas, Civil Rights, and the Declaration of Independence." In Gerber, *Declaration of Independence*, 45–55.

Gerber, Scott Douglas, ed. *The Declaration of Independence: Origins and Impact*. Washington, DC: CQ Press, 2002.

Gibbon, Edward. *The Decline and Fall of the Roman Empire*. Abridged by D. M. Low. London: Chatto and Windus, 1986.

Gienapp, William E. "Abraham Lincoln and Presidential Leadership." In McPherson, *"We Cannot Escape History,"* 63–85.

Goldie, Mark. "The Reception of Hobbes." In Burns and Goldie, *Cambridge History of Political Thought 1450–1700*, 589–615.

Goodhart, Arthur Lehman. "Lincoln and the Law." In Nevins, *Lincoln and the Gettysburg Address*, 38–71.

Graebner, Norman A. "The Politicians and Slavery." In Graebner, *Politics and the Crisis of 1860*, 1–31.

———. *Politics and the Crisis of 1860*. Urbana: University of Illinois Press, 1961.

Grodzins, Dean. *American Heretic: Theodore Parker and Transcendentalism*. Chapel Hill: University of North Carolina Press, 2002.

Guelzo, Allen C. *Abraham Lincoln: Redeemer President*. Grand Rapids, MI: William B. Eerdmans, 1999.

———. "Apple of Gold in a Picture of Silver." In Boritt, *Lincoln Enigma*, 86–107.

———. *Lincoln's Emancipation Proclamation: The End of Slavery in America.* New York: Simon & Schuster, 2005.

Hall, Mark David. "The Declaration of Independence in the Supreme Court." In Gerber, *Declaration of Independence*, 142–60.

Hamilton, Alexander, James Madison, and John Jay. *The Federalist Papers.* Edited by Clinton Rossiter. New York: Mentor, New American Library, 1961.

Hannity, Sean. *Deliver Us From Evil: Defeating Terrorism, Despotism, and Liberalism.* New York: Regan Books, 2004.

Harris, William C. "Toward Appomattox, Toward Unconditional Surrender?" In Boritt, *Lincoln Enigma*, 108–29.

Hart, Jeffrey. *Viscount Bolingbroke: Tory Humanist.* London: Routledge and K. Paul, 1965.

Herndon, William H. *Herndon's Life of Lincoln: The History and Personal Recollections of Abraham Lincoln, as Originally Written by William H. Herndon and Jesse W. Weik.* New York: Albert & Charles Boni, 1930.

———. "Lincoln's Characteristics." *Illinois State Journal* (14 February 1874): 2, c.c. 3–4.

Hertz, Emanuel, ed. *Abraham Lincoln: The Tribute of the Synagogue.* New York: Bloch, 1927.

Hill, Frederick Trevor. *Lincoln the Lawyer.* New York: Century, 1906.

Hitler, Adolf. *Mein Kampf.* Translated by Ralph Manheim. New York: Houghton Mifflin, 1971.

Hoffer, Eric. *The True Believer.* New York: Harper & Row, 1951.

Hofstadter, Richard. *The American Political Tradition: And the Men Who Made It.* 1948. Reprint, New York: Vintage Books, 1973.

Holland, J. G. *Holland's Life of Abraham Lincoln.* 1866. Reprint, Lincoln: University of Nebraska Press, 1998.

Holzer, Harold. "Avoid Saying 'Foolish Things': The Legacy of Lincoln's Impromptu Oratory." In McPherson, *"We Cannot Escape History,"* 105–23.

Holzer, Harold, Gabor S. Boritt, and Mark Neely Jr. "The Lincoln Image: Abraham Lincoln and the Popular Print." In Boritt and Forness, *Historian's Lincoln*, 49–79.

Hubbard, Charles M., ed. *Lincoln Reshapes the Presidency.* Macon, GA: Mercer University Press, 2002.

Huntington, Samuel P. *The Clash of Civilizations and the Remaking of World Order.* New York: Touchstone, 1997.

Ingersoll, Robert G. "The Gentlest Memory in the World." In Rice, *Reminiscences of Abraham Lincoln by Distinguished Men of His Time*, 422–28.

Israel, Jonathan I. *Radical Enlightenment, Philosophy and the Making of Modernity 1650–1750*. New York: Oxford University Press, 2001.

Jaffa, Harry V. "Abraham Lincoln and the Universal Meaning of the Declaration of Independence." In Gerber, *Declaration of Independence*, 29–44.

———. *Crisis of the House Divided: An Interpretation of the Issues in the Lincoln-Douglas Debates*. Garden City, NY: Doubleday & Company, 1959.

———. *Equality and Liberty: Theory and Practice in American Politics*. New York: Oxford University Press, 1965.

———. *A New Birth of Freedom: Abraham Lincoln and the Coming of the Civil War*. Lanham, MD: Rowman & Littlefield, 2004.

Jaspers, Karl. *The Future of Germany*. Translated and edited by E. B. Ashton. Chicago: University of Chicago Press, 1967.

Jayne, Allen. *Jefferson's Declaration of Independence: Origins, Philosophy and Theology*. Lexington: University Press of Kentucky, 1998.

Jayne, William. *Personal Reminiscences of the Martyred President*. Chicago: Grand Army Hall and Memorial Association, 1908.

Jennison, Keith W. *The Humorous Mr. Lincoln: A Profile in Wit, Courage, and Compassion*. Woodstock, VT: Countryman Press, 1992.

Johnson, Paul. *A History of Christianity*. New York: Simon & Schuster, 1995.

Jones, Prudence, and Nigel Pennick. *A History of Pagan Europe*. New York: Routledge, 1997.

Julian, George W. "Lincoln and the Proclamation of Emancipation." In Rice, *Reminiscences of Abraham Lincoln by Distinguished Men of His Time*, 227–45.

Karp, Abraham J. *From the Ends of the Earth: Judaic Treasures of the Library of Congress*. New York: Rizzoli, 1991.

Kens, Paul. Introduction to "Personal Reminiscences of Early Days in California with Other Sketches." *Journal of Supreme Court History* 29, no. 1 (2004): 1–21.

Kimball, Charles. *When Religion Becomes Evil*. New York: HarperSanFrancisco, 2002.

King, Martin Luther, Jr. "I Have a Dream." In Washington, *I Have a Dream*, 102–106.

King, P. D. "The Barbarian Kingdoms." In Burns, *Cambridge History of Medieval Political Thought c. 350–c. 1450*, 123–56.

Koch, Adrienne. *Jefferson and Madison: The Great Collaboration*. New York: Hill and Wang, 1969.

Koch, G. Adolf. *Religion of the American Enlightenment*. New York: Thomas Y. Crowell, 1968.

Kramnick, Isaac. *Bolingbroke and His Circle: The Politics of Nostalgia in the Age of Walpole*. Ithaca, NY: Cornell University Press, 1992.

———. *Lord Bolingbroke Historical Writings*. Chicago: University of Chicago Press, 1972.

Levy, Leonard. "Jefferson as a Civil Libertarian." In Weymouth, *Thomas Jefferson*, 189–215.

Lewis, Joseph. *Lincoln the Atheist* (originally titled *Lincoln the Freethinker*). Austin, TX: American Atheist Press, 1979.

Litwack, Leon F. "The Emancipation of the Negro Abolitionist." In Duberman, *Antislavery Vanguard*, 137–55.

Lund, Roger D. *The Margins of Orthodoxy: Heterodox Writing and Cultural Response, 1660–1750*. Cambridge: Cambridge University Press, 1995.

Luscombe, D. E., and G. R. Evans. "The Twelfth-century Renaissance." In Burns, *Cambridge History of Medieval Political Thought c. 350–c. 1451*, 306–38.

Lynd, Staughton. "The Abolitionist Critique of the United States Constitution." In Duberman, *Antislavery Vanguard*, 209–39.

Macartney, Clarence Edward. *Lincoln and His Cabinet*. New York: Charles Scribner's Sons, 1931.

Manchester, William. *A World Lit Only by Fire: The Medieval Mind and the Renaissance: Portrait of an Age*. Boston: Back Bay Books, 1993.

Marshall, John. *John Locke: Resistance, Religion, and Responsibility*. Cambridge: Cambridge University Press, 1994.

Mathews, Donald G. *Agitation for Freedom: The Abolitionist Movement*. New York: John Wiley & Sons, 1972.

Mayer, David N. *The Constitutional Thought of Thomas Jefferson*. Charlottesville: University Press of Virginia, 1997.

McCollough, David. *John Adams*. New York: Simon & Schuster, 2001.

McGuinness, Arthur E. *Henry Home, Lord Kames*. New York: Twayne, 1970.

McPherson, James M. *Abraham Lincoln and the Second American Revolution*. New York: Oxford University Press, 1991.

———. "Abraham Lincoln: 16th President 1861–1865." In McPherson and Rubel, *"To the Best of My Ability,"* 118–25.

———. *Crossroads of Freedom: Antietam*. New York: Oxford University Press, 2002.

———. "Introduction: Last Best Hope for What?" In McPherson, *"We Cannot Escape History,"* 2–14.

———. "Lincoln as Commander in Chief." In Simon, Holzer, and Ruark, *Lincoln Forum*, 1–15.

———. *The Struggle for Equality: Abolitionists and the Negro in the Civil War and Reconstruction.* Princeton, NJ: Princeton University Press, 1964.

McPherson, James M., ed. *"We Cannot Escape History": Lincoln and the Last Best Hope of Earth.* Urbana: University of Illinois Press, 1995.

McPherson, James M., and David Rubel, eds. *"To the Best of My Ability:" The American Presidents.* New York: Dorling Kindersley, 2001.

Meinecke, Frederich. *Machiavellism: The Doctrine of Raison D'Etat and Its Place in Modern History.* Translated by Douglas Scott. New Haven, CT: Yale University Press, 1957.

Meredith, Roy. *Mr. Lincoln's Contemporaries: An Album of Portraits by Mathew B. Brady.* New York: Charles Scribner's Sons, 1951.

Miller, Keith D. "Frederick Douglass, Martin Luther King Jr., and Malcolm X Interpret the Declaration of Independence." In Gerber, *The Declaration of Independence*, 161–73.

Miller, William Lee. *Lincoln's Virtues: An Ethical Biography.* New York: Alfred A. Knopf, 2002.

More, Louis Trenchard. *Isaac Newton: A Biography.* New York: Charles Scribner's Sons, 1934.

Morel, Lucas E. "America's First Black President? Lincoln's Legacy of Political Transcendence." In Hubbard, *Lincoln Reshapes the Presidency*, 120–52.

———. *Lincoln's Sacred Effort: Defining Religion's Role in American Self-Government.* Lanham, MD: Lexington Books, 2000.

Murley, John A., Robert L. Stone, and William T. Braithwaite. *Law and Philosophy: The Practice of Theory.* Athens: Ohio University Press, 1992.

Neely, Mark E., Jr. *The Last Best Hope of Earth: Abraham Lincoln and the Promise of America.* Cambridge, MA: Harvard University Press, 1995.

Nelson, Janet. "Kingship and Empire." In Burns, *Cambridge History of Medieval Political Thought c. 350–c. 1450*, 211–51.

Nevins, Allan, ed. *Lincoln and the Gettysburg Address.* Urbana: University of Illinois Press, 1964.

Nicolay, Helen. *Personal Traits of Abraham Lincoln.* New York: Century, 1912.

Nicolay, John G. "Lincoln in the Campaign of 1860." In Lincoln, *Oral History of Abraham Lincoln*, 91–106.

Nicolay, John G., and John Hay. *Abraham Lincoln: A History.* Vol. 9. New York: Century, 1890.

Niebuhr, Reinhold. "The Religion of Abraham Lincoln." In Nevins, *Lincoln and the Gettysburg Address*, 72–87.

Noll, Mark A. *America's God: From Jonathan Edwards to Abraham Lincoln.* New York: Oxford University Press, 2002.

Oates, Stephen B. *Abraham Lincoln: The Man behind the Myths.* New York: Harper Perennial, 1994.

———. *With Malice toward None: The Life of Abraham Lincoln.* New York: New American Library, 1978.

Onuf, Peter. "The Scholars' Jefferson." *William and Mary Quarterly,* 3rd ser., 50, no. 4 (October 1993): 671–99.

Orr, John. *English Deism: Its Roots and Its Fruits.* Grand Rapids, MI: Wm. B. Eerdmans, 1934.

Owen, G. Frederick. *Abraham Lincoln: The Man & His Faith.* Wheaton, IL: Tyndale House, 1981.

Paludan, Phillip Shaw. "Emancipating the Republic: Lincoln and the Means and Ends of Antislavery." In McPherson, *"We Cannot Escape History,"* 45–60.

———. "Lincoln and Colonization: Policy or Principle?" *Journal of the Abraham Lincoln Association* 25, no. 1 (Winter 2004): 23–37.

———. *"A People's Contest": The Union and Civil War.* New York: Harper & Row, 1988.

Paulson, Ronald. "Henry Fielding and the Problem of Deism." In Lund, *Margins of Orthodoxy,* 240–70.

Perry, Lewis. *Radical Abolitionism: Anarchy and the Government of God in Antislavery Thought.* London: Cornell University Press, 1973.

Perry, Ralph Barton. *Puritanism and Democracy.* New York: Vanguard, 1944.

Peterson, Merrill D. "The International Lincoln." In McPherson, *"We Cannot Escape History,"* 158–74.

———. *Lincoln in American Memory.* New York: Oxford University Press, 1994.

Piatt, Donn. "Lincoln the Man." In Rice, *Reminiscences of Abraham Lincoln by Distinguished Men of His Time,* 345–75.

Plowden, David, and the editors of the Viking Press. *Lincoln and His America 1809–1865.* New York: Viking Press, 1970.

Pole, J. R. *The Pursuit of Equality in American History.* 2nd ed. Rev. and exp. ed. Berkeley: University of California Press, 1993.

Power, J. Tracy. "'Four Years More': The Army of Northern Virginia and the United States Presidential Election of 1864." In Simon, Holzer, and Ruark, *Lincoln Forum,* 93–111.

Pritchett, John Perry. *Calhoun: His Defence of the South.* Poughkeepsie, NY: Printing House of Harmon, 1937.

Prokopowicz, Gerald J. "'If I Had Gone Up There, I Could Have Whipped Them Myself': Lincoln's Military Fantasies." In Simon, Holzer, and Ruark, *Lincoln Forum*, 77–92.

Randall, J. G. *Lincoln and the South*. Baton Rouge: Louisiana State University Press, 1946.

———. *Lincoln the Liberal Statesman*. New York: Dodd, Mead, 1947.

Randall, J. G., and Richard N. Current. *Lincoln the President: Last Full Measure*. New York: Dodd, Mead, 1955.

Rice, Allen Thorndyke, ed. *Reminiscences of Abraham Lincoln by Distinguished Men of His Time*. New York: Harper & Brothers, 1909.

Rietveld, Ronald D. "Lincoln's View of the Founding Father." In Williams, Pederson, and Marsala, *Abraham Lincoln*, 17–44.

Robertson, J. M. *A History of Freethought: Ancient and Modern to the Period of the French Revolution*. Vol. 2. 4th ed. Rev. and exp. ed. London: Watts, 1936.

Robinson, I. S. "Church and Papacy." In Burns, *Cambridge History of Medieval Thought c. 350–c. 1450*, 252–305.

Sandburg, Carl. *Abraham Lincoln: The Prairie Years and The War Years*. One-volume ed. New York: Harcourt, Brace, 1954.

Schwartz, Barry. "The New Gettysburg Address: A Study in Illusion." In Simon, Holzer, and Ruark, *Lincoln Forum*, 160–86.

Sheldon, Garrett Ward. "The Political Theory of the Declaration of Independence." In Gerber, *Declaration of Independence*, 16–28.

Shutes, Milton H. *Lincoln and California*. Stanford, CA: Stanford University Press, 1943.

Simon, John Y. "Commander in Chief Lincoln and General Grant." In Simon, Holzer, and Ruark, *Lincoln Forum*, 16–33.

Simon, John Y., Harold Holzer, and Dawn Ruark, eds. *The Lincoln Forum: Rediscovering Abraham Lincoln*. New York: Fordham University Press, 2002.

Skinner, Quentin. *The Foundations of Modern Political Thought*. Vol. 2. Cambridge: Cambridge University Press, 1978.

———. *Liberty before Liberalism*. Cambridge: Cambridge University Press, 1998.

Smith, Dennis Mack. *Mussolini*. London: Paladin Graften Books, 1987.

Smith, Jean Edward. *Grant*. New York: Touchstone, 2001.

———. *John Marshall*. New York: Henry Holt, 1996.

Spain, August O. *The Political Theory of John C. Calhoun*. New York: Bookman Associates, 1951.

Speed, Joshua F. *Reminiscences of Abraham Lincoln and Notes of a Visit to California*. Louisville, KY: Printed by John P. Morgan and Co., 1884.

Stampp, Kenneth M. "Lincoln's History." In McPherson, *"We Cannot Escape History,"* 17–32.

Sutherland, Charles W. *Disciples of Destruction: The Religious Origins of War and Terrorism.* Amherst, NY: Prometheus Books, 1987.

Swisher, Carl Brent. *Stephen J. Field: Craftsman of the Law.* Washington, DC: Brookings Institution, 1930.

Tackach, James. *Lincoln's Moral Vision: The Second Inaugural Address.* Jackson: University Press of Mississippi, 2002.

Tarbell, Ida M. *The Life of Abraham Lincoln: Drawn from Original Sources and Containing Many Speeches, Letters and Telegrams Hitherto Unpublished.* Vol. 1. New York: McClure, Phillips, 1902.

Tarnas, Richard. *The Passion of the Western Mind: Understanding the Ideas that Have Shaped Our World View.* New York: Ballantine Books, 1991.

Temple, Wayne C. *Abraham Lincoln: From Skeptic to Prophet.* Mahomet, IL: Mayhaven, 1995.

Thelen, David. "Reception of the Declaration of Independence." In Gerber, *Declaration of Independence,* 191–212.

Thomas, Benjamin P. "Lincoln's Humor: An Analysis." In Burlingame, *"Lincoln's Humor" and Other Essays,* 3–22.

Thurow, Glen E. *Abraham Lincoln and American Political Religion.* Albany, NY: State University of New York Press, 1976.

———. "Abraham Lincoln and American Political Religion." In Boritt and Forness, *Historian's Lincoln,* 125–43.

Trefousse, Hans L. "Abraham Lincoln's Reputation during His Administration." In Simon, Holzer, and Ruark, *Lincoln Forum,* 187–210.

Trueblood, Elton. *Abraham Lincoln: Theologian of American Anguish.* New York: Harper & Row, 1973.

Tucker, Robert W., and David C. Hendrickson. *Empire of Liberty: The Statecraft of Thomas Jefferson.* New York: Oxford University Press, 1992.

Usher, J. P. "Lincoln and Slavery." In Rice, *Reminiscences of Abraham Lincoln by Distinguished Men of His Time,* 203–26.

Volney, C.-F. *The Law of Nature or Principles of Morality Deduced from the Physical Constitution of Mankind and the Universe.* Cheapside: Thomas Tegg, 1811.

———. *The Ruins or a Survey of the Revolutions of Empires.* 4th ed. Cheapside: Thomas Tegg, 1811.

———. *Volney's Ruins or Meditations on the Revolutions of Empires.* Boston: Joshua P. Medum, n.d.

Vorenberg, Michael. *Final Freedom: The Civil War, the Abolition of Slavery, and the Thirteenth Amendment.* New York: Cambridge University Press, 2001.

———. "A King's Cure, A King's Style: Lincoln, Leadership, and the Thirteenth Amendment." In Hubbard, *Lincoln Reshapes the Presidency*, 153–72.

Washington, James Melvin. *I Have a Dream: Writings and Speeches that Changed the World*. San Francisco: HarperSanFrancisco, 1992.

Wells, Damon. *Stephen Douglas: The Last Years, 1857–1861*. Austin: University of Texas Press, 1990.

West, Thomas G. "The Declaration of Independence, the U.S. Constitution, and the Bill of Rights." In Gerber, *Declaration of Independence*, 72–95.

Weymouth, Lally, ed. *Thomas Jefferson: The Man, His World, His Influence*. London: Weidenfeld and Nicholson, 1973.

White, Ronald C., Jr. *Lincoln's Greatest Speech: The Second Inaugural*. New York: Simon & Shuster, 2003.

Whitman, Walt. "Dear Democracy." In Rice, *Reminiscences of Abraham Lincoln by Distinguished Men of His Time*, 413–19.

Williams, Frank J. "Abraham Lincoln and the Changing Role of Commander in Chief." In Hubbard, *Lincoln Reshapes the Presidency*, 9–29.

———. "Abraham Lincoln—Our Ever-Present Contemporary." In McPherson, *"We Cannot Escape History,"* 139–57.

Williams, Frank J., William D. Pederson, and Vincent J. Marsala, ed. *Abraham Lincoln: Sources and Style of Leadership*. Westport, CT: Greenwood, 1994.

Williams, T. Harry. *Lincoln and the Radicals*. Madison: University of Wisconsin Press, 1941.

Williamson, G. I. *The Westminster Confession of Faith for Study Classes*. Philadelphia: Presbyterian and Reformed Publishing Company, 1964.

Wills, Garry. *Inventing America: Jefferson's Declaration of Independence*. New York: Vintage Books, 1979.

———. *Lincoln at Gettysburg: The Words that Remade America*. New York: Touchstone, 1992.

———. *Negro President: Jefferson and the Slave Power*. New York: Houghton Mifflin, 2003.

Wilson, Clyde N. *The Essential Calhoun: Selections from Writings, Speeches, and Letters*. New Brunswick, NJ: Transaction, 1992.

Wilson, Clyde N. Introduction to Wilson, *Essential Calhoun*, pp. xv–xxviii.

Wilson, Douglas, and Rodney O. Davis, eds. *Herndon's Informants: Letters, Interviews, and Statements about Abraham Lincoln*. Urbana: University of Illinois Press, 1998.

Wilson, Douglas L. *Honor's Voice: The Transformation of Abraham Lincoln*. New York: Alfred A. Knopf, 1998.

————. *Lincoln before Washington: New Perspectives on the Illinois Years.* Urbana: University of Illinois Press, 1997.

Winger, Stewart. *Lincoln, Religion and Romantic Politics.* Dekalb: Northern Illinois University Press, 2003.

Wolf, William J. *The Almost Chosen People: A Study of the Religion of Abraham Lincoln.* Garden City, NY: Doubleday, 1959.

————. *The Religion of Abraham Lincoln.* New York: Seabury Press, 1963.

Wood, Forrest G. *The Arrogance of Faith: Christianity and Race in America from the Colonial Era to the Twentieth Century.* New York: Alfred A. Knopf, 1990.

Wood, Gordon. *The Creation of the American Republic, 1776–1787.* Chapel Hill: University of North Carolina Press, 1969.

Yolton, John W. *John Locke and the Way of Ideas.* London: Oxford University Press, 1969.

Zuckert, Michael P. "Lincoln and the Problem of Civil Religion." In Murley, Stone, and Braithwaite, *Law and Philosophy.*

# Index